Studies in Medieval and Renaissance Music

7

YOUNG CHORISTERS, 650–1700

Young singers played a central role in a variety of religious institutional settings: urban cathedrals, collegiate churches, monasteries, guilds, and confraternities. The training of singers for performance in religious services was so crucial as to shape the very structures of ecclesiastical institutions, which developed to meet the need for educating their youngest members, while the development of musical repertories and styles directly reflected the ubiquitous participation of children's voices in both chant and polyphony. Once choristers' voices had broken, they often pursued more advanced studies either through an apprenticeship system or at university, frequently with the help of the institutions to which they belonged.

This volume provides the first wide-ranging book-length treatment of the subject, and will be of interest to music historians — indeed, all historians — who wish to understand the role of the young in sacred musical culture before 1700.

Susan Boynton is Associate Professor of Historical Musicology at Columbia University.
Eric Rice is Assistant Professor of Music History at the University of Connecticut at Storrs.

Studies in Medieval and Renaissance Music
ISSN 1479-9294

General Editor
Tess Knighton

This series aims to provide a forum for the best scholarship in early music; deliberately broad in scope, it welcomes proposals on any aspect of music, musical life, and composers during the period up to 1600, and particularly encourages work that places music in an historical and social context. Both new research and major reassessments of central topics are encouraged.

Proposals or enquiries may be sent directly to the editor or the publisher at the UK addresses given below; all submissions will receive careful, informed consideration.

Dr Tess Knighton, Clare College, Cambridge CB2 ITL
Boydell & Brewer, PO Box 9, Woodbridge, Suffolk IP12 3DF

Volumes already published

1. Machaut's Music: New Interpretations
   edited by Elizabeth Eva Leach

2. The Church Music of Fifteenth-Century Spain
   by Kenneth Kreitner

3. The Royal Chapel in the time of the Hapsburgs:
   Music and Court Ceremony in Early Modern Europe
   edited by Tess Knighton, Juan José Carreras and Bernado García García

4. Citation and Authority in Medieval and Renaissance Musical Culture:
   Learning from the Learned; Essays in Honour of Margaret Bent
   edited by Suzannah Clark and Elizabeth Eva Leach

5. European Music, 1520–1640
   edited by James Haar

6. Cristóbal de Morales:
   Sources, Influences, Reception
   edited by Owen Rees and Bernadette Nelson

Young Choristers
650–1700

❧

edited by

Susan Boynton
Eric Rice

THE BOYDELL PRESS

First published 2008
The Boydell Press, Woodbridge

ISBN 978 1 84383 413 7

The Boydell Press is an imprint of Boydell & Brewer Ltd
PO Box 9, Woodbridge, Suffolk IP12 3DF, UK
and of Boydell & Brewer Inc.
668 Mt Hope Avenue, Rochester, NY 14620, USA
website: www.boydellandbrewer.com

A CIP catalogue record for this title is available
from the British Library

This publication is printed on acid-free paper

Designed and typeset in Adobe Jenson by
The Stingray Office, Manchester

Printed in Great Britain by
CPI Antony Rowe, Chippenham, Wiltshire

CONTENTS

LIST OF ILLUSTRATIONS

LIST OF MUSICAL EXAMPLES

ACKNOWLEDGEMENTS

Many people and organizations deserve thanks for the publication of this volume, among them our respective institutions, Columbia University and the University of Connecticut. Susan Boynton's 2007–8 membership at the Institute for Advanced Study at Princeton University, which was supported in part by the National Endowment for the Humanities, assisted greatly in the final stages of the volume's preparation. Any views, findings, conclusions, or recommendations expressed in this book do not necessarily reflect those of the National Endowment for the Humanities. A School of Fine Arts Dean's Grant from the University of Connecticut funded the archival research for Eric Rice's article, and the travel allotments from the University of Connecticut Research Foundation and the UConn chapter of the American Association of University Professors funded his travel to the 2005 International Medieval Congress at the University of Leeds, UK, for which the conference sessions that spawned this volume were initially conceived. A subsequent School of Fine Arts Dean's Grant from the University of Connecticut supported expert copy-editing by Karen Hiles. We are grateful to Jeffrey Dean for improving the substance of the volume considerably in the course of his editing. Tess Knighton, the series editor, offered invaluable suggestions as the volume took shape, and Caroline Palmer, our editor at Boydell & Brewer, was unfailingly helpful in bringing it to press.

To our children

INTRODUCTION
PERFORMANCE AND PREMODERN CHILDHOOD

Susan Boynton and Eric Rice

Concerning the request of Johannes Sterck, a choirboy of this church, in which he petitioned for release on account of the change of his voice, it is decided that since he can still serve the choir in one way or another, he should remain, [and should] devote between the end of Matins until the high Mass to his course of study.

> (Chapter minutes of the collegiate church of St. Mary in Aachen, December, 1598)[1]

ARCHIVAL entries such as this one have provided music historians with a wealth of information on the education and administration of choirboys in the Middle Ages and early modern period. Such information has traditionally been employed in studies of performance context in which an understanding of young performers' abilities and responsibilities contributes to an overall picture of ecclesiastical and musical life.[2] Mostly unexplored is the experience of young singers as performers and, especially, as children — a social group perceived by their elders as physically, intellectually, and emotionally immature. Given the nature of the surviving sources, this inattention to the experience of young singers is not surprising, for although we possess a great many documents

---

[1] Düsseldorf, Hauptstaatsarchiv, Aachen St. Marien, Akten 11e T. 1; Aachen, Stadtarchiv, K St. Marien 315 8 (photocopies), fol. 90 (December 1598). "𝕵𝖔𝖆𝖓𝖓𝖊𝖘 𝕾𝖙𝖊𝖗𝖈𝖐 vicariolus petiit dimissionem sed non obtinuit:𝕬𝖚𝖋𝖋 supplication*em* 𝕵𝖔𝖆𝖓𝖓𝖎𝖘 𝕾𝖙𝖊𝖗𝖈𝖐 Vicarioli huius Ecclesiae 𝖉𝖆𝖗𝖇𝖊𝖎 𝖊𝖗 propter mutationem vocis dimissionem 𝖌𝖊𝖕𝖆𝖙𝖙𝖊, 𝖛𝖊𝖗𝖆𝖇𝖘𝖈𝖍𝖊𝖎𝖉𝖊𝖙 𝖉𝖜𝖊𝖎𝖑𝖑 𝖊𝖗 𝖉𝖊𝖓 𝕮𝖍𝖔𝖗 𝖓𝖔𝖈𝖍 𝖜𝖔𝖑𝖑 𝖊𝖎𝖓 𝕵𝖍𝖊𝖗 𝖔𝖉𝖊𝖗 𝖊𝖓𝖉𝖑𝖎𝖈𝖍 𝖉𝖎𝖊𝖓𝖊𝖓 𝖐𝖍𝖆𝖓, 𝖉𝖆𝖘 𝖊𝖗 𝖉𝖊𝖘𝖜𝖊𝖌𝖊𝖓 𝖕𝖑𝖊𝖎𝖇𝖊𝖓 𝖘𝖔𝖑𝖑, 𝖘𝖜𝖎𝖈𝖍𝖊𝖓 𝖊𝖎𝖑𝖍𝖎𝖊 post matutinas 𝖇𝖞𝖘 ad summam missam 𝖘𝖊𝖎𝖓 studium 𝖆𝖓𝖟𝖚𝖑𝖆𝖌𝖍."

[2] Examples of this kind that have informed this study include Barbara Haggh, "Music, Liturgy, and Ceremony in Brussels, 1350–1500" (Ph.D. diss., University of Illinois at Urbana-Champaign, 1988); Eric Rice, "Music and Ritual at the Collegiate Church of Saint Mary in Aachen, 1300–1600" (Ph.D. diss., Columbia University, 2002); Reinhard Strohm, *Music in Late Medieval Bruges* (Oxford, 1985); Craig Wright, *Music and Ceremony at Notre Dame of Paris, 500–1550* (Cambridge, 1989); and Craig Wright, *Music at the Court of Burgundy, 1364–1419: A Documentary History* (Henryville, Ottawa, and Binningen, 1979).

pertaining to the administration of choirboys, for the most part we lack first-person accounts by ecclesiastical choirmasters and singers, and we know of none written or dictated by children.[1]

The administrative documents that do survive often raise as many questions as they answer. In the entry above, for example, we learn that Johannes Sterck was denied a request to leave the service of Aachen's collegiate church despite the fact that his voice had broken. The church's canons not only asserted that his service to the choir could and should continue, albeit in a capacity other than performance, but also affirmed their responsibility to educate him. If he could serve the choir in other ways, why did Sterck wish to leave the church's service? Perhaps he understood singing to be his primary function in the church and petitioned for release because he was no longer able to fulfill his duties. Did the canons' affirmation of their responsibility to educate, feed, house, and clothe him constitute concern for his welfare and acknowledgement of his immaturity, or was it simply the means by which the church continued to make use of his labor? In sum, what were church officials' conceptions of childhood and how did these apply to the working lives of young musicians?[2]

In what follows, we address these questions with recourse to the growing body of research on young singers in medieval and early modern Europe. Though the lives and roles of singers varied across time and place, a comparative approach can nonetheless reveal some commonalities in performance traditions and in experiences of childhood before 1700. The evidence suggests that despite young singers' formidable abilities and responsibilities, their experiences — both as performers and as people — reflected conceptions of childhood as understood by the clerics who were their superiors.

Most studies of childhood in the Middle Ages subscribe to one of two positions, known respectively as the "discontinuity" and "continuity" theses.[3] According to the discontinuity thesis, childhood was not considered a distinctive stage of life and children were treated essentially as small adults, subject to the same standards of behavior and expectations as their elders. The continuity thesis holds that notions of childhood were not only well developed, but have changed little since the

---

[1] First-person accounts by adult singers are cited in Richard Sherr, *Music and Musicians in Renaissance Rome and Other Courts* (Aldershot, 1998).

[2] In using the term "childhood," we necessarily exclude adolescents (like Sterck) from the bulk of our discussion in this introduction, since adolescence involves a physical change in the voice that precipitated a change in a choirboy's status, which in turn limits the amount of pertinent archival information. For a discussion of the data for male puberty and vocal change in the late Middle Ages and early modern period, see Richard Rastall's essay in this volume and his *The Heaven Singing: Music in Early English Religious Drama* (Cambridge, 1996), 308–13.

[3] The terms come from Barbara Hanawalt, "Medievalists and the Study of Childhood," *Speculum* 77 (2002), 440–60. For a recent essay that seeks to balance the two opposing views represented by the discontinuity and continuity theses, see Susan Boynton and Isabelle Cochelin, "The Sociomusical Role of Child Oblates at the Abbey of Cluny in the Eleventh Century," in *Musical Childhoods and the Cultures of Youth*, ed. Susan Boynton and Roe-Min Kok (Middletown, Ct., 2006), 3–24.

Middle Ages. Rather than reaffirming either side of the dichotomy suggested by these two perspectives, the historical evidence suggests a more complex reality in which experiences and definitions of childhood change with ideological context and socioeconomic setting. Child singers in ecclesiastical institutions often had considerable responsibility and ability as performers in liturgical and ceremonial contexts. For this reason, some scholars have maintained that choirboys were not perceived as "children" in the current sense of the term (that is, predicated on the notion that childhood is a discrete stage in the life cycle). However, in the medieval and early modern period, documents concerning the supervision of choirboys and methods for their instruction demonstrate widespread awareness of their immaturity and attest a concern for their welfare that extended well beyond their initial utility to the church (as in the case of Johannes Sterck). The balance between children's talents, duties, and liturgical training on the one hand, and the need to account for their immaturity, care, and education on the other, forms one of the central themes of this book. As in our own times, childhood as experienced and imagined in premodern Europe was a measure of a society's self-image; the status of children was as much a function of adult prerogatives as of biological determinants.[1] What it means to be a child in any given time and place tends to be determined primarily by the material conditions and cultural traditions of one's family and community, as well as by the conventions of the polity in which one lives. The profound imbrication of children in ecclesiastical institutions over the *longue durée* and the consequent involvement of young singers in liturgical performance make the study of choristers a fruitful avenue for understanding sacred music in its social and cultural settings throughout medieval and early modern Europe.

YOUNG SINGERS IN THE MIDDLE AGES

Boy singers have been part of Christian sacred music since the beginning of the choral tradition, as they were integral members of the earliest religious establishments in Western Europe. The sixth-century Rule of Benedict refers several times to the treatment of boys in the monastic community. Already in this early monastic document, the special character of children is acknowledged with psychological acuity: for instance, Chapter 30 prescribes corporal punishment for those who are too young to understand the gravity of excommunication. In the early Middle Ages, boys entered monasteries as donations offered to the abbot by their parents in a ritual whose elements are described in Chapter 59 of the Benedictine Rule: the parents wrap the child's hands in the altar cloth, along with a document granting the abbey both the boy and (if possible) some property.[2]

---

[1] On the historical construction of childhood, see Hugh Cunningham, "Histories of Childhood," *American Historical Review* 103 (1998), 1195–1208.

[2] Translation and commentary can be found in *RB 1980: The Rule of St. Benedict in English and Latin*, ed. Timothy Fry (Collegeville, Minn., 1980), 270–73.

The practice of oblation was a central force in the economic and institutional development of medieval monastic communities.[1] Oblation was an unparalleled determinant of social structure, for it required significant numbers of children to be integrated among the adults in the absence of relatives or members of the extended family; as a result, the upbringing of oblates was a constant preoccupation. The passages on boys in the Benedictine Rule just mentioned manifest an awareness that young monks required special treatment. The subject came to occupy an important place in some of the most extensive texts on Western monasticism from the entire Middle Ages, the customaries associated with the Burgundian abbey of Cluny.[2] Customaries are prescriptive texts that address every aspect of daily life in a monastery. The fact that they devote extensive space to the care of young boys is testimony to the priorities of their compilers, who saw the future of their community in its youngest members. The oblates' role in the monastic life took on symbolic dimensions. By giving the children a monastic formation, monks ensured the integrity of their own way of life.

Much of the considerable effort expended on educating these young people was focused on preparing them for participation in the liturgy.[3] The customaries of the central Middle Ages are the most informative source for reconstructing this aspect of liturgical performance.[4] Children performed a range of musical roles in monastic worship, singing both choral and solo chants, intoning psalms, antiphons, and hymns, and chanting lessons. They also collaborated in the preparation of the daily list assigning chants and readings to specific members of the community. On some feast days, child soloists performed special chants including processional hymns, the invitatory, and some propers of the Mass. As a result, the training of young singers was among the principal concerns of those monastic officers most occupied by the direction of music, such as the cantor or *armarius* and his assistants.[5] At the start of the day, after the night office, oblates studied reading and singing under the supervision of their tutors, and when the cantor or armarius arrived, they tried out their readings and responsories for the next Matins service. Most free time between services was spent studying and rehearsing. Like the rest of the monastic community, these young singers lived according to

---

[1] For a general study, see Mayke de Jong, *In Samuel's Image: Child Oblation in the Early Medieval West* (Leiden, 1996). The practice waned somewhat in the high Middle Ages with the advent of new orders that accepted only adults (such as the Cistercians). However, the relatively early entry of children into the religious life (whether as oblates or novices) still continued among the Benedictines.

[2] For the most recent overview of the Cluniac customaries, see the interdisciplinary collection of essays in *From Dead of Night to End of Day: Studies on the Medieval Customs of Cluny*, ed. Susan Boynton and Isabelle Cochelin (Turnhout, 2005).

[3] Susan Boynton, "Training for the Liturgy as a Form of Monastic Education," in *Medieval Monastic Education*, ed. George Ferzoco and Carolyn Muessig (London and New York, 2000), 7–20.

[4] Susan Boynton, "The Liturgical Role of Children in Monastic Customaries from the Central Middle Ages," *Studia Liturgica* 28 (1998), 194–209.

[5] Margot Fassler, "The Office of the Cantor in Early Western Monastic Rules and Customaries: A Preliminary Investigation," *Early Music History* 5 (1985), 29–51.

the daily routine of the liturgy; what made their experience slightly different from that of the adult monks was the constant rhythm of their liturgical training.

Three of the chapters in this volume explore the particularities of young singers' musical education and performance in monasteries. In combination, they present a picture of monastic musical life for both boys and girls. The chapter by Susan Boynton focuses on the period before 1200, when most of the information pertains to boys; chapters by Anne Bagnall Yardley and Colleen Reardon address the later Middle Ages and the early modern period, bringing out the parallels between the musical formation of female and male oblates, as well as the many aspects of continuity across the several centuries encompassed by our chronological framework.

Like the embeddedness of oblates in monastic communities, the functions of choristers in urban churches during the high Middle Ages indicate the place of young singers in the development of ecclesiastical institutions. Along with the cathedral towns in the twelfth and thirteenth centuries there emerged clerical traditions of ritual clowning that emphasized the status of individual clerical orders within the ecclesiastical hierarchy. One such ceremony, that of the Boy Bishop, gave the acolytes license to elect one of their own number as bishop for a day, to choose at least some of the repertory to be sung, and to be received at the residence of the real bishop.[1] This annual event, which occurred on the feast of St. Nicholas (6 December) or that of the Holy Innocents (28 December), gave rise to excesses but also engendered texts and music that form an integral part of the construction of childhood in this period. One such intriguing work involving performance by choirboys is a twelfth-century liturgical drama representing the Massacre of the Innocents and presumably intended for performance on December 28, when the acolytes celebrated a special office (and perhaps also the Boy Bishop's ceremony). The symbolism of this musical play figures the real acolytes as the imagined Innocents.[2] In the thirteenth century, the role of young singers in cathedrals became increasingly formalized and regularized. Their participation in the liturgy and their musical instruction was made more regular through the establishment of choir schools and the endowment of positions for choristers.[3]

---

[1] For the Boy Bishop ceremony in relation to music and drama, see Margot Fassler, "The Feast of Fools and *Danielis ludus*: Popular Tradition in a Medieval Cathedral Play," in *Plainsong in the Age of Polyphony*, ed. Thomas Forrest Kelly (Cambridge, 1992), 68–77.

[2] Susan Boynton, "Performative Exegesis in the Fleury *Interfectio puerorum*," *Viator* 29 (1998), 39–64.

[3] In Toledo Cathedral this process began at the end of the thirteenth century in order to guarantee the choirboys' regular participation in services; see François Reynaud, *Les Enfants de chœur de Tolède à la Renaissance* (Turnhout, 2002), 13, 141–42.

YOUNG SINGERS IN EARLY MODERN ECCLESIASTICAL INSTITUTIONS

THOUGH monastic and collegiate houses share many features with regard to the role of children in the liturgy, the nomenclature used for young singers reflects the differing status they had in these two types of institutions. The use of the term *oblatus* (literally, "the offered one") by a group of monks for a boy in their charge signified the lifetime commitment made by his parents. Collegiate churches seldom received such a commitment, and were apt to refer to their boys as *scholares* (if they had a school as part of the chapter), *chorales* ("choristers"), or simply as *pueri* ("boys"), though terminology varied and was often employed with meanings specific to the institution. For example, by the close of the sixteenth century, the choirboys of Aachen's collegiate church were called *vicarioli*, a plural diminutive of *vicarius* that reflected the hope that they might progress to become adult vicars and perhaps even canons — fully ordained priests who were part of the governing structure of the church.

Despite standardization of official appellations, church documents offer evidence for the notions of childhood prevalent in secular churches. In very general terms, the change of a choirboy's voice was an unmistakable physiological marker of coming maturity and precipitated an important transition in his role within the church (sometimes from that of an active singer to an inactive one, as with Johannes Sterck), though responses to the vocal shift varied widely from church to church and often with each individual case. After singers' voices had broken, they were sometimes able to benefit from tuition scholarships for further musical study financed by individuals within their ecclesiastical institutions, so that musical patronage could be linked to higher education. Several chapters in this volume (Flynn, O'Regan, Rice, Ruiz) discuss systems of educational patronage. The emphasis ecclesiastical institutions placed on further musical training, indeed on education in general, shows that they perceived the need for the continued intellectual development of young singers, that is, for a process of intellectual maturation coinciding with physical growth following the breaking of the voice.

Medieval historians have noted that medical texts distinguish between childhood and adulthood, and late-medieval child-rearing manuals demonstrate an interest in what might reasonably be termed child psychology.[1] That some church officials also held this concern is well demonstrated by the third rule of the *Doctrina pro pueris Ecclesiae Parisiensis* (*Education for the boys of the Church of Paris*), written in 1411 by Jean Gerson, chancellor of Notre-Dame of Paris, regarding the confession of choirboys:

> In addition, they are to be led to confession not just once each year, but four or six times, on the solemn feasts; and then, before they confess, they should be taught from the little books or otherwise how they ought to act

---

[1] Hanawalt, "Medievalists and the Study of Childhood," 443–44.

and what to say in confession. And there should be an appropriate confessor instituted for them, because more prudence is required in confessing well with them than with older people, so that they should not be examined too little or too much.[1]

This passage presents an interesting juxtaposition. Gerson's concern for the boys' spiritual welfare was such that he ordered the boys to be confessed more than once a year (which may have been a previous requirement) and to be taught "how to act and what to say in confession" — the sort of phrase that some might interpret as repressive. But Gerson also advises caution in choosing their confessor, referring to the boys' immaturity. The strict code of behavior cited by proponents of the discontinuity thesis is present here, but so is a distinct perception of children as intellectually and emotionally less developed than adults.[2]

Much of Gerson's *Doctrina*, as Craig Wright has observed, is concerned with keeping the choirboys away from malevolent influence, both within Notre-Dame's walls and outside of them. In this it is similar to many other documents that describe the administration of choirboys. Despite the fact that collegiate churches had administrative procedures and liturgies comparable to those of monasteries, their personnel interacted with all manner of lay worshippers, shopkeepers, and others in the surrounding community to a degree that monks of the period did not. Many canons in urban churches lived outside their church's immediate area, and indeed choirboys were often taught and housed elsewhere in the city as well.[3] The interactions of choirboys with adults who were not immediately responsible for their welfare, even the clerics of the churches they served, were limited and carefully monitored. Though some might be tempted to see such limitations simply as those of a system of control designed for the continued exploitation of children, they also manifest ecclesiastical perceptions of choirboys' vulnerability. In nearly all cases, sets of rules concerning the administration of choirboys discuss the suitability of those who are appointed to teach and care for them, and occasionally the concept of childhood is invoked in such a context. In fourteenth-century statutes concerning the *hôtel* and staff of the choirboys at the Sainte-Chapelle of Paris, for example, we are told that the servants must consist of "a good and honest valet

---

[1] Translated and quoted in Wright, *Music and Ceremony*, 167. The original Latin text is cited at length in F. L. Chartier, *L'Ancien Chapitre de Notre-Dame de Paris et sa maîtrise* (Paris, 1897; repr. Geneva, 1971), 66–70.

[2] Interestingly, the *Doctrina* was held up by Philippe Ariès, the initial proponent of the discontinuity thesis, as "the spirit of the new discipline" leading to a modern view of childhood and child psychology, while liturgists who have studied Notre-Dame have noted its universality in representing traditions of Christian education that date from the twelfth and thirteenth centuries. See Wright, *Music and Ceremony*, 166; Philippe Ariès, *Centuries of Childhood*, trans. R. Baldick (New York, 1962), 106–8; Chartier, *L'Ancien Chapitre de Notre-Dame de Paris*, 65.

[3] Though the original meaning of "canon" derives from the principles of monastic rule, clerics in many collegiate churches were able to own real property, live in their own dwellings, and otherwise enjoy personal freedom beginning in the ninth century. Cathedral canons were similarly "secularized" much later, but in any case by the beginning of the early modern period.

and a chamber-maid old enough to serve and look after them unequivocally, as is needed with children."[1] Whether implicit or explicit, many chapter by-laws concerning the maintenance of choirboys express a similar concern for prudence in selecting those who interact with the church's child-musicians. Evidence that such concern was warranted may be found in the biographies of such sixteenth-century figures as the theorist Giovanni Maria Lanfranco and the composer Nicolas Gombert, both of whom were accused of violating choirboys in their charge.[2]

THE EDUCATION OF CHOIRBOYS

THE primary purpose of most church schools was to teach choristers through musical instruction, grammar, and writing — all means to one end, the correct and diligent performance of the liturgy.[3] This education emphasized upright morals, taught important skills, and was offered at no cost. As such, it was considered highly desirable.

Though the ultimate responsibility for liturgical performance — and, therefore, the education of choirboys — belonged to the cantor, by the early modern period his role was largely supervisory and ceremonial. This was especially true in churches that cultivated notated polyphony, for most clerics lacked the expertise necessary for the instruction of the boys in all but the most basic musical matters. Often, the job of teaching and supervising the choirboys in their day-to-day tasks fell to two people, a master of singing and a master of grammar. In other institutions, the singing master was responsible for teaching Latin as well, and as such bore the ultimate responsibility for the boys' education in the eyes of the collegiate chapter. The singing master was known by a variety of titles, the choice of which depended largely upon his role and the traditions of the church he served. He might be called simply the *magister puerorum* ("master of the boys"), *succentor*

[1] ". . . [U]n varlet bon et honneste et une chamberiere assez ancienne pour les servir et tenir nettement comme besoing est à enfans." Quoted in Denis Escudier, "Des Enfants 'bien appris': L'Enseignement de la grammaire et du chant aux enfants de chœur de la Sainte-Chapelle de Paris d'apres un règlement du xıvᵉ siècle," in *La Tradition vive: Mélanges d'histoire des textes en l'honneur de Louis Holtz*, ed. Pierre Lardet (Paris and Turnhout, 2003), 225.

[2] According to Pietro Aaron, Lanfranco was forced to flee his post as *maestro di cappella* in Verona in 1538 to avoid charges; according to the physician Jerome Cardan, Gombert lost his position at the imperial court and was sentenced to a period of exile on the high seas. On Lanfranco, see Bonnie J. Blackburn, "Lanfranco, Giovanni Maria," in *The New Grove Dictionary of Music and Musicians*, 2nd ed. (London, 2000), 14:231. On Gombert, see George Nugent and Eric Jas, "Gombert, Nicolas," ibid., 10:119.

[3] Jane Flynn, "The Education of Choristers in England during the Sixteenth Century," in *English Choral Practice, 1400–1650*, ed. John Morehen (Cambridge, 1995), 180. Though Flynn's article deals exclusively with the education of choirboys in England, many of her remarks pertain to Continental institutions as well. For a study of education in primarily non-ecclesiastical settings as viewed through printed sources in early modern France, see Kate van Orden, "Children's Voices: Singing and Literacy in Sixteenth-Century France," *Early Music History* 25 (2007), 209–56.

("sub-cantor," i.e., replacement of the cantor in day-to-day functions), or *magister chori*, indicating his responsibility as director of the entire choir. Since choirboys were often a necessary component of a choir engaged in the singing of polyphony, composers were frequently employed to teach and govern them as well as to provide music for the church. A singing master teaching the choirboys and leading them in performance in the Mass and Office had considerable contact with them. He was generally also responsible for recruiting them, though his choices were always subject to the final approval of the chapter.

Information on the recruitment and admission of choristers is often difficult to obtain. Choir schools were sometimes selected as a repository for sons who were not the eldest of a family and therefore did not expect to inherit land. Most churches recruited boys around the age of seven or eight. A religious disposition and legitimate birth were fairly standard eligibility requirements for admission to a choir school.[1] After determining eligibility, the master of choristers would arrange an audition in front of members of the college of canons, who would select or reject a boy based on the quality of his voice and, in some cases, his skill at sight reading.[2] Standards varied widely, for while some institutions strove to engage boys from far and wide with pure voices, others sought to educate the poor of the surrounding region.[3] By the middle of the sixteenth century, physical examination was also possible, for some churches did not admit boys who had been castrated despite the growing predilection for *castrati* in Roman churches.[4] Upon admission, a boy was generally signed over to the church without possibility of release for a period of up to ten years. He received the tonsure, a symbolic shaving of the crown of the head, and suitable vestments, and he was then ordained into minor clerical orders, the lowest ecclesiastical rank. Unlike monastic oblates, however, a chorister at a collegiate church was usually released from service at a certain age, and he could then elect to pursue a lay career — or indeed, to take over his parents' land, if the circumstances in his family (the death of an older brother, for example) suddenly rendered him eligible.

Since the boys' principal duties involved singing liturgical texts, the focus in most church schools was primarily on oral rather than written skills. Scholars have noted that the emphasis on grammar at the early stages of a choirboy's education was to aid in comprehension and thus correct pronunciation of texts that were memorized and sung as part of the divine service. The course of study at this early stage was fairly standardized: most schools employed *De octo partibus*

---

[1] Concerning the minor clerical orders and requirements for ordination, see Denys Hay, *The Church in Italy in the Fifteenth Century* (Cambridge, 1977), 50.

[2] Wright, *Music and Ceremony*, 182; a detailed description of the selection of choirboys at Notre-Dame of Chartres is J.-A. Clerval, *L'Ancienne Maîtrise de Nôtre-Dame de Chartres* (Paris, 1899; repr. Geneva,1972), 37–51.

[3] Barbara Haggh has noted that the *boni infantes* of St. Goedele in Brussels were recruited from among the poorest from the city's public schools, and that recruitment for numerous foundations made for *boni infantes* in the Low Countries and France in the thirteenth and fourteenth centuries was similarly based on need rather than purely on voice quality. See Haggh, "Music, Liturgy, and Ceremony," 156–57.

[4] Wright, *Music and Ceremony*, 170.

orationis of Aelius Donatus, a Latin primer dating from the fourth century, and subsequently Alexandre de Villedieu's *Doctrinale puerorum*, written in Paris in 1199.[1] A choirboy generally learned the texts of the entire Psalter, the canticles for the Divine Office (Magnificat, Nunc dimittis, Benedictus) and the Little Hours of the Virgin, as well as the recitation formulae used to sing them, by rote.[2] It was only after this initial step that the written word and musical notation came to be associated with the processes of singing liturgical texts. Boys who were particularly adept at reading text and music would be taught to write either or both of these.

The alphabet and the notes of the scale were usually taught simultaneously. The scale was presented according to the system devised in the eleventh century by Guido of Arezzo. The Guidonian scale was not eight pitches, but six, which were known collectively as a hexachord, and these were organized in an invariable pattern of whole steps surrounding a single half-step (1, 1, ½, 1, 1). The pitches were assigned syllables — *ut, re, mi, fa, sol, la* — so that the half-step occurred between *mi* and *fa*. With the help of the Guidonian hexachord, the four-line musical staff, and clefs, boys learned to read melodic intervals at sight. Hexachords overlapped to accommodate the two half-steps one encountered when traversing an octave, and by making the transition from one hexachord to another (known as mutation), the boys learned the entire gamut as it was then conceived (G to *e″* and eventually *g″*).

Having progressed this far, most boys were sufficiently skilled to be of good service to the church. The bulk of their responsibility was the chanting of psalms and canticles (which they had memorized) as well as the recitation of scripture readings and the singing of plainchant antiphons and responsories (which they could read at sight). Many churches had long traditions of improvising polyphony for the embellishment of plainchant, and the more advanced boys were engaged in this kind of singing as well. At this point, then, the boys needed to be sufficiently schooled in principles of consonance and dissonance, as well as of rhythm, to allow them to coordinate multiple voice parts. The complexity of the improvised polyphony obviously depended upon the level of expertise of the singers involved (whether boys or men), the nature of the chant to be embellished, and the traditions of the individual church. Jane Flynn has noted that in English churches during the first half of the sixteenth century, mensural notation was taught at this stage, in part to assist in inculcating principles of rhythm and counterpoint,[3]

---

[1] Wright, *Music and Ceremony*, 174; Otto F. Becker, "The *Maîtrise* in Northern France and Burgundy during the Fifteenth Century" (Ph.D. diss., George Peabody College for Teachers, 1967), 81–85.

[2] This method of primarily oral transmission supplemented by written texts was the norm in the Middle Ages and continued largely unchanged in ecclesiastical settings through the early modern period. A notable exception was in England after ca. 1565, when the simpler Elizabethan rite was well enough established that memorization was no longer of paramount importance. See Flynn, "The Education of Choristers," 182–83. A similar emphasis on written texts came to dominate continental Protestant church schools.

[3] Flynn, "The Education of Choristers," 183.

and accomplished primarily through the memorization of prolation tables that explained each notational symbol's durational meaning in context. Boys who excelled in reading mensural notation were employed in the singing of notated polyphony when it was called for by the customs of the church that employed them.

The preceding summary of the curriculum of most early-modern church schools, though heavily abbreviated, presents a glimpse of the day-to-day activities of choirboys in the classroom. The curriculum was rigorous and almost completely practical in nature, since the boys applied nearly everything they learned in the classroom in their performances. Though their days were mostly occupied with the solemn tasks of lessons and services, there are occasional indications of a whimsical approach to their work. Flynn has noted that some published canons were employed for learning mensural notation and principles of consonance and dissonance. She cites one in particular from a 1609 collection by Thomas Ravenscroft that has a text clearly meant to appeal to young singers: "Ut re mi fa mi re ut, hey derry derry, sing and be merry, quando veni, quando coeli, whip little David's bome bome."[1] Such a text, combining solmization and nonsense syllables, liturgy-derived Latin words and childish anatomical references, was very likely used in the context of music lessons in a church school in which the teacher's pedagogy accounted for pupils' emotional and intellectual immaturity.

While it is true that such moments of play scarcely appear in sources pertaining to choirboys, there are clear indications that they existed and were indeed expected. In Jean Gerson's *Doctrina* for Notre-Dame of Paris, the chancellor expresses the chapter's position on games:

> Moreover, all games are prohibited that lead to avarice, indecency or immodest noise, anger or rancor, such as games of dice or chance or all similar things no matter how insignificant they may be, like dominos of lead or copper. Here is seen the truth of the dictum: "Play with a hoop and chase away games of chance." Yet frequent and brief periods of recreation are to be given the boys, as for example shortly after the noon meal and after dinner, which times are of little use for other serious things.[2]

That games of chance and the like were forbidden is not surprising, but against the backdrop of the choirboys' liturgical responsibilities and curriculum, "frequent and brief periods of recreation" are perhaps less expected. Like many early-modern rules for choirboys, Gerson's *Doctrina* presents copious discussion of proper behavior during the divine service, including prohibitions on laughing, chatting, playing games, etc. He surely realized that such prohibitions would be easier for children to follow if they were allowed to engage in such pursuits at other times.

While corporal punishment seems to have been the norm throughout the

---

[1] Ibid., 183–4. The full title of Ravenscroft's work is *Pammelia: Musicks Miscellanie; or, Mixed Varietie of Pleasant Roundelays, and Delightful Catches of 3, 4, 5, 6, 7, 8, 9, 10 Parts in One*.

[2] Quoted and translated in Wright, *Music and Ceremony*, 167.

Middle Ages and early modern period, the degree to which it was used and abused must have varied considerably, and church officials asserted their authority over singing masters who punished their students too severely. A particularly striking case is found in the chapter minutes of Aachen's collegiate church dating from 1712. On 18 October, the succentor appeared before the chapter to complain about the nearly continual absence of five choirboys in his charge, and the chapter responded by reprimanding the truants.[1] Three days later, however, it was the succentor — apparently emboldened by the chapter's support — who was reprimanded:

> Since, indeed, our singing master, after our recent warning, has thus far beaten the said choirboys without discretion with an iron chain or club in the head, which is his custom, wounding the small Bavarian boy with his club, which gave him a black eye, we order our singing master not to punish the choirboys with anything other than a rod on the hand or with something else appropriate in judicious consideration of their offense.[2]

The reprimand reflects the succentor's poor judgment with regard to discipline, but it may also reflect the difficulty of maintaining order among the choirboys at that time, for the archives preserve several documents recording remedies for problems in the performance of the liturgy, many of which involved choirboys. The following entry is typical in that it places the responsibility for the choirboys' lack of discipline squarely on the choirmaster:

> These same choirboys are congregated daily before Vespers in the Chapel

---

[1] Düsseldorf, Hauptstaatsarchiv, Aachen, St. Marien, Akten 11t, fol. 251^{r-v}. "Martis 18. 8bris 1712. Magister Huré Succentor. Lecta supplica magistri Huré Succentoris nostri, conquerentis inter alia, quod Vicarioli nostri ob continuam quasi absentiam a sua schola nil huiusque diducerent; quibus funditus examinatis, dubisque vicariolis desuper audibis, reperto, dictum Succentorem à tempore lucis ad hanc Ecclesiam admissionis dictos vicariolos nullatenus prodebito instruxisse; ordinatum eundem per secretarium nostrum nomine nostro monendum, at in posterum Illos melius, et ab octava usque ad nonam et a fine officij summi sacri de die in diem, exceptis Dominicis et festis diebus constanter instruat, tam in musica, quam cantu gregoriano, alias nunc pro tunc eundem ab officio dimittimus ac dimissum his ee declaramus." ("Having read the requests of Master Huré, our Succentor, complaining that, among other things, our choirboys, on account of their nearly continual absence from his school, may not at all be separated from him; having entirely examined these things, and having heard from the above irresolute choirboys; having perceived that the said Succentor has instructed the said choirboys at this church during the day [and] not for [any other] obligation; we declare that the same boys are to be admonished by our secretary in our name; moreover, in the future that they [are to behave] better, and that [the succentor] may instruct them constantly from the eighth hour until none and to the end of the high Divine Office, day in and day out, in both polyphony and Gregorian chant, except on Sundays and feast days.")

[2] Ibid., fol. 251^{v}. "Cum vero noster phonascus post nuperam nostram monitionem re indiscrete ad eo verberaret dictos vicariolos ferrea catenula aut fuste ad caput, uti in more habet, adhuc nudius tertius parvulum Boverie fuste percutiendo, lividum oculum causarit, ordinamus eidem nostro phonasco — ut non aliter, quam virgis supra manus, aut aliter juxta delicti exigentiam discrete tamen vicariolos puniat."

of St. Nicholas, and there they laugh and play foolishly and also fight. This would be remedied if they never came to the church unless they were in the company of the singing master; they should also not remain in the Chapel of St. Nicholas, but proceed immediately to the choir, where they should modestly and silently await the arrival of the canons. Moreover they should be able to chant the *De profundis* in the aforementioned chapel, with the singing master beginning every other verse and joining the prayer.[1]

This text is from an undated document, but it was probably written during the same period as the previous two entries, and its tenor may well have motivated the succentor's actions. In any case, while the severity of his beatings was clearly unusual, the chapter's specificity with regard to the implement of punishment was not. The *virga* — a rod, twig, or switch — was a common tool for the task, and it was probably seldom used to inflict significant pain. Indeed, in monasteries and elsewhere its primary purpose appears to have been to prevent clerics from touching the boys when guiding them through dressing and undressing, walking through church environs, and the like.[2] Its continued presence and purpose as an implement of punishment in both the classroom and the choir nonetheless served to enforce the strict code of behavior and high standards required of children engaged in the performance of the liturgy.

CHORISTERS' ROLES IN THE LITURGY

CHILD singers took part in many aspects of the liturgy, serving as acolytes, candle-bearers, and censers, to name just a few roles, but they were especially valued for their singing. The belief that boys' voices were akin to those of angels, which was held throughout the Middle Ages and which increased in some quarters during the Counter-Reformation, stemmed from scriptural and patristic writings that emphasized children's innocence and malleability. Their physical and aural presence in church thus represented an idealized Christian purity, and in most places they occupied a prominent place in the ceremonial ritual of high feast days.[3]

---

[1] Aachen, Domarchiv, Stiftsarchiv, IV.3.20; "Defectus Ecclesiae *Aquensis* corrigendi." "ijdem quotidie ante vesperas congregantur in sacello Sti. Nicolai ibidemque garriunt et nugantur aut pugnant. Remedium foret, si nunquam ad templum venirent nisi comitante phonasco, nec haererent in sacello Sti. Nicolai, sed immediate procederent ad chorum, ibidemque modesti et silentes expectarent adventum Canonicorum. Additum possent, quod in praedicto sacello prius de profundis orarent phonasco inchoante alternis versiculis, et subiungente orationem."

[2] Isabelle Cochelin, "Besides the Book: Using the Body to Mould the Mind; Cluny in the Tenth and Eleventh Centuries," in *Medieval Monastic Education*, 21–34.

[3] On the theological basis for the use of choirboys and the various meanings derived from their physical bodies as well as from their voices in Counter-Reformation Spain, see Todd Borgerding, "Imagining the Sacred Body: Choirboys, Their Voices, and Corpus Christi in Early Modern Seville," in *Musical Childhoods*, ed. Boynton and Kok, 25–48.

Choristers performed most often in the daily high Mass and Vespers, services in which lay worshippers were often in attendance at cathedrals and collegiate churches. Their presence at the night office of Matins was generally reserved for Sundays and feast days of elevated rank. At a minimum, choirboys were expected to participate in all choral singing in a given service; those with particular facility could be called upon to sing chant as a soloist or in a small group, or to perform improvised or notated polyphony. Typically, choirboys were responsible for singing one or two of the more complex chants in the Mass, such as the Gradual and the Alleluia, and they were often assigned a reading and a great responsory at Matins. Readings and responsories were usually assigned in ascending order of rank, so it was common for a boy to offer the first reading of Matins, and for a small group of boys to sing the first responsory.[1] Similar performances occurred as part of endowed votive services (which were particularly common in churches dedicated to the Virgin) and annual commemorations of deceased canons.

When the time for such a performance approached, a boy or small group would get up from the benches provided for choirboys, proceed to a large lectern (traditionally in the form of an eagle), and read the lesson or chant — by minimal candlelight if the service was at night. (The psalter and canticles, which the boys were to have memorized, were chanted without the aid of written sources, often in total darkness.)[2] The boy or group would then return to the benches. In the course of this kind of performance, choirboys acted with minimal — if any — direction from an adult master and were regarded no differently from any other celebrant. The expectation was that they would perform as superbly as their adult counterparts. At the time of their performance, then, they were regarded as equal to nearly all the other singers within the service, despite their youth and their low rank within the church hierarchy.

On certain feast days, boys' voices were given pride of place. Christmas and Easter, for example, employed them in elaborate liturgies that were often full-fledged dramas. In some cases, the timbre of their voices was used to represent that of women; in others, that of angels; most of the time, however, the boys' voices had no representational function.[3] A performance practice for Christmas Matins at Aachen's collegiate church will serve as an example of how boys' voices dominated certain liturgies and could be employed to dramatic effect. The first responsory of Matins for Christmas, *Hodie nobis caelorum rex*, refers to Christ as "the king of heaven" who "has deigned to be born of a Virgin for us, so that he may recall lost humankind to the heavenly kingdom." The text of the verse represents the angelic chorus that, according to Luke's Gospel, appeared to the shepherds with the news of Christ's birth, singing "Glory be to God in the highest," etc.

---

[1] For two examples of this practice see Wright, *Music and Ceremony*, 181; Rice, "Music and Ritual," 241.

[2] Clerval notes that Matins clerks at Notre-Dame of Chartres were fined if they were unable to sing the entire Psalter from memory and were required to sing Matins in the dark; see *L'Ancienne Maîtrise de Notre-Dame de Chartres*, 105.

[3] On the use of boys to sing the "roles" of women, angels, and other characters in religious drama, see the essays by Boynton, Kirkman, Rastall, and Ruiz in this volume.

Concerning this piece, the church's ordinals state that two boys sang the first responsory from the church's gallery.[1] By the mid-fifteenth century, lay worshippers would have stood in the church's nave directly below them. Since most of the liturgical singing — much of it by men up to this point in the service — occurred at ground level in the choir, the boys' performance of this responsory was striking both because of its location in the gallery and the sound of the boys' voices in contrast to that of the men. Their location and sound would likely have been deemed particularly appropriate when singing the responsory's verse, since at that moment they recited text associated with singing by the angelic choirs. A late-fourteenth-century polyphonic setting of this verse in three voices that survives in a manuscript today in Erfurt can be linked with Aachen's collegiate church; its composer clearly meant to delineate the portion of the text sung by angelic choirs from the more narrative responsory proper, and he almost certainly also intended boys to sing the setting from the gallery.[2]

Manuscripts of polyphonic music also attest to the level of skill that choristers attained. Scholars have noted the complexity of much of the polyphonic repertory that boys sang, reflecting both their sight-reading ability and their possession of the requisite vocal technique to sing for long periods in a high register. Like adults, boys performed from choirbooks in which the placement of the text was often not indicated with any degree of specificity. Choristers had to know how to fit to music those syllables of text that were haphazardly placed or even omitted altogether (because scribes had left them out or chosen not to repeat the portions of the text that were already written).

Choristers in Context

THE studies in this volume share a number of common themes. On the most general level, they show the manifold ways in which ecclesiastical institutions in medieval and early modern Europe developed structures and spaces for the education and musical training of the young people in their charge. The institutions examined here are representative of the wide range of settings that existed for the formation of young singers: monasteries, cathedral choir schools, collegiate churches, private tutelage, and the apprenticeship system. In monasteries and in secular churches, young singers were in many ways full members of the community, as can be seen from the detailed provisions for their upkeep. Beneficed offices such as that of the cantor's assistant and the master of the choirboys emerged concomitantly with the expansion and adaptation of church precincts and monastic complexes to create special quarters for housing young singers along with their teachers and supervisors as well as designating spaces for study.

In towns and cities, the ever more important role of boy singers reinforced the

---

[1] Aachen, Domarchiv, G 1, fol. 3ʳ; G 2, fol. 11ᵛ. "Et nota quod duo scolares [G 2: scolares vicarii] supra altum monasterium cant*abunt primum Responsorium*."

[2] Rice, "Music and Ritual," 255–58.

intersection of ecclesiastical administration with civic and other urban organizations that spanned diverse functions. In early medieval Rome, such organizations included the *orphanotrophium* and the *schola cantorum* (Dyer); in the early modern period, they encompassed both religious confraternities and the choirs of several of the city's churches (O'Regan). In English towns and cities, choirboys from local churches sang in performances of religious drama alongside members of guilds and corporations (Rastall).

The ways in which young singers were educated exhibit some universal features despite variations across time and place. Training and formation often entailed living with teachers, the community of musicians substituting for the family unit both *de facto* and *de iure*. Monasteries had internal educational systems that accommodated not only oblates and novices, but also, in some female convents, student boarders who were not (yet) committed to a life in the church (Reardon, Yardley). As can be seen in the chapters on Aachen, Cambrai, and Saint-Omer, cathedral and collegiate churches created complex infrastructures for the education of choirboys. Musical and personal relationships among members of these religious communities were interwoven with their corporate identities. Finally, contractual agreements of apprenticeship for singers, which are comparable to such contracts in other trades, reveal the intersection of professional education with paid performance, and point to the teachers' responsibilities for the lodging as well as the instruction of their charges (O'Regan).

Nearly all our information on musical education from the seventh to the seventeenth century shows the central place of memorization and musical literacy in the training of young singers.[1] In some cases we know which texts (musical and grammatical) were used for teaching (Flynn, Ruiz) and in others we even have the specific vocal exercises and other compositions that students learned (Flynn, Reardon, Yardley). In addition to purely musical instruction, choristers' studies focused on Latin grammar and composition. Beyond the education offered by cathedral schools, the administrations of many secular churches enabled choristers to pursue further studies after their voices had broken by providing scholarships for study at school and university (as in Aachen, Cambrai, Saint-Omer, and Seville).

The opportunities and privileges afforded by the scholarship system are only one indication of the powerful influence exercised by ecclesiastical institutions on the social mobility of young singers. The boy singers in the early medieval Roman schola cantorum were prepared for a variety of ecclesiastical careers (Dyer). In the early modern period one Roman confraternity was devoted to the training of orphans (O'Regan). Entry into a choir school such as that of Cambrai offered the possibility of professional advancement to boys who were otherwise underprivileged (Dumont). Indeed, some choirboys from the collegiate church of Saint-

---

[1] On the literacy and musical training of young singers, see also Katherine Zieman, *Singing the New Song: Literacy and Liturgy in Late Medieval England* (Philadelphia, 2008), which became available only as this volume was going to press and therefore could not be taken into consideration here.

Omer embarked on brilliant careers as ecclesiastical singers with the help of elite patronage (Kirkman). The apprenticeship system represented yet another way in which young singers honed their professional skills (Flynn and O'Regan).

The essays in this volume also show how profoundly the important function of young singers in ecclesiastical institutions influenced musical repertories. Children's voices were used to great effect to perform specific music on certain days in the church year such as Christmas, the feast of the Holy Innocents, Palm Sunday, Easter, and Corpus Christi. Choristers played a special role on occasions such as the feast of the Boy Bishop, and they took part in all manner of representational performances including liturgical drama, nonliturgical religious plays, *sacre rappresentazioni*, and dramas composed of *laude*. They often performed the parts of angels. In early modern Rome, boys' voices were used in catechism classes because they symbolized purity.

Choristers performed a wide range of musical genres, both as a separate group and in the choir along with older singers. The chants they sang in the Divine Office included the *Benedicamus Domino*, antiphons, hymns, versicles, and the intonations and solo verses of Matins responsories on high feast days such as Christmas; they also performed the Gradual and Alleluia at Mass. Some of this repertory appears in books prepared specifically for their use (Planchart, Rice, Ruiz). Choirboys sang chant not only in church services but also in religious plays (Rastall). In Italy, they took part in devotional performances of *laude spirituali* (O'Regan, Reardon). Musical repertory and status in a religious institution differentiated groups of young singers from one another; as Colleen Reardon and Anne Bagnall Yardley demonstrate, boarders in convents were allowed to perform a wide variety of genres, whereas the novices sang only chant.

During the fifteenth and sixteenth centuries, choirboys became increasingly important in the performance of polyphony. The choirbooks used by boys contained some of the polyphonic repertory they regularly sang, such as motets for Vespers (Planchart, Ruiz). Particularly beginning in the fifteenth century, boy singers took part in performances funded by private endowments intended to benefit the souls of their donors (Kirkman, Planchart, Rice, Ruiz). The repertory sung in these memorials often consisted of music for the dead (Seville), Marian Masses or Salve services on Saturday or daily private performance of the *Salve regina* (Seville, Saint-Omer), and festal Matins (Cambrai).

While the studies in this volume bring out common experiences among choristers throughout the period from 650 to 1700, they also illustrate regional and institutional differences, demonstrating the richly varied experiences of young musicians. At the same time, they show continuity in the ways churches dealt with the choristers who were such essential members of their institutions. Many of the educational traditions, modes of organization, and musical roles for choristers described here continued well into the eighteenth (and in some cases the nineteenth) century.[1] In our own era, however, public music-making has become primarily the

---

[1] Some recent studies of choristers' roles in ecclesiastical institutions address a slightly later period but nevertheless reveal continuity with the centuries addressed in this book:

purview of adults. This book aims to enrich our understanding of the important role (sometimes unfamiliar to modern musicians) that young singers have played in the history of Western music.

Maîtrises et chapelles aux xviie et xviiie siècles: Des Institutions musicales au service de Dieu, ed. Bernard Dompnier (Clermont-Ferrand, 2003); Carlos Martínez Gil, *La Capilla de Música de la Catedral de Toledo (1700–1764): Evolución de un concepto sonoro* (Toledo, 2003), 137–75.

1

BOY SINGERS OF THE ROMAN SCHOLA CANTORUM

Joseph Dyer

THE first documentary evidence of the presence of boy choristers at Rome occurs near the beginning of Ordo Romanus I, a detailed description of the papal Mass on Easter Sunday at the Roman basilica of S. Maria Maggiore around the beginning of the eighth century. As the pope approached the altar precinct (*presbyterium*), the members of the *schola cantorum* lined up on either side of the processional path.

> Then they [the schola] go according to their rank in front of the altar. They stand in order on either side in two rows — *paraphonistae* on both sides on the outside and the children on both sides in front of them in order.[1]

The rubric assumes that the members of the schola, adults and children, form a "guard of honor" patterned after Byzantine court ceremonial as the papal procession approached the altar for Mass: "et pertransit pontifex in caput scolae."[2] Recent archeological research suggests the presence of a solea leading to the presbyterium at S. Maria Maggiore. This would mean that the members of the schola lined up on both sides of the space within the barriers, the adult singers standing behind the boys, but the presence of a solea at the time the ordo was compiled is by no means essential.[3] The rest of the rubrics in Ordo Romanus I pertaining to the duties of the schola cantorum do not refer separately to the children, and there

---

[1] "Tunc illi elevantes per ordinem vadunt ante altare; statuuntur per ordinem acies duae tantum, parafonistae quidem hunc et inde a foris, infantes ab utroque latere infra per ordinem"; Ordo Romanus I.43; Michel Andrieu, ed., *Les Ordines romani du haut Moyen-Âge*, 5 vols., Spicilegium Sacrum Lovaniense, II, 23–24, 28, 29 (Louvain, 1931–61), 2:81 (hereafter cited as OR and Andrieu, respectively).

[2] OR I.49; Andrieu, 2:83. For the Byzantine equivalent, see *Constantin VII Porphyrogénète: Livre des cérémonies*, 2 vols., ed. Albert Vogt (Paris, 1935): Καταλαβὼν δὲ ὁ πατριάρχης μετὰ τῆς λιτῆς, διέρχεται μέσον αὐτῶν (1.39[30], feast of the Annunciation occurring on the third Sunday of Lent), ed. Vogt, 1:153; virtually the same phrase is found in book 1.10 (Easter Monday), ed. Vogt, 1:67.

[3] Victor Saxer, "Recinzioni liturgiche secondo le fonti letterarie," in *Mededelingen van het Nederlands Instituut te Rome* [Papers of the Netherlands Institute in Rome] 59 (2000),

is no reason to expect that they would do so: the introit was a special case that required precise description. The reiteration of the introit ritual in Ordo Romanus 4 makes no mention of boy singers, though an "honor guard" of subdeacons and the schola is mentioned.[1]

A reference to the Roman schola cantorum occurs in Ordo Romanus 23, a series of brief rubrical notes attributable to a Frankish observer well versed in the liturgy, who was present in Rome for Holy Week, probably in the first half of the eighth century. The intervention of the schola cantorum is mentioned twice at the Easter Vigil: first during the singing of the litany in procession to the baptistery and then at the singing of the Agnus Dei, to which the acolytes make the response.[2] The author does not hint that child singers were involved, but since he noted mainly what struck him as interesting, he may simply have taken the presence of boy choristers for granted.

The "infantes" of the schola had a prominent role in the Paschal Vespers celebrated at the Lateran on Easter Sunday and during the following week.[3] According to Ordo Romanus 27, together with the *primicerius* they chanted the first Alleluia of Easter Vespers, *Dominus regnavit*, to which the adult paraphonistae responded, possibly repeating the introductory alleluia.[4] In the course of the verse the adult singers "announce the words to the children" ("adnuntiant verba infantibus"). The meaning of this rubric is clarified by the Old Roman gradual, Vat. lat. 5319, which contains all the music for the Easter Vespers.[5] This indicates that the paraphonistae preintoned for the boys the first words of two phrases of the Alleluia verse, but not with the melody to which it was sung (Example

71–79, esp. 73; and Federico Guidobaldi, "Struttura e chronologia delle recinzioni liturgiche nelle chiese di Roma dal vi al ix secolo," ibid., 81–99.

[1] OR 4.12–14 ("et transit pontifex cum diaconis per medium scolam"); Andrieu, 2:158–59.

[2] OR 23.28 and 33; Andrieu, 3:273. Subsequently, the Agnus Dei was omitted at the Vigil Mass.

[3] OR 27.67–94; Andrieu, 3:362–72. The archdeacon of Rome, not the pope, presided at the Vespers, which were celebrated with the collaboration of bishops, priests, deacons, and the schola cantorum.

[4] The meaning of the Greek term *paraphonista* remains doubtful; it does not necessarily imply singing in parts. See the discussion of theories in Michael Maier, "Paraphonos, paraphonia," *Handbuch der musikalischen Terminologie* (Auslieferung 34 [2003]), 6–7, to which can be added Guido Milanese, "*Paraphonia–paraphonista*: Dalla lessicografia greca alla tarda antichità romana," in *Curiositas: Studi di cultura classica e medievale in onore di Ubaldo Pizzani*, ed. Antonino Isoala et al. (Naples, 2002), 407–21. (I express my thanks to Günther Michael Paucker for providing me with these references.) Despite the presumption of Eastern origin, the term is not present in any Eastern liturgical or imperial source known to the present writer.

[5] Vatican City, Biblioteca Apostolica Vaticana, Vat. lat. 5319, fols. 84ᵛ–96ᵛ; the chants are transcribed by Margareta Landwehr-Melnicki in Bruno Stäblein, *Die Gesänge des altrömischen Graduale Vat. lat. 5319*, Monumenta monodica medii aevi, 2 (Kassel, 1970), 84*–140*. See also Joseph Smits van Waesberghe, "'De glorioso officio . . . dignitate apostolica . . .' (Amalar): Zum Aufbau der Groß-Alleluia in den päpstlichen Ostervespern," in *Essays Presented to Egon Wellesz*, ed. Jack Westrup (Oxford, 1966), 48–73.

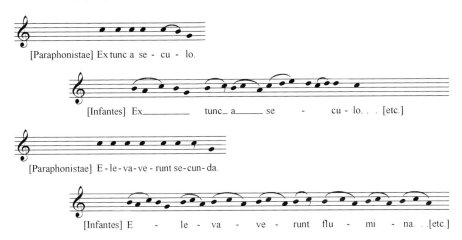

Example 1.1: *Alleluia. Dominus regnavit* [excerpt] (Rome, Biblioteca Apostolica Vaticana, Vat. lat. 5319, fol. 85; rubrics (paraphonistae/infantes) supplied from Ordo Romanus 27.70)

1.1), a practice in some ways similar to that of the prompter in the modern opera house. The gradual does not, like Ordo 27, identify the boys of the schola as the ones for whom the intonation was intended. In that source, the preintonation is preceded by the letter "P" (paraphonistae) and the following phrase by "schol[a]." Ordo 27 specifies that the primicerius leads the concluding alleluia "cum melodiis infantium," to which the adult paraphonistae again "respond." (The music of the final alleluia of *Dominus regnavit* is slightly more extended than that of the first.)

After a station in the baptistery ("ad fontes"), during which two Greek-texted alleluias were sung, a station is made at the oratory of St. John *ad vestem*, one of the chapels adjoining the baptistery, where the primus of the schola sang "cum pueris" the *Alleluia. Venite exultemus*. The same alleluia was repeated at the third station of Vespers, the oratory of St. Andrew *ad crucem*.[1] The participation of the children is not expressly mentioned, the rubric merely indicating "ut supra." Ordo 27 continues with brief rubrical notes about what was sung each day of the week, but the children of the schola are not assigned specific roles on these days.

In the rubrics for Easter Sunday Vespers copied into the Romano-Germanic Pontifical (ca. 960) similar directions are repeated.[2] The Pontifical earlier refers to

---

[1] Pasquale Adinolfi, *Laterano e Via maggiore: Saggio della topografia di Roma nell'età di mezzo* (Rome, 1857), 85–87; Ingo Herklotz, "Der Campus Lateranus im Mittelalter," *Römisches Jahrbuch für Kunstgeschichte* 22 (1985), 1–43.

[2] "Quo finito [*Alleluia. Beatus vir*], primus scolae cum paraphonistis infantibus incipit responsorium gradalem *Haec dies* cum versu *Confitemini*. Quo finito, incipit primus scolae cum melodis [*sic*] infantibus: *Alleluia. Pacha nostrum*; et respondent paraphonistae." Romano-Germanic Pontifical, 99.411; *Le Pontifical romano-germanique du dixième siècle*, ed. Cyrille Vogel and Reinhard Elze, 3 vols., Studi e Testi, 226–27, 269 (Vatican City, 1963–72), 2:116–17 (hereafter cited as RGP and Vogel–Elze, respectively. *Alleluia. Pascha nostrum* in

"infantes paraphonistae" who participate in the Palm Sunday procession, but this is difficult to relate to Roman usage, since a palm procession did not exist in Rome during the late tenth century, at least not in the papal liturgy.

[Ordo de die palmarum] Et **infantes paraphonistae** in loco competenti subsistentes imponant antiphonam *Fulgentibus palmis.*

[Ordo de die palmarum] His recedentibus, ex scola **infantes paraphonistae** iuxta crucem hunc hymnum cantent: *Gloria laus et honor tibi sit, rex Christe,* clero prosequente eundem versum.[1]

This is the extent to which the participation of boy choristers is attested in the Roman liturgical sources and the Romano-Germanic Pontifical. When mentioned, the boys were singled out because of some special function. Their intervention on Palm Sunday symbolized the children among those who welcomed Jesus to Jerusalem.

Boys' Singing outside the Liturgy

CHILD singers might have been involved in the presentation of the long and rather parodistic poem *Cena Cypriani*, performed in the presence of Charles the Bald, when he visited Rome in 875. The poem was shortly thereafter revised by John the Deacon (Himmonides) for his patron, Pope John VIII.[2] (This is the same pope who commissioned a biography of Gregory I that credited him with the foundation of the schola cantorum, as will be discussed below.) In the prologue to the *Cena* John mentions that his version of the poem was presented for the pope's enjoyment "in albis paschalibus" (i.e., on Easter Saturday) and that the prior of the schola (sc. cantorum) was present wearing a headdress resembling horns ("coronatus scolae prior cornibus").

While the participation of child singers is not explicitly mentioned in the prologue to the *Cena Cypriani*, it is in connection with the Roman festival of Cornomania, also celebrated on Easter Saturday in the presence of the pope. By the time the Cornomania festivities were described by Canon Benedict of St. Pe-

---

the Old Roman chant tradition has such *melodiae* (Vat. lat. 5319, fol. 85) and also includes a preintonation of the phrase "Christus qui nos adiuvet."

[1] RGP 99.185 and 187; Vogel–Elze, 2:47 and 2:48. One notes that the "clerus" respond, not a special choir.

[2] The *Cena Cypriani* is edited in *Monumenta germaniae historica: Poetae latini aevi carolini,* 4 vols. (Berlin, 1881–1923), 4:857–900 [870]. See also M. A. Laporte, "Le Souper de Jean Diacre," *Mélanges d'archéologie et d'histoire* 21 (1901), 305–87, and Girolamo Arnaldi, "Giovanni Immonide e la cultura a Roma al tempo di Giovanni VIII," *Bollettino dell'Istituto Storico Italiano per il Medioevo* 68 (1956), 33–89. The *Cena Cypriani* and the Cornomania are treated by Martine Boiteux, "Le feste: Cultura del riso et della derisione," in *Roma medievale,* ed. André Vauchez, Storia di Roma dall'antichità a oggi, 2 (Rome and Bari, 2001), 293–96. See also Ernesto Monaci, "Per la storia della *Schola cantorum* Lateranense," *Archivio della Reale Società Romana di Storia Patria* 20 (1897), 451–63.

ter's in his *Liber politicus*, compiled between 1140 and 1143, the festival was only a memory, having been suppressed by Pope Gregory VII (1073–85).[1] According to Benedict, on Easter Saturday afternoon, the archpriests of the diaconiae led their congregations to the Lateran to sing *laudes* before the pope, whose appearance they awaited near the building that housed the Lateran laundry ("sub follonica"). The *laudes* were followed by considerable buffoonery: e.g., each of the *mansonarii* (sacristans) of the diaconiae, crowned with flowers and dressed in mock-episcopal attire, carried a *phinobolum*, a cornucopia with bells resembling a jester's staff, and led a round dance.

Benedict refers to the presence of children from the nearby schola building: "exeunt pueri de scola ad novum argenzolum."[2] For Easter Saturday he provides only the incipits of the Latin and Greek songs sung by the boys, but the texts can be completed from the *laudes puerorum* sung on the fourth Sunday of Lent, when the boys went from house to house singing these *laudes* and receiving gifts of eggs in return.[3] Benedict transliterated the Greek texts into the Latin alphabet, but in such a confused fashion that it is unlikely he knew what the words meant. Only a skilled reconstruction — several have been attempted — can succeed in making much sense of the text.[4] The song begins with a salutation addressed to the "master of the house" (Οἰκοδέσποτα) from the "scholars" (σχολητές), who also welcome the coming of spring. The children are encouraged to rejoice and to go to school to learn letters (γράμματα μανθάνοντες); from early dawn their assiduous teacher has been writing and reading (γράφει καὶ ἀναγινώσκει). The song continues with a prayer that God will protect their teacher (τὸν διδάσκαλον ἡμῶν, Κύριε, φύλαχον ἡμῖν) and concludes with a comparison between the brightness of spring and the radiance of a world illumined by Christ's Resurrection.

These *laudes* contain nothing that would identify them as exclusively the "property" of the boys of the schola cantorum. Timothy Miller, while maintaining that "the singers who originally chanted this song" belonged to the schola, believed that its ultimate source was Byzantium, presumably passing through the Greek colony in Rome. He was struck by the presence of the word "Romania," generally applied

---

[1] *Le Liber censuum de l'Église romaine*, ed. Paul Fabre and Louis Duchesne, Bibliothèque des Écoles françaises d'Athènes et de Rome, 2nd ser., vi/1–2 (Paris, 1910), 2:171–2 and the introduction (1:107–13). Performance of the *Cena Cypriani* is not mentioned.

[2] Jeffrey Dean surmises that the *hapax legomenon* "argenzolum" belongs to an attested family of medieval agricultural terms beginning "aren-" or "argen-," signifying "field," "vineyard," "plowland." A newly cleared or developed open space adjacent to the schola building may be intended: "The boys go out from the schola to the new (field/garden/piazza?)."

[3] "In the middle of Lent, the students take up staves [*lanceas*] with banners and bells. First they sing *laudes* in front of the church; then they go from house to house singing and receiving eggs as a reward for the *laudes*; thus was it done of old" ("In media quadragesima scolares accipiunt lanceas cum vexillis et tintinabulis. Prius faciunt laudes ante ecclesiam, deinde eunt per domos cantando et accipiunt ova pro beneficio illius laudis; sic antiquitus faciebant"); *Le Liber censuum*, 2:172.

[4] I have followed that in Zoï Patala, "Les Chants grecs du *Liber Politicus* du chanoine Benoît," *Byzantion* 66 (1996), 512–30, esp. 519–23.

to the Christian Empire of the East.[1] The *laudes* ask Christ to bestow on a certain "patriarch" Benedict "many years" (πολλοῖς τοῖς ἔτεσι), a conventional wish in Eastern circles. Was this perhaps Benedict II (684–85), a pope who held office for only a short time a few years after the Sixth Ecumenical Council, which resolved the divisions over monotheletism? This was a period when all could hope for the safety of "Romania."

ROMAN CLERICAL CAREERS

Two of the Ordines Romani (35 and 36) make reference to the initiation of young Roman boys to clerical careers, though neither refers specifically to the schola cantorum. Ordo 35 begins with a short "ordo quomodo in sancta romana ecclesia lector ordinatur."[2] The candidate for the rank of lector, the initial step in an ecclesiastical career, had been prepared by a family with the means to provide private tutoring and of a social status that gave access to the papal presence. The opening of Ordo Romanus 35 reads as follows:

> As soon as a child, given by his parents to a tutor (*magistro*), has been taught sacred letters and has reached the legitimate age to become a cleric and [has been] sagely instructed in reading, if he has a father who can do this on his own, let [the father] suggest the following to the lord pope concerning him, and if he has no father, let a relative or friend intercede on his behalf.[3]

The ordo then provides a specimen of the father's petition, to which the pope replies that he will listen to the young man read at one of the offices ("ad nocturnarum vigilias," according to OR 35). The test having been successfully passed, the pope blessed the new lector with the prayer: "By the intercession of blessed Peter, prince of the apostles, and of St. Paul, the vessel of election, may the Lord save and protect [you] and grant you a learned tongue."[4] The authentically Roman character of the rite is guaranteed not only by the involvement of the *domnus apostolicus*

---

[1] Timothy S. Miller, *The Orphans of Byzantium: Child Welfare in the Christian Empire* (Washington, D.C., 2003), 217–18.

[2] OR 35.1–6; Andrieu, 4:33–4. This passage is regarded as a later interpolation by Bernhard Schimmelpfennig, "Die Bedeutung Roms im päpstlichen Zeremoniell," in *Rom im hohen Mittelalter: Studien zu den Romvorstellungen und zur Rompolitik vom 10. bis zum 12. Jahrhundert*, ed. Bernhard Schimmelpfennig and Ludwig Schmugge (Sigmaringen, 1992), 47–61, esp. 50–55.

[3] "Dum infans, traditus a parentibus magistro, sacris apicibus fuerit edoctus atque clericus iam legitima aetate adultus et ad legendum prudenter instructus, si patrem habet et per semetipsum valet, suggerat de eo ad domnum apostolicum sic; et si patrem non habuerit, propinqui aut amici eius intercedant pro ipso"; OR 35.1; Andrieu, 4:33.

[4] "Intercedente beato Petro principem apostolorum et sancto Paulo vas electionis, salvet et protegat et eruditam linguam tribuat tibi dominus"; OR 35.4; Andrieu, 4:33–4. The grammatical solecisms of the first phrase of the prayer are those of the manuscript London, British Library, MS Add. 15222 (France, ca. 1000).

but also by the note in the ordo that ordinary bishops ("per diversas provintias") use a different prayer, the text of which is given.

The candidate presented to the pope had reached the *aetas legitima* and level of learning required to enter the clergy as a lector and to make a mature commitment to the clerical estate. Epitaphs of Roman lectors indicate that many were in their twenties when they died; most were attached to a *titulus* (local church), not to an entire ecclesiastical region.[1] Ordo 35 cannot be later than the first quarter of the tenth century, since, as Michel Andrieu pointed out, it was a source for the editors of the Romano-Germanic Pontifical. But the ritual just described must be many centuries older, perhaps no later than the early sixth century, since it assumes that the lectorate is still a function to be discharged rather than just a stage on the path to higher orders.[2] There is no indication of what the next step for the new lector would be. As the scion of one of Rome's better families, he may have continued his education privately, while offering his services to his titulus. Alternatively, he may have been admitted forthwith to the household of the pope for further initiation to the obligations of the clerical estate and the functions of the Lateran administration. The passage in Ordo 35 is incidentally an argument against the existence of a hypothetical Roman "schola lectorum" that allegedly metamorphosed into the schola cantorum.[3]

A comparable career path is anticipated by Ordo Romanus 36 ("De gradibus romanae ecclesiae"):

> In whatever school are found boys who sing the psalms well, let them be taken and trained in the schola cantorum; afterwards let them become *cubicularii* [members of the papal household]. If they happen to be sons of the nobility, let them immediately be trained in the *cubiculum*.[4]

The first sentence might be construed as a set of instructions to a "talent scout" whose responsibility it was to recruit for the papal choir the best vocal talent Rome had to offer, but this interpretation hardly seems likely. If it were the case, how can one explain that the career path depended primarily on social standing — the schola cantorum for ordinary "pueri" and the papal *cubiculum* for "nobilium filii"? The main criterion of selection, described as "bene psallentes," almost certainly refers not to a gift for singing but to the ability to memorize a large portion

[1] Henri Leclercq, "Diacre," *Dictionnaire d'archéologie chrétienne et de liturgie*, 8/2: 2249–66, esp. 2249 (epitaph of Pope Liberius, 352–66).

[2] "On passe de la fonction conçue comme un service de la communauté à la fonction conçue comme étape d'une carrière"; Alexandre Faivre, *Naissance d'une hiérarchie: Les Premières Étapes du cursus clérical*, Théologie historique, 40 (Paris, 1977), 339.

[3] Enrico Josi, "Lectores — schola cantorum — clerici," *Ephemerides liturgicae* 44 (1930), 282–90.

[4] "Primum in qualicumque scola reperti fuerint pueri bene psallentes, tolluntur et nutriuntur in scola cantorum, et postea fiunt cubicularii. Si autem nobilium filii fuerint, statim in cubiculo nutriuntur"; OR 36.1; Andrieu, 4:195.

of the Psalter at an early age — an achievement regarded in the Middle Ages as an unmistakable sign of intellectual ability.

In this regard the *Liber pontificalis* praised Pope Leo II (682–83) as "distinguished for his chanting and psalmody, which he interpreted elegantly and with the most sensitive and subtle touches" ("cantelena ac psalmodia praecipuus et in earum sensibus subtillissima exercitatione limatus"). Nearly identical words appear in the biographical sketch of Gregory III (731–41): "knowing by heart all the psalms in order and interpreting them elegantly with the most sensitive and subtle touches" ("psalmos omnes per ordinem memoriter retinens et in eorum sensibus subtilissima exercitatione limatus").[1] The apparent musical emphasis of the earlier entry is changed to what was probably the original meaning: both popes possessed a remarkable mastery of the Psalter and its spiritual significance. Gregory had committed the Psalter to memory, perhaps not a singular achievement for an adult, but noteworthy in a child of tender years.

The distinction made in Ordo 36 between education in the schola cantorum and the *cubiculum* (or *patriarchium*, as the papal household is called in the *Liber pontificalis*) is an essential one. In his survey of early medieval monastic and clerical education in Italy, Georg Hörle overstated the importance of the Roman schola cantorum, asserting that "for the most part, the popes of the following period [i.e., after Leo II] received their education in Gregory's schola cantorum."[2] He came to this conclusion by failing to distinguish between education in the *patriarchium/cubiculum* and that received in the quite separate schola cantorum. In this he was followed by Gerhard Pietzsch, who quoted extensively from biographies of popes who were educated *in patriarchio* (Gregory II, 715–31) or *in patriarchio Lateranense* (Stephen IV, 816–17), assuming (incorrectly) that this was identical to the schola cantorum.[3] Young boys admitted directly to the papal household, typically the offspring of prominent families, were marked for early advancement towards high ecclesiastical office. The lives of those destined to be popes were by no means typical, and it might be doubted whether many of the schola's alumni gained admission to the papal *cubiculum*.

---

[1] Louis Duchesne, ed., *Le Liber pontificalis: Texte, introduction et commentaire*, 2 vols. (Paris, 1886–92), complemented by Cyrille Vogel, *Additions et corrections* (Paris, 1957), 1:359 (Leo), 1:415 (Gregory); hereafter cited as LP. *The Book of Pontiffs (Liber Pontificalis): The Ancient Biographies of the First Ninety Roman Pontiffs to AD 715*, trans. Raymond Davis, rev. ed., Translated Texts for Historians, 5 (Liverpool, 2000), 80 (Leo); and *The Lives of the Eighth-Century Popes (Liber Pontificalis): The Ancient Biographies of Nine Popes from AD 715 to AD 817*, trans. Raymond Davis, Translated Texts for Historians, 13 (Liverpool, 1992), 19 (Gregory).

[2] Georg H. Hörle, *Frühmittelalterliche Mönchs- und Klerikerbildung in Italien*, Freiburger theologische Studien, 13 (Freiburg im Br., 1914), 27.

[3] Gerhard Pietzsch, *Die Musik im Erziehungs- und Bildungsideal des ausgehenden Altertums und frühen Mittelalters*, Studien zur Geschichte der Musiktheorie im Mittelalter, 2 (Halle an der Saale, 1932; repr. 1969), 52–54. The necessary correction was made by Fedor Schneider, *Rom und Romgedanke im Mittelalter: Die geistigen Grundlagen der Renaissance* (Munich, 1925; repr. 1952), 110–12.

Only two popes are known to have spent any time as students in the schola cantorum. In both instances the *Liber pontificalis* gives an insight into what was taught to children enrolled there. The future Pope Sergius I (687–701), son of a Syrian émigré, arrived in Rome from Sicily during the pontificate of Adeodatus (672–76), and "because he was studious and competent in the task of chanting, he was handed over to the prior of the singers for education."[1] Given the fact that he was almost immediately accepted into the ranks of Roman clergy upon arrival, he must have already been a member of the clerical state in Sicily. Within a few years, Pope Leo II (682–83) ordained him cardinal priest of S. Susanna. Four years later Sergius ascended the papal throne. Since he must have been of mature years when he arrived in Rome from Sicily, one might imagine that he was sent to the schola not for basic education or lessons in singing but to improve his command of Latin. An institution designed to train future members of the clergy would surely have offered not only language instruction and biblical studies but whatever pertained to the obligations of clergy.

Another future pope, Sergius II (844–47), orphaned at the age of twelve, attracted the attention of Pope Leo III (795–816), who, "recalling his parents' nobility" ("parentum eius nobilitatem recolens"), assigned him to the schola cantorum "for general education and to be instructed in the sweet melodies of chant" ("ad erudiendum communes tradidit litteras et ut mellifluis instrueretur cantilenae melodiis").[2] Sergius, who could not have been entirely destitute if his parents enjoyed high social standing, apparently had no relatives willing or able to care for him. Only the schola cantorum had the facilities necessary to provide for the needs of an orphan.

The Schola Cantorum and the Orphanotrophium

THE fact that Sergius II was an orphan when assigned to the schola cantorum brings up the question of its association with an *orphanotrophium* (orphanage). That an orphanage existed in Rome by the end of the seventh century is confirmed by the record of legal action (*privilegium*) taken to recover property of which the orphanotrophium had been wrongly deprived by the *avaritia* of its previous director. Preserved in the *Liber diurnus*, a collection of formulae used in the papal *scrinarium* (chancery), the *privilegium* asserts that the income from this property, whose location and extent are not specified, was needed to provide for the sustenance of the children ("pupillorum alimentorum necessitatibus").[3] Since fewer children could be supported on the diminished income, there was a further

---

[1] "Quia studiosus erat et capax in officio cantilenae, priori cantorum pro doctrina est tradita"; LP 1:371; trans. Davis, *The Book of Pontiffs*, 85.

[2] LP 2:86. Sergius was related to the family of Pope Stephen IV (816–17).

[3] Theodor von Sickel, ed., *Liber diurnus romanorum pontificum ex unico codice Vaticano* (Vienna, 1889), 127–29 (no. 97); the text is also available in Jacques-Paul Migne, ed., *Patrologiae cursus completus: Series latina*, 225 vols. (Paris, 1844–55), 105:115–16; hereafter cited as PL.

danger "lest the order of singers should disappear and shame be inflicted thereby on the church of God" ("ne ergo cantorum deficeret ordo atque hinc dei ecclesia contumelia irrogaretur"). This statement identifies the orphanotrophium as an institution expected to produce boy singers to participate in regular liturgical observances, and the wording of the document suggests that they performed music during the papal liturgy. Indeed, the *privilegium* is couched as a papal initiative: "we deem this [demand for restoration of the property] to be just by the authority of blessed Peter, prince of the apostles, in whose place, although unworthy of divine graciousness, we act" ("iustum fore decernimus auctoritate beati Petri apostolorum principis, cuius meritis impares dignatione vero divina vices gerimus"). Can it be an accident that this *privilegium* dates from the pontificate of Sergius I, who would have had good reason to look after the welfare of the "alma mater" that had assisted him early in his brilliant career in the Roman church?

Pope Sergius II had a similar motivation some years later for restoring the house of the schola cantorum, "which was formerly called the orphanotrophium," since the old building had fallen into a precarious state of disrepair ("prae nimia vetustate iam emarcuerat et pene in ruina posita et confracta a priscis temporibus").[1] As an alumnus, Sergius would have taken a very special interest in the schola cantorum and its apparently venerable building. He donated a precious textile as well as a silver paten and chalice to the schola's oratory, which was dedicated to the Roman martyr, St. Stephen.

Judging from the use of the word "formerly," however, the orphanotrophium had ceased to function as such during the lifetime of Sergius II. Pope Stephen V (885–91) donated a book of sermons to a hospice at the Vatican dedicated to the memory of Gregory I and a copy of the Heptateuch to the schola cantorum "which was formerly called the Orphanotrophium."[2] By a deed dated 911 a certain Johannes, identified as "a subdeacon of the Holy Roman Church and primicerius of the schola cantorum, which is called the orphanotrophium," conceded land near the Porta Maggiore to the archpriest Merco and to the "honesta femina" Petronia.[3] He must have done this in his official capacity, for it required the approval of both the administration of the schola ("consentiente scola cantorum") and Pope John X (914–28). As late as the end of the twelfth century the memory of a connection between the schola cantorum and the orphanage remained alive:

[1] LP 2:92; *The Lives of the Ninth-Century Popes (Liber Pontificalis) : The Ancient Biographies of Ten Popes from AD 817 to AD 891*, trans. Raymond Davis, Translated Texts for Historians, 20 (Liverpool, 1995), 85–86.

[2] "Reverentiam b. Gregorii precessoris sui prae oculis cordis habens, tribuit idem summus pontifex [Stephanus] in hospitale ipsius beati Gregorii in porticu b. Petri apostoli Sermonum sanctorum librum 1, et in Scola cantorum quae pridem Orphanotrophium vocabatur Eptaticum 1"; LP 2:195.

[3] "Iohannes venerabilis subdiaconum sancte romane ecclesie et primicerio scole cantorum qui appellatur orphanotropio"; *Il regesto Sublacense del secolo XI*, ed. Leone Allodi and Guido Levi (Rome, 1885), 159 (no. 112); see LP 2:102 n. 18, and *Codice topographico della città di Roma*, ed. Roberto Valentini and Giuseppe Zucchetti, 4 vols., Fonti per la Storia d'Italia, 81, 88, 90, 91 (Rome, 1940–53), 2:318 n. 1. The connection is here placed in the present tense (*appellatur*).

the *Liber censuum* records a gift of six *denarii* made to the oratory of the schola, called "Sancto Stephano Orfanotrofi."[1]

The mention of an oratory dedicated to St. Stephen allows us to locate the schola cantorum / orphanage building near the beginning of the old via Merulana (not the present avenue laid out by Gregory XIII in 1575 and originally named via Gregoriana). The Turin Catalogue of the churches of Rome (ca. 1320) lists the *ecclesia sancti Stephani de Scola Cantoris* immediately after the church of S. Matteo de Merulana, but notes that by then it had been abandoned.[2] The location of S. Matteo is depicted on several sixteenth-century maps of the city, but there is no trace of the schola building or its oratory, which had long since disappeared.[3]

The Roman Orphanotrophium and its Byzantine Model

ORPHANOTROPHIUM, the name by which the orphanage was known in Roman sources, points unmistakably to a Byzantine model, a relationship that can now be reevaluated thanks to the studies of Timothy Miller on the Orphanotropheion of Constantinople.[4] The establishment of that orphanage by a certain Zotikos took place during the reign of the Emperor Constantius (337–61) as part of the social program undertaken by Bishop Makedonius (340–48 and 350–60). It attracted substantial private philanthropic support and soon became one of the most prominent institutions of the Byzantine capital. In 472 the *orphanotrophos* (director of the orphanage) was elected patriarch of Constantinople, and in that same year the Emperor Leo I (457–74) bestowed on the institution singular financial and legal privileges, incidentally confirming Zotikos as its founder. The preeminence of the institution and its relationship to the by then sainted Zotikos is also attested by a decree of the Emperor Herakleios (610–41). The operation of the Orphanotropheion was later assumed by the imperial administration, and its administrator became a prominent court official. The orphanotrophos bore responsibility for managing not only the properties owned by the institution but

---

[1] *Le Liber censuum*, 303.

[2] The Paris catalogue of the churches of Rome (ca. 1230) also mentions "S. Stephanus Orphontrofium [*sic*]. Both lists are edited in Valentini and Zucchetti, *Codice topographico*, 3:310 (Turin) and 281 (Paris). In his sixteenth-century description of St. Peter's, Tiberio Alfarano seems to confuse this building with an orphanage associated with St. Martin's monastery at the Vatican; see *Tiberii Alpharani de Basilica Vaticanae antiquissima et nova structura*, ed. Michele Cerruti, Studi e Testi, 26 (Rome, 1914), 38.

[3] Views from the maps are conveniently assembled in Ferruccio Lombardi, *Roma: Le chiese scomparse; La memoria storica della città* (Rome, 1996), 89 (no. 95); see also ibid., 107 (no. 134). On the history of S. Matteo in Merulana, see Mariano Armellini, *Le chiese di Roma dal secolo IV al XIX*, rev. ed. Carlo Cecchelli, 2 vols. (Rome, 1942), 304–6.

[4] Timothy S. Miller, "The Orphanotropheion of Constantinople," in *Through the Eye of a Needle: Judeo-Christian Roots of Social Welfare*, ed. Emily Albu Hanawalt and Carter Lindberg (Kirksville, Mo., 1994), 83–104; Miller, *The Orphans of Byzantium*, 209–46 and 283–300 ("Epilogue: The West").

also for property held in the name of those orphans who would eventually become heirs to substantial estates.

Timothy Miller has drawn attention to the esteem in which the orphans' singing was held while the priest Akakios occupied the post of orphanotrophos during the patriarchate of Gennadios (485–72). Akakios' brother, a poet and composer, wrote hymns for the children to sing.[1] The Emperor Justinian II (685–95 and 705–11) appointed as orphanotrophos one of the Byzantine Church's greatest hymnodists, Andrew of Crete (ca. 660–740). Andrew's most celebrated work, the penitential "Great Kanon" (250 strophes), is sung at Matins on "Thursday of the Great Kanon," a date that falls within the fifth week of Lent.[2] It is more than likely that such a person would have had the children in his charge perform his own works. The *Book of Ceremonies* of the emperor Constantine VII Porphyrogenitos (913–59) contains a few references to the singing of orphans at important court festivals. On the feast of the Hypapante (Purification), the orphans, lined up on either side of the entry to the church of the Theotokos in Blachernae, acclaimed the emperor in song, "as is customary," before the beginning of the liturgy (ὀρφανά φωνοβολοῦντες ὑπερεύονται τὸν βασιλέα). Before the liturgy on the Annunciation, the orphans, along with the metropolitans and bishops, paid homage to him,[3] but their singing never assumed a role in the liturgy like that of the Roman "paraphonistae infantes."

The Schola Cantorum / Orphanotrophium and the Eastern Presence at Rome

BEGINNING in the first half of the seventh century, successive incursions by Persians, Avars, and Arabs created turmoil in the Christian East and North Africa. Marauding bands of Arabs pillaged the countryside, and the great cities of Syria and Palestine fell before Muslim armies. Jerusalem was lost by 638, and Egypt was wrested from Byzantine control by 646. Profoundly split by doctrinal differences (monophysitism, monotheletism), the Empire could not present a united front against the invaders: some Christians became willing collaborators against neighbors with whom they were in dispute over theological matters.[4] Defenseless monasteries were frequent targets of the invaders, and monks found

[1] Miller, "The Orphanotropheion," 90.

[2] *Triodion katanyktikon, periechon hapasan tēn anēkousan autō akolouthian tēs hagias kai megalēs Tessarakostēs*, 2nd ed. (Venice, 1863), 258–74; *Patrologiae cursus completus: Series graeca*, ed. Jacques-Paul Migne, 161 vols. (Paris, 1857–66), 97:1305–1444. For an English translation, see *The Lenten Triodion*, trans. Mother Mary and Kallistos Ware (London, 1977), 377–415.

[3] Constantine VII Porphyrogenitos, *De ceremoniis* 1.36 (27), 1.39 (30), and 1.10; ed. Vogt, *Le Livre des cérémonies*, 1:140 [Hypapante], 153 [Annunciation], 69 [Easter Monday]; see p. 19 n. 2 above.

[4] For a vivid recent account of this period and the doctrinal controversies see Andrew J. Ekonomou, *Byzantine Rome and the Greek Popes: Eastern Influences on Rome and the Papacy from Gregory the Great to Zacharias, A.D. 590–752* (Lanham, Md., 2007), 43–112.

themselves at odds with bishops and emperors they regarded as heretics. The same dilemma faced members of the secular clergy who, like the monks, adhered to the teaching of the Council of Chalcedon (451) that Jesus, consubstantial with the Father, possessed the fullness of both divine and human natures.

From the standpoint of safety and orthodoxy, many Eastern monks and clergy viewed Rome as the destination of choice, and Greek monasteries were established in Rome beginning in the last half of the 640s.[1] Well trained in theology and expert controversialists, the monks served the papacy well at a crucial moment by their vigorous participation in the Roman synod of 649 that condemned monotheletism: the theological position that Christ had but a single will, the divine necessarily predominating over the human, a view that diminished Christ's human nature.[2] Excellent education, determination to uphold orthodox belief, and diplomatic skills made the Easterners a preferred group from which popes were elected. The era of the "Greek" popes, elected from the secular clergy, lasted more than a century, coming to a close with the death of Zacharias in 752. A foreign-born secular community of indeterminable size must have also existed in the city. Ordo Romanus II anticipates that some children presented for baptism came from families whose primary language was Greek.[3] The officiating presbyter asks the acolyte in what language the candidates for baptism will confess the Lord: either Greek or Latin is foreseen as an answer.

With such a notable Eastern presence in Rome, Constantinopolitan institutions would have been familiar. In the last third of the seventh century the first *monasteria diaconiae* were established in Rome by Pope Benedict II (684–85).[4] Unknown in Rome before the arrival of the Easterners, these served as warehouses and as points of distribution for food. They were staffed by monks, many (if not most) of Eastern origin, though administered by a Roman *pater diaconiae*. The founding of the network of diaconiae offers evidence of the kind of impulse to provide social services that could have also sparked the founding of an orphanage along the lines of the Orphanotropheion at Constantinople (and adopting its name).[5] It is not difficult to imagine that the Romans might have desired to emulate a Byzantine institution that was as celebrated as it was practical. The continued presence of the Greek *laudes* for Cornomania in the schola's repertoire

---

[1] Jean-Marie Sansterre, *Les Moines grecs et orientaux à Rome aux époques byzantine et carolingienne (milieu du VIᵉ s. – fin du IXᵉ s.)*, 2 vols., Académie Royale de Belgique: Mémoires de la Classe des Lettres, 2nd ser., 66/1 (Brussels, 1983), 22–29.

[2] Ekonomou, *Byzantine Rome and the Greek Popes*, 113–57.

[3] OR 11.62–66; Andrieu, 2:434–35.

[4] Ottorino Bertolini, "Per la storia delle diaconie romane nell'alto medioevo sino alla fine del secolo VIII," *Archivio della Società Romana di Storia Patria* 70 (1947), 1–145 (repr. in *Scritti scelti di storia medievali*, 2 vols., ed. Ottavio Banti (Livorno, 1968), 1:311–460); Raimund Hermes, "Die stadtrömischen Diakonien," *Römische Quartalschrift für Antike und Christentum* 91 (1996), 1–120.

[5] There is no way of ascertaining whether or not female orphans were accepted at the Roman orphanotrophium.

prompted Timothy Miller to argue "that those who organized the Roman orphanage patterned it on the older Orphanage on the citadel of Constantinople."[1]

The Schola Cantorum and the Gregorian Legends

THE earliest claim that Pope Gregory the Great founded the schola cantorum assumes that the presence of boy singers was an integral part of Gregory's scheme.[2] Johannes Diaconus, active at Rome during the last half of the ninth century and thus nearly three centuries after Gregory's lifetime, produced an extensive account of Gregory's life and achievements. John VIII (872–82) commissioned the biography as a Roman alternative to the narratives of Paulinus of Nola, Paul Warnefrid (ca. 720–99), and Bede, none of which refer to Gregory's supposed interest in music or to the schola cantorum.

Though John had access to documents in the papal archives now lost, he had a tendency to assume that situations familiar in the late ninth century traced their origins back to Gregory himself. No surviving contemporary evidence connects Gregory with the schola cantorum, nor do his letters ever refer to an orphanage at Rome, though he expressed several times his solicitude for the plight of orphans. Since John's brief report on Gregory's founding of the schola takes for granted that boy singers were involved, it merits an examination in the present context. According to John:

> [Gregory] founded the schola cantorum, which even today according to the same traditions sings in the Roman church; and he endowed [the schola] with several properties. He built two dwellings, one at the steps of the basilica of blessed Peter the apostle, the other indeed near the buildings of the Lateran patriarchate, where are preserved until the present day his bed, on which he reclined while singing, and the rod with which he threatened the boys, along with the authentic antiphoner.[3]

---

[1] Miller, *The Orphans of Byzantium*, 218.

[2] For more on the history of the institution, see Joseph Dyer, "The Schola Cantorum and its Roman Milieu in the Early Middle Ages," in *De Musica et Cantu: Studien zur Geschichte der Kirchenmusik und der Oper; Helmut Hucke zum 60. Geburtstag*, ed. Peter Cahn and Ann-Katrin Heimer, Musikwissenschaftliche Publikationen, Hochschule für Musik und Darstellende Kunst, 2 (Hildesheim, 1993), 19–40; idem, "Schola cantorum," in *Die Musik in Geschichte und Gegenwart* (2nd ed.): *Sachteil* 8:1119–23.

[3] "Scholam quoque cantorum quae hactenus eisdem institutionibus in sancta Romana ecclesia modulatur constituit, eique cum nonnullis praediis; duo habitacula, scilicet alterum sub gradibus basilicae beati Petri apostoli, alterum vero sub Lateranensis patriarchii domibus fabricavit, ubi usque hodie lectus eius, in quo recubans modulabatur et flagellum ipsius quo pueris minabatur veneratione congrua cum authentico antiphonario reservatur"; Johannes Diaconus, *Vita S. Gregorii Magni*, 2.6; PL 75:90. On John's biography of Gregory, see Claudio Leonardi, "La 'Vita Gregorii' di Giovanni diacono," in *Roma e l'età carolingia: Atti delle giornate di studio, Roma 3–8 maggio 1976* (Rome, 1976), 381–93. John is sometimes described (inaccurately) as having been a monk of Monte Cassino.

Nothing could be clearer: Gregory founded the eminent papal choir, suitably endowing each of its twin habitations and even taking an interest in training the young singers. A Gregorian foundation of the celebrated papal choir would have fit neatly with the existence of a sacramentary attributed to Gregory and the prologue to two Mass antiphoners approximately contemporary with John's biography. These claimed Gregory had "composed this book of musical art of the schola cantorum."[1] A third witness, the Antiphoner of Mont-Blandin, says that it was "ordered by St. Gregory for the yearly cycle" ("ordinatus a sancto Gregorio per circulum anni").

It is evident that John knew of locations in Rome associated with Gregory's memory. As we have seen, the schola building near the Lateran had been renovated just a few years before by Sergius II (without any reference to Gregory as founder), but the nature of Gregory's connection with a *domus* for the schola cantorum at the Vatican is not clear. John recorded the presence at the Lateran site of three relics that tradition associated with the sainted pope. While it would be unreasonable to dispute what he saw, his interpretation of them merits closer scrutiny. John understood the first of these relics, a bed, to be a place where Gregory was wont to sing — a remarkable conclusion in itself! The bed is mentioned again in the early twelfth century in the *Descriptio Lateranensis ecclesiae*, but now it is to be seen in the oratory of S. Gregorio in Martio, to the west of the Lateran Baptistery.[2] The *Descriptio* describes the object as nothing more than a bed on which Gregory rested. Since the pope's frail health kept him confined to bed for many months of his pontificate, one can well imagine why this bed might be preserved as a relic, though it had nothing whatsoever to do with Gregory's presumed musical interests.

John believed that Gregory had the time, during a stressful pontificate weighed down with many cares, to offer instruction in singing to choirboys.[3] He assumed further that Gregory threatened the boys (presumably choirboys, since this is a "musical" portion of the biography) with a *flagellum*. This word is often translated "whip" or "scourge," but it could also mean "rod or staff, a sign of authority" ("virga

---

[1] René-Jean Hesbert, *Antiphonale missarum sextuplex* (Brussels, 1935), 2–3 (no. 00); for a comprehensive discussion and bibliography, see David Hiley, *Western Plainchant: A Handbook* (Oxford, 1993), 503–13.

[2] "Est iterum huic oratorio [S. Crucis] satis proximum alius sancti papae Gregorii oratorium [S. Gregorio in Martio], ubi usque hodie lectulus, in quo ipse sanctus solebat quiescere, videtur iuxta aram permanere"; *Descriptio Lateranensis ecclesiae* 12, ed. Valentini and Zucchetti, *Codice topographico*, 3:355 [= PL 194:1555]; Lombardi, *Roma: Le chiese scomparse*, 66 (no. 53, with two maps).

[3] I am unconvinced by the theory of John R. C. Martyn, "Gregory the Great: On Organ Lessons [and on Equipping Monasteries]," *Medievalia et Humanistica*, n.s. 30 (2004), 107–113, that Gregory's touching letter to his friend Leander of Seville (Ep. 5.53a, July 595) "seems to reveal Pope Gregory himself as an experienced choirmaster, even conducting solo singers, while using an organ to accompany them." In the letter, Gregory refers with rhetorical flourish to the poor health that has so weakened his voice, which he compares to a "pipe split with cracks" ("scissa rimis fistula"), that it hinders the ability of the "organum cordis" to express itself.

seu baculus, jurisdictionis insigne").[1] Might this staff (we have no idea what it looked like) have been Gregory's *ferula*, a baton that symbolized papal authority?[2] Finally, the "authentic" antiphoner (necessarily lacking musical notation) seen by John was obviously a book of chants for the Mass (and possibly the Office) but no more than this can be determined about the object or its age.[3] Would John have recognized a book that actually dated back to the time of Gregory, or was its connection to the sainted pope just as legendary as that of the other two "relics"?

GREGORY AND THE ROMAN SYNOD OF 595

ONE of the items in the dossier of texts allegedly relating to Gregory the Great's attitude towards music and to the founding of the schola cantorum is a decree forbidding deacons to sing at Mass, promulgated at a Roman synod held on 5 July 595. According to the terms of this decree, deacons were expected in the future to confine themselves to the chanting of the Gospel. It has also been claimed that liturgical reassignments pursuant to this led to the formation of the schola cantorum. The relevant passages of the decree, the first of six that Gregory promulgated on that day, read as follows:

> In this holy Roman church, over which the divine dispensation has willed that I preside, there has recently arisen an extremely reprehensible custom: that certain singers are chosen for ministry at the holy altar and, having been appointed to the order of deacon, they attend to the modulation of the voice, when it would be more suitable for them to occupy themselves with the office of preaching and almsgiving. . . . This being the case, I decree that in this see ministers of the holy altar ought not to sing and should carry out only the office of reading the Gospel at Mass. I think that psalms and other readings should be done by subdeacons or, if necessity demands, by [clerics in] minor orders.[4]

It has been argued that the assignation of "psalms and other readings" to sub-

---

[1] W.-H. Maigne d'Arnis, *Lexicon manuale ad scriptores mediae et infimae latinitatis . . .* (Paris, 1866), col. 935.

[2] Pierre Salmon, "La 'Ferula,' bâton pastoral de l'évêque de Rome," *Revue des sciences religieuses* 30 (1956), 313–27.

[3] The term "authentic" formed part of the rhetorical arsenal used in the introduction of the Roman liturgy into Gaul.

[4] "In sancta hac Romana ecclesia, cui divina dispensatio praeesse me voluit, dudum consuetudo est valde reprehensibilis exorta, ut quidam ad sacri altaris ministerium cantores eligantur, et in diaconatus ordine constituti modulationi vocis serviant, quos ad praedicationis officium elemosinarumque studium vacare congruebat. . . . Qua de re praesenti decreto constituo ut in sede hac sacri altaris ministri cantare non debeant solumque evangelicae lectionis officium inter missarum sollemnia exsolvant. Psalmos vero ac reliquas lectiones censeo per subdiaconos vel, si necessitas exigit, per minores ordines exhiberi"; *Gregorii I papae Registrum epistolarum*, ed. Paul Ewald and Ludwig Hartmann, Monumenta germaniae historica: Epistolae 1–2, (Berlin, 1887–99; 2nd ed., Berlin, 1957), 1:363.

deacons and clerics in minor orders created the conditions that gave birth to the schola cantorum, primarily on the grounds that the principal officers of the schola held the rank of subdeacon (as did many other Roman clerics). Though there is quite enough that is puzzling about this regulation, devoid as it is of any context, it cannot be read as the foundation charter of the Roman schola cantorum.

I have argued elsewhere that Gregory's intention was not primarily to discourage the ordination of candidates with exceptional voices.[1] Indeed, how could such a criterion be fairly applied, especially at a time when there seems to have been a shortage of vocations in Italy?

Since deacons, particularly archdeacons, were the favored candidates for promotion to the episcopate, it was in Gregory's interest as a churchman to discourage the ordination to this rank of poorly qualified candidates. Even his own see of Rome had not been exempt from the practice of this "extremely reprehensible custom." The situation would have been exacerbated by the fact that Rome, conforming to an ancient tradition that stretched back to apostolic times, restricted the number of deacons to seven.[2] After a while this restriction was relaxed, but the other deacons who served the church of Rome, known as "diaconi forenses," did not share the eminent status and privileges of the seven. For more than a century preceding Gregory's election, popes were chosen from the restricted circle of the seven deacons. Between the years 483 and 615, for example, only two popes, John 11 (533–35) and Silverius (536–37), were demonstrably *not* deacons before their election. Thus Gregory's concern with what deacons did at Mass veiled a larger purpose: to protect the episcopal office, not least of all the papacy itself, from unworthy candidates. Gregory practiced what he preached. Although the number of ordinations to the diaconate reported in the papal biographies of the *Liber pontificalis* was always notably inferior to the number of ordinations to the episcopate or the priesthood, it is noteworthy that over the course of a pontificate of thirteen years Gregory ordained thirty-nine priests but only five deacons.[3] Discouraging clerics with good voices, or founding a choir or choir school, were the furthest things from his mind.[4]

---

[1] Dyer, "The Schola Cantorum and Its Roman Milieu," 28–32.

[2] According to an early-sixth-century forgery, the *Constitutum Sylvestri*, "diaconi non essent plus nec amplius per paroeciarum examen nisi duo, et diaconi cardinales urbis Romae septem;" *Constitutum Sylvestri* 6 (PL 8: 835. The fifth-century historian Sozomenes mentions only seven deacons at Rome (*Historia ecclesiastica* 7.19; PG 67:1476).

[3] LP 1: 312.

[4] Though it is not relevant, I cannot refrain from quoting the opinion of the Russian theologian Lev Gillet, "Deacons in the Orthodox East," *Theology* 58 (1955), p. 420 n. 2, on the "professional" diaconate in the Orthodox Church of Russia: "the professionalism in mind is that which looks upon a deacon as primarily a cantor. This error was common in Imperial Russia, where the first quality the public required in a deacon was a powerful bass voice. To some young men it was a matter of indifference whether they became deacons or opera singers."

CONCLUSIONS

ALL of the evidence points to the last half of the seventh century as the period when both the schola cantorum and the orphanotrophium were established at Rome — independently of each other, as far as one can determine. Whatever the connection between the two institutions might have been, there is of course a vast difference between commissioning a college of adult singers to assist at papal ceremonies and the founding of an orphanage. The former requires little more than an administrative decision, an organizational structure, and a system of financial support. An orphanage requires a building which must be physically maintained, personnel to provide administrative services, sustenance, discipline, and education, as well as a dependable system for financing the operation.

If the schola cantorum, like the other scholae of the Lateran administration (notaries, defensors, papal subdeacons), was a guild of professionals, it would have accepted talented young associates as apprentices. Apprenticeship was the normal method of learning any craft. Even though advanced degrees in music are essential today, a church musician still acquires important skills in apprenticeship situations, perhaps first as a choirboy and then as an assistant to an organist-choirmaster. Thus it might have seemed only natural, once the decision had been made (almost certainly under Byzantine influence) to establish an orphanage in Rome on the Constantinopolitan model, to link it with an institution like the schola cantorum that already provided musical services and prepared Roman boys for clerical careers. Very little is known about the careers of ordinary Roman clergy who did not become popes, high-ranking clergy, or important officers in the Lateran administration.[1] If ordained acolyte, a graduate of the schola could have provided a variety of pastoral service in one of the Roman tituli. A more serious step was ordination to the subdiaconate, which carried with it (since the time of Leo I) the obligation of chastity. Subdeacons not only performed many different functions in the papal Mass liturgy, as described in Ordo Romanus I, but also carried out responsible administrative tasks, either in the service of the papacy or in one of the ecclesiastical regions into which Rome was divided. If boy singers did not remain members of the schola cantorum — and few could have found permanent places as papal singers — their years of training in the schola prepared them for a variety of ecclesiastical careers.

[1] Michel Andrieu, "La Carrière ecclésiastique des papes et les documents liturgiques du Moyen Âge," *Revue des sciences religieuses* 21 (1947), 90–120.

2

BOY SINGERS IN MEDIEVAL MONASTERIES AND CATHEDRALS

Susan Boynton

YOUNG boys were present in monastic communities in Western Europe by the early Middle Ages. The sixth-century Rule of Benedict refers to the practice of child oblation (the parents' offering of a child as a donation to a monastery), which was the most common form of entry into the religious life until around 1200.[1] Oblates continued to form an important part of such populations through the twelfth century, but a decline in oblation accompanied the emergence of new religious orders (such as the Cistercians) who accepted only adult vocations. Benedictine monasteries continued to accept boys, although in diminishing numbers and at an increasing age.[2] In the 1230s, Pope Gregory IX set the minimum age for entry into a monastery at eighteen.[3] The practice of oblation for girls lasted longer, through the early modern period.[4]

As members of monastic communities, child singers took part in the performance of the Office and Mass. Some of the earliest vestiges of their role in monastic musical performance come from the Carolingian period, when monasteries took on an increasingly important role as centers of ritual commemoration, while educating growing numbers of young boys.[5] The presence of child oblates in

---

[1] On the history of oblation in the early Middle Ages, see Mayke de Jong, *In Samuel's Image: Child Oblation in the Early Medieval West* (Leiden, 1996).

[2] As of 1175, the Cistercians prohibited novices under eighteen years old; similarly, in 1186, the Benedictines of St. Augustine's at Canterbury obtained a papal decree requiring that novices had to be at least eighteen; see Nicholas Orme, *Medieval Children* (New Haven and London, 2002), 225; Nicholas Orme, *Medieval Schools: From Roman Britain to Renaissance England* (New Haven and London, 2006), 256–57.

[3] John Doran, "Oblation or Obligation? A Canonical Ambiguity," in *The Church and Childhood: Papers Read at the 1993 Summer Meeting and the 1994 Winter Meeting of the Ecclesiastical History Society*, ed. Diana Wood (Oxford, 1994), 127–41; see also Nora Berend, "La Subversion invisible: La Disparition de l'oblation irrévocable des enfants dans le droit canon," *Médiévales* 26 (1994), 123–36.

[4] See the contributions to this book by Anne Bagnall Yardley and Colleen Reardon.

[5] See Mayke de Jong, "Carolingian Monasticism: The Power of Prayer," in *The New Cambridge Medieval History*, ii: *c.700–c.900*, ed. Rosamond McKitterick (Cambridge, 1995),

this period is mentioned in prescriptive texts and in some cases is evident in the physical environment, as in the ninth-century abbey church of Corvey, where some graffiti in the western gallery of the upper level of the westwork have been interpreted as musical notation. Charles McClendon has pointed out that this notation could have been a pedagogical aid for the boys who were being taught to sing there, and he suggests that the sound of their voices, possibly perceived as dangerously seductive, might have inspired the frescoed image of the Sirens situated in the lower level directly below that part of the westwork.[1]

Already in this period, boys' elementary education consisted of learning to read and sing the psalms and hymns. An early prescription for this first phase of training appears in the Murbach Statutes of 816, preliminary acts to the synod of Aachen that described the school reforms of Abbot Atto of Reichenau. The Statutes stipulated that students should begin by learning the psalms, hymns, and canticles, then proceed to the Benedictine Rule, and from there to Scripture and patristic writings:

> after the psalms, canticles and hymns will have been memorized, students
> should go through the rule, with their teachers listening to them; after the
> rule, the text of the lectionary, and meanwhile the history of divine authority
> and its exegetes as well as the sermons of the fathers and their lives.[2]

Boys in monastic communities did not necessarily move beyond these basic texts to attain a high level of education in the liberal arts. Some, however, became skilled poets and composers. One of the best-known in the central Middle Ages was Notker Balbulus (ca. 840–912), a monk at the abbey of Saint Gall. The prologue to his *Liber hymnorum* describes the difficulty he experienced as a young person ("cum adhuc iuvenulus essem") in memorizing very long melismas ("longissimae melodiae"). Imitating the compositions in a manuscript brought to the abbey, he began to write Latin verse to fit the melodies of the melismas, and eventually one of his teachers wrote them down and gave them to the *pueri* to sing ("et pueris cantandos aliis alios insinuavit").[3] In the ninth, tenth, and eleventh centuries, writers of the Saint Gall school produced numerous pedagogical texts as well as poetry intended for liturgical performance. For instance, Ekkehard IV (ca. 980 – after 1057), a teacher, poet, and chronicler at Saint Gall, wrote two poems

---

622–53. On the life of oblates in a ninth-century monastery, see Mayke de Jong, "Growing up in a Carolingian Monastery: Magister Hildemar and his Oblates," *Journal of Medieval History* 9 (1983): 99–128.

[1] Charles B. McClendon, *The Origins of Medieval Architecture* (London, 2005), 192–93.

[2] "Actuum praeliminarium synodi primae aquisgranensis commentationes sive Statuta Murbacensia (816)," in *Consuetudines saeculi octavi et noni*, ed. Josef Semmler, Corpus consuetudinum monasticarum, 1 (Siegburg, 1963), 442: "ut scolastici, postquam psalmi, cantica et hymni memoriae commendata fuerint, regula, post regulae textum liber comitis, interim uero historiam diuinae auctoritatis et expositores eius necnon et conlationes patrum et uitas eorum legendo magistris eorum audientibus percurrant."

[3] Wolfram von den Steinen, *Notker der Dichter und seine geistige Welt* (Bern, 1948), Editionsband, 8–10.

in couplets to be sung by the boys following the cross in procession around the cloister on Sundays.[1]

Pedagogical texts and their commentary traditions, including some treatises on music theory, can tell us a great deal about the character of musical learning in the Middle Ages. Among the few theory treatises that specifically mention the training of boys are the writings of Guido of Arezzo, who devised an early system of staff notation as well as solmization syllables for use in teaching the chant repertory more efficiently.[2] Since the predominantly oral transmission of chant in the early and central Middle Ages meant that singers spent considerable amounts of time learning melodies by ear, Guido's writings mark a significant turning point. His pedagogical methods reflect a broader phenomenon observable in the eleventh century, namely a gradual shift to greater reliance on the written record, including musical notation.[3]

For the most part, however, the medieval texts of music theory offer only limited insight into the social context and institutional setting of practical musical training, the roles and responsibilities of teachers, and the practical organization of instruction or the times and places in which it took place.[4] For information on such pragmatic aspects of medieval musical education, one must often turn to texts such as monastic customaries, which offer the most extensive information on the daily life of children in monasteries from the tenth to the thirteenth century, and therefore constitute the most important sources for the process by which students learned to read and sing. Varied in length and scope, these texts contain a wealth of information on all aspects of life in a monastery, including innumerable details on the performance of the liturgy. The first detailed customaries were written down in the eleventh century, on the basis of oral customs that had developed throughout the central Middle Ages.[5] Customaries are partly prescriptive in

---

[1] "Versus de natale domini pueris circa claustrum post crucem in dominicis canendi" and one about other feasts: see *Der Liber benedictionum Ekkeharts iv nebst den kleinern Dichtungen aus dem Codex Sangallensis 393*, ed. Johannes Egli (Sankt Gallen, 1909), 391–92. I am grateful to Peter Stotz for bringing this text to my attention.

[2] See Guido of Arezzo, "Epistola ad Michahelem" and "Prologus in Antiphonarium," in *Guido d'Arezzo's Regule Rithmice, Prologus in Antiphonarium, and Epistola ad Michahelem: A Critical Text and Translation with an Introduction, Annotations, Indices, and New Manuscript Inventories*, ed. Dolores Pesce, Wissenschaftliche Abhandlungen, 73 (Ottawa, 1999), 405–531.

[3] On orality and literacy in the eleventh century in relation to chant transmission, see Susan Boynton, "Orality, Literacy, and the Early Notation of the Office Hymns," *Journal of the American Musicological Society* 56 (2003), 99–167.

[4] In some cases, music theory may be interpreted as commenting symbolically on the nature of musical education, such as the account of the Orpheus myth that links the treatises *Musica enchiriadis* and *Scholica enchiriadis*; see Susan Boynton, "The Sources and Significance of the Orpheus Myth in 'Musica enchiriadis' and Regino of Prüm's 'Epistola de harmonica institutione,'" *Early Music History* 18 (1999), 47–74.

[5] The most recent overview of the customaries as a genre is Isabelle Cochelin, "Évolution des coutumiers monastiques dessinée à partir de l'étude de Bernard," in *From Dead of Night to End of Day: The Medieval Customs of Cluny*, ed. Susan Boynton and Isabelle Cochelin (Turnhout, 2005), 29–66.

nature, for they sometimes set forth recommendations for an ideal organization of monastic life rather than recording the reality of a single institution. Nevertheless, many customaries are to some extent also descriptive texts, illustrating details of practice in particular monasteries. Even those customaries written specifically for the use of particular institutions reflect teaching methods and traditions of performance that may have been common.

The earliest truly extensive and detailed monastic customary, containing dozens of references to liturgical performance by boys, is the *Liber tramitis* from the abbey of Farfa (located northeast of Rome), compiled in the first half of the eleventh century on the basis of customs at the Burgundian abbey of Cluny.[1] However, the richest single source for the musical role and the daily life of child oblates is the customary written at Cluny around 1080 by a monk known to us only as Bernard.[2] This text, both descriptive and prescriptive, conveys practical details of boys' participation in the liturgy. Another major customary, which appears to be based on Bernard's, is the decretal that Lanfranc, Archbishop of Canterbury (1070–89), originally compiled for Canterbury Cathedral but which appears also to be intended for use in a monastery: it contains several references to an abbot. Lanfranc's decretal refers to the children as *infantes* and assigns them numerous chants including the hymn *Inuentor rutili*, to be performed by two boys in a cathedral church. According to this customary, boys are assigned simpler chants (such as the *Benedicamus Domino* and short responsories) and more complex ones, including the gradual during the morrow Mass on the feast of All Saints.[3]

While certain customaries are more informative than others regarding the role of boy singers, oblates had a significant musical and liturgical role in the daily services of all Benedictine communities. In addition to singing along with adults in the monastic choir, they also performed separately, judging from the prescriptions that assign chants to them as a group or as individuals. Boys were also responsible for liturgical readings as well as carrying books and candles. One of the most prominent roles for boys was during the procession on Palm Sunday, when they sang the processional hymn *Gloria laus*, a performance that was often made more colorful and impressive by a particular architectural setting such as the monastery gates or the city walls. Often, boys sang the strophes of the text, alternating with adults singing the refrain. At other moments in the procession, they might be assigned chants associated with children in the scriptural account of Palm Sunday, such as the antiphon *Osanna filio Dauid*.[4] Through their performance on Palm

---

[1] On this customary as a source of information on musical performance, see Susan Boynton, "Les Coutumes clunisiennes au temps d'Odilon," in *Odilon de Mercœur, l'Auvergne et Cluny: La "Paix de Dieu" et l'Europe de l'an mil; Actes du colloque de Lavoûte-Chilhac des 10, 11, et 12 Mai 2000* (Nonette, 2002), 193–203.

[2] The only widely available edition of the text is "Ordo cluniacensis per Bernardum scriptorem saeculi XI," in *Vetus disciplina monastica*, ed. Marquard Herrgott (Paris, 1726; repr. Siegburg, 1999). A diplomatic edition with English and French translations by Susan Boynton and Isabelle Cochelin is in preparation (Turnhout, forthcoming).

[3] *The Monastic Constitutions of Lanfranc*, ed. and trans. by David Knowles, revised by Christopher N. L. Brooke (Oxford, 2002), 66, 76, 96, 98.

[4] For the *infantes'* performance of this antiphon and the *Gloria laus*, see ibid., 38.

Sunday, boys in religious communities symbolically represented the children mentioned in the Gospel narrative and in liturgical texts commemorating the entry into Jerusalem.[1]

Even after the twelfth century, when child oblation had passed its historical peak, boys played an important liturgical role in some Benedictine monasteries. The thirteenth-century ordinal from the abbey of St. Arnulf in Metz, possibly based on a twelfth-century model, describes the boys' numerous duties; among the most musically complex genres they sang were the responsories of Matins and Lauds. A boy soloist sang the first responsory of Matins on Ember Wednesday in Advent, and the responsory at Lauds, as well as the gradual at Mass. On certain feast days, a pair of boys or two pairs of boys sang the fourth, eighth, and twelfth responsories of Matins.[2] The ordinal from St. Arnulf also describes the antiphonal performance of the Kyrie by boy soloists in the darkened church on Maundy Thursday, a tradition found also in much earlier monastic customaries such as the tenth-century *Regularis concordia*.[3]

Monastic customaries enable us to situate the musical training and activities of children within the ongoing assimilation of behaviors through imitation of their elders and the internalization of hierarchies that were fundamental to life in a monastic community.[4] Highly ritualized and occupying numerous hours a day, the Divine Office was the most important setting in which young monks were instructed in many things besides singing and reading: they learned proper bodily comportment, where and how to stand, and also the correct order in which to sing and read according to the date of one's entry into the monastery.[5] Liturgical performance entailed such extensive preparation and rehearsal that it constituted the very essence of medieval monastic education.[6]

Customaries indicate which members of monastic communities were responsible for training children to perform in the liturgy as well as the times and methods of instruction. Supervised practice took place at various times of the day with teachers who seem to have been responsible primarily for surveillance of the children. Oblates learned much of their chant by listening and then repeating after their teachers, as in the traditional method of instruction specifically

---

[1] Susan Boynton, "The Liturgical Role of Children in Monastic Customaries from the Central Middle Ages," *Studia liturgica* 28 (1998), 194–209 at 205–8.

[2] *Der Liber ordinarius der Abtei St. Arnulf von Metz (Metz, Stadtbibliothek, Ms. 132, um 1240)*, ed. Alois Odermatt, Spicilegium Friburgense, 31 (Freiburg, 1987), 68, 295, 296, 313, 315.

[3] Boynton, "The Liturgical Role of Children," 205.

[4] On the hierarchical structure of monastic communities, see Isabelle Cochelin, "Étude sur les hiérarchies monastiques: Le Prestige de l'ancienneté et son éclipse à Cluny au XIᵉ siècle," *Revue Mabillon*, n.s. 11 (2000), 5–37.

[5] See Susan Boynton and Isabelle Cochelin, "The Sociomusical Role of Child Oblates at the Abbey of Cluny in the Eleventh Century," in *Musical Childhoods and the Cultures of Youth*, ed. Susan Boynton and Roe-Min Kok (Middletown, Ct., 2006), 3–24.

[6] See Susan Boynton, "Training for the Liturgy as a Form of Monastic Education," in *Medieval Monastic Education*, ed. Carolyn Muessig and George Ferzoco (Leicester, London, and New York, 2000), 7–20.

mentioned in the Cluniac customary written by Ulrich of Zell around 1080: "the boys sit in chapter, and learn the chant from someone singing it before them."[1] In the eleventh and twelfth centuries, a single person often taught both reading and singing, and this teacher was frequently also the librarian, whose responsibilities included correcting and annotating the monastery's liturgical books. The armarius was ultimately responsible for the education of the oblates as well as for the library and the organization of the liturgy. Presumably because of his full schedule, most of the instruction of the oblates was entrusted to an assistant, and the armarius listened to the children sing and read only after his assistant had already trained them. Thus the customary from the abbey of Fleury written just after the year 1000 mentions the "armarius qui et scolae praeceptor vel librarius", a librarian who is also the teacher,[2] but it was the precentor's assistant, the succentor, who taught chant: "For assistance [the precentor] is given a brother of demonstrable talent who is called the succentor. For the master of the school is the guardian of the children. Careful in every study of chants and in daily practice, he arranges the definitions of the tones and differentiae of the psalms and is accustomed to take forcefully to the chapter those treating the Divine Office negligently."[3] As Margot Fassler has shown, the *Liber tramitis* (which reflects customs at the abbey of Cluny between 1027 and 1048) expands the role of the armarius to absorb functions previously fulfilled by the cantor or precentor.[4] Several customaries of the late eleventh and early twelfth centuries similarly combine the responsibilities of the armarius and cantor.[5]

A Cluniac customary from the 1080s and an early-twelfth-century one from Fruttuaria both provide for silent reading practice, or the memorization of psalms and hymns, during the celebration of Mass.[6] The Fruttuaria customary also refers to the use of books during the oblates' daily lesson in preparation for the liturgy, prescribing that "no one looks at the book there, except a boy who is so old that he cannot learn otherwise; and if there are two of them, they take a board, put it between them, and place the book on top of it."[7] According to this customary,

---

[1] PL 149: 687: "Pueri sedent in capitulo, et per aliquem praecinentem cantum addiscunt."

[2] *Consuetudines floriacenses antiquiores*, ed. Anselme Davril and Lin Donnat (Siegburg, 1984), 17.

[3] Ibid., 15: "Huic frater probabilis ingenii solatio datur qui succentor nuncupatur. Nam scole magister est acceptor infantum. In omni studio cantilenarum et cotidiana cura tonorum diffinitiones et psalmorum distinctiones providus disponit et divinum officium negligenter tractantes propellare in capitulo solet."

[4] Margot Fassler, "The Office of the Cantor in Early Western Monastic Rules and Customaries: A Preliminary Investigation," *Early Music History* 5 (1985): 29–51; Peter Dinter, *Liber tramitis aevi Odilonis abbatis* (Siegburg, 1980), 238–39.

[5] *Consuetudines fructuarienses*, ed. L. G. Spätling and Peter Dinter (Siegburg, 1987), 138.

[6] "Ordo Cluniacensis per Bernardum," 204; *Consuetudines fructuarienses*, 1:21.

[7] *Consuetudines fructuarienses*, 2:150–151: "Nullus ibi aspicit in librum, nisi tam magnus puer sit, qui aliter discere non possit, et si duo sunt, apprehendunt tabulam et inter se ponunt et librum desuper mittunt."

literate novices were lent a psalter and hymnary, which they could borrow for up to a year.[1]

The prevalence of the basic approach to education found in customaries is confirmed by other didactic texts of the eleventh and twelfth centuries such as the scholastic colloquies of the English monastic writer Ælfric Bata from the early eleventh century.[2] Although they are set dialogues intended for memorization and declamation, these texts can be seen as reflections (albeit stylized ones) of the daily life and education of boys in an Anglo-Saxon monastery. One dialogue refers to the memorization of responsories, antiphons, and lessons for the Divine Office; another mentions the incipits of the versicles the boys will perform at Compline.[3]

By the twelfth century, boys' voices were becoming a regular component of cathedral choirs. In this period, English secular cathedrals supported a number of choristers.[4] Thirteenth-century ordinals from some northern French cathedrals attest the importance of boy singers in almost every aspect of the liturgy. In the Norman cathedral of Bayeux, boys had an extensive array of responsibilities quite similar to the duties of monastic oblates. On ferial days, cathedral choristers intoned all but the first antiphons of Vespers, Matins, and Lauds. They also sang all the versicles and the *Benedicamus Domino* (except at Prime and Compline, when boys sang the versicles but a priest said the *Benedicamus*). On simple feasts of nine lessons, two boys intoned the second and third antiphons of Matins, and three boys read the first three lessons. During Lent and on other non-festal occasions, a single boy sang the responsory at Lauds. The chapter *Tu in nobis es Domine* and the verse *Custodi nos Domine* were always sung by a single boy. At Prime, a single boy sang the verse, read the martyrology entry, and recited the obits that were to be commemorated on the next day.[5] In the ordinal of Laon Cathedral (written about the same time), the young singers who fulfilled many of the same duties are referred to as *clericuli*.[6]

In the late thirteenth century, as boy singers became increasingly important to cathedral chapters, some chapters established endowments for a fixed number of choirboy positions. In Toledo Cathedral at the end of the thirteenth century, Archbishop Gonzalo García Gudiel (1280–99) established ten regular positions for choirboys (*clerizones perpetuos*) to sing in the choir and to perform the Marian

---

[1] Ibid., 2:265.

[2] *Anglo-Saxon Conversations: The Colloquies of Ælfric Bata*, ed. Scott Gwara, trans. with an introduction by David W. Porter (Rochester, N.Y., 1997); *Latin Colloquies from Pre-Conquest Britain*, ed. Scott Gwara, Toronto Medieval Latin Texts 22 (Toronto, 1996).

[3] *Anglo-Saxon Conversations*, 94, 106.

[4] Kathleen Edwards, *The English Secular Cathedrals in the Middle Ages*, 2nd ed. (Manchester, 1967), 303–17; Orme, *Medieval Children*, 226; Orme, *Medieval Schools*, 63; Nicholas Orme, "The Medieval Clergy of Exeter Cathedral, II: The Secondaries and Choristers," *Reports and Transactions of the Devonshire Association* 115 (1983), 85–100.

[5] *Ordinaire et coutumier de l'église cathédrale de Bayeux (XIIIᵉ siècle)*, ed. Ulysse Chevalier, Bibliothèque liturgique, 8 (Paris, 1902), 5, 6, 7, 9, 13, 21.

[6] *Ordinaires de l'église cathédrale de Laon (XIIᵉ et XIIIᵉ siècles)*, ed. Ulysse Chevalier, Bibliothèque liturgique, 6 (Paris, 1897).

Mass celebrated in the chapel of St. Ildefonsus. As the group expanded over time, more complex structures for their upkeep and participation in the liturgy were developed, with the first major codification of the regulations (after the foundation document) being redacted in 1388.[1] By the early fourteenth century there were also six paid choirboys in the choir of the Sainte-Chapelle in Paris. Their presence is apparent already in a document of 1305, and in the second quarter of the fourteenth century a set of regulations was established prescribing both their musical obligations and their education in singing and grammar under the guidance of two chaplains who were their teachers.[2]

The thirteenth and fourteenth centuries witnessed the development of English almonry schools, in which monasteries provided education for boys who were tonsured but were not required to become monks. The resident boys received lodging in the almonry, food left over from the alms, and education in exchange for their assistance in the church. There were also nonresident students who paid tuition fees. The earliest evidence for almonry schools dates from the last third of the thirteenth century, but already several decades earlier some monasteries had allowed students to stay in their almonries in order to attend school nearby.[3] Thus the institution of the almonry school seems to have developed naturally from preexisting uses of monastic almonries. Joan Greatrex has shown that the boys described in the customary of the cathedral priory of Norwich (written about 1260 and still in use in 1311) were being educated in the monastery but were not actually monastic oblates. They participated in the liturgy but were not highly trained singers. A decade later, there was an almonry school at Norwich in which boys were trained in singing as well as in grammar.[4] Around 1300 the almonry schools became particularly important to the liturgical life of Benedictine abbeys because the students could act as servers at Mass, facilitating the daily celebration of Mass required of each individual ordained monk. Eventually, two distinct groups of

---

[1] François Reynaud, *Les Enfants de chœur de Tolède à la Renaissance* (Turnhout, 2002), 13; the foundation document is transcribed on 141–42, and the constitutions (from a seventeenth-century copy) on 143–44. Reynaud also discusses the role of the choirboys in the sixteenth and seventeenth centuries in his "Les Fonctions des enfants de chœur à la cathédrale de Tolède au début du xviiᵉ siècle," in *Maîtrises et chapelles aux xviiᵉ et xviiiᵉ siècles: Des Institutions musicales au service de Dieu,* ed. Bernard Dompnier (Clermont-Ferrand, 2003), 495–508.

[2] For an analysis of this text, see Denis Escudier, "Des Enfants 'bien appris': L'Enseignement de la grammaire et du chant aux enfants de chœur de la Sainte-Chapelle de Paris d'après un règlement du xivᵉ siècle," in *La Tradition vive: Mélanges d'histoire des textes en l'honneur de Louis Holtz,* ed. Pierre Lardet (Paris and Turnhout, 2003), 223–33.

[3] For an excellent recent account of almonry schools, see Roger Bowers, "The Almonry Schools of the English Monasteries, c.1265–1540," in *Monasteries and Society in Medieval Britain: Proceedings of the 1994 Harlaxton Symposium,* ed. Benjamin Thompson, Harlaxton Medieval Studies, 6 (Stamford, 1999), 177–222.

[4] Joan Greatrex, "The Almonry School of Norwich Cathedral Priory in the Thirteenth and Fourteenth Centuries," in *The Church and Childhood,* 169–81. For further discussion of the almonry school at Norwich, building in part on Greatrex's study, see Bowers, "The Almonry Schools," 182–87. Bowers argues that the boys mentioned in the Norwich customary were monastic novices, not secular schoolboys as Greatrex stated.

boys emerged within the same school, one trained particularly in singing. By the end of the fourteenth century, some boys in almonry schools were trained to sing the daily Lady Mass and votive Marian antiphon (both in plainchant). In the later fifteenth century, as boys' voices became more prominent in polyphony, almonry-school students were trained to perform the complex repertory of monastic Lady chapel choirs.[1]

Continental ordinals from the later Middle Ages also attest the musical role of boys in cathedral choirs. Even texts that contain very few specific references to boy singers mention their performance of *Gloria laus* on Palm Sunday, a tradition that seems to have been in continuous use from the monasteries of the central Middle Ages (see above) to the cathedrals of the fifteenth century. In the thirteenth-century ordinal from Bayeux, the boys greet the procession standing above the church door with palm branches in their hands as they sing the *Gloria laus*; the boys perform the verses in alternation with others singing the first verse as a refrain.[2] The 1346 ordinal of Besançon states that the boys sing the hymn from (possibly inside) the closed door of the church.[3] The ordinal of Aosta Cathedral, copied around 1470, states that the boys sang the *Gloria laus* from atop the city walls.[4] A late-medieval ordinal from Eger Cathedral in Hungary (printed in 1509 with contents from the fifteenth century) contains extensive information on the liturgical roles of the *pueri* (boys under 12 years of age), *iuuenes* (older boys in minor orders but not necessarily destined for an ecclesiastical career), and *precedentes* or *procedentes* (youths committed to the church and preparing for the diaconate). The *pueri* sang complex solo chants such as the verses of the great responsories on the first Sunday of Advent and the tracts during Lent, and directed the choir on minor feasts, whereas older boys and youths fulfilled these duties on feasts of higher rank.[5]

Ordinals are also the best source of information on the special performances in which young singers participated during the clerical festivities of the minor orders during the period around Christmas. Two days particularly associated with boy singers were the feasts of St. Nicholas (December 6) and the Holy Innocents (December 28). Both provided occasions for the ceremony of the Boy Bishop, in which one of the acolytes or choirboys was named bishop for a day, and the choirboys as a group could choose certain elements of the liturgy for that day.[6]

---

[1] Bowers, "The Almonry Schools," 189–93, 208–11.

[2] *Ordinaire et coutumier de l'église cathédrale de Bayeux*, 119–20.

[3] *L'Ordinaire liturgique du diocèse de Besançon (Besançon, Bibl. Mun, MS 101): Texte et sources*, ed. Romain Jurot, Spicilegium friburgense, 38 (Fribourg, 1999), 262: "Post hec cantant pueri porta templi clausa Gloria laus prout moris est."

[4] *L'Ordinaire de la Cathédrale d'Aoste (Bibliothèque Capitulaire, Cod. 54, fol. 93–240)*, ed. Robert Amiet and Lin Colliard, Monumenta liturgica ecclesiae augustanae, 4 (Aosta, 1978), 244: "incipiant pueri super muros civitatis Gloria laus."

[5] László Dobszay, "*Pueri vociferati*: Children in Eger Cathedral," in *International Musicological Society Study Group Cantus Planus: Papers Read at the 6th Meeting, Eger Hungary, 1993* (Budapest, 1995), 1:93–100.

[6] On the Boy Bishop, see particularly E. K. Chambers, *The Medieval Stage* (Oxford, 1903), 1:336–71; Shulamith Shahar, "The Boy Bishop's Feast: A Case-Study in Church

The Boy Bishop's feast, like other clerical festivities, involved playful reversals of the ecclesiastical hierarchy that were acted out through ritual gesture and musical performance.[1] The thirteenth-century ordinal of Bayeux Cathedral contains a lengthy account of the liturgy for the feast of the Innocents, including the ceremony of the Boy Bishop.[2] After Vespers on the feast of St. Stephen the boys celebrate First Vespers of Innocents' Day. They process to the altar of St. Nicholas, showing all due reverence to their boy bishop, who during his tenure performs all the offices of a real bishop except for the celebration of Mass. The boys' cantor begins the responsory *Centum quadraginta* (for the Holy Innocents) with the verse *Cantabant* and the responsory prosula *Sedentem in superne*; the boy bishop pronounces a prayer, and after the *Benedicamus Domino* he gives the blessing. At the conclusion of the office the boys take their places in the high stalls normally reserved for the clergy, while the boy bishop takes the dean's stall. After Compline, which they perform with modifications of their own choosing ("sicut eis placuerit"), the boys accompany the boy bishop to the lodging of the real bishop, constantly singing *Sedentem in superne*. They sing the same prosula after the final responsory of Matins, with the choir repeating the melody melismatically after the boys sing each verse of the prosula.[3] After Terce, the boys perform a procession into the nave of the church where they sing once again the responsory *Centum quadraginta* with a verse and prosula. During Mass, the boys' cantor fulfils all the functions of an adult cantor. During the performance of the Magnificat at Second Vespers, the boys repeat many times the verse "Deposuit potentes" to emphasize the role reversal that was integral to the day.[4] Thus, in churches with boy singers, the chant repertory for the feast of the Innocents was associated with particular performance traditions such as the Boy Bishop's ceremony.

Music for the feasts of the Christmas Octave also suggests ways in which the presence of young singers in religious communities may have influenced medieval repertories of chant, liturgical poetry, and drama. The texts of many tropes for the Proper of the Mass on Innocents' Day explicitly refer to performance by boys.[5] Several twelfth-century music dramas representing the Massacre of the Holy Innocents appear to be linked with the clerical celebrations on the feast of

Attitudes towards Children in the High and Late Middle Ages," in *The Church and Childhood*, 243–60; Karl Young, *The Drama of the Medieval Church* (Oxford, 1933), 1:106–10.

[1] Margot Fassler, "The Feast of Fools and *Danielis ludus*: Popular Tradition in a Medieval Cathedral Play," in *Plainsong in the Age of Polyphony*, ed. Thomas Forrest Kelly (Cambridge, 1992), 65–95, esp. 68–77.

[2] What follows is taken from the description of the feast in *Ordinaire et coutumier de l'église cathédrale de Bayeux*, 69–72.

[3] On the performance of responsory prosulas, see Thomas Forrest Kelly, "Melisma and Prosula: The Performance of Responsory Tropes," in *Liturgische Tropen: Referate zweier Colloquien des Corpus troporum in München (1983) und Canterbury (1984)*, ed. Gabriel Silagi, Münchener Beiträge zur Mediävistik und Renaissance-Forschung, 36 (Munich, 1985), 163–80.

[4] On the significance of this ritual gesture, see Fassler, "The Feast of Fools."

[5] Susan Boynton, "Performative Exegesis in the Fleury *Interfectio puerorum*," *Viator* 29 (1998), 44–45.

the Innocents. The exegete Gerhoh of Reichersberg referred to performances of such dramatic representations in the cathedral chapter at Augsburg in the first half of the twelfth century.[1] One of the best known of these works, preserved in the thirteenth-century "Fleury Playbook" (a manuscript of unknown origin that made its way into the library of the abbey of Fleury), establishes an equivalence between the Innocents as *pueri* (children) and the singing boys who presumably represented the Innocents. The opening rubric states "for the killing of the children the innocents should wear white stoles, and [processing] rejoicing through the church, let them pray to God, saying: 'O how glorious is the kingdom.'"[2] While many of the rubrics refer to the singers as *innocentes*, some call them *infantes*, as when they are slaughtered: "afterward, as the children remain prostrate, an angel from on high says, as if admonishing them: 'You who are in the dust, rise up and cry out.' The children, prostrate [sing]: 'Why, our Lord, do you not defend our blood?'"[3] Beginning with the part of the text comprising Rachel's lament, the supine boy singers are called *pueri*: "then Rachel is led in, with two consolers, and standing over the boys, she weeps, sometimes falling . . ."[4] One further rubric referring to multiple boys makes it clear that these *pueri* designate not only the sons that Rachel mourns, but also the actual singers: "Rising at the voice of the angel, the boys enter the choir, singing . . ."[5] The Fleury *Interfectio puerorum* makes a richly symbolic use of boy singers, building on the commentary traditions associated with the scriptural account of the Massacre and with the feast of the Innocents to create visual, musical, and liturgical connections between the boys of an ecclesiastical choir and the New Testament child martyrs.[6]

A more tenuous association is that between the emergence in the eleventh and twelfth centuries of an innovative musical genre based on the *Benedicamus Domino* and the fact that young singers often performed this versicle at the conclusion of the office.[7] In the late eleventh, twelfth, and thirteenth centuries, new versions of the *Benedicamus Domino* appeared, particularly in manuscripts from what is now

---

[1] Ibid., 42.

[2] "Ad interfectionem puerorum induantur innocentes stolis albis, et gaudentes per monasterium, orent deum dicentes: O quam gloriosum est regnum"; text in Orléans, Bibliothèque Municipale, MS 201, 214, quoted from the transcription in Boynton, "Performative Exegesis," 62.

[3] "Postea, iacentibus infantibus, angelus ab excelso ut moneatur eos, dicens: Vos qui in puluuere estis, expergescimini et clamate. Infantes iacentes: Quare non defendis sanguinem nostrum, deus noster?" Transcription from ibid., 62–63.

[4] "Tunc inducatur Rachel, et duae consolatrices; et stans super pueros plangat cadence aliquando . . ." Ibid., 63.

[5] "Ad uocem angeli surgentes pueri intrent chorum dicentes . . ." Ibid., 64.

[6] For a fuller discussion of the play, its exegetical and liturgical background, and its symbolism, see ibid., 39–61.

[7] Anne Walters Robertson, "Benedicamus Domino: The Unwritten Tradition." *Journal of the American Musicological Society* 41 (1988), 5–9; *Iohannis Beleth Summa de ecclesiasticis officiis*, 31e, 53c, ed. Herbert Douteil, Corpus christianorum continuatio mediaeualis, 41 (Turnhout, 1976), 61, 92. I am grateful to Gunilla Björkvall for bringing my attention to Beleth's commentary on the *Benedicamus Domino*.

France. Some are melodically elaborate settings of the versicle itself,[1] but there emerged a new musical genre based on the *Benedicamus Domino* with a structure incorporating refrains and featuring prominent use of rhyme. These songs can be classified in some cases as tropes on the liturgical versicle, with florid melodies and interpolated text, but some depart further from the base text, developing more extended structures.[2] These "Benedicamus" compositions constitute many of the earliest examples of a larger musical corpus emerging around 1100 in a style often called the "New Song."[3] Perhaps the custom of having younger singers perform the *Benedicamus Domino* fostered some of the musical experimentation that was a precondition for the emergence of the "New Song" corpus.

While in these cases boys may have played a subtle role in the development of musical repertories, at later times the influence proceeded in the opposite direction, with stylistic change in certain genres augmenting the involvement of boy singers. For example, as polyphony in English Lady chapels began to require boys' voices, beginning in the middle of the fifteenth century, ecclesiastical institutions (first cathedrals, then collegiate churches, private chapels, and abbeys) increased the quality and number of choristers so as to ensure a sufficient quantity of voices capable of performing the high parts in a demanding repertory.[4] Until this period, which saw the development of music that clearly required the voices of boys, we would know little about boy singers in the Middle Ages without the information provided by the prescriptive texts (such as monastic customaries and cathedral ordinals) discussed here. We are fortunate that the ecclesiastical institutions concerned with training and rearing boys took care to record the manifold ways in which musical performance by the young was a central component of the liturgy in monasteries and secular churches alike.

---

[1] Several such melodies for the *Benedicamus Domino* appear in Michel Huglo, "Les Débuts de la polyphonie à Paris: Les Premiers organa parisiens," in *Aktuelle Fragen der musikbezogenen Mittelalterforschung, Forum musicologicum* 3 (1982), 93–164 at 150–54.

[2] Wulf Arlt, *Ein Festoffizium des Mittelalters aus Beauvais in seiner liturgischen und musikalischen Bedeutung*, 2 vols. (Cologne, 1970), Darstellungsband, 160–206.

[3] On the "New Song," see Arlt, *Ein Festoffizium*; Arlt, "Das Eine und die vielen Lieder: Zur historischen Stellung der neuen Liedkunst des frühen 12. Jahrhunderts," in *Festschrift Rudolf Bockholdt zum 60. Geburtstag*, ed. Norbert Dubowy and Sören Meyer-Eller (Pfaffenhofen, 1990), 113–27; Arlt, "Neues zum neuen Lied: Die Fragmente aus der Handschrift Douai 246," in *Sine musica nulla disciplina: Studi in onore di Giulio Cattin*, ed. F. Bernabei and A. Lovato (Padua, 2006), 89–110; James Grier, "A New Voice in the Monastery: Tropes and Versus from Eleventh- and Twelfth-Century Aquitaine," *Speculum* 69 (1994), 1023–69.

[4] Bowers, "The Almonry Schools," 281–83; Roger Bowers, "To Chorus from Quartet: The Performing Resource for English Church Polyphony, c.1390–1559," in *English Choral Practice, 1400–1650*, ed. John Morehen (Cambridge, 1996), 20–31; Orme, *Medieval Children*, 227–28; Orme, *Medieval Schools*, 65–66.

3

THE MUSICAL EDUCATION OF YOUNG GIRLS IN MEDIEVAL ENGLISH NUNNERIES

Anne Bagnall Yardley

It is requested that those who are to be received as nuns will be taught and instructed in reading and singing before they are admitted.[1]

> (From a nun's comment at the visitation to Burnham Priory, Diocese of Lincoln, 1520)

SOURCES from medieval England make it abundantly clear that the primary requisite skills for each nun are the ability to read and to sing. Nuns themselves, as evidenced in the above citation from visitation records, emphasized that new nuns should be able to participate fully in monastic life and do their share of the convent's work — matters of deep concern for them. Yet the processes through which nuns mastered these skills are considerably less clear. Evidence from a variety of primary and secondary source materials shows that throughout the Middle Ages, despite the increasing availability of written materials, instruction in liturgical music for English nuns continued to flourish within a culture of oral transmission, memorization of vast quantities of chant, and the gradual absorption of each young woman into the nunnery.[2]

Reading in the medieval period was much more an oral/aural experience than a visual one and relied on the individual's development of great stores of memorized material.[3] At a minimum, a nun was able to recognize the letters of

---

[1] "Petitur . . . quod ille que in moniales recipiuntur sint docte et informate in lectura et cantu antequam admittantur."

[2] The classic text on nunnery life is Eileen Power, *Medieval English Nunneries, c.1275 to 1535* (Cambridge, 1922). For an excellent listing of sources containing references to the existence of schools for children in nunneries, see Power's Note B, 568–81. Susan Boynton, "Training for the Liturgy as a Form of Monastic Education," in *Medieval Monastic Education*, ed. George Ferzoco and Carolyn Muessig (London, 2000), 7–20, describes the teaching of children in monasteries, emphasizing sources from eleventh- and twelfth-century France.

[3] For recent studies on medieval methods of learning and the role of memory, see Nicholas Orme, *Medieval Children* (New Haven, 2002); Nicholas Orme, *English Schools*

the alphabet and sound out basic syllables, and had learned to read the Psalter —
learning also implied reading aloud and memorizing.

Nuns were also expected to read aloud (and listen to) sacred texts during
meal times. Numerous bishops' injunctions remind nuns of the importance of
this custom. For example, Bishop Alnwick issued this injunction to the nuns at
Catesby Priory in 1442: "Also that while you are eating in the refectory, one of you,
at the assignment of the prioress, should read a saint's life or another writing of
holy Scripture so that you will avoid and eschew idle words and the breaking of
silence."[1] On these daily occasions, texts for reading included the rule of the order,
the bishop's injunctions (pronounced quarterly), and readings from the church fathers and the lives of saints. While some and possibly much of this reading would
have been in the vernacular by the fifteenth and sixteenth centuries, nuns clearly
read and heard a lot of Latin. Since the position of reader rotated on a weekly
basis, we can assume that even those nuns whose understanding of the Latin was
less than comprehensive had the ability to recite the text correctly.

There is little if any evidence that most nuns moved to the next normative stage
of education for males — the learning of Latin grammar. Katherine Zieman suggests that nuns inhabited an area between the literate clergy and the often illiter-
ate laity, a realm she designates "liturgical literacy":

> The nuns' (desired) literate status, required solely for the purpose of litur-
> gical performance, is thus not an authorized form of literacy without un-
> derstanding; it is rather an authorized form of literacy in which the nature
> and necessity of understanding is not specified. This is the mode of textual
> interaction I would like to call "liturgical literacy," the performance of sacred
> Latin texts in which the relationship to grammatical understanding is am-
> biguous. . . . Unlike grammatical literacy, it did not imply a clearly defined
> set of skills. Liturgical performance could draw upon a number of learned
> abilities, from those we might qualify as musical (such as solmization), to
> phonetic decoding skill, to mnemonic techniques, to a variety of grammati-
> cal proficiencies, yet there was no systematically articulated hierarchy or
> sequence of these skills, as they were effectively subordinated to the impera-
> tive to perform.[2]

---

in the Middle Ages (London, 1973); Mary Carruthers, The Book of Memory: A Study of
Memory in Medieval Culture, Cambridge Studies in Medieval Literature, 10 (Cambridge,
1990); Michael Clanchy, From Memory to Written Record: England, 1066–1307, 2nd ed.
(Cambridge, Mass., 1993); Katherine Zieman, "Reading, Singing and Understanding: Con-
structions of the Literacy of Women Religious in Late Medieval England," in Learning and
Literacy in Medieval England and Abroad, ed. Sarah Rees Jones, Utrecht Studies in Medieval
Literature, 3 (Turnhout, 2003), 97–118.

   [1] A. Hamilton Thompson, ed., Visitations of Religious Houses in the Diocese of Lincoln, 3
vols., The Publications of the Lincoln Record Society, 7, 14, and 21 (Lincoln, 1914–29), 2:52:
"Also that in the tyme of your refeccyone atte mete oon of yowe at thassignacyone of the
prioresse rede som seynts lyfe or an othere lessone of holy wrytte to thentent to eschewe
and voyde idle wordes and brekyng of sylence."
   [2] Zieman, "Reading, Singing, and Understanding," 105–6.

While Zieman is concerned as much with the perception of nuns' literacy as with their actual abilities,[1] the description she proposes covers a range of abilities and skills that accords well with the evidence. It also suggests that the questions scholars usually raise about monastic education and learning are more pertinent to monks than to nuns, and that we therefore should be looking for evidence of nuns' literacy in places other than the grammatical treatises. Were nuns able to understand their services? Were they able to read as called for by the Benedictine Rule? Did they encourage a body of devotional materials written in English? The precise relationship of nuns' liturgical literacy to grammatical literacy is, in this context, ambiguous. Because the purpose of the nuns' literacy was liturgical performance, it is precisely their ability to render the liturgy accurately that becomes the measure of their literacy.

If we wish to assess that literacy, however, David Bell suggests a scale on which to measure a nun's proficiency in Latin:

> When speaking of Latin literacy therefore, it is best to divide it into a number of levels. The first and simplest level is the ability to read a text without understanding it (this is not difficult in Latin and requires only a few minutes of instruction); the second level is to read and understand a common liturgical text; the third level involves reading and understanding non-liturgical texts or less common texts from the liturgy; and the fourth level is the ability to compose and write a text of one's own.[2]

Bell underestimates the amount of time needed to learn to read Latin when one has never read in any language, but these levels describe a progression of skills that fits Zieman's definition of "liturgical literacy." While we will never be able to specify exactly how many nuns attained each level, it is evident that nuns represented the whole range of these categories, probably with a heavy concentration at level two and level three.

The levels of literacy implied by the injunction to read have attracted a good deal of scholarly attention, but much less attention has been paid to the other half of the equation — the question of what it meant to be "docte et informate in cantu" (taught and instructed in song). If we can assume that nuns probably developed a range of skills in singing as in reading, what would those skills be and what evidence do we have that nuns possessed those skills? Certainly the intersection of reading and singing in the performance of the Divine Office indicates that they are inextricably bound together.

I propose the following four levels of musical literacy as corollaries to Bell's steps in Latin literacy:

1) The ability to sing the basic psalm tones, litanies, and antiphons of the Divine Office with accurate relative pitch and from memory.

---

[1] Ibid., 104 n.
[2] David N. Bell, *What Nuns Read: Books and Libraries in Medieval English Nunneries*, Cistercian Studies Series, 158 (Kalamazoo, Mich., 1995), 60; the entire chapter on "Literacy and Learning" is important for this discussion.

2) The ability to remember the repertoire, including intoning chants, choosing the appropriate chant for the occasion, and consulting liturgical manuscripts. At this level a nun could read music at least as an *aide-mémoire*.

3) The ability to read notated music, to explain the system of hexachords and mutation, to teach music, and to compose chants.

4) The ability to compose and/or to sing polyphony.

Source material from English nunneries provides evidence that at least some English nuns attained all four levels of musical literacy during the later Middle Ages.

1) The ability to sing the basic psalm tones, litanies, and antiphons of the Divine Office with accurate relative pitch and from memory

This first level of musical achievement would have been what bishops and others envisioned when they called for the ability to read (i.e., pronounce) and sing as preconditions of entry into the convent. The skills listed here, especially the ability to chant the psalms, were part of the elementary curriculum offered to children by their parents, parish priests, and nuns themselves as part of learning to read.

The ordinal from the Benedictine abbey at Barking distinguishes among three levels of girls and young women: *infantes*, *iuvenculae*, and *scolares*. No definition of these terms is articulated, but from the context we can make an educated guess as to what they signify. Laurentia McLachlan writes:

> At Barking the term [*scolaris*] seems to designate a novice, because in the directions for the profession of a nun (p. 350 infra) the *Magistra scolarium* instructs the newly professed in her duties. . . . The *juvencule* were most probably girls receiving their education in the Abbey, and the *infantes* must certainly have been children. There was a strong presumption that most of these would eventually become religious, and custom in mediaeval monasteries required their presence in church for the greater part of the choir office, special parts of which were allotted to them.[1]

While McLachlan's conclusion is based on the ordinal, the question can also be approached through medieval concepts of the "ages of man." As Nicholas Orme points out, schemes consisting of six or seven stages for the entire lifespan usually include one each for very young children (birth to age seven), childhood (seven to fourteen), and adolescence.[2] These stages correspond closely with what we know of Barking Abbey as well as with bishops' comments on children in nunneries. The standard age categories are also consistent with statements in bishops' registers suggesting that girls should not remain in the convent after their fourteenth

---

[1] J. B. L. Tolhurst, ed., *The Ordinale and Customary of the Benedictine Nuns of Barking Abbey (University College, Oxford, MS 169)*, Henry Bradshaw Society, 65–66 (London, 1927), 369. McLachlan wrote the notes to this volume.

[2] Orme, *Medieval Children*, 6–7.

(or in some cases twelfth) birthdays without special license. As they reached the age of adolescence, they were expected to stay in the nunnery only if they wished to become a professed nun.

We can assume that Barking Abbey educated many girls who ranged in age from five to fourteen, as well as incorporating multiple novices. If we accept that *infantes* refers to girls (and probably also boys) up through age seven and that *iuvenculae* refers to girls up through about the age of fourteen, what can we learn about their musical training?

The *infantes*, as might be expected, appear very rarely in the ordinal. On a couple of occasions they are instructed to receive a snack along with the infirm. This instruction appears frequently for the *iuvenculae* and *scolares* as well, demonstrating a constant concern that those who are either young or very old could not go for as long a period without food as the rest of the nuns. There are two instances that confirm the *infantes'* occasional participation in liturgical activities at Barking. The instructions for Christmas Day describe the order of the procession: "First two older sisters go out and then the young children [*infantes*] with their mistresses, two by two, then the younger nuns and after that the older ones."[1] From these instructions, it would appear that even the younger children were included in the festivities on Christmas Day.[2] Regardless of whether *infantes* is used here as a catchall term for all of the children, it would at least have included those in the youngest category.

The other occasion on which the *infantes* participate is Vespers on the Feast of the Innocents. On this day, the *scolares* and *iuvenculae* play the roles usually associated with nuns, i.e., one novice serves as abbess, another as the *cantrix*, etc. The *infantes* sing the final *Benedicamus Domino* — a short chant performed by the *scolares* on other occasions. In other words, the very young children are used here to contrast with the greater age and experience of the novices.

From this we learn that by the age of six or seven a child could be expected to sing the *Benedicamus Domino*, which calls to mind the *clergeon* (schoolboy) described in the "Prioress's Tale" within Chaucer's *Canterbury Tales*. In a description of this seven-year-old boy, we learn how he absorbs the sounds of the older children's lessons while studying his own primer:

> This little child, learning his little book,
> as he sat with it and studied it at school,
> heard *Alma redemptoris mater* sung
> as [older] children learned their antiphons.
> He dared draw near and then again more near,

[1] Tolhurst, *Ordinale*, 27: "Primo exeant due senes sorores et postea infantes cum magistris bine et bine deinde minores et postea seniores."

[2] This practice would accord with the instructions at Origny-Saint-Benoîte for certain feasts on which younger novices were supposed to vest (Saint-Quentin, Bibliothèque municipale, MS 86, 346–47).

and listened ever to the words and notes,
until he knew the first verse all by rote.[1]

This portrait of a young scholar demonstrates the large role one's absorption in the surrounding environment played in medieval learning; from the other children who were learning antiphons, the boy could learn both the words and the music by heart without understanding the text.

Once girls at Barking reached the stage of *iuvenculae* (aged eight to fourteen, approximately), they clearly participated much more frequently in the liturgy. As well as appearing on several occasions as part of the group receiving an extra snack ("uadant accipere mixtum"[2]), the *iuvenculae* served as additional participants when the number of novices was insufficient. The ordinal mandates this involvement especially on the Feast of the Innocents: "If, however, the number of novices is less than the number of antiphons then the psalms and versicles for many martyrs should be begun by the schoolgirls."[3] Clearly, the schoolgirls were expected to have sufficient musical skill to sing the antiphon incipit and begin the recitation of the psalm. They may, of course, have practiced diligently for this occasion, which undoubtedly loomed large as a chance to imitate their elders publicly. Therein lay one of the benefits of the Feast of the Innocents: an opportunity to learn adult roles. Similarly, on weekdays following Trinity Sunday — ordinary time in the liturgical year — certain readings and chants were to be read or sung "ab alia scolari uel iuuencula" (by another novice or schoolgirl). This relatively unimportant liturgical occasion was another chance for young girls to hone their skills.

We do not know exactly when or if schoolchildren were in the choir with the professed nuns. While many injunctions forbid the presence of children in the dormitory, only a few mention the presence of children in the choir.[4] To name just one instance, a nun at the visitation of Catesby Priory in 1530 complained, "It is not appropriate that the children should play in the cloister, nor that they should sit in the choir, and yet the majority do that; and there are many children in the monastery, some boys and some girls."[5] Unfortunately, neither this complaint nor

---

[1] Translation by Paul Strohm, whom the volume editors thank for his help. Chaucer, *The Canterbury Tales*, ll. 516–22, in *The Riverside Chaucer*, 3rd ed., ed. Larry D. Benson (Boston, 1987), 210: "This litel child, his litel book lernynge, / As he sat in the scole at his prymer, / He Alma redemptoris herde synge, / As children lerned hire antiphoner; / And as he dorste, he drought hym ner and ner, / And herkned ay the wordes and the noote, / Til he the firste vers koude al by rote."

[2] Tolhurst, *Ordinale*, 14, for examples.

[3] Ibid., 34: "Si uero scolarium fuerit paucior numerus quam antiphone, tunc incipiantur a iuuenculis, Psalmi et uersiculi plurimorum martirum." Although *iuvenculis* could be either feminine or masculine, its use in other places in the ordinal is usually in feminine form (*iuvenculae*).

[4] See Power, *Medieval English Nunneries*, Note B, for prohibitions against children sleeping in the dorms.

[5] A. Hamilton Thompson, ed., *Visitations in the Diocese of Lincoln, 1517–1531*, The Publications of the Lincoln Record Society, 35 (Hereford, 1944), 103: "... non est consonum quod pueri ludent in claustro nec sedeant in choro, et tamen ita plerumque faciunt; et sunt plures pueri in monasterio aliqui masculi et alie femine."

the bishop's injunction to fix the problem stipulates where the children should be during the service. Two centuries earlier, in his 1314 visitation, Bishop Henry Woodlock told the nuns at Wintney Abbey, "And we wish and command that neither male nor female children should be in the choir when you sing the Divine Office."[1] It is likely that the children were to be in the church but not actually in the choir with the nuns, just as they were supposed to be in separate sleeping quarters.[2] In many cases, children, like Chaucer's little clergeon, would seem to have absorbed their musical education by listening to services.

Very little extant evidence sheds any light on the development of vocal stamina in young people preparing to becoming novices, yet there must have been some work in this initial phase on good vocal production. Nuns spent approximately six hours a day in services, the vast majority of which included singing. The chantress at Syon Abbey is specifically instructed to choose pitch and tempo so that her sisters can continue to sing:

> Also to start the song smoothly and moderately, neither too high nor too low,[3] neither too fast nor too slow, but steadily and reverently after the due ceremony of the feast or day, and according to the length of both the services of the sisters and brothers, and according to the attitude of their hearts; because to sing so high one day that they cannot sing any more, or so slowly and low that they grow tired and put both themselves and their listeners to sleep — that lacks prudence and knowledge of the Lord, who teaches in his holy rule that things should be done with good sense.[4]

This attention to the spiritual and physical aspects of liturgical performance presumably affected the teaching of schoolchildren as well. One's physical condition and spiritual state are closely related. The duty of the *cantrix* was to make sure that her musical choices did not adversely affect the spiritual condition of the nuns or their audience.

---

[1] A. W. Goodman, ed., *Registrum Henrici Woodlock diocesis Wintoniensis* (A.D. 1305–1316), Canterbury and York Society, 43–44 (Oxford, 1940–41), 758: "Et voloms et comaundoms qe enfans madles ne femeles ne soyent menes en queor taunt come hom chaunte le seruice Dieu."

[2] See Susan Boynton, "The Liturgical Role of Children in Monastic Customaries from the Central Middle Ages," *Studia liturgica* 28 (1998), 194–209 at 197–99, on the placement of children; she suggests that they sat separately near the altar.

[3] Medieval Latin and various vernacular equivalents of "high" could imply both loud and high in pitch, while "low" implied both soft and low in pitch.

[4] "Also to sette the songe euen and mensurably, neyther to hyghe nor to lowe, neyther to faste nor to slowe, but sadly and deuoutly after the solennyte of the feste or day, and after the lenghte of bothe seruyses of sustres and brethren, and after the disposicion of ther brestes; ffor to syng so hyghe oo day, that they may nomore, or to longe and lowe, that they enwery and brynge a slepe bothe themselves and ther herers, thys wantethe discrecion and doctryne of our Lord, whiche techethe in hys holy rewle that al thynge scholde be done resonably." This description is from the instructions to the *cantrix* at Syon Abbey (hence the reference to the brethren); see George J. Aungier, *The History and Antiquities of Syon Monastery, the Parish of Isleworth, and the Chapelry of Hounslow: Compiled from Public Records, Ancient Manuscripts, Ecclesiastical and Other Authentic Documents* (London, 1840), 359.

One final aspect of the musical skills required at this early stage was the expectation that children learn the Psalter. Such a task seems formidable now, but nuns and monks sang all 150 psalms weekly (some even more often), and memorizing them was a key part of preparation for the monastic life as well as a cornerstone of lay piety.

Hugh of St. Victor, writing in Paris in the twelfth century, offers the memorization of the psalms as an example of how to memorize biblical material.[1] He suggests that students create a mental map or grid of the numbers from one to 150 and memorize a short text incipit for each number. The number one would call to mind the incipit "Blessed is the man." In this way, the learner constructs a mental map of where each psalm is stored. As the student proceeds to memorize each psalm, similar techniques are used so that at each point only the amount that can be stored in memory is memorized. Since this memorization is done aloud, the student has both a visual aid — imagining the numbers on a grid — and an aural aid — voicing them.[2]

This first level of musical literacy would seem to be a reasonable minimum that would be expected of nuns entering their year of profession as a novice. The quality and capabilities of the novice mistress and the *cantrix* as well as the innate ability of the novice herself probably determined which of the other levels she reached.

2) The ability to remember the repertoire, including intoning chants, choosing the appropriate chant for the occasion, and consulting liturgical manuscripts. At this stage a nun could read music at least as an aide-mémoire.

If the first level of musical literacy was a precondition for admission to the novitiate, then surely it was the work of the novice year to teach the young woman the skills outlined in level two. Novices were supposed to spend no more than one year in the convent before deciding to make a full profession or to leave. In many cases, however, nuns seem to have spent multiple years in the condition of "tacite expressa," meaning that a nun who had worn the habit for a whole year was considered to have made a tacit profession.[3] During that time, they were supposed to be under the care of the novice mistress. Some descriptions lump together

---

[1] My use of Hugh of St. Victor's material is prompted by its presence and translation in Mary Carruthers and Jan M. Ziolkowski, eds., *The Medieval Craft of Memory: An Anthology of Texts and Pictures* (Philadelphia, 2002).

[2] A common contemporary parallel would be the memorization of the Qur'an by young Muslim boys today. Schoolboys aged eight to fourteen will take two to three years to study nothing but the Qur'an and memorize it. Like young people in the Middle Ages, they often do not understand the meaning of the text they memorize; the sound of the words is itself a holy sound. On such schools in the New York area, see Michael Luo, "Memorizing the Way to Heaven, Verse by Verse," *The New York Times* (Wednesday, August 16, 2006), A18 (national edition).

[3] For a discussion of Peckham's *Sanctimoniales* and this rule, see Thompson, ed., *Visitations of Religious Houses in the Diocese of Lincoln*, 3:348 n.

younger professed nuns with novices. For example, the injunctions issued to Malling Priory in 1299 by Robert Winchelsey, archbishop of Canterbury, require the diocesan bishop to celebrate the profession of nuns who have finished their year of probation. He further enjoins "that the novices and the rest of the younger nuns should be shaped assiduously through regular observances so that they, provoked towards humility through the Divine Office, do not extol themselves."[1] The participation of novices and young nuns in the Divine Office formed appropriate levels of humility in them, and their participation was considered a requisite part of growth and development in the convent.

In the Barking ordinal, several specific roles are entrusted to the *scolares*. An examination of these provides a window onto their musical formation. During Advent, the novices intone the antiphons on weekdays at Lauds.[2] Two novices sing the litany in procession on Ash Wednesday.[3] On Monday after the first Sunday in Lent, one scholar begins the Vespers responsory *Participem me* and sings the solo verse.[4] At Lauds on the octave of Easter, the novices sing together a short versicle.[5] On the Rogation Days and the feast of St. Mark, they sing the short litany.[6] In the weeks of ordinary time following Trinity Sunday, the novices sing the short responsories.[7] They sing the *Benedicamus Domino* at Vespers at the feast of St. Nicholas.[8] They chant the *Resquiescant in pace* on All Saints' Day.[9] In addition to these musical duties, the novices also participated by reading lessons, bearing tapers, adoring the cross, and performing various other liturgical activities. The portions assigned to the novices expanded their musical repertoire and prepared them to assume the role of *ebdomadaria* after they were professed.

The role of the *ebdomadaria* best exemplifies the level of musicianship required of the professed nun.[10] The position of *ebdomadaria* rotated weekly and the *cantrix* assigned each nun to this role in turn. The *ebdomadaria* read or chanted prayers and lessons and intoned several chants. At Barking, she frequently began the introit in the middle of the choir for the principal Mass. She prepared for her week as *ebdomadaria* by consulting with the *cantrix* and reviewing the appropriate chants. While not necessarily fluent in reading musical notation, she presumably

---

[1] Rose Graham, ed. *Registrum Roberti Winchelsey Cantuariensis Archiepiscopi*, A.D. 1294–1313, Canterbury and York Society, 52 (Oxford, 1956), 834: ". . . quod novicie et cetere juniores moniales in regularibus observanciis studiosius informentur ut per occupacionem divini officii ad humilatatem provocate non extollant se."

[2] Tolhurst, *Ordinale*, 15.

[3] Ibid., 64: "Peractis autem antiphonis, due scolares concineant letaniam et intrantes chorum consistant in medio donec illam finierint" (When these antiphons are finished, moreover, two novices sing together the litany and entering the choir they stand together in the middle until they have finished it).

[4] Ibid., 71.

[5] Ibid., 117.

[6] Ibid., 125, 127, and 220.

[7] Ibid., 148.

[8] Ibid., 167.

[9] Ibid., 329.

[10] For a fuller discussion of this role, see Anne Bagnall Yardley, *Performing Piety: Musical Culture in Medieval English Nunneries* (New York, 2006), 66–69.

could consult the liturgical manuscripts to remind herself of the beginning of each melody.

The role of *ebdomadaria* invites us to ask how the nuns gained a rudimentary knowledge of reading music. The notation of music and the notation of speech both involve the symbolic representation of aural events. Just as letters invoke speech sounds, notes on the staff provide the representation of musical sounds. Historically, the invention of a way to notate musical sounds occurs much later than systems for representing spoken sounds. But by the mid eleventh century, both a system of staff notation and the mnemonic device known as the "Guidonian hand" were in place. Their invention stemmed from the interaction of memorization and writing.[1]

The medieval mind was regularly trained to remember things by storing them in a visual location — often a building of some sort — and the Guidonian hand served that function for remembering music. While the hand was the most frequently used image for teaching note names, other designs involved a ladder or scale, or used other visual images. With any of these techniques, the purpose was the same: to enable the singer to read notated music and to understand the modes on which chant is based.

A manuscript from the Benedictine house at Wherwell includes a very rudimentary Guidonian hand, a tantalizing indication that nuns there learned by this method (see Figure 3.1).[2] While the hand is far from complete, it does include the basic note names. Further information in the manuscript offers more theoretical material. This method of teaching musical notes seems to have been the one most widely used at the time. Since the teacher could use her own hand as the model, she would not need written materials to teach note names, the concept of the scale, or an elementary understanding of interval structure.

Two intriguing musical items, also from Wherwell, indicate that the nuns there learned a form of vocal warm-ups not unlike those used today. Six lines of these exercises appear at the end of a psalter that belonged to Johanna Stretford, a nun at Wherwell.[3] Using the G hexachord, the first line goes right up the scale and back down, fixing the sounds of each note in the ear. The second line moves up three notes by step and then traces the leap from G to B, followed by a scalar passage and leaps up the intervals of the fourth, fifth, and sixth. This short exercise would train both the voice and the ear, helping to provide a visual and aural connection between the intervals and their representation on the staff. Line three comprises descending scales and leaps of the fourth, fifth, and sixth. Line four moves by thirds up and down the hexachord. Finally, lines 5–6, shown in Example 3.1, introduce the *f* below the hexachord in what is possibly an exercise in mutating from the F hexachord to the G hexachord. (Mutation is the process by which one moves from one hexachord to another, with the note that was "re" in the first hexa-

[1] Karol Berger, "The Guidonian Hand," in *The Medieval Craft of Memory* (see p. 56 n. 1 above), 71–82.

[2] St. Petersburg, National Library of Russia, MS Q. v.i., 62, fol. 11ᵛ.

[3] London, British Library, MS Additional 27866, fol. 147ʳ. See Yardley, *Performing Piety*, 63, fig. 2.4.

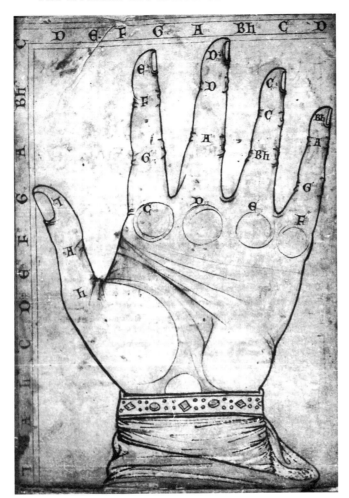

Figure 3.1: St. Petersburg, National Library of Russia, MS Q. v.i., 62, fol. 11ᵛ: Guidonian hand from Wherwell Abbey. Copyright © National Library of Russia. Used with permission.

Example 3.1: Vocal exercise from the Wherwell Psalter (London, British Library, Add. MS 27866, fol. 147ʳ; syllables added by author)

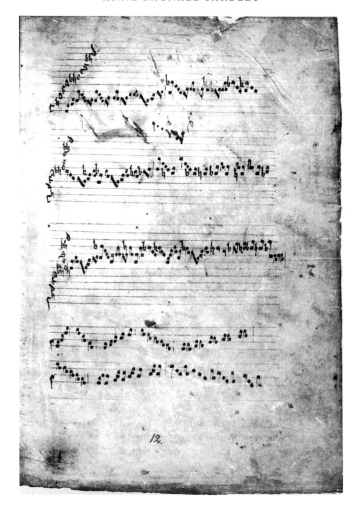

Figure 3.2: St. Petersburg, Public Library, MS Q. v.i., 62, fol. 12ʳ: Vocal exercises from Wherwell Abbey. Copyright © National Library of Russia. Used with permission.

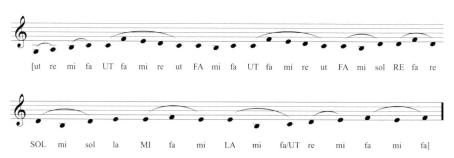

[ut re mi fa UT fa mi re ut FA mi fa UT fa mi re ut FA mi sol RE fa re

SOL mi sol la MI fa mi LA mi fa/UT re mi fa mi fa]

Example 3.2: Vocal exercise from Wherwell Abbey (St. Petersburg, National Library of Russia, MS Q. v.i., 62, fol. 12ʳ; syllables added by author)

chord, for example, becoming "ut" in the next. I have indicated mutations through the use of capitals.) This single page could effectively trigger the mental organization of material that the nun had presumably memorized. These exercises appear in a psalter that has musical notation for all of the included antiphons as a useful reference for a nun leading worship.

While the exercises in the psalter are relatively rudimentary, the notations found in the same manuscript as the Guidonian hand are far more complex (see Figure 3.2).[1] Initially, the visual appearance of this page offers a ladder to allow the student to absorb the full gamut of notes. It also moves in meticulous detail through the mutation possibilities. In the first phrase, it mutates nine times, as can be seen in Example 3.2. (Mutations are again indicated by the use of capital letters.) In the second phrase, the mutations between the soft (F) and hard (G) hexachords help the student practice the differences in the use of B-flat and B-natural.

After the completion of this mutation exercise through the full two and a half octaves, another set of exercises begins. These stay in the lowest hexachord and resemble those found in the Wherwell Psalter cited earlier. They seem in many ways more useful as vocal warm-ups than as theoretical material, although they do explore the hexachord in great detail.

These folios offer important insight into the teaching of music in the nunnery, suggesting to us that novices and young nuns developed their competency in music through three principal avenues: the absorption of the entire repertoire through participation, the development of specific skills in singing and leading through the assignment of chant intonations and litanies on specific occasions, and the intellectual understanding of the musical gamut through the teaching of basic music theory. Learning in these three ways, the novice who entered at level one would master level two by the time of her profession or shortly thereafter.

While it is not realistic to suggest that all nuns possessed the same level of proficiency, one can assert that almost all nuns had access to the first two avenues (absorption and practice in short solos) and could fulfill the expectations that they would serve as *ebdomadaria* in the rotation.

One of the principal means by which girls improved their musicianship was self-correction. The Benedictine rule states clearly that all in the monastic community had to kneel down and acknowledge their mistakes. The *Additions to the Rule* of Syon Abbey classify mistakes into several categories ("lyght," "grievous," "more grievous," "most grievous"). Among the "lyghte defawtes" are two that apply to musical performance:

> If anyone, after she makes a mistake in reading or singing in the choir, does not humble herself immediately, kneeling down to the ground devoutly . . .

> If any person presumes to read or sing in the choir differently than what

---

[1] St. Petersburg, National Library of Russia, MS Q. v.i., 62, fol. 12ʳ. For a transcription of this folio, see Yardley, *Performing Piety*, 241–42.

is written or noted in the corrected books after the use and custom of the order . . .[1]

It is striking that the fault lies not so much in making the mistake but in failing to acknowledge the mistake. The nun herself had the greatest responsibility for identifying such errors. Because the chant was sung in unison, mistakes would have been quite noticeable; the nun trained her ear by noticing her own faults and atoning for them immediately. Even today, some choir directors ask singers to raise their hands in rehearsal when they have made a mistake to show they are aware of the error. Children pick this up very easily and learn from it. Kneeling is an even more disruptive action and would have reinforced the need for accuracy in performance. Before the *cantrix* or novice mistress corrected the young woman, she had a chance to identify her own mistakes.

This passage from the *Additions* also indicates the authority represented by "corrected books" in the later Middle Ages. Syon Abbey put an especially strong emphasis on bringing its liturgical books into agreement with one another, perhaps because the Bridgettine liturgy was created by its founder. Nevertheless, this instruction is a clear indication that the notated book was the final arbiter of the correct practice and that the nuns were expected to know its contents.

The competence and knowledge of both the novice mistress and the *cantrix* also affected the curriculum for the novice, as evidenced by source materials from several nunneries.[2] The extant rule from the Franciscan house at Aldgate suggests that "If there be a sister who is proper and of good intelligence, the abbess, if she thinks it appropriate, should assign a proper and honest mistress to teach them singing, so that they can perform the office and service of God steadfastly."[3] An injunction from the Dean of St. Paul's Cathedral in London to the nuns at St. Helen's describes the need for a teacher in much the same terms:

> Also we decree and enjoin you, that you appoint and choose one of your sisters, honorable, able, and learned in sound judgment, who can, may, and shall be in charge of the teaching and instruction of your sisters who are ignorant, to teach them the service and the rule of her order.[4]

---

[1] Aungier, *History and Antiquities*, 252: "If any after that sche fayleth in redyng or syngynge in the quyre, meke not herself anone knelyng down to the grounde religiously . . . If any presume to rede or to synge otherwyse in the quyer, than is wryten or noted unto her in the corrected bokes after the use and custom of the religion."

[2] For a more comprehensive discussion of the role of the *cantrix*, see Yardley, *Performing Piety*, 53–66.

[3] *A Fifteenth-Century Courtesy Book, edited from the MS by R. W. Chambers . . . and Two Fifteenth-Century Franciscan Rules, edited from the MS by Walter W. Seton*, Early English Text Society, o.s. 148 (1914; repr. Oxford, 1962), 85: "ȝif þer be any sustris couenable & of gode witte, The abbes, ȝif sche þentkiþ hem goode, to ordeyne & assigne a maystresse couenable & honeste for to teche hem songe, to performe þe office & seruise of god stedfastli."

[4] William Dugdale, *Monasticon Anglicanum: A History of the Abbies and other Monasteries . . .*, new ed. (London, 1849), 4: 554: "Also we ordeyne and injoyne yow, that ye ordeyne, and chese on of yowre sustres, honest, abille, and cunnyng of discrecyone, the which can

Nunneries required excellent musical leadership in order to form the next genera-tion of nuns for the proper rendition of the liturgy. While such nuns were not always available, the ideal, especially in the larger houses, would be to find a nun who had reached level three to serve as *cantrix*.

> 3) *The ability to read notated music, to explain the system of hexachords and mutation, to teach music, and to compose chants. At this level the nun has a thorough understanding of the liturgy and a knowledge of the repertoire for all the feast days.*

Very few girls or young women would have reached this level of musical knowl-edge, yet the presence of some who had attained this level indicates that young girls had competent teachers available to them. As the *Additions to the Rule* at Syon Abbey so aptly put it:

> The chantress and sub-chantresses should one and all be knowledgeable [erudite] and flawless in reading and singing, having an expert knowledge of the ordinal and of creating the table for the choir, and with excellent vocal ability.[1]

In other words, the person in charge of music for the abbey had to exhibit the musical abilities of what I have called level three. She had to be well educated, mu-sical, and a good vocalist, and she had to know the liturgy extremely well. To these abilities, mentioned explicitly in the *Additions*, I would add that she had to be able to compose a chant if required for a particular liturgical occasion.[2]

We must remember that the size and nature of nunneries varied dramatically in the British Isles during the Middle Ages. Some houses had fewer than five nuns at the time of the Dissolution, whereas others housed more than thirty. Thus, it is fair to assume that some houses were lucky to have even one nun who reached level two in her musical abilities while such others as Barking, Dartford, Syon, and Shaftesbury may have housed multiple nuns who were capable of serving as *cantrix* with all of the capabilities described in the *Additions*.

The ability to teach music to other nuns is perhaps the most salient character-istic of nuns who have reached this level. Manuscripts associated with Wherwell Abbey offer the most convincing proof of the systematic teaching of music. In addition to the folios previously described, a manuscript now in St. Petersburg also includes a treatise on the gamut.[3] This folio offers an unusual depiction of

---

may and schall have the charge of techyng and informacyone of yowre sustres that ben un-cunnyng for to teche hem here service, and the rule of here religione."

[1] Aungier, *History and Antiquities*, 359: "The chauntres and subchauntresses euerychone owe to be cunnyng and perfyte in redyng and syngynge, hauynge experience of the ordinal and mayng of the table for the quyer, with habilite of voyce." The "table for choir" was the document or tablet listing the nuns responsible for leading chants each week.

[2] Here I refer to composing a melody, but it is quite possible that nuns composed both text and music.

[3] See Yardley, *Performing Piety*, 62, fig. 2.3, for a reproduction, and app. C, 239–41, for

basic musical grammar. Each note is shown as a circle: the note name is given with its corresponding syllables — e.g., C *sol fa ut*. Above the circle, an instruction in French indicates whether the note would be written on a line or in a space of the staff. Below the note name is the indication of which part of the gamut it inhabits — low (grave), middle (acute), or high (superacute). Above the note name is an indication of which form of B (soft or hard, i.e., flat or natural) is used in the hexachord. So in the case of C *sol fa ut*, when C is *sol*, the B (which is *fa*) is soft or flatted. When C is *fa*, then the B (which is *mi*) is hard or natural; when C is *ut*, B is not in the hexachord. All of this information — which has taken a long paragraph to decode — is contained in one short mnemonic device. Taken in concert with the other circles, the graphic depiction imparts the entire hexachord system in half of one folio. Once the system has been explained, one can memorize it by calling the drawing to mind.

Young women learning music at Wherwell Abbey received an excellent education in music theory. Through the Guidonian hands, the circle graphs, the treatise, and the vocal exercises, they had many opportunities to understand music in a systematic way. Another important method for systematizing chants comes in the tonaries. Anna Maria Busse Berger argues that "the purpose of the tonary was simply to organize the repertory for memorization."[1] There are, however, no extant tonaries from English nunneries, so we have no indication of whether or not English *cantrices* had access to such volumes. We do know that they were expected to understand all the rules for the liturgical year and to find the appropriate chants. In addition to the statement from Syon Abbey that the chantress should have "experience of the ordinal," the Barking ordinal specifically charges the chantresses with monitoring the church calendar: "The *cantrices* should be diligent and should examine the calendar with watchful care lest — God forbid — due to their carelessness or negligence the Divine Office be performed irrationally."[2]

Along with the responsibility for the calendar came that of knowing which chants were to be sung and then assigning them to nuns. The *cantrix* had to know the mode of the antiphon preceding and following a psalm so that the singers would sing the correct psalm tone. (Tonaries helped to classify this information.) Whether or not the house owned a tonary, nuns had to hold vast numbers of chants in their memory in a way that allowed them to retrieve the appropriate chant and know its mode. They also had to consult the volumes of liturgical chant owned by the nunnery and read the music in them. The average nun could probably follow along, but someone needed to take the lead.

A nun who reached level three would also be able to execute accurate, pleasing

a transcription of the treatise. The word "gamut" comes from the name given to the lowest note of the theoretical scale in medieval music — *gamma ut* — and came to represent the entire hexachord system.

[1] Anna Maria Busse Berger, *Medieval Music and the Art of Memory* (Berkeley, 2005), 60.

[2] Tolhurst, *Ordinale*, 151: "Sollicite sunt *cantrices* et cura diligenti kalendarium inspiciant . . . ne quod absit incuria illarum uel negligencia diuinum officium irracionabile fiat." The omitted portion details the number of Sundays that fall in certain periods of the year depending on when Easter occurs.

singing and to hear and identify the mistakes of others. If a novice did not correct her own mistakes, the *cantrix* identified them for her. The *cantrix* was also expected to balance the two sides of the choir, as the Syon *Additions* suggest: "Also, it is her role to see that the choir is balanced on the two sides in number, voice, and skill, by calling over nuns from one side to the other as need be, and doing this in as suitable a time as possible."[1] Thus the *cantrix* had to be able to hear the whole balance of the ensemble, to know and understand the capabilities of each nun, and to make the music as perfect as possible. She had to teach the nuns at a "suitable" time, perhaps between services. These acts required a high level of musicianship. A young nun in the choir would learn from corrections by the *cantrix* as well as by correcting herself.

Finally, a nun at this level had the ability to compose new chants as needed for particular liturgical occasions. Since virtually all such music from the Middle Ages is anonymous, it is hard to prove specific authorship, but three unique hymns from Barking Abbey and the *Visitatio* from the Wilton Processional indicate that some English nuns did compose.[2] While there is no indication that young nuns were taught specifically in composition, some may well have learned by example. We can recall that the beautiful compositions of Hildegard of Bingen come to us from a nun who claimed to have received no instruction.[3]

4) The ability to compose and/or to sing polyphony

Did young nuns receive instruction in the performance of polyphonic music? There is very little evidence to suggest that polyphony formed an important part of the repertoire in English medieval nunneries, although there are a few tantalizing hints. Additionally, several Continental sources attest to a much more common use of polyphony across the Channel.

The early-fourteenth-century polyphonic codex from the Monasterio de Las Huelgas in Burgos, Spain, records a highly unusual polyphonic pedagogical exercise. Both parts of this two-part composition use solmization syllables, demonstrating how mutation between hexachords functions in a polyphonic context. The text of the lower voice then continues, "You Carthusian virgins and nuns, adorned with gold, because you are suitably talented for all this, take care

---

[1] Aungier, *History and Antiquities*, 360: "Also it is her parte to se that the quyer be euen on euery syde in nowmber, voyce, and kunnyng, by kallyng oyer from oo seyde to another as nede is, and this in moste conuenient tyme sche may."

[2] See Yardley, *Performing Piety*, 153–55, for the *Visitatio*, and 192–98 for a discussion and transcription of the Barking hymns.

[3] For further information on Hildegard as a musician, see Margot Fassler, "Composer and Dramatist," in *Voice of the Living Light: Hildegard of Bingen and Her World*, ed. Barbara Newman (Berkeley, 1998), 149–175. Two other articles that deal with Hildegard's pedagogy are Beverly Mayne Kienzle, "Hildegard of Bingen's Teaching in her *Expositiones evangeliorum* and *Ordo virtutum*," and Carolyn Muessig, "Learning and Mentoring in the Twelfth Century: Hildegard of Bingen and Herrad of Landsberg," in *Medieval Monastic Education* (see p. 49 n. 2 above), 72–86 and 87–104 respectively.

to produce polyphony, with the other voices sounding along in this way."[1] The community at Las Huelgas consisted primarily of women of noble lineage who brought a high level of education to the cloister. The presence of this exercise at the end of an entire corpus of polyphony indicates that nuns received some particular instruction in this art.

Most instruction in polyphony, however, involved the memorization of patterns of notes that could appropriately accompany melodic patterns in the chant. Busse Berger offers a detailed look at the ways in which singers created a memorial archive of potential note choices for creating improvised polyphony. She argues that most musical treatises of the medieval period were written to be memorized, much as students memorized declensions of nouns in the study of grammar.[2] Throughout the period, improvised polyphony formed a major part of polyphonic performance and is thus very difficult to document.

In England, the nuns at Syon Abbey were specifically prohibited from singing polyphonic music. The *Additions to the Rule* state that their singing is to be "sadde, sober, and symple with out brekyng of notes and gay relesynge with alle mekenes and devocion; but organs schal thei never have none."[3] "Organs," in this case, probably refers to polyphony, *organa*, rather than to the instrument. "Breaking of notes" is also sometimes used as a term to describe polyphony. The fact that the rule bans this behavior probably points to some past history of including polyphony. Since the Bridgettine order emphasized simplicity and the restriction of the nuns' liturgy to their particular Marian devotion, it is not surprising to find this ban at Syon.

Once again, a source from Wherwell Abbey provides the strongest evidence of musical erudition. Two three-voiced Marian antiphons are bound with the fourteenth-century cartulary from Wherwell.[4] The ability to perform polyphony is one potential result of the attention to music pedagogy evidenced in the theoretical treatises also associated with this nunnery. Nuns who had been systematically trained to read notation could have applied that skill to singing polyphony. Thus there surely were English nuns who reached this fourth level of musical proficiency.

The teaching of music to English girls and young women in medieval nunneries relied upon the traditional oral pedagogy of the time. Schoolgirls learned to memorize the Psalter, sing in unison with their peers, and assimilate the repertoire of the Divine Office. Novices absorbed the tradition through their presence at serv-

---

[1] Burgos, Monasterio de Santa Maria la Real de Las Huelgas, MS 9, fol. 154ᵛ: " Et huius modi cetera voce resonare, vos, virgines Cartucenses, moniales deaurate ad hec apte, quia nate, organizare curate."

[2] Berger, *Medieval Music*, 111–58.

[3] Augnier, *History and Antiquities*, 319.

[4] London, British Library, MS Egerton 2104A, fol. 14ᵛ, 2. For a discussion of other English sources, see Yardley, *Performing Piety*, 109–11. For a partial list of polyphony from continental sources, see Anne Bagnall Yardley, "'Ful weel she soong the service dyvyne': The Cloistered Musician in the Middle Ages," in *Women Making Music: The Western Art Tradition, 1150–1950*, ed. Jane Bowers and Judith Tick (Urbana, Ill., 1986), 26–27.

ices and through opportunities to intone chants, lead litanies, and sing solo verses. In some houses, novices learned to name the medieval gamut and memorized the Guidonian hand. By the time of their profession, most nuns had an extensive store of memorized chants ready to be called into use on an appropriate liturgical occasion. Nuns who excelled in this area could become teachers of younger nuns and serve as *cantrices*. Some evidence suggests that English nuns may also have sung polyphony. Through the constant bodily absorption of the sounds of chant, the responsibility for monitoring their own performance, and the systematic learning of music theory, young nuns developed a musical literacy that surpassed that of most members of the literate world today.

4

CHOIRBOYS IN EARLY ENGLISH
RELIGIOUS DRAMA

Richard Rastall

INTRODUCTION

THIS essay examines the role of choirboys in vernacular religious drama in England around 1400–1600. Setting aside the choirboy companies of the late sixteenth and early seventeenth centuries and the boys employed in the adult professional theatres, the residual repertory is that of the civic and parish dramas. The evidence is scanty and difficult to interpret, especially in the still-emerging area of parish drama; but the financial accounts concerning drama in the larger towns and cities provide some information from which a broad picture can be developed.

The plays concerned are the anonymous biblical, saint, and morality plays, which used or may have used choirboys in two main ways. First, because community and commercial drama in England used only male actors (unlike France, for instance, where females are well documented), female roles were played by males. The great majority of these roles, which presented young females, were taken by young male actors with treble voices: only such roles as the prophetess Anna (in the Presentation plays) and the Blessed Virgin at the end of her life (plays of the death of Mary) are known to have been taken by older actors.[1] The young male actors might be apprentices or journeymen of the trade guilds concerned or choirboys from a local church, although some may have belonged to neither of these categories.

Second, many plays required solo singers or small groups of singers to perform items of plainsong or, more rarely, polyphony. While some items were obviously

---

[1] David Wulstan, "Vocal Colour in English Sixteenth-Century Polyphony," *Journal of the Plainsong and Mediaeval Music Society* 2 (1979), 19–60, esp. 25–26; Richard Rastall, "Female Roles in All-Male Casts," *Medieval English Theatre* 7/1 (1985), 25–51; Richard Rastall, *The Heaven Singing* (Cambridge, 1997), 308–27; and Richard Rastall, "Young Wives Played by Males: The Case of Percula in York Play 30," in *Mainte belle œuvre faicte: Études sur le théâtre médiéval offertes à Graham A. Runnalls*, ed. Denis Hue, Mario Longtin, and Lynette Muir (Orléans, 2005), 433–37.

intended to be sung by members of the cast who were not professional singers, most demanded professionals. This is clear from both the repertory (liturgical chant normally performed by trained singers, or polyphony, which demanded a high level of specialist training) and the quality of performance demanded by the dramatic situation (such as the music of angels). Often it is impossible to tell who the professional singers were, but sometimes they can be identified as local church singing-men, and sometimes as choirboys. To some extent this second use of boys overlaps with the first, as a professional singer was sometimes needed to play a female role (such as that of the Virgin Mary) that demanded high-quality singing. Liturgical items were sometimes sung by other characters, including angels, which also might demand a professional singer. Angels were regarded as male — the Bible refers to them as "young men" — but they were usually depicted as androgynous creatures with young, rather feminine, faces. Written music for them is sometimes for tenors and sometimes for trebles, so it is clear that both men and boys played angelic roles.[1]

Boys and children

It is likely that the majority of boys taking female roles were prepubertal. This is, however, impossible to quantify — and in an age when the voice change apparently happened quite slowly, there was often little disruption to a boy's ability to sing: the voice simply moved gradually from treble to alto and on down to tenor and bass.[2] For this reason the precise stage of the actor's development was not necessarily crucial, since a transitional boy might still be speaking and singing well in a low treble or alto voice. While we should expect a stable prepubertal voice to be used in a female role, therefore, a transitional voice might still be similar to that of a young female. Such a boy would normally be physically capable of the visual impersonation as well, given the possibility of a wig and a small amount of padding.[3]

It is therefore important to know precisely what sort of actor and singer was involved. Although some scholars are still skeptical, it seems to me beyond doubt that puberty in boys, prior to the twentieth century, generally took place rather later than we now expect it, and over a wider age range. Certainly some boys experienced the growth spurt at the age of thirteen or fourteen, this being followed by the change of voice and other physical changes associated with puberty at fourteen or so — but most were older than that, and some as old as twenty, before the treble

---

[1] Richard Rastall, "The Musical Repertory," in *The Iconography of Heaven*, ed. Clifford Davidson, Early Drama, Art, and Music Monograph Series, 21 (Kalamazoo, Mich., 1994),162–96; Rastall, *The Heaven Singing*, 328 ff.

[2] D. A. Weiss, "The Pubertal Change in the Human Voice," *Folia Phoniatrica* 2 (1950), 126–59, esp. 134; J. M. Tanner, *Growth at Adolescence*, 2nd ed. (Oxford, 1962), 34.

[3] On the physical characteristics associated with puberty in boys and girls, see Rastall, *The Heaven Singing*, 313; Martin H. Johnson and Barry J. Everitt, *Essential Reproduction* (Oxford, 1980), 145 and 149.

voice changed. There may have been local and chronological differences — that has not been investigated, as far as I know — but in general it is safe to say that the change of voice happened between the ages of fourteen and twenty, with the average at about seventeen and a half.[1]

This higher average age for the onset of the voice change has several important consequences. Although choirboys might be as young as ten, or even younger, the generally higher average age of choristers means that we cannot assume *little* boys when dealing with them. Even when the growth spurt was delayed to the mid or late teens, a choirboy's general growth would ensure that he had a larger chest capacity than he had had as a fourteen-year-old. The growth of a prepubertal boy was probably not unlike that of a girl of the same age, and his lung-capacity there-fore increased with the years, even before the noticeable growth spurt signaling the onset of puberty. Individuals varied, of course, but given a class of prepubertal males up to the age of twenty, it was certainly possible for members of that class to impersonate females of the same age or rather older.

One indication of this — perhaps the only objective evidence there is — lies in the constitution of choirs. Such documentary records as we have show that boys and men sang in the ratio of roughly 3 : 2 by part. This is in considerable distinc-tion from modern choirs, where far more than three boys are required to balance two men by part: a present-day cathedral choir typically has six or more boys in each part to balance two or three men.[2] My evidence for this is taken from choirs in England, but it is the case that the smaller ratio was expected also in sixteenth-century Rome. The constitution of the papal chapel dated 27 September 1589 described a choir of

> twelve singers: four basses, four tenors, and four [falsettist] contraltos, and in addition, for the voice that is called soprano, four eunuchs, if skilled ones can be found; if not, six boys . . .[3]

This shows a choir of 4/4/4/4 (or 2/2/2/2 on each side) if the top part was sung by castrati, or 6/4/4/4 (3/2/2/2 on each side) if boys were used. Not every choir had quite this ratio of boys to men: but, relative to the men of the time, the larger lung capacity of choirboys, compared with that of modern boys, cannot be in doubt.

This class of older prepubertal and transitional boys, which has been virtually absent from twentieth-century and twenty-first-century society, must have ac-counted for a considerable proportion of the population in earlier centuries and is therefore of some importance in any study of music or drama. In the context of a choir it includes all "children" and "boys"; in the context of a trade guild it

---

[1] For the results of S. F. Daw's study of Bach's choir at St. Thomas's, Leipzig, see Rastall, *The Heaven Singing*, 311–12.

[2] Ibid., 338–39.

[3] Extract from the bull *Cum pro nostro pastorali munere*, quoted in Nicholas Clapton, *Moreschi: The Last Castrato* (London, 2004), 10–11.

includes most apprentices ("boys") and some journeymen ("men"). Note that the meaning of "man" and "boy" is different in these two contexts.[1]

Boys as actors in civic drama

This class of actor, which included both trained choirboys and apprentices (and probably some journeymen) from the guilds, was crucial in the production of community drama. Such roles as Trowle, the anarchic apprentice shepherd in Chester 7, would be ideal for an energetic apprentice to play. So too would other such roles: Iak Garcio, the apprentice shepherd in Towneley 12; Lamech's boy (*Adolescens*) in the N-Town *Noah* play (N-Town 4); and Cain's apprentice Pike-harness (*Garcio*) in Towneley 2, *The Murder of Abel*, for instance. Most of the spoken roles as angels would be possible for an apprentice actor, too, as would such female roles as the Mothers of the Innocents, Noah's daughters-in-law, and Pilate's wife Dame Percula.[2] These already offer a wide range of characters, with plenty of scope for a good actor.[3]

These roles would not generally demand the participation of choirboys, although trained choristers had certain advantages purely as actors: being trained in liturgical ceremony, they not only understood the performance of ceremonial actions but also knew more generally how to move in public. The vocal training acquired in learning to sing would also stand them in good stead for public speaking. Such a role as that of the twelve-year-old Christ in Towneley play 18 (*Christ and the Doctors in the Temple*) demands a young actor of considerable presence and ability, capable of holding the audience's attention through a long speech. An apprentice or journeyman might well be found to take this role: but it certainly demands skills that a choirboy would normally learn, so it is not clear from the script alone that a choirboy was considered necessary. The financial records for performances of this play would no doubt tell us the answer, but unfortunately they do not survive.

Another role that looks suitable for an energetic apprentice with a good stage personality is that of the Priest's assistant in *Mary Magdalen*. However, this is not a play that was mounted by the trade guilds: it also has a good deal of music in it, including a final performance of the *Te Deum* by the "clerks," who are presumably a small group of professional singing-men. The actor taking the part of the Priest was probably one of them, for he was responsible for the "office of the day" sung by himself and the Boy. In this unsuccessful performance the Boy sang a "treble" to the Priest's tenor — that is, a counterpoint, not necessarily written down, to the

---

[1] See E. J. Dobson, "The Etymology and Meaning of 'Boy,'" *Medium Aevum* 9 (1940), 121–54.

[2] We know that the Mothers of the Innocents were played by three mature males (or possibly two mature males and a transitional one) in the late Coventry play, but that is unlikely to have been the case everywhere. On Dame Percula, see Rastall, "Young Wives."

[3] Texts used are Martin Stevens and A. C. Cawley, ed., *The Towneley Plays*, Early English Text Society, s.s. 13, 14 (Oxford, 1994); Stephen Spector, ed., *The N-Town Play*, Early English Text Society, s.s. 11, 12 (London, 1991). For Chester, see below.

plainsong sung by the Priest. This suggests two professional singers, and the fact that the performance goes disastrously wrong does not negate that supposition: only professional singer-actors could perform a truly comic failure to sing a service, as this apparently is. Moreover, the Boy has previously read a lesson, which suggests that the actor knows how to read in public. This, it seems to me, is a role for a highly competent older choirboy, well trained in all the usual skills and with a considerable stage presence. It is a great pity that the place of performance of this play is unknown and no financial records of it are known to survive.

There can be less doubt that professional boy singers (i.e., choirboys) were used when characters had to sing at a level that marked them out as "holy." This broad distinction seems to be borne out by the records, which show payments to professional singers where there is a musical performance by one or more angels, by such a character as Simeon (who sings the *Nunc dimittis* in the Purification plays) or the Virgin Mary (singing the *Magnificat* at the Visitation). Simeon, obviously, was played by a mature male, as angels sometimes were; the young Virgin Mary and some angels were surely played by boys.

Boys as singers in religious drama

To some extent it is possible to match those plays that demand groups of singers with financial accounts that show relevant payments. This match is between the dramatic requirements of the play and the musical resources of one or more local churches, but it can be made only where the provenance of a play is securely known and the financial records of that place survive. This is unfortunately not the case for any of the saint plays or moralities, but several of the biblical plays can be considered. Both texts and documentary evidence survive for the civic plays of York, Chester, Coventry, Norwich, and Newcastle, while we have records but no texts for the plays of Beverley and Hull. There are no banns or guild records for the Beverley cycle, however, and so we have no information on music in those plays; nor is there any evidence of singers in the Newcastle plays, for which the only surviving text is that of the Shipwrights' play of *Noah's Ark*.[1]

In no case does the evidence survive in sufficient quantity or detail for certainty about who sang what, but it is possible to build up a picture of the relationships between church choirs and plays. In the rest of this essay, therefore, I shall discuss the matches that indicate the use of choirboys in various plays.

Plays from Coventry, Norwich, and Hull

Two play-texts and some detailed guild accounts survive for the Coventry plays, which included a considerable amount of music. While it is possible that boys took some of the angelic roles, the only singers specified in the records

---

[1] See Richard Rastall, *Minstrels Playing* (Cambridge, 2001), 350–54.

are singing-men, and it seems likely that all the singers were mature males. This may seem odd, in view of the major churches in Coventry, which presumably supported boy choristers. On the other hand, in the middle of the sixteenth century, to which many of the records belong, the town waits also sang in one of the churches, and James Hewitt and his colleagues may have exerted something of a stranglehold on the supply of singers to the plays.[1] It is noticeable that the surviving notated music for the Mothers of the Innocents — the famous "Coventry carol" *Lullay lullay, thou little tiny child* — is for a group consisting of alto, tenor, and bass, the same as for the shepherds' song.[2] There may have been a tradition in Coventry, therefore, of using adolescent and mature males even for singing in female roles.

The Norwich Grocers' play of *The Expulsion from Eden* requires Adam and Eve to sing, and so almost certainly used a choirboy in the role of Eve.[3] Unfortunately the notation has not survived, and no singers appear in the surviving records, which are seventeenth- and eighteenth-century selections from a book of Grocers' accounts now lost. Norwich had two churches that maintained choirs in the relevant period (ca. 1530–65) and from which suitable singer-actors could have been supplied: St. Peter Mancroft and the collegiate church of St. Mary. There is evidence that the former was the church concerned, however. The Grocers' accounts for the performance of 1533 contain a payment of 12*d.* to Sir Stephen Prowett "for makyng of a newe ballet," which seems to be the song of Adam and Eve.[4] The composer Stephen Prowett was working in Norwich by 1526 and was stipendiary priest at St. Peter Mancroft from 1547: the "Sir" of the accounts shows him to have been in priest's orders by 1533. Prowett became rector of St. Peter Mancroft in 1556 and held the post until his death in 1559.[5] It therefore seems likely that in the period 1547–59, Stephen Prowett was involved in the music for the Grocers' play and supplied singer-actors from the choir of St. Peter Mancroft to play Adam and Eve — the latter presumably one of the boys of the choir.

The Noah play of Kingston-upon-Hull, a play performed on Plough Day, has not survived, but the accounts of the Trinity Guild give some information about its staging between 1461 and 1551.[6] The last twenty years of accounts are only summaries, however, as are those for some earlier years, so that we have non-continuous detailed accounts for 1461–1531. Material published by Anna J. Mill

---

[1] See Rastall, *The Heaven Singing*, 341–42.

[2] The Coventry songs are discussed in *The Heaven Singing*, 137–52.

[3] For the Norwich text, see Norman Davis, ed., *Non-Cycle Plays and Fragments* (London, 1970), 8–18.

[4] For the circumstances of this performance, see *The Heaven Singing*, 74–75.

[5] Roger Bowers, "Prowett, Stephen," in *The New Grove Dictionary of Music and Musicians*, 2nd ed. (London, 2001), 20:445.

[6] Plough Monday was usually the Monday after Epiphany (6 January), and the Hull play is known to have been performed in snow one year, but Hull's Plough Day was evidently not firmly fixed and seems to have occurred at various times between Christmas and Easter. See Anna J. Mill, "The Hull Noah Play," *Modern Language Review* 33 (Oct. 1938), 489–505, esp. 490.

shows that between 1468 and 1501, payments of 18*d*. or so were regularly made to "the parish clerk and his children."[1] It is unlikely that these would be hired as actors only — a singing role seems certain. It may be that they were to sing during the Flood (as happened also at Chester). If they were out of sight in the ship, the singers could impersonate Noah (the parish clerk), his three sons, and their wives. Possibly the children acted their roles as well: although there are separate payments to the actors playing Noah, his wife, and God, there are none for the sons of Noah and their wives.

If the children played the roles of Noah's family, the parish clerk would still be needed as the man in charge of them who was also their teacher. However, he may also have had a singing role, perhaps leading the audience in a song of praise at the end of the play. From 1512 onwards the payments to the clerk and children change, and there are also additional payments to clerks. In 1512–14 "vj chylder" were paid 12*d*., "the clarke" 12*d*., and "the prestes" 8*d*. In 1520/21 the priests and clerks were given a single payment of 2*s*. 4*d*. and the six children 2*s*. The following year the same sums were expended, but the children are noted as "Noye chylder": the "chylder" of the 1522/3 accounts are noted as "Noye chylder" in a duplicate account for that year, so they are certainly the same group. In a similar way, "the prestes and clarkes" also appear as "the syngeres" (1523/4, 1527/8) and "the prestes and clarkes that sange" (1522/3, 1525/6). Which of these payments includes the parish clerk? It ought to be that to the children (18*d*. is raised to 12*d*. + 12*d*. = 2*s*.), but in the context of a later general increase of expenditure on music one cannot be sure.

These payments continue in the accounts until 1531, after which summary accounts are all that survive. The fee for the children remained at 2*s*., but that for the priests and clerks was raised to 2*s*. 8*d*. from 1527/8 onwards. The accounts show a considerable rise in expenditure on music, then, but mainly to hire more singers in their maturity (the "priests and clerks"). The money paid to the parish clerk and his children (16*d*. in 1468/9, 20*d*. in 1469/70, and 18*d*. from 1471/2 onwards) rose to 2*s*. in 1520/21 and remained there. Of course, the number of singers in this group remained static at six, presumably because they were playing the roles of Noah's sons and their wives. Although this is not certain for the fifteenth-century performances, the scale of payments suggests continued use of the children in the play.

These boy choristers were evidently from Holy Trinity Church, where the shipmen's guild, later the Trinity Guild, was situated. The parish clerk would be in charge of the music at the church, effectively the boys' master and music-teacher. I have found no records of the parish clerks and choirboys at the church, but on this evidence the choir normally included at least six boys, and one would assume more than that if it was always able to supply six competent boy actor-singers for the play.

The remaining plays to be considered come from the York and Chester cycles,

---

[1] Mill, "The Hull Noah Play," and a summary in R. W. Johnson, "Noah at Hull," *The Dalesman* (1963), 105–7.

which have the most studied texts and the most extensive documentation.[1] Payments to singers are usually to a single performer or to a very small group. The case of female roles usually demanded a boy, as already noted; in the case of the roles of angels these solo performers must usually have been singing-men from a local church, although a senior choirboy may have been an alternative. Where there are more than two or three singers performing as a group, I should expect these to be boys. Part of the reason for this is cost, the men being so much more expensive. However, when boys were hired it was necessary to arrange this through the precentor or parish clerk (or his deputy), which probably incurred an extra payment. The example of boys performing at Hull is a case in point, as are certain pageants at Chester.

In the discussions below I shall note some plays in which I think choirboys were probably not involved. Some of these are arguable cases, sometimes because it is not clear that the boys would have to be professionals and sometimes because it seems more likely that the singers were men. The relevant information is set out in the two volumes of my *Music in Early English Religious Drama*.[2]

The York Cycle

Play 9: The Flood   Noah and his family sing in praise of God after the Flood is over. I doubt that professional singers were required for this, although the three daughters-in-law were presumably played by boys. (Mrs. Noah could well have been played by a man.) One indication that the three daughters were played by apprentices or journeymen from the guild concerned (the Fishers and Mariners) is found in the text. As we shall see in considering play 45 below, the role of the singers as actors in that play allowed them to function as a group, as choirboys would need to. A group of choristers would have different timetables from the guild actors and could not always rehearse at the same time: the demands of church services to be sung, rehearsals for those services, and the boys' normal lessons would require them to rehearse for extracurricular events such as a play according to their own schedules.

For any substantial involvement in a play, then, it was best if the boys could rehearse separately from the other actors, not just for the musical contribution (which was necessary anyway) but for the play itself. The ideal would be for the boys to perform in a scene that is more or less self-contained and thus could be thoroughly rehearsed with only minimal involvement (if any) from other actors.

---

[1] The Towneley, N-Town, and Cornish cycles, as well as other plays, would offer much detailed information on music if we knew their places of origin and had accounts from the performances. Texts used here are Richard Beadle, ed., *The York Plays* (London, 1982); and R. M. Lumiansky and David Mills, ed., *The Chester Mystery Cycle*, Early English Text Society, s.s. 3, 9 (Oxford, 1974, 1986).

[2] *The Heaven Singing* and *Minstrels Playing*, passim. On this specific point, see the discussion of the forces needed to play angels in the York and Chester plays, *The Heaven Singing*, 328–38.

This is certainly not the case here, where the roles of the three daughters are completely integrated with the other roles. Even if Noah's sons were also played by choristers, the problem would not be solved: the sons have considerable roles that are fully integrated with those of Noah and his wife. I conclude, then, that all the roles in this play were performed by actors from the guild and that no professionals were needed for the singing.

Play 11: Moses and Pharaoh   The Israelites sing a hymn of praise at the end, but here, too, there is no reason to think that professional singers were involved.

Play 12: The Annunciation and the Visitation   It should be assumed that the Virgin Mary as a young girl would be played by a boy, even in a possible early version of this play in which the *Magnificat* may have been spoken. It seems most likely that the piece was sung, however, at least by the mid sixteenth century, the directions for singing being in the hand of John Clerke, the servant of the Common Clerk of York between 1538/9 and his death in 1580.[1] In that case a well-trained choirboy was needed to play the role.

The other singing part in the play (also shown by stage directions added by Clerke) is that of the angel Gabriel. We should expect this role to be played by a singing-man.

Play 15: The Shepherds   The shepherds themselves sing, but they did not need to be professionals. A leaf missing from the play must have contained the angelic *Gloria* sung to the shepherds. If this was sung by a single angel, one would expect him to be a singing-man; if, as is much less likely, by a group of angels, then the performers would have been choirboys.

Play 17: The Purification   There are no music cues in the text of this play, and it would be possible to play it without music. If some liturgy is added, with two processions, as seems likely, professional singers would not necessarily be required. If professionals were used, it would be one or two singing-men at most.

Play 21: The Baptism of Christ   Two angels sing *Veni creator* immediately after the baptism. These were probably professionals, but men rather than boys.

Play 22: The Temptation of Christ   As in the previous play, two angels sing *Veni creator*. There is reason to think that this may not be the correct piece,[2] but in any case the angels here, too, must be men.

---

[1] For John Clerke's work on the York plays, see Peter Meredith, "John Clerke's Hand in the York Register," *Leeds Studies in English* n.s. 12 (1981), 245–71.

[2] Discussed in Rastall, *Minstrels Playing*, 52–4.

Play 25: The Entry into Jerusalem   Roger Burton's *Ordo paginarum* of 1415 specifies "viij pueri cum ramis palmarum cantantes Benedictus &c."[1] These eight boys
were probably trained choristers, although the necessity for this depends on the
repertory, which is uncertain. The Palm Sunday antiphon *Osanna filio David*
seems the most likely piece at line 287, and the boys had to sing an unnamed piece
at line 544 (for liturgical reasons, perhaps the responsory *Ingrediente Domino*).[2]
It is true that one could train apprentices or prepubertal journeymen to sing
a syllabic-neumatic item like *Osanna filio David*, but who would train them, how,
and over what period of time? Even supposing that eight suitable boys could be
found from within the guild, the time and expertise needed to train them to sing
plainsong well enough for public performances would be considerable. I believe
that a guild would take the sensible option and hire some trained singers.

A group of eight singing boys might be difficult to find in any church but the
Minster, which needs to be considered further if information about the number
of boys in various York churches can be found. As the twelve angels in Play 45
(see below) must almost certainly have come from the Minster, use of the same
boys in Play 25 would require them to return to the starting point of the plays in
time to perform in *The Assumption* after finishing their work with *The Entry into
Jerusalem*. In fact, I believe that they would not have been able to perform in both
of these plays,[3] nor that they could even be in time to perform in play 47. To do so,
they not only had to cross the city to the starting point, but also had to change cos-
tumes from that of children to the robes of angels. In any case, if such an arrangement were possible it supposes that a group of choirboys had time to learn the
material and rehearse with two separate guilds, in addition to their normal work.

It is also worth considering whether two or more churches might have joined
together to supply such a group of choristers. In theory this is possible, and practical problems might be minimal if the two churches worked to similar timetables.
There is no evidence for it, however.

Play 37: The Harrowing of Hell   The prophets sing in Limbo, immediately after
their release, and a third time at the end of the play. On the last occasion they are
led away by the Archangel Michael, who has only a very short speech and who
does not necessarily join in the singing. On this occasion there is no reason to
think that Michael is played by a singing-man, nor that the prophets should be
professional singers or led by a professional. Guildsmen would be able to learn
suitable music, although it is unclear what the repertory should be. *The Harrowing
of Hell* is a spectacular play, however, in which it is possible to include a great deal
of liturgical procession with music, so there could well be an onstage choir.[4] The

---

[1] Facsimile in Richard Beadle and Peter Meredith, ed. *The York Play*, Medieval Drama
Facsimiles, 7 (Leeds, 1983).

[2] Rastall, *Minstrels Playing*, 54–5.

[3] The question of doublings is discussed in *The Heaven Singing*, 330. Timings for the
York cycle are in Margaret Dorrell, "Two Studies in the York Corpus Christi Play," *Leeds
Studies in English* n.s. 6 (1972), 63–111.

[4] On possible liturgical additions to this play, see Rastall, *The Heaven Singing*, 278–83.

composition of this, whether men, boys, or both, would presumably depend on who was available and how much the guild concerned (the Saddlers) was prepared to pay. No relevant records survive.

Play 38: The Resurrection   An angel, described in line 225 as "a ʒonge childe," sings at the Resurrection of Christ. The intention to have singing there may be an old one, but the direction is one supplied in the mid sixteenth century by John Clerke: the obvious piece to sing, perhaps indicated by the directions, would be *Christus resurgens*. Of the four pieces with this incipit, one seems too long for the purpose, two probably do not demand a trained singer, and the fourth certainly would have to be sung by a professional. It is an exposed item, however, at a crucial point in the narrative, and I imagine that a director would certainly hire a professional. A singing-man would be the obvious choice, except for the description of the angel as "a young child," which surely demands a choirboy.

Play 42: The Ascension   Two angels sing after the Ascension, probably a liturgical piece with the incipit *Viri Galilei*. One would expect professionals for this — probably men rather than boys.

Play 43: Pentecost   Two angels sing *Veni creator spiritus* — probably men.

Play 44: The Death of the Virgin   The last scene of this play is for four angels, sent by Jesus to bring his mother to Heaven after her death. This is a self-contained scene, in which each angel has one short speech (2, 2, 4, and 4 lines), at the end of which they sing *Ave regina celorum*. This scene, which can be rehearsed separately, is suitable for a non-guild group, and in any case the music would require professional singers. Four men would be expensive, and boys would be perfectly suitable. The antiphon *Ave regina celorum* would be sung to plainsong; a polyphonic setting of *Ave regina . . . mater regis* might be in two parts, as is the setting sung by four angels in the Washington *Assumption* painting (ca. 1485) by the Master of the St. Lucy Legend.[1]

Play 45: The Assumption of the Virgin   This play is justly famous both for the spectacular nature of its staging and for the music that survives for it in the play manuscript.[2] There are three songs performed by angels: the first two (*Surge proxima mea* and *Veni de Libano*) are part of a self-contained scene in which twelve angels address the Blessed Virgin; a third song (*Veni electa mea*) is performed in the gap between subsequent scenes, when the apostle Thomas journeys between the place of his vision of the Virgin and the place where the other apostles are. As this third song would be easy enough to insert into the play during a late rehearsal,

[1] For this setting, see Rastall, "The Musical Repertory," 162–96, esp. 172–73; and *The Heaven Singing*, 380–83 and plate 8.

[2] London, BL Add. MS 35290: for a facsimile, see Beadle and Meredith, *The York Play*; for an edition, see Richard Rastall, ed., *Six Songs from the York Mystery Play "The Assumption of the Virgin"* (Newton Abbot, 1985).

the angels' roles are effectively self-contained and were evidently written that way. We can therefore consider the angels to have been twelve professional singers.

We should expect a group of this size to be choirboys for reasons of cost: twelve men would have been prohibitively (and unnecessarily) expensive. In fact, the musical settings for this play show that the singers were boys, being for equal voices in the treble or mean range.[1] Settings of the three song-texts are written into the play-text at the appropriate places in the manuscript, and another group of settings of the same texts appears at the end of the play. The settings in the body of the text are relatively simple, those at the end more complicated. This may reflect the location intended: certainly the simpler settings are more appropriate for performance out of doors, while the second settings could have been intended for performance indoors on some civic occasion other than the usual cycle production. Alternatively, the settings may reflect less and more experienced groups of boys. However, both sets of songs demand professional singers: they are written in black mensural notation with red coloration, suggesting singers of considerable experience.

This raises the possibility that not all of the twelve choirboy-angels sang the music. Finding a coherent group of twelve choristers would be difficult enough, and I shall return to this question: but if so many could be found — and the twelve speaking parts demand it for practical reasons — then there is still a doubt about the ability of the younger and less experienced boys to perform polyphony written in the mensural notation of ca. 1463–77, when the manuscript was copied. It does make better sense to assume that, of the twelve speaking angels, some would be too inexperienced to sing this music. Although the settings are in only two parts, at least four singers were needed for the second setting of *Veni de Libano*, in which both parts divide, producing a four-part chord. As noted under Play 44, to have four of the most senior boys performing two-part music would reflect the situation seen in the Washington *Assumption* picture, although the singers depicted there were post-pubertal and singing in the tenor range.

What institution could supply a group of twelve boys? It is possible that some of the larger monastic houses maintained such a large choir, although the information is unavailable. However, the Minster was certainly a contender. In 1425 the Minster choir included seven boys, but then the Archdeacon of Richmond, Thomas Dalby, paid for the number of boys to be increased to twelve. This must have been the largest group of choirboys in the area and may well be the group for which the angelic scene in the Assumption play was designed.[2]

Play 46: The Coronation of the Virgin   This play has speaking parts for six angels, who sing towards the end of their almost self-contained scene and again at the end of the play. While these conditions may suggest that the angels were played by six boys, all of whom sang, other factors throw doubt on this. The speeches

[1] Richard Rastall, "Vocal Range and Tessitura in Music from York Play 45," *Music Analysis* 3/2 (1984), 181–99. The music is discussed in Rastall, *The Heaven Singing*, 121–37.

[2] Rastall, *The Heaven Singing*, 328–9.

are considerably larger than those of the angels in Play 45, and while they were probably not outside the capabilities of choirboys, they are perhaps an indication that guildsmen played most of these roles, perhaps only two being played by professional singers. If this is correct, then the singers were probably men, not boys. There is no indication of what texts they sang and whether it was plainsong or polyphony.

Play 47: The Last Judgement This play includes three speaking angels, two of whom are the trumpeters. Angels sing on two occasions. The play was evidently performed in a lavish production — the Mercers being a very wealthy company — and the second song marks the end not only of this pageant but of the whole cycle.[1] Although the speaking angels do not have long speeches and the trumpeters may not actually have played their instruments, the authority with which they speak suggests that these roles were played by mature guildsmen, a separate group of singers performing the music.

There is no doubt that the singing angels must have been played by professionals: whatever they sang, the circumstances of this performance surely demanded very high-quality singing to match the spectacular staging. As already noted, it is just possible, in theory, that the eight choristers performing in Play 25 could return to the start in time to sing in this play. Margaret Dorrel's timings, however, which have proved quite accurate in practice, show that there would not be enough time for the eight choirboys playing the children in Play 25 to change costume (from children to angels) and cross the city to start again in the Mercers' pageant (Play 47). There was surely too much at stake for the Mercers to rely on a group of choirboys who might well be late and almost certainly would be tired — if not after twelve or more performances of Play 25, then almost certainly after a few performances of *The Judgement*. On balance, I am inclined to believe that the Mercers hired two or more singing-men for their play.

What is the minimum requirement of choirboys for the York cycle, then? We have seen that several plays required boys who were professionally trained as singers and/or actors:

Play 12	*The Annunciation and the Visitation*	1 boy
Play 25	*The Entry into Jerusalem*	8 boys
Play 38	*The Resurrection*	1 boy
Play 44	*The Death of the Virgin*	4 boys
Play 45	*The Assumption of the Virgin*	12 boys

Thus a minimum of twenty-six boys is required for the cycle. Since very little doubling is possible and probably none is desirable, and because the groups of four, eight, and twelve boys are significant numbers for any church, it is likely that these represent a minimum of three church choirs. The actual number of choirboys

---

[1] On the staging of this play, see Alexandra F. Johnston and Margaret Dorrell, "The York Mercers and their Pageant of Doomsday, 1433–1526," *Leeds Studies in English* n.s. 6 (1972), 11–35.

performing in any one year could certainly be higher than this, as several of the plays discussed might have used boys rather than men. The whole matter raises interesting questions about how many York churches had choirs with boys and therefore about the total choirboy population in York.

The Chester Cycle

UNLIKE the York cycle, the Chester cycle includes music cues for minstrels, so although the play-text has more music cues than any other cycle or play, there are fewer potential cues involving choirboys.[1]

Play 1: The Fall of Lucifer   The angels sing twice or three times in this play, the first and third occasions probably being the antiphons *Dignus es Domine Deus* and *Gloria tibi trinitas*. There are speeches for eight out of the nine orders of angels (the seraphim are omitted), which might suggest eight singer-actors. In this case the use of singing-men seems unlikely, while the use of choirboys for such important (although small) roles does not seem probable either. If the antiphons were sung — there are other, and more difficult, possibilities for *Dignus es Domine Deus* — they are both largely syllabic settings and might be sung by well-trained guildsmen. On balance, however, I think it most likely that a small choir of perhaps two or three men, or four or more boys, sang on behalf of the whole angelic body.

Play 3: Noah's Flood   Mrs. Noah's gossips sing a drinking song, which should not require professional singers. These roles were no doubt taken by guildsmen, probably postpubertal ones. Later, Noah and his family sing during the flood itself: one manuscript names "Save me, O God," which is probably John Hopkins's metrical version of Psalm 69 (68, *Salvum me fac*, in the Latin psalter). As this is an easy tune that was well known at the time, there is no reason for the guild (the Waterleaders and Drawers of Dee) to have employed professional singers. The roles that we should expect to be played by boys, Noah's daughters-in-law and perhaps his sons, are well integrated throughout the play and not suitable for an external group of singer-actors. Although professional singers should not be discounted entirely, it seems probable that the singing was undertaken by guildsmen.

Play 6: The Salutation and Nativity   Mary has a crucial role in this play, and she is required to sing at least the first verse of the *Magnificat*. A prepubertal guildsman could perhaps undertake this, singing the text to a congregational chant. However, it is quite likely that she sings the whole of the *Magnificat*, interspersed with the English translation — the text does not demand this, but strongly suggests it. In this case a professional singer might well have been used, an experienced older choirboy being needed. The roles of Gabriel and another angel were

---

[1] Angels in the Chester cycle are discussed in *The Heaven Singing*, 332–8, and music generally in *Minstrels Playing*, chap. 6.

probably taken by men. The angel is required to sing and was probably played by a singing-man.

Play 7: The Shepherds   The text hardly suggests that professional singers were needed for this play, except for the role of the angel, who evidently sang an impressive setting of *Gloria in excelsis Deo*. He was presumably played by a singing-man. The shepherd-boy Trowle, called Garcius in the speech-headings, is certainly musical and famously teaches a song to the audience, but this does not need a professional singer: a young, outgoing, confident guildsman with a good ear and a loud, accurate singing voice, adolescent or just postpubertal, would be ideal. It is a large and important role, demanding energy and stage presence rather than musical training.

Professional singers were used in this play, however. Financial accounts of the Painters' guild survive for the years 1568, 1572, and 1575,[1] and show that the guild hired both singers and minstrels. In 1568 the guild spoke to the precentor of Chester Cathedral, John Genson, "for Shepertes Boyes" and hired four of them at a fee of 2s. 8d.; 2d. was spent on them (probably for refreshments) during a rehearsal. In 1572 they hired boys again at a fee of 4s. and spent 2d. on "the iiij syngares" at an audition or rehearsal; and in 1575 they hired three boys at a fee of 3s., when they also spent 1d. "for synges" and 6d. "for pouder [food?] for the sengers."

From these accounts we can be sure that the Painters hired four boys from the Cathedral in 1568 and 1572, and three of them in 1575. We can also be sure that they were hired as singers, for although the accounts do not make that absolutely certain, the fees involved were too high unless paid for a specialist skill such as singing. Since these shepherds' boys were also singers, they must be the "helpers" who in one manuscript of the play are required to sing with the shepherds when Garcius teaches a song to the audience.[2] In this case the shepherds sing an "hilare carmen," the "mery songe" of line 443, but the other manuscripts show this as a "Trolly lolly lo" song. Whatever the song performed, Garcius presumably taught the audience by lining out the song in the manner of a parish clerk teaching a metrical psalm to a church congregation, with the shepherds and their boys supporting the audience.[3]

Play 10: The Slaughter of the Innocents   The Angel sings twice in this play and has a substantial acting role (36 lines) that interacts with Joseph and Mary. Moreover, the second song seems to be performed in procession at the end of the play. While an experienced boy might have taken the role, therefore, a singing-man seems much more likely.

---

[1] The Chester accounts are in Lawrence M. Clopper, ed., *Records of Early English Drama: Chester* (Toronto, 1979). For a detailed discussion of the records for Play 7, see Rastall, *Minstrels Playing*, 292–94; I give here only a *précis* concerning the singers.

[2] MS H, after line 447: "Tunc omnes pastores cum aliis adjuvantibus cantabunt hilare carmen."

[3] On "lining-out" in this and another song taught to an audience, see Rastall, *The Heaven Singing*, 377.

Play 11. The Purification of the Blessed Virgin   The role of Simeon was almost certainly taken by a professional singer, since he is required to sing the whole of the *Nunc dimittis* besides having a considerable speaking role. This is a task for a mature male, not a boy — Simeon is after all an old man — and there is some evidence that the role was played by the composer Robert White in 1567 and 1568.[1] Other possibilities for music in this play include liturgical processions and angelic singing.

Financial accounts survive for six years in the period 1546–1575.[2] In 1546, the Smiths paid 3s. 4d. to "Barnes and the syngers," apparently Thomas Barnes from the Cathedral and singers in his charge: the latter could be mature singing-men, but this wording indicates a group of boys. As the actor playing Simeon was paid the usual 3s. 4d. this year — a high sum that presupposes a special skill such as singing — the singers were clearly not required to sing the *Nunc dimittis*, and so we return to the other possibilities. The accounts for 1561 include payments to two senior members of the Cathedral clergy and five boys for singing, but in 1567, 1568, and 1572 there are no entries for a group of singers, and the vocal music was evidently provided by singing-men. These are described as "clarkes of the menster" in 1567 and variously named in these years as John Genson (the precentor), Randle Barnes (a canon), and Mr. White (probably the composer Robert White, organist for three or four years until 1570). The accounts for 1575 are unhelpful in identifying singers, but there were apparently more than three of them, so a group of boys may again have been involved.

The absence of boys in some years may be due to the hiring of them by the Painters. Their use of four boys in 1568 and 1572 (there are no extant Painters' accounts for 1567) apparently prevented the Smiths from hiring the five previously employed. The reduced group of three boys in 1575 may show that the Painters had come to an agreement with the Smiths so that both guilds could hire boys. If this is a correct reading of the accounts, we see that in 1568 and 1572 the Cathedral could not supply two groups of boys totaling nine singers, and that in 1575, assuming that the Smiths did hire boys, the total number available was only seven or eight.

Play 14: Mary Magdalene, and the Entry into Jerusalem   The singing of *Osanna filio David* would seem an obvious context for the use of a group of boys, as in York play 25, but the surviving Shoemakers' accounts, probably for the performance of 1550, show no payments to singers. We must therefore assume that this singing was undertaken by the cast generally.

---

[1] R. M. Lumiansky and David Mills, *The Chester Mystery Cycle: Essays and Documents, with an Essay, 'Music in the Cycle', by Richard Rastall* (Chapel Hill, N.C., 1983), 135.

[2] The earliest account is usually dated 1554, but John Marshall convincingly assigned it to the performance of 1546: "The Chester Whitsun Plays: Dating of Post-Reformation Performances from the Smiths' Accounts," *Leeds Studies in English* n.s. 9 (1977), 51–61, esp. 56.

Play 17: The Harrowing of Hell   Any liturgical music in procession here might need professional singers, but it could certainly be accomplished without; and the singing of the *Te Deum* at the end of the play could similarly be performed entirely by guildsmen. Professionals, including boys, could have been involved, therefore, but there is no evidence of any kind.

Play 18: The Resurrection   Two angels sing *Christus resurgens*. As at York, this has to be an impressive performance, requiring professionals. These might be boys or men.

Play 20: The Ascension   This play includes substantial material, both spoken and sung, for three angels, requiring professional singer-actors. This would be possible for experienced senior choirboys, but singing-men are much more likely.

Play 23: The Coming of Antichrist   The Archangel Michael has a speaking role integrated with other roles, and he sings in leading a procession at the end of the play. It would be possible for an experienced senior choirboy, but a singing-man is more likely.

Play 24: The Last Judgement   The two angels have quite small roles as far as speech is concerned, but they also blow the trumpets (which, of course, they may not actually be playing), separate out the good souls from the bad, and sing while they are doing so. These seem suitable roles for two singing-men, although senior boys cannot be ruled out.

The minimum number of choirboys needed in the Chester cycle, then, seems to be:

Play 6	*The Salutation and Nativity*	1 boy
Play 7	*The Shepherds*	4 boys (3 in 1575)
Play 11	*The Purification of the Blessed Virgin*	5 boys (more than 3 in 1575)

Other plays required singers, who might or might not be boys: in particular, there must be question marks over the singers needed for plays 14 and 17, and yet other plays might have raised the number of choirboys used. However, we have noted (under play 11 above) that the Cathedral may have found it difficult to supply more than seven or eight boys at most in any year and was probably limited to supplying four or five in most years. This may mean that any boys other than those hired for plays 7 and 11 had to come from some other church.

As in York, it is possible that some of the singers could perform in more than one play, and the timetable does make some doubling possible in theory. Between 1531 at the latest and the early 1570s, the Chester plays were performed over three days, divided, it seems, as plays 1–9, 10–17 (the current play 16 was two separate plays at that time), and 18–24. Thus the Cathedral boys could have performed in both of plays 7 and 11 — and indeed, a group of five could have encompassed play

6 as well.[1] The plays were spread over four days in 1575, and the rather special circumstances of that performance (which turned out to be the last one) may be responsible for the reallocation of boys in plays 7 and 11. But the fact is that the accounts for plays 7 and 11 suggest that the Cathedral boys did not usually play on both days, which would have caused logistical problems as well as taking a great deal of the boys' time. The smaller commitment of boys to the plays at Chester, compared with that at York, may reflect both the smaller population of Chester and, more specifically, the smaller number of city churches, although the nature of the evidence makes our conclusions highly speculative in any case. This discussion, in fact, helps to underline those areas where our knowledge is still inadequate. Our picture of how the guilds prepared for plays, who performed in them, and how the auditions and rehearsals were undertaken is still very fragmentary; similarly, the details of how the normal mechanism of boys, precentor, master of the children, and other church dignitaries interacted with civic processes such as the plays is still insufficiently understood.

[1] See Rastall, *The Heaven Singing*, 337–38.

5

FROM *MOZOS DE CORO* TOWARDS *SEISES*
BOYS IN THE MUSICAL LIFE OF SEVILLE CATHEDRAL IN THE FIFTEENTH AND SIXTEENTH CENTURIES

Juan Ruiz Jiménez

THE involvement of a group of boys in the daily rituals of the cathedral of Seville goes back to the restoration of its diocese, whose cathedral was dedicated on 11 March 1252.[1] My aim in this essay is to synthesize the various ways in which this important and indispensable group formed part of the daily life of the cathedral and to incorporate a new perspective based on recent studies of the archival sources.[2] The statutes promulgated on 29 May 1261 by Archbishop Remondo and his chapter already provide evidence for the existence of such a group in the designation *alumni cori*, who along with the *clerici cori* were under the jurisdiction of the cantor and the supervision of his vicar or succentor, who assisted him in his duties.[3] The financial support for the maintenance of the choirboys derived from the income willed to the cathedral by King Fernando III,

---

[1] All studies on the role of boys in the liturgical life of the Church of Seville are, like this one, indebted to Simón de la Rosa y López, *Los seises de la catedral de Sevilla: ensayo de investigación histórica* (Seville, 1904, rep. Seville, 1982). Herminio González Barrionuevo, *Los seises de Sevilla* (Seville, 1992), is not of central importance for the period that is the focus of the present essay. The most recent publication pertaining directly to the *seises* in this period focuses on a specific aspect of their participation in the feast of Corpus Christi in the context of recent studies on the early modern body; see Todd M. Borgerding, "Imagining the Sacred Body: Choirboys, Their Voices, and Corpus Christi in Early Modern Seville," in *Musical Childhoods and the Cultures of Youth*, ed. Susan Boynton and Roe-Min Kok (Middletown, Ct., 2006), 25–48.

[2] To avoid confusion, references here to the acts of the cathedral chapter of Seville will not be taken from those published in Robert Murrell Stevenson, *La música en la catedral de Sevilla (1478–1606): Documentos para su estudio* (Madrid, 1985), because they are incomplete, sometimes contain errors, and do not correspond to the present numbering of the volumes in the cathedral archive.

[3] These Constitutions follow in the wake of others emanating from various Castilian-Leonese chapters, the model being the Constitutions of the cathedral of León, given by Honorius III on 25 May 1223. See Enrique Costa y Belda, "Las constituciones de Don Raimundo de Losaña para el cabildo de Sevilla (1261)," *Historia, instituciones, documentos 5* (1978), 169–235 at 195, 201–2, 223.

conqueror of the city, and by his son Alfonso x, who left income proceeding from the tithes of his *almojarifazgo* (1252).[1]

It has not been possible to determine the origin of the position of the *magister puerorum* in the cathedral of Seville. The office existed as a salaried post by at least the beginning of the fifteenth century and is documented as being held in 1419 by Alfonso Sánchez, the cathedral's first known choirmaster. The definitive impetus for establishing a master of the choirboys would come from Pope Eugenius iv in the course of the reforms he promoted during the 1430s. In these years, the diocese of Seville obtained the promulgation of the bulls *Ad exequendum* of Eugenius iv (1439) and *Votis illis* of Nicholas v (1454).

Various conclusions may be drawn from the bull of Eugenius iv. This document was granted at the request of the dean of the cathedral chapter and does not appear to establish anything new regarding the functions carried out by the choirboys or their master. The person who received the prebend had to be skilled in grammar and chant ("in gramatica et canto perito") and would be selected by the chapter. The stipend would not be paid in perpetuity; rather, the master could be relieved of the office and replaced by someone else at the discretion of the chapter. The number of boys was fixed at six (hence the designation *seises*). The master was supposed to direct and teach them and look after their health and nourishment ("dirigeret, instrueret, reficeret et nutriret"); they were likewise to be selected by the chapter. The text emphasizes the requirements for the master's academic preparation, his behavior, and his participation in the stipulated daily liturgical obligations, all of which would contribute to the splendor of ceremonial in the cathedral. The *ración* would be Prebend 20, the income from which would be divided in half between the salary of the master and the maintenance and education of the boys.

The difficulty of finding a person competent in both grammar and chant obliged the chapter to ask the pope if it could choose a master who was accomplished in chant but not in grammar, in light of the priorities and needs of the cathedral and the fact that instruction in language was already covered by someone else (as we shall see). This request was granted by the abovementioned bull of Nicholas v (1454).[2]

The bull of Eugenius iv makes it clear that the sustenance of the choirboys depended on the *magister puerorum*. At least since the establishment of this benefice, the person who held it was responsible for the boys' education and care and was also supposed to lodge and feed them in his own home. When someone other than the holder of the prebend temporarily took charge of the choirboys for some reason, he automatically received the income from the prebend and was to be called the *magister puerorum*.[3] In the course of the fifteenth century,

[1] Rosa y López, *Los seises*, 30–31. The *almojarifazgo* was the tax paid for goods or merchandise exported from the kingdom, for items imported into the kingdom, or for goods traded from one port to another within Spain.

[2] These bulls are translated by Rosa y López, *Los seises*, 65–70. The originals, along with that of Julius iii (cited below) are found in the Archivo de la catedral de Sevilla (hereafter A.C.S.), sección ix, leg. 125, piezas 15–17.

[3] I believe that occasional ambiguous expressions confirm this fact. In 1464, the

most beneficiaries of this *ración* held it only temporarily, continuing to serve the cathedral of Seville in other salaried or beneficed positions once they had finished performing the functions of the office.[1]

In the first half of the fifteenth century, the number of choirboys rose from five in 1414 (the earliest date at which their precise number was fixed) to seven in the 1430s and to eight in 1440, an increase that probably reflects the gradual specialization discussed below. Their number reached an exceptional maximum of twelve in the first years of the sixteenth century, although it usually remained between eight and ten.[2]

As the members of the cathedral choir multiplied and became specialized, the original nucleus of choirboys split into two groups. One consisted of those designated from the end of the fifteenth century by some variant on the diminutive of *cantor* (*cantorcito* or *cantorcillo*); they were under the choirmaster's jurisdiction. The other group, supervised by the boys' master of plainchant, continued to be called *mozos de coro*. Beginning in the 1570s, the first of these groups was distinguished by the characteristic Castilian term *seise*, which clearly alludes to the number of choirboys mentioned in the bull of Eugenius IV. In the first quarter of the sixteenth century, the terminology remained quite ambiguous, with the expression *mozo de coro* used generically for both groups, while the terms *maestro de los mozos* and *maestro de capilla* appear occasionally as synonyms.[3] Although

---

statement that Mateo Ximénez "took charge of the choirboys" could indicate that they already lived with him. The following statement from 1499 is clearer: "The Lord Schoolmaster called Francisco de la Torre was in charge of the choirboys, as your worship knew, for which they gave him a stipend in this Church" ("El señor Maestrescuela dijo Francisco de la Torre cómo tenía los mozos, como sabían sus mercedes, de lo cual le daban una ración en esta Iglesia") [in the margin:] "Magister puerorum"; A.C.S., sección I, libro 5, fol. 65ᵛ (1499); sección II, libro 249 (1464).

[1] This was the case for Alfonso Sánchez (1419–41), Esteban Alfonso (1444–58), Nicola Brachio de Fierro (1464–81), and Mateo Ximénez (1444–79†), who were cantors and masters of the choirboys; and of Pedro Martínez de la Caridad (1420–58†), Pedro Sánchez de Santo Domingo (1474–1502†), and Francisco de la Torre (1464–1507†), who received both Prebend 20 (corresponding to the *magister puerorum*) and another *ración* unrelated to this position throughout the time they served the cathedral; see Ruiz Jiménez, "Los sonidos de la montaña hueca: Innovación y tradición en las capillas musicales eclesiásticas de la corona de Castilla durante los albores del Renacimiento; el paradigma sevillano," in *La música en tiempos de Isabel la Católica*, ed. Soterraña Aguirre Rincón (Valladolid, forthcoming).

[2] In 1414, each received a weekly salary of 12 *maravedís*; A.C.S., sección II, libro 1075; sección IV, libros 20 (1505), 21 (1506), 22 (1507), 30 (1513), 33 (1514), 35 (1516).

[3] The evidence suggests that this process was already defined by 1467. In this year, one of the votive endowments received by the chapter (on which see more below) refers to "the succentor with the boys, whom he shows, and the teacher of the boys with his singing students" ("el sochantre con los mozos que el muestra, e el maestro de los mozos con sus discípulos cantores"). In 1474, orders of payment (*libramientos*) for Nicola Brachio de Fierro referred to him as the master of the "singing" boys. In the capitular agreement of 5 January 1478, in which Pedro Sánchez de Santo Domingo was named as a replacement for Nicola Brachio de Fierro as master of the choirboys, the word "coro" was altered to read "canto de órgano" (polyphony). These are all clear indications of the existence of a possible specialization of the child singers already by this time. A.C.S., sección I, libro 1, fol. 2ʳ. Alonso Pérez

already consolidated many years before, this process of separation culminated in 1532 when the choirboys (not the *seises*) entered the shortlived Colegio del Cardenal, founded a few years earlier by Cardinal Alonso Manrique to house youths preparing for an ecclesiastical career. Its regulations state that the choirboys should wear

> purple clothing, not red, because they should be distinguished from the other six, and not grey, because they should also be distinguished from the students, and that these twenty boys should be called the choir collegians, and so that they do not displease the cantor or succentor, we request that these [officials] name the said boys and inform the rector, and that the master come there to teach them and give lessons to the College, and that in the church he punish and correct those who belong to the College in everything pertaining to the divine service.[1]

Another distinguishing element was the fact that the *seises* did not enter the Colegio del Cardenal; instead, they continued to live with the choirmaster or whoever was responsible for their instruction, until 1 January 1636, when they joined the Colegio de San Isidoro (founded in the capitular residences of the Estudio de San Miguel), where they lived with the *mozos de coro*.[2]

ACADEMIC TRAINING

DOCUMENTATION from as early as the fourteenth century sheds light on the Colegio or Estudio de Gramática de San Miguel, which was installed close to the cathedral. A grammar teacher (a cleric or priest whose salary was drawn from the budgets of both the cathedral chapter and the city council) and an assistant with a bachelor's degree were entrusted with teaching grammar to the residents of

---

de Alba, throughout his trajectory as *magister puerorum* in the cathedral of Seville, was designated interchangeably, albeit with a clear development, as master of the choirboys (1492), master of the singing boys (1496), and finally choirmaster (1503): A.C.S., sección 1, libro 1, fol. 2^r (1478), libro 4, fol. 172^v (1492), libro 6, fol. 5^v (1503); sección II, libro 682 (1496), libro 719 (1503); libro 1077, fols. 168^r, 175^v.

[1] "[r]opas moradas e no sean coloradas, porque haya diferencia de los otros seis, e no sean pardillas, porque también haya diferencia de los otros colegiales, e que estos veinte mozos se llamen los colegiales del coro, e porque no hagan agravio al chantre ni a su sochantre, queremos que ellos nombren los dichos mochachos e lo hagan saber al rector; y el maestro que suelen tener que los venga allí a enseñar e dar liciones al Colegio e que a quien pertenesce los castigue e corrija en la Iglesia en todo lo que conviene al culto divino." Rosa y López, *Los seises*, 43.

[2] An account of the legislation and changes that took place in the government and teaching of the *seises* upon entering this institution lies outside the chronological limits of the present study. The most important archival source for this subject is the *Libro de la Fundación del Colegio de San Isidro de la Sancta Iglesia de Sevilla y de la entrada y salida de los colegiales y seises. Dispuesto por el Doctor Pedro del Bosque, su primer rector* (A.C.S., sección v, libro 362). See also Rosa y López, *Los seises*, 145–48; González Barrionuevo, *Los seises de Sevilla*, 16, 78–94.

the city.[1] Among the students who attended this institution were the choirboys, who were taught the reading and grammar skills essential to the comprehension and pronunciation of the texts they had to read and sing. One room in the school, called "la Galea," was granted by the chapter to the boys so that they could stay there to study.[2]

The musical education of the boys developed and became more specialized in the course of the fifteenth and sixteenth centuries, paralleling the development of the original group of choirboys. At first, throughout the fifteenth century, the *magister puerorum* or succentor (both usually also singers of polyphony in the cathedral choir) were responsible for teaching the boys, although the specific details of what they taught are not known. It remains difficult to determine whether these two officers taught the choirboys at the same time, from the outset. All indications suggest that they were teaching separately by the 1460s. The choirboys' lessons with the succentor centered on plainchant, differing from the *cantorcicos'* lessons with the *magister puerorum* (a position held in these years by Nicola Brachio de Fierro and Pedro Sánchez de Santo Domingo).[3] In the sixteenth century, the proliferation of archival sources makes it possible to confirm this situation. The official responsible for teaching the choirboys chant is called *maestro de canto llano*, a position that would become the *cátedra de melodía* in the seventeenth century. Teaching the *cantorcicos* was the responsibility of the *maestro de capilla*, a title that became established as a designation for this official, or for his assistant, who was also called the *maestro de facistol*, and who would occupy the position known as the *cátedra de canto de órgano* towards the end of the sixteenth century.[4]

Although there are no concrete references to the type of musical instruction the choirboys received from their teachers in the fifteenth century, their responsibilities and performances in the cathedral suggest that their musical education was not significantly different in the first half of the sixteenth century.

Already in 1408 there is an allusion to the fact that the boys were taught in a chapel of the cathedral, possibly that of San Clemente where the cibary was located,[5] probably continuing until work began on the construction of the new

---

[1] José Sánchez Herrero, "Centros de enseñanza y estudiantes de Sevilla durante los siglos XIII al XV," *En la España medieval* 5 (1984), 875–98 at 878–82.

[2] A.C.S. Sección 1, libro 4, fol. 139ᵛ (1488); sección IV, libro 18, fol. 22ᵛ (1499), libro 29, fol. 4ʳ (1512).

[3] Between at least 1408 and 1459, the succentor, *magister puerorum*, a cantor, or some undesignated person who "teaches the boys of the cathedral choir" ("enseña a los mozos de la capilla") received an annual salary of 900 *maravedís*. In the 1470s, the succentor's salary for his teaching had increased to 3,000 *maravedís*. A.C.S., sección II, libros 1074, 1075, 1079.

[4] Herminio González Barrionuevo, *Francisco Guerrero (1528–1599): Vida y obra; La música en la catedral de Sevilla a finales del siglo XVI* (Seville, 2000), 133, 170, 175–77.

[5] A.C.S., sección II, libro 1075, fols. 2ʳ, 199ʳ. The Librería Capitular was situated in this space at the beginning of the fifteenth century, when one of its sacristans (at least between 1401 and 1410) was Fernando Estevan, "teacher of plainchant, counterpoint, and polyphony" ("maestro de canto plano, e de contrapunto e de canto de órgano"), whose musical treatise written in Castilian in 1410 may represent his teaching in this period. See

Gothic church, when the choirboys and their teacher must have moved to a space in the new location of the cibary (tabernacle), which had been moved from the center of the Mudejar cathedral to the chapels situated in the back of the Nave del Lagarto in the Patio de los Naranjos. Beginning in 1533, musical instruction (like the singers' and *ministriles'* rehearsals with the choirmaster) took place in the Capilla de la Granada, situated in the Nave de los Caballeros, in one of the wings of the Patio de los Naranjos, the modern-day location of the Iglesia del Sagrario.[1] The choirmaster at the time, Pedro Fernández de Castilleja, had to teach two lessons of *canto de órgano* (polyphony). A few years later, in 1540, it was specified that these were to be lessons of *canto llano* (plainchant), *canto de órgano* (polyphony), and *contrapunto* (counterpoint).[2]

In 1551, the cathedral of Seville hired Francisco Guerrero as assistant to Pedro Fernández de Castilleja. At this time the assistant's duties were formulated in detail, including those related to the boy singers. First, he would have to teach them to read, write, and sing the responses, verses, antiphons, lessons, and the martyrology; the remainder of the assistant's duties pertained to service in the cathedral choir. Second, he would have to teach them to sing plainchant, polyphony, counterpoint, "the same for plainchant as well as for polyphony" ("así sobre canto llano como sobre canto de órgano"), and composition, so they would become capable musicians and composers. Third, he would have to see to their lodging, meals, and clothing until they were dismissed or their voices changed. The chapter specified that they would not be used for performances except for those in the cathedral, or for any performances that were not strictly musical. The assistant also had to make sure there were boys in sufficient number for the needs of the liturgy. The chapter checked each month to ensure strict observance of these orders. The compensation offered to Guerrero maintained the salary he had received as a contralto singer and gave him half the income of the choirmaster's *ración*, guaranteeing him this position at the death of Pedro Fernández de Castilleja. All this, at the request of the dean, the chapter, and Guerrero himself, was ratified by the bull *Pastoralis officii*, issued by Julius III on 1 June 1554. On 6 February 1555, the chapter raised Guerrero's salary by 20,000 *maravedís* and granted him a house large enough to live in with the *seises*, along with the express permission to maintain a school there and to give private lessons for as long as he did not receive the full salary of the choirmaster.[3]

At the end of the chronological period that concerns us here, the chapter compiled two detailed statutes of 1597 and 1598 listing all the agreements that traditionally had been drawn up regarding the choirboys and the *seises* along with their respective teachers. The first statute describes their training in plainchant and lists

---

Juan Ruiz Jiménez, *La Librería de Canto de Órgano: Creación y pervivencia del repertorio del Renacimiento en la actividad musical de la catedral de Sevilla* (Granada, 2007), 8.

[1] Throughout the history of the cathedral, despite changing times and locations, these two spaces continued as the sites for instruction and the choir rehearsals.

[2] A.C.S., sección 1, libro 13, fols. 272^r, 279^r; libro 17, fol. 19^v.

[3] For the text of the agreements and a translation of the bull, see Rosa y López, *Los seises*, 81–96.

their various functions, both musical and liturgical. The regulations for the *seises* describe the care of their clothing, their nourishment, and their lodging, and the financial resources that the master had to dedicate to them. He had to attend not only to their musical education (which took place in the cathedral for one hour in the morning and another in the afternoon), but also to their behavior, controlling their trips outside. The *seises* owed him absolute respect and obedience, but if any of them felt aggrieved, he could turn to the dean who, after listening, would see that justice was done.[1]

The substance of the boys' instruction in plainchant can be deduced from treatises by two choirmasters of Seville Cathedral: the *Arte de canto llano* of Juan Martínez (Alcalá de Henares, 1532) and the *Breve instrucción de canto llano para aprender brevemente el artificio del canto* of Luis de Villafranca (Seville, 1565). For the musical education of the *seises* the teacher needed, among other materials, books of polyphony and plainchant that were duplicates or that could not be used in the choir for some reason, as well as some volumes from the rich collection of music theory treatises and printed books that came to the cathedral from the Biblioteca Colombina.[2]

PROFESSIONAL ACTIVITIES

THE participation of the choirboys in a private ceremony is documented for the first time in 1311, indicating that they were involved early on in various rituals resulting from individual donations. In this particular case they had to participate along with the clerks of the *veintena* (*clerici cori* or *clerici vicenarii*) in the performance of the canticles of Matins and the litany at the grave of the deceased woman who made the donation.[3] As we will see, these votive endowments constituted an important source of external revenue for the maintenance and academic training of the choirboys, besides giving a significant boost to the cathedral's musical activities both inside and outside the choir. Thanks to the proliferation of such donations, the chapter decided in 1363 on a sum of 300 *maravedís* for those who wished to establish in perpetuity a solemn celebration of their anniversary in the cathedral, with a vigil at the tomb and a Requiem Mass the following day. The money was to be divided among those participants who remained until the choirboys said *Requiescat in pace*.[4]

The *Regla Antigua de Coro*, compiled in the course of the fourteenth and fifteenth centuries and preserved in a parchment copy completed in 1551, describes the frequent participation of the choirboys, called *pueri*, in the liturgical activities

---

[1] For the transcription of these Statutes, see Rosa y López, *Los seises*, 56–57; González Barrionuevo, *Los seises de Sevilla*, 293–96.

[2] Ruiz Jiménez, *La Librería de Canto de Órgano*, 13, 17, 220, 306–7.

[3] A.C.S., sección IX, leg. 58, pieza 34. The clerks of the *veintena*, or *veinteneros*, specialized in liturgical chant and, at least since the beginning of the fifteenth century, appear frequently as singers of both plainchant and polyphony.

[4] A.C.S., sección I, libro 370, fol. 10^v.

of Seville cathedral.[1] This document offers precise details regarding the specific chants, the number of boys who had to sing them (ranging from one to six), and where they were to sing. These prescriptions vary considerably according to the rank of the feast being celebrated, highlighting the extent and particular significance of their participation in liturgical actions of both the Office and the Mass. The *Regla Antigua* also describes the participation of the choirboys in the numerous processions inside and outside the church in which they carried candles, censers, crosses, and other liturgical objects. This continued activity meant that they spent most of their time in the cathedral. The chapter had a room with beds on its premises so that the boys appointed to sing Matins could rest.[2] The boys' ordinary duties, determined by the succentor, followed a weekly rotation for which he prepared the choir list designating the two boys in charge, the two with candles who sang the responsories and verses of the choir, and a fifth who had several duties: reading the daily martyrology entry, ensuring that all the books were returned to their cupboards, and keeping the lectern in the center of the choir lit.[3]

From the choirboys' role in the liturgy emerged a repertory that was occasionally copied in books intended specifically for them. The earliest evidence for such books is a reference from 1434 to a binding in boards and silver repoussé of a book for the choirboys that only a few months later would be stolen from its place in the choir. In 1454, there is another reference to the binding of a book of the "five histories" (*çincostodias*) "from which the boys read in the chapel" ("en que leen los mozos en la capilla"), probably used for teaching.[4] In 1485, the prebendary Gonzalo Sánchez had to provide the choirboys with a psalter and a volume containing the "five histories."[5] The Biblioteca Capitular preserves some of the books intended for the choirboys, among them a volume copied in the fifteenth century entitled *Versiculos puerorum*, which includes several melodies for versicles, antiphons, hymns (*Gloria laus* and *Vexilla regis*), and other chants (see Figure 5.1).[6] In 1555, Francisco Guerrero was paid for the binding of a book of responses and verses for the *cantorcicos*.[7]

The participation of the choirboys with adult singers in the performance of

---

[1] A.C.S., sección III, libro I.

[2] A.C.S., sección I, libro I, fol. 14ʳ (1478); libro 3, fol. 54ᵛ (1481), libro 6, fol. 51ᵛ (1503).

[3] These functions appear together in the chapter heading for the office of cantor in the *Libro Blanco* of the cathedral, copied in 1411, which reflects the traditional functions of the boys throughout the fourteenth century. A.C.S., sección II, libro 1477, fol. 69ʳ.

[4] This term, which is repeated to refer to various volumes produced within the cathedral precinct and outside it, alludes to a *Commune sanctorum*. The prologue of Cardinal Francisco Jiménez de Cisneros to the *Commune sanctorum* (Alcalá de Henares, ca. 1516) states: "We have administered the publication of the Commune sanctorum, which others call the five histories" ("curavimus imprimendum Commune sanctorum quod alii quinque historias appellant"); quoted in Julián Martín Abad, *Post-incunables ibéricos* (Madrid, 2001), 202. This is also confirmed by Juan Bermudo in his *Declaración de instrumentos musicales* (Osuna, 1555) fol. 124ᵛ: "Los communes, que otros dizen cinco historias."

[5] A.C.S., sección I, libro 3, fol. 29ᵛ (1485); sección IV, libro 2B, fols. 9ʳ, 46ᵛ (1434), libro 7, fol. 16ʳ (1454).

[6] Biblioteca Capitular y Colombina (hereafter B.C.C.), MS 59-4-15.

[7] A.C.S., sección VI, leg. 11354.

Figure 5.1: Seville, Institución Colombina, MS 59-4-15, s.f.

polyphony is documented as an established practice from the beginning of the fifteenth century. It must have taken root in the previous century, but the absence of certain types of documents before this date precludes further specificity for the moment.

In 1419, the master of the choirboys, Alfonso Sánchez, with five singers and the five choirboys, sang the *chanzonetas* (villancicos) of Christmas Matins, for which each received extra remuneration. A few years later, in 1440, the choirboys' participation in the Corpus Christi procession is also documented. Brought by the tenor singer Íñigo Sánchez, they sang *canto de órgano* in front of the platforms on which the monstrance was carried, perhaps along with the other seven singers who were paid for the same reason.[1]

From the middle of the fifteenth century, private donations that included the choirboys in devotional or liturgical performances (whether as an independent group or along with other singers) increased in both number and size. With the construction of the new Gothic church, new ritual spaces emerged to accommodate the diversification of musical practices, which in turn affected the growth of ensembles necessary for performance and the need for new musical repertory, both local and imported.

In 1450, a canon of Seville Cathedral, Ruy González Bolante, founded the chapel of St. Francis, one of the first Gothic spaces to be built, for his burial in the cathedral. Among other things, he endowed four Masses to be said in the morning, so as not to interfere with the liturgy of the hours. Three of these Masses were to be celebrated in the chapel of St. Francis; the fourth would take place at the altar of Santa María de la Antigua, which at this time was situated in the chapel of St. Clement. One of the chaplains from the chapel of St. Clement would officiate at these Masses, and the master of the choirboys would sing with the six boys and two other singers from the cathedral choir. Each Mass was endowed with 120 *maravedís*, which would be divided among the participants.[2]

A short while later, in 1456, Pedro Martínez de la Caridad, who was the first designated for the prebend of *magister puerorum*, established a foundation that expressly required the presence of the choirboys. He wished to be buried in front of the altar of the Virgen de la Antigua, and in this place he established a ritual to be celebrated every Saturday, when the succentor, accompanied by the choirboys, would sing the antiphon *Salve regina* "solemnly" ("solemnemente"). Afterwards, two of the boys would sing *Ergo pro nobis ora dei genitrix pia*, followed by a prayer, and then all would sing a response "solemnly" and pronounce the appropriate prayer over the tomb of Pedro Martínez.[3] It is difficult to determine whether both the antiphon and the response would be sung polyphonically. It is likely that they were, because the choirboys would sing the superius and altus parts, while the succentor, who at the time of the foundation was Miguel Rodríguez (and who was usually also a singer in the cathedral choir), would perform the lower part, creating

---

[1] Ruiz Jiménez, "Los sonidos de la montaña hueca."
[2] A.C.S., sección II, libro 1477, dotación nº 79.
[3] A.C.S., sección II, libro 1477, dotación nº 92.

a sufficiently versatile ensemble for singing the repertory already well established in Seville Cathedral around the middle of the sixteenth century (see below).

Particularly significant for our knowledge of the repertory for the dead is the donation of Gonzalo Sánchez de Córdoba, archdeacon of Jerez and canon of Seville Cathedral. On 25 September 1467, the chapter agreed on the manner in which the anniversary of this important canon would be celebrated. Sánchez de Córdoba was interred in the chapel of St. James. The Vigil would be celebrated in the choir with an invitatory and two high-ranking clerics wearing copes. The Requiem Mass on the following day, 17 July, would take place in the chapel where the canon was buried and would be attended by the chapter and all the beneficed clergy. The foundation makes special reference to the participation of the clerks of the *veintena* in the responses of both the Vigil and of the Mass:

> The succentor, with the boys he teaches and the master of the boys with his singing pupils, are to take part in the responses of the Vigil and the Mass of this anniversary, and then the succentor and the master of the boys, on the following day, must say his Requiem Mass, and either one of them may celebrate, and the boys officiate, and for this they are to be paid 100 *maravedís*.[1]

Everything seems to indicate the polyphonic performance of the responsories of the dead, *Libera me domine* and *Ne recorderis*, which opened and closed these ceremonies, probably along with some element of the Requiem Mass — all at about the time that the lost Requiem of Dufay (the earliest known example of the genre) is thought to have been composed.[2] In this context, the donation of the canon Hernán Gómez de Solis (recorded in his will dated 29 August 1526) leaves no room for doubt. The foundation stipulates that Vespers of the Dead should be sung at his tomb: "one polyphonic response and on the next day a polyphonic mass with its response" ("un responso de canto de órgano y otro día una misa de canto de órgano con su responso"). At this Mass, the succentor would officiate and the choirmaster would sing with his choirboys and other singers of the cathedral selected by him to receive the payment stipulated by the foundation.[3]

Around 1480, the cathedral canon Pedro Díaz de Toledo began to fund the *Salve* service that was performed every Saturday afternoon in the chapel of the Antigua. To guarantee its continuation, in 1499, when he was already bishop of Málaga, he established a special foundation that explicitly dictated the payment of four *maravedís* to each of the six boy sopranos (*tiples*) who would take part in the performance of the various polyphonic pieces in this ceremony.[4] This endowment

---

[1] A.C.S., sección ii, libro 1477, dotación nº 202: "el sochantre con los mozos que el muestra, e el maestro de los mozos con sus discípulos cantores han de estar a los responsos de la vigilia e misa del dicho aniversario, e después el dicho sochantre e el maestro de los mozos, otro día siguiente, han de decir su misa de réquiem e celebrar cualquiera de ellos e los mozos oficiarán, e estos han de haber ciento maravedís luego pagados."

[2] On the composition of the choir in these years and the liturgy and repertory of these anniversaries, see Ruiz Jiménez, *La Librería de Canto de Órgano*, 278–84.

[3] A.C.S., sección ix, leg. 70, pieza 1.

[4] A.C.S., sección ii, libro 1477, dotación nº 392.

became the model for others that would be founded later on in the same place and in the cathedral's other ritual spaces. At least three books of polyphony can be linked to this devotional foundation in the period under consideration here. Two of them (now lost) contained motets, settings of the *Salve regina*, masses, "and other things" ("e otras cosas") — and were already in the chapel in 1517; the third, copied in 1553, is still extant and contains a repertory both native and foreign for the celebration of this ceremony.[1] One *Salve regina* by Guerrero (Figure 5.2) and his motet *Virgo prudentissima* for four voices are scored for SSSA. The same manuscript contains another *Salve regina* by Guerrero and a considerable number of motets by various composers, scored for SSAT.[2]

In 1498, Pedro Mejía, archdeacon of Écija and canon of Seville, endowed the singing of the antiphon *Sanctissimae trinitatis* by the choirboys.[3] The donation was supplemented in 1549 by the canon Diego Vázquez Alderete.[4] This practice continued in the choir of Seville Cathedral, after Prime and before Vespers, until the closing of the Colegio de San Isidoro in 1960. The melody appears at the end of the *Arte de canto llano* of Juan Martínez, whom the chapter named master of plainchant for the choirboys in 1525.[5] Comparable donations, albeit with slightly different ritual prescriptions, include funerary responses endowed in 1503 by the canon Diego Alfonso de Sevilla and in 1505 by the cathedral organist Bernal de Cuenca — in both cases the antiphon *Gaude Dei genitrix*, which was to be sung by the choirboys with their master: the first in front of the altar of Our Lady of the Pomegranate and the second in front of the altar of Our Lady of the Remedies, situated behind the choir (*trascoro*).[6]

In 1502, the cathedral cantor Juan de Vergara endowed the Matins services of Easter and, after the office, a procession to the chapel of the Virgen de la Antigua with the monstrance over a chalice. These festal Matins entailed the participation of the singers, choirboys, and the organist. At the beginning of the procession, the cathedral choir sang the antiphon *Crucifixus surrexit a mortuis*; upon reaching the door of the chapel, they began to sing the antiphon *Regina celi letare*. At the conclusion of the antiphon, the boys sang the verse *Surrexit Dominus de sepulcro*. In the chapel, the priest said the prayer *Mater Dei rogamus te*, after which they returned to the choir, accompanied by the singing of the *Regina celi*. After the host was placed on the altar, shown to the people, and deposited in the monstrance, the priest would say the prayer *Concede nos famulos tuos*, and the boys would finish the

---

[1] Ruiz Jiménez, *La Librería de Canto de Órgano*, 38–40.

[2] See ibid., 111.

[3] This donation was reinforced at the beginning of the sixteenth century when another one was established by the agent of the lonja Pedro Ortiz, who left 1,000 *maravedís* a year for the choirboys to sing this antiphon after Prime and None. A.C.S., sección 11, libro 1517.

[4] A.C.S., sección 11, libro 1477, dotación nº 453.

[5] The melody is recorded by Rosa y López, *Los seises*, 40–42; González Barrionuevo, *Los seises de Sevilla*, 45; A.C.S., sección IV, libro 8, fol. 6ʳ.

[6] A.C.S., sección 11, libro 1477, dotaciones nº 355 and nº 384.

Figure 5.2: Seville, Institución Colombina, Libro de Polifonía no. 1, fols. 25ᵛ–26ʳ.

ceremony by singing the *Benedicamus Domino* with a reprise of the Alleluia. The choirboys were paid 50 *maravedís* from the total donation of 5250 *maravedís*.[1]

The last donation I will mention here reflects the participation of the choirboys in the polyphonic performance of votive Masses, which confirms the diversification of the repertory they sang as well as the process by which they became divided into the two groups described earlier. Around 1514, the canon Luis Ordóñez began to fund a Mass of the Sacrament celebrated in the cibary of the cathedral on the first Thursday of each month at the same time and in a manner comparable to the one sung polyphonically in the chapel of the Virgen de la Antigua on Saturday afternoons. In 1518, Ordoñez endowed his donation in perpetuity, simultaneously founding two monthly Masses, also dedicated to the Sacrament and celebrated in the cibary, which would be said on Fridays by the master of the choirboys, accompanied by the choirboys. The chapter ordered "that the choirmaster and the master of the choirboys, each with his boys, should celebrate these offices," and according to the foundation, they would be paid the amount stipulated for this service.[2]

In addition to the work performed by the boy singers in the choir and in other ceremonial spaces of the cathedral, they acquired a prominent role in the diverse dramatic performances that took place over the course of the liturgical year. I have not been able to document conclusively the participation of a costumed choirboy in the song of the Sibyl during Matins on the feast of the Nativity. On the contrary, as already stated, beginning in the early fifteenth century the choirboys sang in the *chanzonetas* during Christmas services, and from the end of the century it is clear that they played a very active role singing and dancing in the performances of the *Officium pastorum*. By the middle of the sixteenth century, these performances had gradually been transformed into theatrical productions that were very popular with the citizenry.[3]

There is also no doubt about the role played by the choirboys, dressed as the Marys, during the representation of the *Visitatio sepulchri*, or the sequence of the Mass, *Victimae paschali laudes*, on Easter Sunday. The first references date from 1434, when the carpenter Bartolomé Sánchez was paid to build the floor of the tomb and the scaffolding for the image of Mary, where it had to be located so as to be more easily seen. Payments for gloves, ribbons, the Crown of Thorns, and a person especially enlisted to make up and dress the choirboy for his participation in this performance, all appear sporadically in the chapter records.[4] In 1504 and 1505, we know that the figures of Jesus, the Virgin Mary, Mary Magdalene, and six apostles appeared in this representation; in 1506, the scene was completed

---

[1] A.C.S., sección ii, libro 1477, dotación n° 409.

[2] A.C.S., sección i, libro 10, fol. 196ʳ (1518): "al maestro de capilla e al maestro de los mozos de coro que cada uno de ellos, con sus mozos, hagan estos dichos oficios."

[3] Jean Sentaurens, *Seville et le théâtre: De la fin du Moyen Âge à la fin du XVIIᵉ siècle* (Lille, 1984), 21–23.

[4] A.C.S., sección iv, libro 2ʙ, fols. 3ᵛ, 4ʳ (1434); libro 8, fol. 14ʳ (1458), libro 10, fol. 23ʳ (1464); libro 18, fol. 27ᵛ (1498); libro 19, fol. 52ʳ (1504); libro 20, fol. 58ᵛ (1505); libro 21, fol. 57ʳ (1506).

with the three Marys. The female characters must have been played by choirboys, as was the custom.

A theatrical performance of particular importance in Seville Cathedral was that which took place on the feast of Pentecost beginning in the fourteenth century.[1] Even absent an analysis of all its components, it is clear that it became ever more complex as the sixteenth century approached. Many of its elements are common to representations associated with several ecclesiastical institutions in the Crown of Aragón.[2] The most familiar elements to scholars include the temporary structure called a "castle" (*castillo*) that was placed in the chancel, a wheel representing heaven to which eight seraphs and other ornamental elements were attached, and mechanical doves, all accompanied by fireworks, the release of a white dove, hundreds of turtledoves, wafers, sunbeams, etc. In the most elaborate form of the spectacle, the characters were God the Father, the twelve apostles, and the Virgin Mary. Singers, *ministriles*, trumpets, drums, and tambourines participated in the performance; in 1506 and 1508, a payment is specified for the "six little singers who went up in the wheel" ("seis cantorcillos que anduvieron en la rueda, arriba").[3]

It is difficult to determine the beginnings of the Boy Bishop ceremony in Seville Cathedral. It is listed already in the *Regla Vieja* and documented by other sources beginning in 1414 in the oldest volume of payment registers preserved in the cathedral.[4] We know the details of the ceremony and how it was organized by Archbishop Diego de Deza in 1512, in thanksgiving for the fact that the dome of the cathedral harmed no one when it collapsed on 28 December 1511 — the feast of the Holy Innocents when the actions involving the Boy Bishop and his entourage traditionally took place. According to Ortiz de Zúñiga, the ceremony continued to be performed until 1563. Developed, transformed, and not exempt from various scandals, it survived in the *Colegio de Maese Rodrigo* (University of Seville) as a student festival until 1654 and in the cathedral until well into the eighteenth cen-

---

[1] In the *Regla Vieja de Coro* of Seville Cathedral, the writing of which (as stated above) must have begun in the fourteenth century, the Mass of Terce on the feast of Pentecost refers to what could have been the origin of the performances associated with this feast. The celebrant begins the first verse of the sequence *Veni sancte spiritus* "facing the choir, and throws a white dove from his hands, and after these verses are played on the organ, that first verse should be repeated by the choir, and afterwards by the organ, and finally the entire sequence is sung in alternation with the organ. While it is sung, turtledoves and fire and water and hosts are thrown" ("uersa facie ad chorum, et proiiciat de manibus suis columbam albam et post istimet versus pulsatur in organis iste primus versus repetatur in choro et post in organis et post modum dicatur tota prosa in organis alternatim. Interim autem dum cantatur proiinciantur turtures et ignis et aqua et oblee"); A.C.S., sección III, fol. 144ᵛ.

[2] Francesc Massip i Bonet, "Cerimònia litúrgica i artifici teatral en el jorn de Pentecosta (segles XIII–XVI)," in *Actes del Congrés de la Seu Vella de Lleida* (Lleida, 1991), 257–63.

[3] A.C.S., sección I, libro 7, fol. 34ʳ (1508); sección IV, libro 2B, fol. 5ᵛ (1434); libro 18, fols. 27ᵛ–28ᵛ (1498); libro 19 fol. 52ʳ⁻ᵛ (1504); libro 20, fol. 59ʳ⁻ᵛ (1505); libro 21, fols. 57ᵛ–58ʳ (1506).

[4] A.C.S., sección II, libro 1075, fol. 10ʳ; sección III, libro 1, fol. 275ʳ.

tury, when it involved a *seise* who acted as the choirmaster and other clerks who acted as master of ceremonies and succentor on the feast of the Innocents.[1]

At particular moments and for occasional ceremonies celebrated in the cathedral, the choirboys appeared costumed, usually as angels. Thus, at the funeral in 1545 of María Manuela of Portugal, the first consort of King Philip II, the boy singers, "like angels" ("como ángeles") with wings and garlands on their heads, standing around the tomb, sang the response of the second lesson *Qui Lazarum* and the *Requiescat in pace*.[2] The "via triumphalis" designed for the wedding in 1526 of Emperor Charles V and Maria of Portugal terminated in a magnificent arch financed by the cathedral chapter and positioned above the cathedral's Puerta del Perdón. At the center of this arch was a "heaven" from which the boy singers, some dressed as angels and others representing the Virtues, sang "with skilled and sweet harmony" ("con diestra y suave harmonía").[3]

I have reserved for the end of this essay my discussion of the participation of the choirboys in the procession of Corpus Christi (which in Seville assumed exceptional solemnity and splendor) because it is the best known aspect of their history.[4] In the complex civic-religious spectacle of this processional parade, the choirboys played various roles that changed and even on occasion were superimposed throughout the fifteenth and sixteenth centuries. Their presence among the musical personnel participating in the procession is already recorded in the cathedral's earliest preserved account books, which date from 1434, when eight choirboys were paid for singing in the procession along with the eighteen singers of the cathedral.[5] The number of choirboys and adult singers varied annually for practically the entire period considered in this study. In addition to their role within the cathedral choir, they appear from the middle of the fifteenth century in the "roca," a kind of decorated float carried in the procession on the shoulders of a dozen men. On the "roca" the choirboys were costumed as Mary, St. Dominic, and St. Francis, or as singing angels. Along with this official structure, the procession included other *castillos* similar to the "roca" but sponsored by some of the city's guilds. In these there also occasionally appeared boy singers whose origins are not specified.[6]

---

[1] Rosa y López, *Los seises*, 45–59.

[2] B.C.C., MS 59-1-3, fol. 151ʳ.

[3] Sentaurens, *Seville et le théâtre*, 32.

[4] In addition to the bibliography cited on the *seises*, various scholars, some of them art historians, have addressed this theme; see especially José Gestoso y Pérez, *Curiosidades Antiguas Sevillanas: Serie II* (Seville, 1910; repr. Seville, 1993); John Brande Trend, "The Dance of the Seises at Seville," *Music & Letters* 2 (1921), 10–28; Vicente Lleó Cañal, *Arte y espectáculo: La fiesta del Corpus Christi en la Sevilla de los siglos XVI y XVII* (Seville, 1975); Lynn Matluck Brooks, "'Los Seises' in the Golden Age of Seville," *Dance Chronicle* 5 (1982), 121–55; Sentaurens, *Seville et le théâtre*, 35–77, 155–68; María Jesús Serrano Sanz, "El Corpus en Sevilla a mediados del siglo XVI: Castillos y danzas," *Laboratorio de Arte* 10 (1997), 123–38.

[5] A.C.S., sección IV, libro 2B, fol. 6ᵛ.

[6] In 1514, in the entourage that accompanied them to the *castillo* subsidized by the guild of the tailors, knitters, and bodice-makers, there were two boy singers who were supposed

In the sixteenth century the structure of the "roca" was transformed into triumphant chariots — moving stages that allowed for the display of a greater number of characters with more complex staging. On these surfaces, veritable dramatic works such as the *autos sacramentales* could be performed, allowing the *seises* temporarily to become actors.[1] The last element of the *seises'* participation in the Corpus Christi procession, the dance, is also the one whose origins and configuration throughout the sixteenth century is most controversial. The first explicit allusion occurs in 1508 in the cathedral fabric's account books, which record the payment of 136 *maravedís* to the boy singers who "were singing and dancing in the procession." The figure indicates that there were eight singers, since each usually received 17 *maravedís* (half a *real*). The reduced number (in comparison to the twelve singers in 1507) can be explained by the terrible epidemic of the plague that devastated the city that year and decimated the cathedral choir as much as the rest of the citizenry. Nothing in this reference suggests novelty except the specification of dancing, which is repeated in 1509, 1510, and 1512, when there were eleven choirboys. The records specify that they danced in front of the Custodia, but this is repeated only very sporadically until the practice became established in the seventeenth century.[2] Everything indicates that 1508 was not the first year in which the choirboys danced and that, at the beginning, they did not have to dance every year, nor did all those who participated in the procession take part in the dance. The dances must have had a prearranged choreography, which entailed the presence (mentioned occasionally) of a person charged with teaching it to the *seises*.[3] The high point of this tradition — the codification and the introduction of the *seises'* dance in the cathedral during the celebration of the octave of Corpus Christi (in front of the high altar), the Immaculate Conception, and the three days of Shrovetide — came about through private donations of 1613, 1654, and 1679 that lie outside the chronological limits of this study.[4]

What happened to the choirboys after their voices changed? What were their prospects for professional advancement? For the fifteenth century, very little is known; the academic training they had received enabled them to continue in ecclesiastical careers and enter the regular or secular clergy as singers in the choir of Seville Cathedral or in one of the other ecclesiastical institutions of comparable

---

to sing the Magnificat. In the *castillo* of the carpenters' guild in 1530, four singers were supposed to represent the office of the Nativity: Joseph, Mary, an angel, and a shepherd (plus a small child). The contract stipulates that the singers had to be the youngest available and that they had to rehearse their performance in advance. Sentaurens, *Seville et le théâtre*, 52, 54.

[1] In the performance of the *auto sacramental El triunfo de la Iglesia* (1560), there were six *cantorcicos* on stage, but their precise role in the dramatic action cannot be determined; Sentaurens, *Seville et le théâtre*, 165–67; Rosa y López, *Los seises*, 231–32; José Sánchez-Arjona, *Noticias referentes a los Anales del Teatro en Sevilla desde Lope de Rueda hasta fines del siglo XVII* (Seville, 1898; repr. Seville, 1994), 23.

[2] A.C.S., sección IV, libro 23, fol. 17ʳ; libro 24, fol. 20ᵛ; libro 25, fol. 26ʳ; libro 28, fol. 27ʳ.

[3] Rosa y López, *Los seises*, 234, 236, 240–44.

[4] Ibid., 248–52, 256–59.

or inferior rank. The situation became regularized and institutionalized thanks to two individual foundations established by two beneficed members of the cathedral clergy who were former *seises*. The first of these was established by the prothonotary and canon Diego de Ribera in his will of 10 December 1551. One of the clauses created two scholarships of six thousand *maravedís* a year for those boy singers whose voices had changed and who had served four years in the cathedral. The youths had to continue their studies in the Colegio de San Miguel and their residence in the choir. In order to receive the scholarship, they were examined each trimester to check on their performance. If their progress was inadequate, they would be paid their salaries and dismissed. The scholarships would last for four years. Only two years later, in 1553, another former *seise*, the dean Diego de Carmona, increased Canon Ribera's donation by four thousand *maravedís* for each of the two existing scholarships and established two more of equal size, lowering to three the prior years of service as *seise* that were required for the scholarship.[1] These donations propelled and enhanced the prestige of the group, and above all, favored its formation, promotion, and employment — the most famous example in the period under study here being the composer Alonso Lobo de Borja. The Colegio de San Isidoro and other foundations established in the seventeenth century improved their standards of living, and the chapter focused still more attention on this group of children essential to the musical development of Seville Cathedral.

[translated by Susan Boynton]

[1] For the details of these donations, see ibid., 120–31.

6

THE SEEDS OF MEDIEVAL MUSIC
CHOIRBOYS AND MUSICAL TRAINING
IN A LATE-MEDIEVAL MAÎTRISE

Andrew Kirkman

6 JUNE 1491 was a day of high drama at the collegiate church of Saint-Omer in northern France.[1] At a meeting held that day, the chapter officially fired the succentor, Malin Alixandre, from his post as master of the church's six choirboys and ordered his removal from the house that he shared with them. This action stimulated a quick and strident response from the church's cantor, Jehan de Hemont, who was emphatic that the right of hiring and firing the master of the boys was his alone.[2] For its part, the chapter claimed that the cantor's business was limited to overseeing the maintenance and instruction of the boys and their house, and that the right of appointment was theirs alone. Enraged at what he perceived as an infringement of his rights of office, the cantor walked out of the chapter meeting saying that he would resort to the process of law.[3]

That Hemont was indeed within his rights seems clear repeatedly from the wording of chapter entries detailing appointments of masters of the boys, including one whereby, little more than three months earlier, Alixandre had himself been assigned to the position from which he was now being ejected:

> On the twenty-first of February the lord and master Johannes de Hemont, cantor of this church to whom it concerns by reason of his office to present a master learned in singing for the instruction of the six choirboys, this day

Thanks are due to Barbara Haggh and Philip Weller for reading this text and offering suggestions, to Bonnie Blackburn, Barbara Haggh, Leofranc Holford-Strevens, David Marsh, and Philip Weller for assistance with the documents, and to John Harper for answering specific questions concerning the duties of choirboys.

[1] Throughout this paper I use the hyphenated "Saint-Omer" for the city, and "St. Omer" for the church itself.

[2] For a similar case from late fifteenth-century Poitiers see Paula Higgins, "Musical Politics in Late Medieval Poitiers: A Tale of Two Choirmasters," in *Antoine Busnoys: Method, Meaning, and Context in Late Medieval Music*, ed. Paula Higgins (Oxford, 1999), 155–74.

[3] The fracas is recounted in chapter acts recorded in Saint-Omer, Archives municipales [as for all subsequent documents with the 11. G. call number], 11. G. 355, fols. 83ᵛ–85ʳ.

in the accustomed fashion presented to my lords in chapter lord Malin Ale-xandre, whom the lords graciously admitted.[1]

It would seem that here, as in general,[2] all administrative matters concerning the boys and their master, the succentor (literally "sub-cantor") stood under the jurisdiction of his immediate superior, the cantor. However, the reason for the sacking, as recorded in the minutes of the next chapter meeting that was held just four days later, reveals the incident in a rather different light. Here it emerges that Alixandre's removal was occasioned by the fact that he had violently beaten one of the choirboys and, as the document says, hated him ("quemdam de sex pueris vio-lenter verberaverat et [in] odio Ipsum habebat"). In spite of the cantor's protesta-tions that he would make amends if Alixandre's sacking were repealed, the chapter stuck by its decision, affirming that if Hemont would not remove the master, they would do so themselves. Yet more than a month later the cantor had still failed to remove Alixandre and replace him, and in the face of this intransigence it emerges that the chapter members had decided to remove him themselves.

It is worth dwelling briefly on the identity of their new appointee to Alixandre's post: Grigorius Bourgois, sometimes known by the alias "Scripure" and frequently referred to in the Saint-Omer accounts as "tenorista."[3] Bourgois had been in Saint-Omer since 1473, when the archives record his appointment to a chaplain-cy.[4] Before that, though, he had led a rather different life. A record concerning him, dated the previous year, has survived in Ghent, recounting how he had appeared before a magistrates' court trying to sue a certain Arend vanden Couden for selling him an unruly horse; indeed, the horse had been so intractable that it had injured several of Bourgois's companions. Bourgois's suit, which demanded that vanden Couden take back the horse, return his money, and pay for the injuries, was unsuc-cessful, but the record does give us an important piece of information because it names him as a tenorist of the king of Naples.[5]

It is tempting to speculate, therefore, as to how Bourgois's career might have led him to Saint-Omer. The answer must surely be that he had been there in 1471, when the court of Naples met Charles the Bold, duke of Burgundy, in Saint-Omer in order to form an alliance with him. For some reason, perhaps

[1] II. G. 355, fol. 83ᵛ: "Die xxia februarii dominus et magister Johannes de hemont Cantor huius ecclesie cui interesset ratione sue dignitatis presentare magistrum doctum in Cantu ad Instruendum sex pueros chori hac die more solito presentavit dominis meis in capitulo dictum Malinum Alexandre quem domini gratiose admiserunt."

[2] For the prevailing nature of this situation, see for example Otto Frede Becker, "The Maîtrise in Northern France and Burgundy During the Fifteenth Century," (Ph.D. disserta-tion, George Peabody College for Teachers, 1967), 189–95.

[3] For discussion of the role and duties of the "tenorist" see Rob C. Wegman, "From Maker to Composer: Improvisation and Musical Authorship in the Low Countries, 1450–1500," *Journal of the American Musicological Society* 49 (1996), 444–49; Barbara Haggh, "Music, Liturgy and Ceremony in Brussels, 1350–1500," 2 vols. (Ph.D. dissertation, University of Illinois at Urbana-Champaign, 1988), 1:189–91.

[4] II. G. 354, fol. 172ʳ.

[5] For this information, see Rob C. Wegman, *Born for the Muses: The Life and Masses of Jacob Obrecht* (Oxford, 1994), 67–68.

connected with his place of origin, as in so many other cases, Bourgois must have sought favour with the chapter on that occasion, thus explaining his appearance in the church archives shortly thereafter. Clearly some special consideration had not only brought Bourgois to Saint-Omer but had kept him there: the archives record his appointment to a series of positions, including various stints (the earliest beginning in 1478) as master of the boys, and he remained in the town until his death in 1496.

In the event, however, his 1491 appointment was short-lived: as so often in such cases, after much disagreement and vituperation, the injured parties decided to bury the hatchet, and on 13 July Hemont's alternative candidate, Robert Poilly, was accepted. As the account states, Hemont had acted contrary to the express command of the chapter in seeking to maintain Alixandre in his position, and had allowed him to remain in the boys' house for three days after his dismissal. Yet in spite of this, and notwithstanding Hemont's own protestations at being "offended in [his] proper rights and dues," the injured parties decided to revert to the situation as it had been before the dismissal, although, perhaps prudently, they are unspecific about what the precise nature of that situation had been. Neither do the stated reasons for the cessation of hostilities — a claimed desire to cultivate peace and love, and the difficulty in a time of prevailing war of conducting the necessary legal proceedings — seem especially persuasive, much less unforeseeable. Certainly this is far from the only surviving record of violence towards a choirboy, and harsh treatment seems to have been relatively commonplace.[1] Perhaps, then, there were other dynamics in play here: the office of master of the boys, which was the subject at this period of a game of almost continuous musical chairs, was a focus of frequent dispute during Hemont's tenure as cantor, with masters not infrequently failing to meet the requirements of their position or being absent without having made proper provision. Clearly Hemont's relationship with the chapter was not an easy one, and there are hints that he may have been a generally difficult figure.[2]

On the other hand, it is possible that the chapter considered themselves in some sense indebted to Hemont and that he, in turn, felt a certain amount of righteous indignation. It would appear that he had been instrumental, and clearly took some pride in, the negotiations that had led to a significant advance in the development of the Saint-Omer maîtrise, one that indeed was of very recent vintage at the time of the dispute. Its outcome had been announced at an earlier chapter meeting on 31 December:

---

[1] For some particularly egregious examples of both at Rouen Cathedral, see Chanoine A. Bourdon and l'Abbé A. Collette, *Histoire de la maîtrise de Rouen* (Rouen, 1892; repr. Geneva, 1972), 107–10.

[2] This much is suggested by Hemont's dealings with the chapter concerning his housing. On 30 Sept. 1476 he acquired a house in the cloister (11. G. 354, fol. 206ʳ). By 12 April the following year, however, he was complaining to the chapter about the state of it and gave it back to them for renovation. Whatever was done clearly did not meet with his approval, since on 7 Dec. he received the house of the deceased canon Thierry de Vitry (11. G. 354, fol. 223ʳ).

On the last day of the aforesaid month [of December] with the dean and canons congregated in chapter, having received certain apostolic and legal letters thundered from above by the venerable man lord Johannes de Hemont, cantor, concerning the reservation of the suppressed fruits and revenues of the canonry and prebend that he was accustomed to receive, to be received on the capitular table by the said cantor, which shall support the use and maintenance of the master of song and the six choirboys — in measure and form as if he held the canonry in person, just as this and other things may be established in greater detail by apostolic letters and processes received from above. Which apostolic letters he, appearing in person in the said chapter in the presence of myself the notary, the said lords the dean and canons, reported, made known and published according to the form or measure of the assigned process, on which account the lords duly wishing to proceed held the said letter to have been communicated, drawn up and published and decreed themselves to have been duly informed.[1]

While it is undoubtedly safe to say that Hemont was compensated for the renunciation of his prebend,[2] it is equally clear that he had been closely involved in this development and felt a certain ownership in its outcome. The negotiations at the papal see leading to the suppression and reassignment of the income from Hemont's canonry was the work, however, of other hands. Like other musically related machinations during this period, these negotiations had been conducted and expedited by Nicolas Rembert, a former *contratenorista* of St. Peter's, Rome, a lawyer and notary in the papal curia, and also a canon of St. Omer from 1484 and, from 1494 until his death ten years later, dean.[3]

The suppression of Hemont's prebend was an event of considerable signifi-cance in the history of the maîtrise: unlike other offices and entitlements sup-pressed for its maintenance during the same period, this was a "grande prebende," a benefice carrying considerable financial weight. This much is clear from the

---

[1] My thanks to Leofranc Holford-Strevens for this translation.

[2] His involvement on 4 March 1491 in the triangular permutation of a chaplaincy was surely part of this arrangement, though other details of such putative compensation have apparently been lost (see II. G. 355, fol. 83ᵛ).

[3] A record on fol. 26ʳ of the fabric accounts for 1490/91 records how he has "Impetré obtenu et despechié en ladite court de Rome les bulles de la suppression de la prebende dichelle eglise." The Chapter Acts record Rembert's frequent leaves of absence in Rome, where his influence explains his efforts (albeit unsuccessful, as witnessed by a document dated Sept. 1489 found by Jeremy Noble) to obtain an expectative benefice in Saint-Omer for Josquin; see Jeremy Noble, "New Light on Josquin's Benefices," in *Josquin des Prez: Pro-ceedings of the International Josquin Festival-Conference*, ed. Edward E. Lowinsky and Bon-nie J. Blackburn (Oxford, 1976), 80–84. This may not have been his only attempt to secure a prebend in Saint-Omer for a singer with a long-standing connection with the papal choir: a record in the Saint-Omer Chapter Acts dated only a month before the Josquin document details his involvement in appointments to a Saint-Omer prebend held briefly by Gaspar van Weerbeke. It appears unlikely, though, that Rembert was himself professionally in-volved in singing after his period in the choir of St. Peter's; certainly there is no hint in his enormous executors' accounts that he had ever been involved in music at all.

subsequent fabric accounts, where the distributions and other incomes arising from the prebend, now directed to the maîtrise, are annually recorded. Clearly its importance was not lost on the dean and chapter, whose discussion, where its inaugural document is frequently referred to as the "bulle conservatoire," reveals a certain self-consciousness about the status and significance of the suppression and the application of its income.

As elsewhere, such suppressions provide a barometer for the growth in prestige and wealth of the maîtrise, which in turn reflects the changing patterns in the devotional and ritual, not to mention musical, practices it served. Expense lavished on the maîtrise stands in direct proportion to the expanding number and elaboration of the public and, particularly, private devotions to which it made such a central contribution. In Saint-Omer, as elsewhere, such developments accelerated exponentially during the fifteenth century, especially in the later part of the century and on into the next. In contrast to many other foundations, however, the unusual completeness of the surviving accounts at Saint-Omer allows us to trace that growth with unusual precision.

The Growth of the Maîtrise

THE 1490 suppression was not the only one in the history of choral provision at Saint-Omer, and neither was it the first. An entry in the Chapter Acts for 30 September 1476 reveals the intention of the chapter to suppress the first vicariate becoming vacant through death, subject to agreement by the pope (the collegiate foundation depended for its authority directly on the Holy See), and to use its income for the upkeep of the boys. That papal approval for this move was indeed forthcoming is evident from a bull issued by Sixtus IV in December of the same year suppressing "one of the twenty-eight perpetual *sine cura* vicariates," plus, upon its relinquishment by its present incumbent, a minor prebend.[1] Yet it is clear that by the early sixteenth century the existing incomes were proving insufficient for the maîtrise's ever expanding role in the church's observances and devotions:[2] a further bull from 1506 details the similar redirection of the income from the vicariate formerly associated with Hemont's suppressed prebend.

The most tangible reflection of the growing importance of the master and boys takes the form of the physical expansion of their dwelling. The 5,000 bricks, in addition to sundry other materials, bought for work conducted in 1439/40 clearly indicate a program of major rebuilding; similarly the payments for materials and for workmen who, in 1468/69 "extended the said house upward" ("ont Ralongié ledit maison par [le] hault") suggests the addition of a new floor, perhaps an upstairs schoolroom.[3]

[1] The text of this bull is preserved in an eighteenth-century copy in II. G. 53, which also contains contemporary copies of the other bulls of suppression under discussion.

[2] Inflation or reduction in the value of endowments could lead to similar developments; see for example Becker, "The Maîtrise," 187–88.

[3] As has been the arrangement at Notre-Dame of Paris since the fifteenth century; see

The fabric accounts offer a running commentary on the maintenance of the boys and of the house in the cloister which they shared with their master. Detailed payments relate the making and provision of their clothes, beds, and other necessities, while records of the purchase and repair of their books provide insight into their education and liturgical duties, information that closely complements other contemporary information including that provided by iconography.

Generally, notwithstanding the potential hazards threatened by an irascible master, life as a choirboy seems, by the standards of the time, to have been reasonably comfortable. Although, as elsewhere, the boys were billeted two to a bed,[1] they were well housed, well fed, and well placed, as we shall see below, to advance in the ecclesiastical hierarchy. Records suggest that some care was expended on their comfort; for example, a document records that at a meeting on 4 May 1474 the chapter ordered that a garden formerly used by a mason be given over to the house of the boys, and that a door be provided for their access.[2] And information, gleaned from the fabric accounts for 1446/7, concerning some windows they had broken reveals that not all their waking hours were devoted to the serious pursuits of study, liturgy, singing, and worship.

By the standards of today, of course, these were hard times, and the privilege of being a choirboy could not render one immune to the considerable vicissitudes of life in northern France in the later Middle Ages. On at least two occasions the provisions of the boys became seriously compromised by prevailing financial hardship, in one case to the point where, as we learn from the fabric accounts of 1459/60, the chapter declared itself unable to meet their financial requirements, levying half of the costs on their parents and friends.[3] The periodic outbreaks of plague, sadly, touched the choirboys as well, as in 1513/14 when pestilence claimed the life of the choirboy Jehennet Deubry and, for the sake of their health, the remaining boys were packed off for a month to the nearby town of Esques.[4]

In general, though, things only got better. With the advent of ever more lavish endowed observances, the boys, and the perceived value of their performances, seem increasingly to have been viewed as an emblem of prestige. This process is

ibid., 76; Craig Wright, *Music and Ceremony at Notre Dame of Paris, 500–1550* (Cambridge, 1989), 169. For these building accounts, see II. G. CF 31, fol. 5[r] and II. G. CF 59, fol. 50[r].

[1] This is clear from accounts that speak of their three beds (see, for example, the records for the making of their three beds in the fabric accounts for 1495/6): throughout the period in question their number remained fairly stable at six.

[2] II. G. 354, fol. 177[v]: "Messeigneurs . . . ont ordonné que le gardinet de le carpenterie que soloit obtenir le machon deloyle soit attribué a le maison des enffans de coeur et que on fache au mur dele maison desdits enffans ung huis pour entrer audit gardin."

[3] II. G. CF 50, fol. 13[r]: "Au maistre de chant pour le gouvernance des vi enfans de cuer pour chaqun xii l courant lan/ la fabricque ne peut porter Icelle despenses pour la petitte Revenue quelle a de present laquelle ne souffise pour entretenir lanchienne revenue de leglise Pourquoy la moittié dicelle despense est mise sur les tailles dicelle eglise Et les parens et amis desdits enfans payent lautre Et pour ce cy Neant." Similarly the report on the chapter meeting of 6 March 1478 bemoans their "raritatem victualium." (II. G. 354, fol. 215[r].)

[4] II. G. CF 100, fol. 29[v]: "pour cest an a cause de la peste et que lung desdits enfans en morut/ assavoir Jehennet deubry."

most vividly revealed in the expense and sheer bulk of their annual provisions: while expenses on the choirboys are buried among the "despenses extraordinaires" in the earliest surviving fabric accounts from the late fourteenth and early fifteenth centuries, by the early 1460s their financial outgoings had expanded to the point of meriting a section of their own. Yet the first such dedicated accounts, those of 1462/3, covering half a page and with expenditure totalling £8 9s. 3d., pales into insignificance beside those for, say, 1516/17, whose three and a half densely packed pages outline expenses weighing in at no less than £72 11s. 6d., most of it for material and clothing.[1] While on its own this is a rather crude measure of the developments of the intervening period, which of course experienced fluctuation, it is nevertheless indicative of the general shift visible across the intervening half century.

The fact of the matter is that, during this period and beyond, more and more money was spent on more and more elaborate garments and other provisions as the boys' liturgical and singing duties became ever more varied and, as a consequence, more remunerative. As a particularly vivid example, we might juxtapose two accounts, a little more than forty years apart, for the making of garments. In the accounts of 1472/3, a certain Kateline is paid 18s. "for the making of six aubes and six amices for the children made from the old linen of the said organs." Set against this hand-me-down approach the records entered into the accounts of 1515/16 look like the height of extravagance: here expenses on materials and garments in lambs' fur alone total almost £5.[2]

DUTIES OF THE CHOIRBOYS

SUCH a radical advance in fortune raises the question as to what, beyond the daily round of mass and office, the choirboys' duties might have entailed. How could such sums have been afforded, and what could the boys have been doing to merit their outlay?

It seems clear that, as elsewhere, their specific singing duties included the intonations and solo verses in certain chants including responds at Matins on high feast days, including Christmas.[3] Such duties emerge in the fabric accounts in payments for the copying of such items into books for the boys' use. A representative early example is the following record entered on folio 7 recto of the accounts for 1428/9: "Item: Paid for a book of song for the choirboys containing the incipits

---

[1] The total sum of £180 12s. 6d. for the latter account includes salaries of the two (successive) masters of the boys; in earlier documents such salaries appear elsewhere in the ledger. Money is reckoned in *livres*, *sous*, and *deniers*, analogous but not equal in value to English pounds, shillings, and pence. The monetary standard was *tournois* unless *parisis* is specified.

[2] 11. G. CF 63, fol. 9ᵛ and 11. G. CF 102, fol. 30ᵛ.

[3] Wright, *Music and Ceremony*, 181, describes the similar, highly challenging duties of boys at Notre-Dame of Paris.

and verses of the responsories for the entire year, 32s."[1] This was a difficult repertory requiring considerable vocal skill, and the high cost for copying the book also gives some indication of its extent. The periodic recurrence of such records might suggest a relatively high turnover of such books resulting from what was surely their heavy usage, though the variety in copying costs may also indicate a number of distinct volumes containing different parts of the repertory. At any rate, these later records add to the one already quoted some detail concerning the specifics of the boys' responsibilities:

1444/5, fol. 4ᵛ: Item: for writing the new book of responses and for entering the music; also that it is paid to master Ghuy the instructor priest as appears in the bill, £8 8s.[2]

1451/2, fol. 14ᵛ: To master Thomas le Becourt for having written a book in which are the lives of the saints and responses for the choirboys, £5 12s. To master Guillaume Durant for having entered the music for the responses of the said book, 29s.[3]

1494/5, fol. 31ᵛ: Item: for a quire of paper provided to the older Tingry for writing the lessons of the boys and the responses, because they have no book and need to have a new one made, for this 18d.

Fol. 32ᵛ: Item: for having remade the leather [straps/covers/cases?] that support/cover/house the trumpets of the choirboys on Christmas Day when they sing the Respond at Matins, 8s.[4]

In a less vocally challenging sphere, but again in reflection of wider practices, the boys were clearly also called upon to take part in liturgical drama, in which

---

[1] "Item paiee pour ung livret de cant pour les enfans de coeur contenant les komenchemens et verses des Respons de toute lannee xxxii s."

[2] "Item pour escripre le nouvel livre de respons et le avoir noté aussi quil est payet a sire ghuy le maistre prestre comme apparoit par cedule viii l viii s."

[3] "A Sire thomas le becourt pour avoir escript ung livre ou quel sont les legendes et respons pour les enfans de coeur v l xii s / A Sire guillaume durant pour avoir noté les Respons dudit livre xxiiii s." The boys would have been required to intone certain readings ("les lychons"), probably, as at Notre-Dame of Paris, at Matins on feasts of nine lessons or of higher rank (see Wright, *Music and Ceremony*, 180). "Legendes" refers to the extracts from the Martyrology that they would likewise have been expected to read during the office.

[4] "Item pour une main de pappier baillié au grant tingry pour escripre les lychons des enffans et les respons A cause quilz navoient point de livre et que lon en faisoit Ung nouvel pour ce xviii d"; fol. 32ᵛ: "Item pour avoir refait les cuirs qui portent les grelles Des enffans de coeur au jour de nowel quant ilz chantent le Re[spond] a matines viii s." I am most grateful to John Harper (private communication, Oct. 24, 2007) for his help concerning the likely meaning in this context of "grelles." He has pointed out to me the use of the French *gresle* for trumpet and suggested that this instance is likely a reference to the use of such trumpets as props carried by the boys during their singing of the *Gloria in excelsis* (the song of the angels) in the guise of angels as part of the first respond at Christmas matins. The "cuirs," he notes, could then logically refer either to covers for the instruments, straps used to carry them, or cases used to house them when not in use.

they assumed the roles of angels (at Christmas and Easter) and, it would seem, the three Marys (at Easter), the latter clearly as part of the *Visitatio sepulchri*.[1] Many generations of choirboys must have donned the wings made for these purposes, at least to judge from the repeated records concerning them, of which the following are typical:

> 1407/8 (rotulus): Item: to remake and repaint the wings and the caskets which serve for the choirboys on Easter Day at Matins for the resurrection, etc.[2]

> 1425/6, fol. 6ᵛ: Item: to Wauter Pinque, painter, for completely remaking and repainting the four wings serving for the choirboys at Matins on Christmas and Easter days and for remaking and regilding the three caskets of the three Marys which are used on Easter Day at Matins, for everything, 36s.[3]

> 1442/3, fol. 6ʳ: Item: to Colard de Santy, painter, for having properly repaired the wings of the angels belonging to the boys, etc. And also for cleaning the angels . . . [the entry goes on to detail other painting work].[4]

As we shall see below, furthermore, these dramatic roles were extended in 1535 by the terms of the will of the cantor and former choirboy Robert Fabri.

But as far as the fifteenth and early sixteenth centuries are concerned, there can be little doubt that, as was the case generally during this period, the increasing importance of the choirboys was closely entwined with the concurrent enhancement in the importance and scope of polyphony. The accounts reveal the instigation of ever-increasing outlets for their polyphonic skills, both in public and, especially, in privately endowed observances.

A particularly obvious and familiar case in point is their involvement in the foundation's regular Marian observances, most obviously the singing of the *Salve regina* in front of the much-venerated local statue of "Notre Dame des Miracles."

---

[1] This topic is clearly much too large and ramified to be addressed in detail here. Suffice it to say that boys had been used to impersonate angels from the earliest phase of Christmas drama in the eleventh century. Their assumption of the role of angels at the Easter Sepulcher seems to have begun rather later, but became fairly common by the thirteenth century. The range of their roles expanded towards the end of the Middle Ages: in the fifteenth century, a number of ecclesiastical foundations, as at St. Omer, cast boys as the three Marys, and, as in the example initiated by Robert Fabri and discussed below, as participants in the Annunciation drama of the so-called *Missa aurea*. For a useful summary of developments in the roles of boys in ecclesiastical drama, see Dunbar H. Ogden, *The Staging of Drama in the Medieval Church* (Newark, N.J., and London, 2002), 154.

[2] "Item pour refaire et repaindre les eles et les boystes qui servent a[u]s enfans de cheur le Jour de pasques a matines pour le Resurexion etc."

[3] "Item a wauter pinque paintre pour refaire et repaindre tout de nouvel les iiii elles que servent aux enfans du coeur aux matines du jour de noel et pasques et pour refaire et redorer les iii boistes des trois maryes qui servent au jour de pasques aux matines pour tout xxxvi s." The "iii boistes" are presumably the three jars carried by the Marys to the sepulcher containing oil to anoint Christ's dead body.

[4] "Item A Colard de Santy paintre pour avoir remis apoint les eles des angles appartenant aux enfans etc. Et aussy pour nettoyer les angles."

This icon, which survives, now resides in the church (now cathedral) of St. Omer itself, its surrounding walls and pillars covered with accounts of its eponymous miracles. Until the destruction in 1792 of the separate chapel of "Notre Dame sur le marchiet," the image was kept in this building, and the master, boys, and other clerics would process there each Saturday to perform the *Salve* service. Performance of the antiphon itself in polyphony is affirmed in the annual payments concerning the ritual, and this was clearly the purpose of "the book from which the choirboys sing the *Salve*" ("le livre ou les enfans de coeur chantent le salve") for the rebinding of which Thomas de Boucoud was paid in 1463/4.[1]

But the major change in the late fifteenth and early sixteenth centuries was the endowment of devotions on behalf of the souls of deceased canons, with or without polyphony, that frequently involved the boys. The scale of these frequently elaborate and expensive endowments at St. Omer is clear enough from the complexity and sheer bulk of its fabric accounts, in which, for each fiscal year, the more involved endowments are enumerated individually, each receiving a separate section. A comprehensive treatment of this very large topic is beyond the scope of this article; here it will suffice to offer two contrasting examples, one comparatively simple, the other unusually lavish.

At the more modest end of the spectrum stand such endowments as the following, according to which a certain Simon Acthe requested the performance by the choirboys in a chapel of his choice (which in practice was frequently the burial chapel) of an annual Requiem Mass for his soul. As was typical in such directives, the service was to be paid for by rents from property:

> 1458/9, fol. 1ʳ: From Simon Acthe for two measures of land lying in the said place of Lannoy of which the borders are declared as above, each year at the said term of St. Michael, 4*s*. 11*d*. in money of Paris, which the said deceased gave to the choirboys in order that they be obliged each year to say and sing (*dire et chanter a note*) the day after Trinity in the chapel of St. Mary of Egypt a Requiem Mass for his soul. And for this here the said 4*s*. 11*d*. in money of Paris which are worth 5*s*. 6*d*.[2]

While it is often difficult to tell whether such payments for singing "a note" were for chant or polyphony, no such doubt pertains to the following example, which unquestionably stands at the opposite end of the financial scale. To consider this takes us back to a major figure in the musical life of St. Omer whom we have encountered already: the canon and later dean Nicolas Rembert. In Rembert's case we have the advantage not only of the annual accounts for his endowments

---

[1] 11. G. CF 54, fol. 49ᵛ. For a complete survey of Boucoud's work in copying and rebinding the books of St. Omer, see Marc Gil and Ludovic Nys, *Saint-Omer gothique* (Valenciennes, 2004), 378–79.

[2] "De Simon Acthe pour deux mesures de terre gisant audit lieu de lannoy dont les aboutz sont declairies comme dessus chaqun an audit terme St michiel iiii s xi d parisis/ que ledit feu donna aux enfans de cuer moyennant quilz sont tenus chaqun an de faire dire et chanter a note lendemain de le trinité en le cappelle Ste Marie// degypte une messe de Requien [*sic*] pour lame du lui Et pour ce cy lesdits iiii s xi d par. qui valent v s vi d."

in the fabric, but also of his enormous and unusually detailed executors' accounts, which survive in the Saint-Omer archives as MS II. G. 484. Rembert's endowments merit a separate study; for now, though, it will suffice to note that he dedicated a very large proportion of his considerable estate to devotions for his soul, a number of them involving polyphony.

Rembert's most visible posthumous memorial was his personal side chapel, dedicated to the Conception of Our Lady, which survives in the south aisle of the church. This, as the accounts inform us, was the location for his endowed daily performance of the *Salve regina*. Rembert's *Salve* must have rivalled in lavishness even the Saturday *Salve* at Notre Dame sur le marchiet: as the payments for its performance (entered annually in the fabric accounts) reveal, its performing forces were no fewer than five male voices and the choirboys (presumably the full complement of six), plus an organist, the latter raising the possibility that the performance may have been accompanied, though organ introductions or *alternatim* performance are also possible. Clearly this was a foundation of great significance to its endower: Rembert provided for its execution the staggering sum of £1,000, more than one-eighth of his total estate at the time of his death. The records of its execution from the fabric accounts of 1509/10 can serve as well as any:

> Fol. 24ᵛ: To master Jehan Cambelin, master of the choirboys for this year, for having sung, with the said boys, the said *Salve* every day during the time of this accounts, £9.
>
> Item: to masters Pierre Somelart, G. Grisel, Jo[hannes] Tingry and master Jan de Monte, vicars, for having helped in singing the said *Salve* every day of the year of this accounts, to each 60s., [which] here is £12.
>
> Fol. 25ʳ: To master Josse Narhel who has played the organs at the said *Salve* during the time of this accounts, £6.[1]

Not content solely with magnificent and sonorous devotions at side chapels, however, Rembert also donated £1,000 to what, as was clearly the case with the *Salve*, must have been a polyphonic performance at the daily high Mass: thus, as we learn from his executors' accounts, the choir was instructed to perform "before the high altar each day their *O salutaris hostia* or *O sacrum convivium*, which may be performed before or as soon as possible after the Pater noster [or] before the Agnus Dei if my lords do not wish to permit it here."[2]

Although Rembert's foundations were unusually lavish, by the time of his death in 1504 they joined a considerable and growing roster of privately endowed masses and other devotions, all of them augmenting the visibility and cachet

---

[1] "A Sire Jehan Cambelin maistre des enffans de coeur pour cest an pour avoir aueuc lesdits enffans chanté ledit salve tous les jours durant le temps de ce compte ix lbz"; "Item a Sires pierres Somelart g grisel Jo. tingry et maistre Jan de monte vicaires pour avoir aidiet a chanter ledit Salve tous les jours lan de che compte a chaqun lx s est Icy xii lbz"; "A Sire Josse Narhel le quel a joué des orgues audit salve durant le temps de che compte vi lbz."

[2] II. G. 484, fol. 4ᵛ. I discuss the context and particular relevance of the timing and location of this foundation in a forthcoming study.

of the boys as well as, of course, the receipts of the fabric. Foundations such as Rembert's give the true measure of the economic value of the maîtrise during this period: if fear of purgatory and desire for its speedy transition provided the economic engine for the spread of such devotions generally and of polyphony in particular, then a principal component in the "fuel" for that engine was supplied by the boys. Underpinned by such biblical commonplaces as "Out of the mouth of infants and of sucklings thou hast perfected praise," and "Suffer the little children, and forbid them not to come to me, for theirs is the kingdom of heaven," the image fostered by their singing was one of heavenly innocence on earth and its attendant promise of future salvation.[1] Such was the characterization that doubtless informed the 1425 document in which Philip the Good founded his Burgundian court maîtrise for "four little children, innocent and of good behavior, for the service of the chapel" ("quatre petis enfans innocens, de bonnes mœurs, pour le service de la chappelle").[2] To this emphasis on innocence, however, may be added a further dimension of their role: as suggested by their casting as angels in the church's liturgical dramas, they were earthly metaphors for the choirs of cherubim whose singing they fore-echoed and whose hearing the endowers of such foundations aimed to expedite.[3] All the more reason, then, for their training to be sufficiently streamlined and strict as to produce the maximum degree of polish, thereby adumbrating the sounds of their heavenly counterparts to the greatest possible extent. From this perspective, furthermore, we begin to perceive the degree to which, by means of foundations with polyphony, the prestige of the contribution of choirboys was itself instrumental in driving the enormous contemporary expansion of polyphony generally.

Upward Mobility

I F the skills of the boys were becoming increasingly desirable for the purgatorial advancement of departed souls, an entering chorister, for his part, became part of a powerful support network with considerable potential advantages for his future. One of the most signal of these — especially, perhaps, from our perspective of soaring college fees — was the benefit offered in terms of education. That benefit did not cease on the breaking of the voice: on the contrary, the St. Omer archives, like those of other large ecclesiastical foundations, bear repeated and diverse witness to the provision of funds for university study, usually at Paris or Louvain, but also as far away as Cologne.

---

[1] "Ex ore infantium et lactantium perfecisti laudem" (Psalm 8:3; quoted by Christ in Matthew 21:16); "Iesus vero ait eis sinite parvulos et nolite eos prohibere ad me venire talium est enim regnum caelorum" (Matthew 19:14). For these latter points and the biblical references, see Wright, *Music and Ceremony*, 165, and Becker, "The Maîtrise," 64.

[2] Jeanne Marix, *Histoire de la musique et des musiciens de la cour de Bourgogne sous le règne de Philippe le Bon* (Strasbourg, 1939; repr. Baden-Baden, 1974), 162. My thanks to Philip Weller for reminding me of this.

[3] See Becker, "The Maîtrise," 64.

But the maîtrise was also the first step on a path of upward ecclesiastical mobility, one that, as we shall see below, could lead to a profitable and sometimes
eminent career. For some, that mobility was instigated by circumstances of birth:
there is no question but that admittance as a choirboy, here as elsewhere, was
aided enormously by family circumstance. Thus in October 1493, for example,
Nicolas Rembert secured a place as one of the choirboys for a certain Johannes
Rembert, perhaps a nephew. But one clearly did not need to be related to a major
canon in order to reap benefits of this nature: the four named choirboys "who
were tonsured" ("lesquelz furent tonsuré") according to an entry on folio 28 verso
of the fabric accounts for 1510/11 included one Sebastien Doudeville, presumably
a relative of the Robert Doudeville who, as recorded in the accounts for 1507/8,
had recently been paid for copying two new polyphonic masses.[1]

As elsewhere, at St. Omer there seems to have been a system of finding vicariates for boys when their voices broke. Thus we learn that when Julian de Berghes
celebrated his first Mass in July 1495, he was provided with bread and wine free
of charge because he was a former choirboy, "as is the custom in such cases."[2]
A record of 21 November 1458 offers a snapshot of the chain of promotion that
a diligent choirboy might expect to enter: on that day a vicariate vacant through
the death of Johannes Robert was given to Johannes Caignart; in turn, Caignart's
"scotterius" passed to Petrus Marcel, while the *parva vicaria* that Petrus had held
went to Psalmonus de Caille, who had been a choirboy.[3] Certain positions were
clearly reserved for former choirboys. On 2 August 1492, a scotterius vacated by
the death of the former choirboy Pierre Godin went to the similarly trained Julien
de Berghes, "provided that the cleric in his place in the capella will be Philippe du
Hecq, one of the choirboys."[4] This pattern of advancement reveals, in addition to
their intrinsic eschatological significance (discussed above), another central function of the choirboys: their use and training guaranteed an abundance of adults
with the necessary skills and knowledge to serve as the adult male voices — not to
mention the composers — of the future, and furthermore, to become candidates
for higher clerical office generally.[5]

---

[1] II. G. CF 94, fol. 37ʳ.

[2] II. G. 355, fol. 111ʳ.

[3] II. G. 353, fol. 45ʳ. While the term "scotterius" or "escotier" clearly denotes someone
fulfilling minor ecclesiastical duties, I have not been able to ascertain their precise nature. It
may be that this rank was peculiar to St. Omer.

[4] II. G. 355, fol. 95ᵛ.

[5] See Wright, *Music and Ceremony*, 165, and Becker, "The Maîtrise," 65. Becker's
eloquent encapsulation of this function is worth quoting in full: "The church also saw in
the young singers, lectors and acolytes the promise of future servants who would fill the
positions of vicars, canons, priests, deacons — and even cardinals and popes. What better
preparation could be conceived for a candidate for the priesthood than the benefit of having
sung in the choir daily for eight to ten years? During this period he had become initiated
to the rigor of the cloistral life, he had celebrated the daily offices, he had sung for the brilliant festivals and the most solemn rites. It was only a step from the choir to the altar, and,
without apology, the maîtrise was an instrument for the recruitment of clerical leaders for
succeeding generations."

Unfortunately, Du Hecq, who died in the year 1505/6, did not live long enough to capitalize fully on the potential inherent in his advancement. No such misfortune halted the progress, however, of one of his chorister predecessors, a certain Robert Fabri or Le Fevre. Fabri's life provides a textbook case of a successful ecclesiastical career beginning in the maîtrise. On 17 January 1463 a vicariate vacated by the death of its prior incumbent was given to "Roberto Fabri puero chori." That Fabri's musical capabilities were highly regarded is clear from a record in the executors' accounts of Toussaint de le Ruelle, former papal singer and long-time member of the Burgundian court chapel, who held a canonry at Saint-Omer from 1425 until his death in 1470. Among the items given by Toussaint according to the terms of his will are two music books, lent to Fabri while the testator was alive and now bequeathed to him.[1] By 28 February 1474 he had made the logical progression for a gifted former choirboy when the cantor presented "Robert le Fevre, priest, vicar" ("Robertum le fevre presbiterum vicarium") "for the governance of the singing school" ("ad regimen scolarum cantus").[2] And in more than one case in the same year Fabri is named as one of the sponsors in putting forward candidates for vacant offices. He was clearly also a scribe of music: the fabric accounts of 1490/91 include a payment to him "pour avoir notte" a Gospel book.[3] By 1491/2 he is still listed, in a payment for saying daily Masses for the soul of the deceased canon Baugois le Beghin, as "prestre et vicaire."

But his advance was far from over: by 7 June 1504 he is referred to as cantor and canon of St. Omer, a position he was to retain until his death in 1535, at what must have been for the time the uncommonly advanced age of around 85. Fabri's influence on Saint-Omer did not, moreover, end with his death: at his demise he endowed the performance of a *Missa aurea*, the dramatic representation of the Annunciation staged, as elsewhere, as part of Mass on the Ember Wednesday after the third Sunday in Advent.[4] As in other manifestations of this tradition,

[1] It is possible that the two were linked by familial or at least pseudo-familial ties: one of the other gifts bequeathed in Toussaint's will was the sum of £6, "a clay le fevre pour toussains le fevre son filz et filleul dudit feu." (II. G. 476, no. 11, fol. 24ᵛ) While Fabri / Le Fevre was of course one of the commonest French surnames, the combination of its presence here and the frequency of references to Robert Le Fevre in the same accounts is suggestive.

[2] Such progression of a talented boy via minor clerical positions to ultimate assumption of the role of master of the boys seems to have been commonplace. For a comparative case, see the career of Jacques Barre at Notre Dame of Paris, who, apparently like Fabri, seems to have risen to that position in his twenties (see Wright, *Music and Ceremony*, 173). For the advancement of various former choirboys to the rank of master of the boys at the Cathedral of Rouen, see Bourdon and Collette, *Histoire de la maîtrise de Rouen*, 106–12.

[3] II. G. CF 78, fol. 22ᵛ. Presumably work on books was what led to his possession, as noted in his executors' accounts, of "Une presse a lier livres" (II. G. 482, no. 7, fol. 6ᵛ).

[4] Edition in Karl Young, *The Drama of the Medieval Church*, 2 vols. (Oxford, 1933) 2:482–83, after L. Deschamps de Pas, in *Mémoires de la Société des Antiquaires de la Morinie* 20 (1886–7), 209–10. Young likewise reprints from Deschamps de Pas the inventory (dated 1557) of items stored in a leather coffer that were used in the performance, a number of which are "armoiez des armes dudit Sʳ Fabri." The inventory survives in the archives as MS II. G. 1557. Fabri's endowment comes rather late in the history of this popular Mass-*cum*-drama: Anne Walters Robertson mentions the tradition in a number of locations, including,

and surely in acute reminiscence of his own experience as a boy in the church, boys are specified in the roles of the archangel Gabriel ("dressed as an angel as one does on the day of the Resurrection"; "acoustré en angele comme on faict le jour de la resurrection") and the Virgin ("dressed as a maiden"; "accoustré [sic] comme une pucelle"). They are to be instructed by the master "to do this and to sing with fine tone and softly" ("a ce faire et chanter a bon ton et a loisir") and "thoroughly devoutly" ("bien dévotement"), and are required, in a remarkably satisfying turn of the wheel, to "pray to God for the soul of the said founder" ("prier Dieu pour lame dudict fondateur"), their eminent choirboy predecessor.[1]

To achieve the status of cantor, one of the highest offices of the church, was no mean feat, and stands as eloquent testimony to the advancement possible for a talented choirboy. But the success of an individual can of course be measured in ways other than according to advancement in his parent institution, and my final examples concern two instances in which the talent of choirboys trained at St. Omer was sufficient to gain them attention far beyond the city walls.

A series of letters to the collegiate church from the early sixteenth century testifies to its dealings with Charles v and his regent in the Netherlands, his sister Mary of Hungary. Among these are, by some miracle of survival, three letters (presented in full in the Appendix below) that address in a very direct fashion issues involving choirboys. Two letters from 1534 recount what, from the point of view of musical advancement, must surely count as an epic missed opportunity.[2] On 29 March of that year Mary of Hungary, still fairly new in her post as Regent of the Netherlands and in the process of building the chapel choir for which she would become renowned,[3] wrote to the chapter of St. Omer concerning a certain Michelet de Cobrize, choirboy. The letter relates how she has heard of this boy and commands that he be sent back "with this messenger" so that she can hear him sing. Sadly, however, Michelet failed to make the grade: less than a month later, as we learn from a letter returned with the boy himself, he was packed off back to Saint-Omer. The queen relates how, "although we have found him to be well versed in his music, because he is a little old/tall [grand] and because he could not well adapt himself to what we desire for the song of our chapel, we have not retained the child." She goes on to request that this decision not stand against Michelet at his home church, and that he will be granted his regular income as if he had not been summoned to Brussels.

in her earliest citation, performances in nearby Tournai as early as 1231 (see her "Remembering the Annunciation in Medieval Polyphony," *Speculum* 70 (1995), 284–86). See also the discussion of the *Missa aurea* and its performance in various churches of Bruges in Reinhard Srohm, *Music in Medieval Bruges*, 2nd ed. (Oxford, 1990), 46, 52–53, and 158.

[1] See Young, *The Drama of the Medieval Church*, 2:482–83.

[2] Since the year in Brussels changed at Easter, the date "ce xxixᵉ de mars anno xxxiii avant pasques" would mean our 1534, not 1533. My thanks to Leofranc Holford-Strevens for this detail.

[3] On Mary's noted love for music and particularly her cultivation of the Netherlands court chapel, see Glenda G. Thompson, "Music in the Court Records of Mary of Hungary," *Tijdschrift van de Vereniging voor Nederlandse Muziekgeschiedenis* 34/2 (1984), 132–73.

It seems highly likely that such occurrences were commonplace, and that Mary, who is known to have supported choirboys in schools throughout the Low Countries,[1] kept a keen eye out for new young talent and auditioned choirboys in this fashion on a regular basis. It may be that, as elsewhere, choirboys in her court chapel were normally admitted at a certain age, an age that Cobrize, being "un peu grand," may have exceeded.[2] Equally, the considerable feat, which was surely demanded, of memorizing new chants and new liturgical practices,[3] and the virtuosity — particularly in tackling such difficult genres of chant as that of the Matins responds discussed above — demanded for their performance must have rendered such a trial situation severely challenging to a young child. Equally, though, this level of interest from one of the most powerful political figures in Europe gives some measure of the cachet — in terms not just of musical but also of visual devotional and indeed political display — that attached to the skill of a gifted choirboy during this period.[4]

The potential rewards for choirboy success in such a forum as this could be considerable, as is amply revealed by my final example. On 16 June 1516, the chapter was sent a demand from Brussels from the sixteen-year-old Charles v on behalf of a certain "Ernoulet du Brœuck." This figure, clearly the composer Arnold von Bruck, and at that time a "clerk of our private chapel," had formerly, the letter relates, been a choirboy at St. Omer, which was apparently his home town.[5] On account of this familial background, Charles, desiring "his apt promotion and advancement in the holy church," now required that the chapter grant him "the first

---

[1] Ibid., 135.

[2] See for instance the stipulation of the Chapter of Lyon Cathedral that "the habit of the church would not be given to boys more than eight years of age or to those who could not read well." Jean Marie H. Forest, *L'École cathédrale de Lyon* (Paris, 1885), quoted in Becker, "The Maîtrise," 139.

[3] On the feats of memory demanded of choirboys at Notre Dame of Paris, see Wright, *Music and Ceremony*, 174–76.

[4] The frequent documentation of the impressment of choirboys into royal chapels reveals that Mary's interest, if rather more nurturing than what seems to have been the norm, was far from unusual among crowned heads. Examples include the story of a choirboy of Chartres who so impressed Anne of Brittany on a visit there in 1510 that she asked to take him with her, in return providing the cathedral with an inscribed bell, and the rather more brutal abduction, in 1517, of two choirboys of Rouen Cathedral who had impressed Francis I. (See M. L'Abbé Clerval, *L'Ancienne Maîtrise de Notre-Dame de Chartres* (Chartres, 1899), 107, and Bourdon and Collette, *Histoire de la maîtrise de Rouen*, 50–51.)

[5] The statement of Othmar Wessely that von Bruck had been a choirboy in Charles's own chapel may therefore need correction; see "Bruck, Arnold von," *Grove Music Online* ed. L. Macy (http://www.grovemusic.com; accessed Aug. 20, 2007). For an alternative possibility, however, see below. It seems clear from the archives that Arnold/Ernoult came from a family of long local tradition. The fabric accounts of 1431/2 record the appointment to an escoterie of a "maistre brixe du broeuc" (ii. G. CF 26, fol. 2ᵛ). The numerous payments in the second decade of the sixteenth century to a "pierre du broecq drapier" (possibly the boy's father) for clothing for the choirboys, suggests that he may have come from a family of tailors. It is tempting to speculate that Pierre, who in the year 1516/7 was paid for the making of "une Robe et chaperon . . . pour Jennes hanon a son presentement du coeur," may have done the same, at his own presentation, for little Ernoulet (ii. G. CF 103, fol. 27ʳ).

vicariate that as from now will become vacant in your said church at your collation and disposition." Charles went on to request that the chapter fulfill his wish

> without hesitating to do this under the pretext that he departed from the same your church without your seal or licence of leave, the which, as we understand, he did more through youth than out of any malice, and, moreover, at the urgent pressing and request of certain of our special servants, and to enter into our service.

The latter suggests that von Bruck had earlier, perhaps while still a choirboy, been impressed into Charles's own choir. At any rate his service under Charles clearly provided a substantial early boost to his future career, and it must have been this early association with a Habsburg chapel that allowed him ultimately to assume his major post at the court of Charles's brother Ferdinand I. This case is reminiscent of the similar care taken by Pope Leo X on behalf of Jean Cunsel, or Conseil, one of the various French choirboys he had acquired from Louis XII. In a case exactly analogous to that of von Bruck, Leo wrote in 1517 to Francis I to request a canonry for Cunsel in the Sainte-Chapelle of Paris, the foundation in which the boy had received his training.[1] Such instances suggest that a certain obligation was felt to be implicit in the impressment of choirboys, and that such efforts to safeguard their future progress in the institutions from which they hailed may have been more commonplace than the known documentation suggests.

Impressment of the better choirboys into more eminent and wealthy chapels was of course a hazard for ecclesiastical foundations across fifteenth- and early sixteenth-century Europe, especially those in Northern France and the Low Countries, where the effectiveness of the maîtrise training was widely acknowledged and admired.[2] In another sense, though, it was an acknowledgment of success: that boys from St. Omer could attract the attention of the royal and imperial chapels was a clear sign of the efficacy of its training. If St. Omer was no Cambrai Cathedral or St. Donatian, Bruges, the success of its choirboys nonetheless proves, as do other aspects of its musical establishment, its high professional standing and the possibility for its choirboys, at least insofar as they could avoid the iron hand of the choirmaster, of a bright future.

---

[1] See André Pirro, "Leo X and Music," *The Musical Quarterly* 21 (1935), 8.

[2] For a discussion of the effect of this practice in Liège and elsewhere, see for example Antoine Auda, *La Musique et les musiciens de l'ancien pays de Liège* (Brussels, Paris, and Liège, 1930), 49–50.

Appendix:
DOCUMENTS CONCERNING CHOIRBOYS AND THE COURT
CHAPELS OF CHARLES V AND MARY OF HUNGARY

II. G. 112

1.) Marie par la grace de dieu royne douairiere dhongrie et de bohesme Regente et gouvernante

Venerables treschiers et bien ames Pource quentendons/ quaves ung enffant de cueur appelle michielet de cobrize/ que desirons oyr chanter/ Nous vous Requerons le nous envoyer avec ce porteur/ Et vous nous feres plesir A tant venerables tres chiers et bien amez nostre seigneur soit garde de vous. De Bruxelles ce xxixᵉ de mars anno xxxiii avant pasques

Marie

2.) Marie par la grace [de] dieu royne douairie[re] de hongrye de bohesme Regente et gouvernante

Venerables tres chiers et bien aimes/ Nous vous aiyons escript nous envoyer michelet de cobrize enffant de cueur de v[ost]re esglise porteur de cestes pour loyr chanter/ Ce quaves fait dont vous scavons bon grez et combien que layons trouve bien saichant sa musicque/ neantmoings pour ce quil est ung peu grand et quil ne se pourroit bonnement plyer selon que desirons pour le chant de n[ost]re chapelle ne lavons Retenu enffant dicelle dont vous avons bien voulu adverter/ Et Requerir que sa venue icy ne luy soit aucunement preiudiciable avis que nonobstant Icelle Il ait son jour de provision comme sil ne eust este par nous mande Et vous nous feres plesir.

A tant venerables tres chiers Et bien amez n[ost]re seigneur soit garde de vous De bruxelles ce xiiiᵉ davril

Marie

Mary by the grace of God Queen dowager of Hungary and Bohemia, Regent and Governor

Venerable, dear, and well-beloved: Insofar that it has come to our attention that you have a choirboy called Michielet de Cobrize, whom we desire to hear sing, we require that you send him with this messenger, and you will give us pleasure. To [our] so venerable, dear, and well-beloved, may Our Lord be your protector. From Brussels this 29 March in the year [15]33 before Easter [1534 modern style]

Mary

Mary by the grace of God Queen dowager of Hungary and Bohemia, Regent and Governor

Venerable, dear, and well-beloved: We have written to you to send us Michelet de Cobrize, choirboy of your church [and] bearer of this [letter] to hear him sing. The which you have done and of which we know you to be well consenting. And although we have found him to be well versed in his music, nevertheless because he is a little old/tall and because he could not well adapt himself to what we desire for the song of our chapel, we have not retained the child, whom we have wished to return to you. And we require that his coming here will not in any way count as a prejudicial judgment towards him, [and] that notwithstanding the same he may have his provision as if he had not been summoned by us. And you will give us pleasure.

To [our] so venerable, dear, and well-beloved, may Our Lord be your protector. From Brussels this 13 April.

Mary

II. G. 110

De par le Roy

Venerables Chiers et bien amez Pour ce
que avons en singuliere Recommandacion
n[ost]re bien ame ernoulet du broeucq
a present clerc de n[ost]re chappelle dome-
stique et lequel a parcidevant este enfant de
cueur en v[ost]re eglise/ et desirons son bien
promocion et avancement en sainte eglise/
Nous vous Requerons bien affectueusment
et acertes que en faveur de nous et a ceste
n[ost]re requeste vous luy vueillez liberale-
ment donner et accorder la premiere vicairie que derienavant [dorenavant] vaquera
en v[ost]re dit egliese a v[ost]re collacion et
disposicion par quelque moyen que ce soit
et en contemplacion de nous le preferer
a ce avant tous autres sans differer de ce
faire soubz umbre quil se seroit parti dicelle v[ost]re eglise sans v[ost]re sceu con-
gie ou licen[ce] Ce que comme entendons
il fist plus par jonesse que sans aucun
malice et aussi a linstante poursuyte et Requeste daucuns nos esp[ec]eaulx serviteurs
et pour venir en n[ost]re service/ Parquoy
vous Requerons y avoir Regart et nous accorder n[ost]re dit Requeste Et vous nous
ferez singulier honneur service et plaisir
Ce scet dieu qui venerables Chiers et bien
amez vous ait en sa sainte garde Escripts en
n[ost]re ville de bruxelles le xviiie jour de
juing anno xvc xvi

Charles

From the King

Venerable, dear and well-beloved: Insofar that we have in singular esteem our
well-beloved Ernoulet du Brœucq, pres-
ently clerk of our private chapel and who
heretofore was a choirboy in your church,
and we desire his apt promotion and advancement in the holy church, we require
that, with apt affection and in good ear-
nest, you, in good will to us and to this
our request may wish freely to give and
accord to him the first vicariate that as
from now will become vacant in your said
church at your collation and disposition by
whatever means that this may be, and in
deep consideration of us to prefer him for
this before all others, without hesitating to
do this under the pretext that he departed
from the same your church without your
seal or licence of leave, the which, as we
understand, he did more through youth
than out of any malice, and, moreover, at
the urgent pressing and request of certain
of our special servants, and to enter into
our service. Wherefore we require you to
take this into account and accord us our
said request. And you will render us singular honor, service and pleasure. This God
knows; may he hold you, venerable, dear,
and well-beloved, in his holy protection.
Written from our city of Brussels the 18th
day of June, in the year 1516.

Charles

7

CHOIRBOYS IN CAMBRAI IN THE FIFTEENTH CENTURY

Alejandro Enrique Planchart

IN the late fourteenth and fifteenth centuries, the city of Cambrai was one of the most important musical centers in what is now northern France and Belgium. The city was the political and religious hub of an immense diocese that extended east as far as Brussels and Antwerp, and its cathedral was regarded as one of the architectural wonders of the entire region. The cathedral was richly endowed, supporting fifty prebendary canons and a large number of chaplains,[1] but there were also two important collegiate churches in the city with an active musical life: the church of Ste. Croix, which was technically a dependent of the cathedral boasting ten canons and a number of chaplains, and the parish church of St. Géry, which was built on a hill just outside the walls and supported some thirty canons and a small number of chaplains. All three of these churches maintained an active *maîtrise*, recruiting and training choirboys. The documentation from all three churches survives, though with relatively large lacunae, and in all three cases there is enough information to permit the drawing of a provisional picture of the education and the careers of the choirboys in each of these establishments.

At the outset it may be useful to describe the nature of the primary sources as they survive. The richest material with regard to information about choirboys comes from three areas within the cathedral's primary sources. First, there are the chapter acts from 1364 to 1503, which survive in fifteen volumes.[2] These refer to the hiring and dismissal of the *magistri puerorum* and grammar teachers and occasionally to the help offered to a choirboy or his family. From these occasional

---

[1] The fundamental studies of the cathedral remain André le Glay, *Recherches sur l'église métropolitaine de Cambrai* (Paris, 1825), and Jules Houdoy, *Histoire artistique de la cathédrale de Cambrai, ancienne église métropolitaine Notre-Dame* (Paris, 1880).

[2] Cambrai, Médiathèque municipale (henceforth CBM), MSS 1052 [old register A], 1053 [unsigned], 1054–56 [B–E], 1057 [E]; Lille, Archives Départementales du Nord (henceforth LAN), 4G 1090 [I]; CBM 158–60 [K–M], and 1061–65 [O–S]. Old registers F (1428–35), H (1439–42), and N (1468–76) are lost, while the unsigned register CBM 1053 covers the same period as register B (CBM 1054, 1388–95) but with no duplication of the material.

entries, we can learn the name of a few of the choirboys who, by and large, remain anonymous in most other accounts. A particularly important entry, however, is a record of the ordinances for the governance of the choristers that is addressed to the *magister puerorum* and dated 22 September 1458.[1] These rules are in turn reflected and amplified in a series of ordinances drawn up in 1739 and 1754,[2] apparently codifying practices dating back several centuries.

The second important group of sources comprises the accounts of the office of the *petits vicaires*. These men, together with the choirboys, formed the basic singing ensemble of the cathedral. The accounts survive from 1361 to 1498, though with enormous lacunae.[3] They transmit summaries, week by week, of the number of vicars and choirboys present at services, but seldom give names.[4] In the case of the *petits vicaires*, a list of their names is given twice a year: once before All Saints, when they received cloth for their robes, and once before Lent, when they received money to buy herring. Occasionally a present to a minor cleric or to a choirboy is recorded and the recipient's name is given.

The third group of sources is the accounts of the office of the *aumosne*. This office covered half of all the expenses of the *petits vicaires* and the choirboys, among other things, so that in many ways it complements the information of the surviving registers of the *petits vicaires* and allows us to fill many of the large lacunae in the other series.[5] The accounts of the *aumosne* record presents and graces granted to numerous people, including the *petits vicaires*, the choirboys, and the families of the choirboys, and many of these relate to their travel to and from Cambrai and the often fatal illnesses that struck their ranks with some frequency. These accounts offer the largest number of names for the choirboys in the cathedral, but again, the names that have been recorded represent a small fraction of the dozens of choirboys who went through the *maîtrise* in a given year.

After their voices broke, a number of choirboys were sent to schools with a gift from the chapter, but others became *petits vicaires* and remained part of the clergy of the cathedral. After 1439, the accounts for the cathedral's wine and bread record the number of vicars present at the services, including their names, week by week. These accounts survive complete from 1439 to 1500,[6] and although the *petits vicaires* are named just with their first name or with a sobriquet, a detailed collation of these names with those recorded in three sources — the acts, the lists

[1] CBM 1060, fol. 25ᵛ.

[2] LAN 4G 94, piece 1372.

[3] The modern shelf signatures are LAN 4G 6787–91. Accounts survive for the following years: 1361/2, 1386/7, 1393/4, 1399/1400, 1409/10, 1411/12, 1453/4, 1458–60, 1462–65, 1466–70, 1474/5, 1483/4, 1485–88, 1491–96, 1497/8.

[4] An astonishing exception is the note in the accounts of 1409/10, LAN 4G 6789 (1409/10), fol. 4ʳ, of the reception of Willemet [Du Fay] in the tenth week of the fiscal year.

[5] The modern shelf number of the *aumosne* registers for the fifteenth century is LAN 4G 7757–72, covering the years 1378–1500 with some lacunae. Registers survive for 1378/9, 1383/4, 1385/6, 1387/8, 1391–94, 1395–1402, 1403–6, 1407–36, 1438–43, 1444–64, 1465–67, 1468–88, 1490–95, 1496–1500.

[6] LAN 4G 7439–73; the register for 1450/51 is missing.

of members in the grand community of chaplains, and references to Cambrai clerics in the registers of supplications in the Vatican Archives — allows the recovery of their full names and often of the span of their clerical career.

The situation for St. Géry and Ste. Croix is slightly different, and their archives are not as rich in information concerning the singing-men or the choirboys as those of the cathedral. Neither of these churches had a series of accounts comparable to either the accounts of the *petits vicaires* or the accounts of the *aumosne* in the cathedral, although the chapter acts, particularly those of Ste. Croix, record much of the same kind of information found in the chapter acts of the cathedral. The principal sources for St. Géry that record information about choirboys are the chapter acts, which survive from 1381 to 1503. Although the registers are often a disorganized mixture of financial accounts, lists of collations, and actual notes from the chapter deliberations,[1] there are also the accounts of the *bourse*, which survive in relatively complete form for 1410–18 and for 1446–1503,[2] and the accounts of the community of chaplains, which survive for intermittent spans throughout the century.[3] The sort of information given in the acts is similar to what we find for the cathedral, and the kind of information found in the registers of the *aumosne* in the cathedral usually appears in the section of the *expensae foraneae* in the accounts of the *bourse*. St. Géry had a group of singing-men similar to the *petits vicaires* of the cathedral; they were referred to as *socii chori*, and their number is often listed in the accounts of the *bourse* and those of the chaplains, but their names are virtually never given.

The principal sources for Ste. Croix are the chapter acts from 1406 to 1506[4] and the accounts of the fabric, which survive essentially uninterrupted from 1418 to 1500.[5] Again, the acts of Ste. Croix give the same kind of information found in those of the cathedral, while the accounts of the fabric provide a summary of the annual expenses for the *petits vicaires* and choirboys similar to the accounts of the *petits vicaires* in the cathedral.

In all, the information on the singing-men and the choirboys in St. Géry and Ste. Croix is considerably more scattered and fragmentary than what we have for the cathedral. Accordingly, this essay will concentrate on the situation in the cathedral, with occasional references to the situation at St. Géry and Ste. Croix whenever possible.

By the beginning of the fifteenth century, the cathedral and the two main collegiate churches at Cambrai had well-established choir schools. The staff of the cathedral's choir school consisted of a *magister puerorum* (master of the boys), essentially the music teacher and the head of the school; possibly a master of grammar, who taught the children Latin and possibly some basic arithmetic;

---

[1] LAN 7G 572–79.

[2] LAN 7G 2411–17.

[3] LAN 7G 2908–70; the records survive for 1402/3, 1405–08, 1409–11, 1412/13, 1414–20, 1421–27, 1428–31, 1432–38, 1439–44, 1456–61, 1462–71, 1472–75, 1478–83, 1487/8, and 1489–97.

[4] LAN 6G 177–8, old registers F and G.

[5] LAN 6G 702–9.

a *dominus*, probably one of the chaplains, who instructed the children in catechism once a week; and a female servant, who cleaned the children's house and probably prepared their meals. In the accounts, the choirboys' house is called *la maison des enfants d'autel*, indicating that it also housed children who were in the service of the cathedral, but who were not singers. The house was also the residence of the *magister puerorum* and was thus considered to be the *maîtrise* of the cathedral.

In his pioneering study of the canons of the cathedral, Damien Lourme notes that Cambrai had what he terms *petites écoles* and *grandes écoles*, and that it even had what one could call a proto-*studium*, in which canons with advanced degrees in theology or law and a license to teach gave lectures to their fellow canons and other clergy at their houses. The cathedral provided those who attended lectures with a certificate of completion.[1] It may be that the grammar school was institutionally and physically separate from the *maîtrise* and thus open to students other than the cathedral's choirboys. The grammar school also may have included a curriculum beyond a primary education, a fact that can be deduced from a number of references in the chapter acts and other accounts throughout the fifteenth century to men listed not as *magister puerorum*, but as *rector scholarum, rector scholarum grammaticalium, rector magnarum scholarum*, or else *magister scholarum* — all references that may indicate the wider function of the school. Additional references are *magister domus bonorum puerorum* or *maistre des bons enfans*, indicating in this case a building, the *domus bonorum puerorum*, which was apparently the site of the school and was different from the house where the choirboys lived. The choirboys' house was maintained by the offices of the *aumosne* and the assize and is always called *la maison des enfants d'autel* in these accounts.[2]

The *domus bonorum puerorum* was apparently not administered, in terms of its physical maintenance, by the cathedral chapter. The *Collège des Bons Enfants* of Cambrai had been founded in 1278, and although its rector and teachers were under the authority of the cathedral's *scholasticus*, the institution had its own foundation.[3] Further evidence that the grammatical instruction did not take place in the house of the choristers, as did the music and religious instruction, comes from one of the regulations set down in the chapter acts in 1458:

> Item: That he do diligence to those whom he will teach, so that the children

---

[1] Damien Lourme, "Chanoines, officiers et dignataires du Chapitre Cathédral de Cambrai (1357–1426): Étude prosopographique et institutionelle," 3 vols. (archivist and paleographer thesis, École nationale de Chartes, 1990), 1:105–6. LAN 4G 1086, fol. 21ᵛ, no. 36, is a copy of such a certificate, issued on 12 July 1422 to Jacques de Metz Guichard, the dean of the cathedral and doctor of laws, who had pursued a course in theology with Philippe Parent, a Master of Theology.

[2] For example, LAN 4G 5409, fol. 39ʳ (assize, 1437/8), 4G 7761, fol. 17ʳ (*aumosne*, 1438/9), such entries appear virtually every year in these accounts in the section on repairs to the houses.

[3] This was probably the most popular name for a school in France in the late Middle Ages; references to such schools are found in the records of several dozen French and north Italian cities. A summary history of the Cambrai school appears in Eugène Bouly, *Dictionnaire historique de la ville de Cambrai: Des abbayes, des chateaux-forts et des antiquités de Cambresis* (Cambrai, 1854; repr. Brussels, 1979), 43 and 75.

have decent surplices that are not worn, and that they wear long robes in the choir, that he make them go to the grammar school all together and thus progress straight there, without diverting elsewhere if it is not for a reasonable purpose.[1]

The fifteenth-century regulations largely concern the need for the choristers to have the proper religious instruction, to observe decorum at all times, and to be taught the traditional plainsong. The rules also emphasize that the choristers are to have healthful food and drink without pastries and sweets, clean linens throughout the year, and proper heat in winter. The master should also ensure that the choristers did not "overheat" themselves during the periods that they were free to play, and that they observe proper behavior when there are other adults at their meals. A more specific rule indicates that the choristers were encouraged (and eventually required) to speak Latin rather than French, even among themselves.

The eighteenth-century regulations expand upon the earlier ones, presenting a relatively detailed daily schedule of instruction, rehearsal, and attendance at services that left precious little free time. They appear to have been part of an effort to codify the traditions of the cathedral with a historical and almost antiquarian bent. The statutes set down in the eighteenth century are written in the same hand as the regulations for the choristers and consist by and large of citations from the chapter acts, the *Livre rouge*, and the *Livre poilou*, two medieval collections of charters and regulations.[2] In fact, the regulations give the clear impression that the routine was deliberately designed to fill all of the choristers' available time. Given what their duties were, not only in terms of regular attendance in the choir but also their increased employment in newly endowed services (which grew dramatically throughout the fifteenth and sixteenth centuries),[3] it is more than plausible to project the detailed regimen described in the eighteenth-century regulations back to the fifteenth century, since just such a fully regimented schedule survives in a number of French *maîtrises* well into the twentieth century. A summary of the schedule in the eighteenth-century regulations is as follows:[4]

    Waking up and dressing before Matins

---

[1] CBM 1060, fol. 25^r: "Item faire diligence a ceulx quil apprehendera que les enfans ayent soupplis honnestes et non trauwez/ et qui ils portent en cuer longues robes/ quil les face aler a lescole de grammaire tous ensemble et qui ansi remengerent tout a droit sans ailleurs duvertir se nestoit poure aucune cause raisonable."

[2] LAN 4G 1995, 1^r–66^r (Statutes of the eighteenth century), 4G 1085 (*Livre poilou*); the *Livre rouge* apparently does not survive.

[3] See Barbara Haggh, "Itinerancy to Residency: Professional Careers and Performance Practices in 15th-Century Sacred Music," *Early Music* 17 (1989), 359–67; Christine K. Forney, "Music, Ritual and Patronage at the Church of Our Lady, Antwerp," *Early Music History* 7 (1987), 1–58; and Reinhard Strohm, *The Rise of European Music, 1380–1500* (Cambridge, 1993), 269–83 and 287–90.

[4] LAN 4G 94, piece 1732. See also the narrative presentation in Sandrine Dumont's contribution to this volume, pp. 151–52 below.

Getting the church robes (which had been laid out in the common room the night before)

Leaving for the church under the guide of the eldest chorister, receiving holy water at the door from the *bénitier*

Matins: During winter the master must be sure that a proper fire is lit for when the choristers return from Matins

Return to the house, recitation of morning prayers

Washing

Breakfast (*déjeuner*)

Rehearsal of the pieces for the Mass until prime

[Return to the church for Mass]

Mass

After Mass: Latin class until midday, on Sundays the catechism [probably at the grammar school]

Midday: Lunch (*diner*) and recreation until one

One: Study of the Latin lesson delivered in the morning

[Return to the church for Vespers and Compline]

At the return of Compline and until supper: music lesson

Supper (*souper*): At 6:30 from 1 April to 1 October, and at 6:00 from 1 October to 1 April

After supper: half an hour of free time

At 7:00: Rehearsal for Matins and the daily Office, the obits, and the Office of the BVM for the next day

At 8:00: Evening prayer, bedtime, and silence

An aspect of the eighteenth-century regulations, one that has no obvious echo in their fifteenth-century counterparts but can nonetheless be detected in isolated comments in the chapter acts and even in the contemporary chronicles, concerns a certain alarm on the part of the chapter that the choristers were often used by the canons and by visiting dignitaries for private, secular festivities, and that family relationships sometimes interfered with the choristers' daily routine. Accordingly, the eighteenth-century regulations seek to forbid or curtail the choristers' performances in anything other than the church services and to isolate them socially from their relatives and even from each other. Visits in the city were restricted and discouraged, as was contact with family members, and the choristers were forbidden to visit among themselves in their rooms. An adult had to be with them at all times. From comments in the fifteenth-century chapter acts, we can infer that a similar attitude existed at that time, and that the life of a chorister was highly regimented and strenuous, both physically and psychologically. An ambiguous entry in the chapter acts of 1485 comments that the choirboys should not be allowed to sing songs in public or play games unless these had been examined by the head of the *grand métier*.[1] The entry is ambiguous because it is so laconic.

---

[1] CBM 1061, fol. 243ʳ: "Infantes chori carmina non permittantur canere in publico neque iniquos ludos ludere nisi prium tam ludorum quam carminum verba fuit pandita et ostensa magno ministro." Craig Wright, "Performance Practices at the Cathedral of

Clearly the choirboys were traditionally allowed certain public songs and games, but the concern was to avoid those that could cause scandal.

The full responsibility for the upbringing and education of the choristers fell squarely upon the *magister puerorum*, who had his meals with the choirboys most of the time and was often responsible for one or more of the supernumeraries. Some of the masters, particularly those who ruled the choirboys for a decade or more, such as Nicolas Malin, Pierre de Castel, Jehan Hemart, and Denis de Hollain, could do this quite competently. A few of them had trouble imposing discipline upon their charges, particularly if they had undertaken the task while still very young, as was the case, for example, with Robert le Canoine during his first stint (1458–60); some, like Jacob Obrecht (1484–85), were incompetent administrators. Not only was Obrecht incapable of maintaining discipline, but during his tenure, lice spread among the choirboys so severely that the boys required extensive treatment, and all of the bedding and linens in the house had to be burned and replaced.[1]

A recurring break in the daily routine of the choirboys, documented extensively in the accounts of the *aumosne* and in the chapter acts, was a consequence of illnesses (including outbreaks of the plague), which were all too frequently fatal. Sick choristers were taken out of the house and placed under the care of an apothecary and in the house of someone who was then paid to nurse them back to health. Probably closely related to this enduring problem was the practice, documented extensively in the accounts of the *petits vicaires* and the *aumosne*, of always having a few boys (the supernumeraries) beyond the official number, which was six early in the fifteenth century and seven at least from about 1407.[2] The supernumeraries were virtually always housed with the other choristers, and the *magister puerorum* was provided with extra funds for them,[3] but an additional chaplain was responsible for their instruction while they were being prepared to enter the *maîtrise*. This is, for example, how we know that Guillaume Du Fay was taught by

---

Cambrai, 1475–1550," *The Musical Quarterly* 64 (1978), 322 n. 56, gives the year erroneously as 1483.

[1] CBM 1061, fol. 223ᵛ.

[2] The documentation is not entirely clear. Neither the regulations of 1739 nor the entry in the acts in 1458 indicate the number of choirboys. It is possible that at the outset a "nominal" number of choirboys was established; this was the case with the number of *petits vicaires*, for instance, which varied in the fifteenth century from as few as eight to as many as seventeen, but the office was on more than one instance called "the office of the twelve *petits vicaires*" (LAN 4G 1086, no. 306). In the *aumosne* registers as early as 1407/8, "a seventh choirboy" is mentioned (LAN 4G, 7758, fol. 7ʳ), which implies that the notional number was six. Still, a "seventh choirboy" is routinely mentioned in the accounts after 1407. By 1423/4, the yearly purchase of livery for the choirboys simply indicates that cloth was bought for the robes of seven choirboys (LAN 4G 7760, fol. 7ʳ). In September 1461, the *magister puerorum* was paid 24 lb [livres?] for the expenses of Gerard de Torteil, a choirboy "beyond the number of seven," for the entire year (LAN 4G 7764, fol. 14ʳ), and by 1466/7, some choirboys are referred to as being "beyond the usual number of seven" (LAN 4G 7764, fol. 14ᵛ).

[3] The accounts of the *aumosne* include numerous such entries in the course of the fifteenth century.

Jehan Rogier de Hesdin for eleven weeks prior to his admission as a choirboy in August of 1409.[1]

What kind of repertory did the choirboys sing at the cathedral and the other churches of Cambrai? The regulations tell us nothing of it, and the few ordinals that survive from churches in Cambrai are silent on this subject. We can assume that boys took part in the daily liturgy, which was sung largely in plainsong until well into the fifteenth century, since there was little polyphonic singing *in choro* at any of Cambrai's churches until relatively late in the fifteenth century. But there are two important additional sources of information. One is the accounts of the cathedral fabric, which report the copying and repair of the cathedral's liturgical books. The choirboys as a group had their own missals and antiphoners, which were often repaired and rebound; one is tempted to assume that they got rougher and more frequent use than the other books. Liane Curtis, in her excellent study on the production of music manuscripts in fifteenth-century Cambrai, gives a chronological summary of the entries in the fabric that mention books for the choirboys, reproduced in Table 7.1.[2]

That the choirboys had graduals and antiphoners is not surprising; they had to sing in the liturgy and probably stood in a separate group with the *magister puerorum*. The Cambrai books are silent on this point, but it was a normal procedure in most French cathedrals and collegiate churches. In any case, they would often not be tall enough to read from the choirbooks on the high eagle lecterns used by the singing-men. The reason for the absence of missals from Table 7.1 becomes evident once we note that every single missal mentioned in the accounts of the fabric belonged either to the main altar or to one of the side chapels. The two exceptions to this are mentions of the "missal[s] of the *petits vicaires*,"[3] probably meaning a different location for the missals of the chapel of St. Stephen, which was the chapel of both the *grands* and *petits vicaires*. The homiliaries and martyrologies were most likely used for the religious instruction of the boys or to prepare them to understand the Matins lessons, particularly those not taken from the Bible.

Two kinds of books found in Table 7.1 are unusual. The first of these is an *alleluyer* mentioned in 1417 and again in 1429 and 1454; in addition, in 1472 there is a reference to a manuscript containing the graduals and alleluias for the whole year. Although alleluias were often copied as a group in early manuscripts, this practice had generally disappeared by the thirteenth century, and the only *group* of alleluias was to be found in the *commune sanctorum*, in which the proper chants in each category were copied together. Still, in the high and late Middle Ages, there was one book in which the chants were grouped by category, namely the *cantatorium* and its successor, the troper. The late tropers, that is, those copied in the twelfth

---

[1] David Fallows, *Dufay*, 2nd ed. (London, 1987), 7.

[2] Liane Curtis, "Music Manuscripts and their Production in Fifteenth Century Cambrai" (Ph.D. dissertation, University of North Carolina at Chapel Hill, 1991), 175. Curtis follows the distinctions made in the entries between "choirboys," "altarboys," and simply "boys" (which she labels as "unspecified"), but the boys who served at the altar were also in fact choirboys.

[3] E.g. LAN 4G 4642, fol. 31ʳ (1436/7), 4G 4669, fol. 26ʳ (1459/60).

Table 7.1: Chronological mentions of books for the boys in the accounts of the fabric

1411/12	pro liber responsoriorum pro pueris noviter facto	LAN, 4G 4616, fol. 21ʳ
1412/13	Iohanni Engelberti . . . pro religando librum vigiliarum puerorum altaris	LAN, 4G 4617, fol. 20ᵛ
	item pro simil factionem in tribus libris puerorum altarisᵃ	
1413/14	Item l'omelier dez enfans d'autel, reloyer . . .	LAN, 4G 4618, fol. 36ᵛ
1415/16	Gerardo Scriptori pro religando cooperiendo et recolando graduale In quo pueri altaris repetunt [entry ends here]	LAN, 4G 4620, fol. 34ᵛ
1416/17	Gerardo clerico Sancte Crucis pro religando reparando rescribendo et recollando graduale puerorum altaris	LAN, 4G 4621, fol. 29ᵛ
1417/18	Payments to Jehan L'Escripvain for repairs	LAN, 4G 4622, fol. 31ᵛ
	1 dez livres des enfans d'autel	
	le grant omelier des enfants	
	reloyer nettoyer et recouvrir le livre de motez des enfans	
	Item l'alleluyer des enfans	
1429/30	Item Nicolao clerico revestiarii pro minutando in papiru unum librum continentem omnia responsoria totius anni pro pueris altaris qui pro antea consumebant libros ecclesie ad ordinationem Nicolai Malin de Cayot qui liber fuit postea grossatus in pergameno	LAN, 4G 4634, fol. 34ᵛ
		LAN, 4G 4635, fol. 32ᵛ
	Item domino Nicolao Rutoire pro grossando notando et illuminando rotum hunc librum	
	Item eidem pro religando et reparando graduale puerorum laceratum in pluribus locis	
	Item eidem qui religavit de novo librum alterum puerorum ubi cantant les alleluia [sic]	
1431/2	Item Iohanni le Roingniet librario pro religando unum librum longum in quo pueris altaris repetunt suas lectiones	LAN, 4G 4637, fol. 27ʳ
1434/5	Item eidem Thome [le Roingniet] pro religando de novis asseribus et chorio tanato librum omeliarum puerorum altaris . . .	LAN, 4G 4640, fol. 27ʳ
1435/6	Item religando de novo et rescribendo plura folia martyrologii [MS: matrolog] puerorum . . .	LAN, 4G 4641, fol. 30ʳ
1444/5	Item Willermo Caudel scriptori grace pour avoir recollet en plusieurs lieux et reloyer le livre des lechons de prime pro pueris altaris . . .	LAN, 4G 4651, fol. 34ᵛ

1446/7	Item clerico Sancti Gengulphi pro religando et reparando libro in quo parvi pueri cantant graduale et cetera . . .	LAN, 4G 4653, fol. 22^r
1450/51	Item prefato Willermo scriptori^b pro reficiendo religando recolando et rescribendo xxvii folia nova in libro omeliarii puerorum altarium	LAN, 4G 4657, fol. 22^v
1453/4	Item domino Bertholdo Mauchion pro reparando religando de novo et rescribendo in pluribus locis graduale puerorum . . .	LAN, 4G 4660, fol. 22^r
1454/5	Item a mesire Berthoul pour avoir recolet enluminet reloyet rescript et notte ung viel alleluyer ou les enfans d'autel cantent . . .	LAN, 4G 4661, fol. 23^r
1460/61	Item a Jehan Rongnet escrivain et leyeur de livre pour avoir reloyet 1 grant antiphonier ou aprendent les enfans de cuer	LAN, 4G 4668, fol. 23^v
	Item au devandit messier Simon Mellet pour avoir escript et enlumine vii livre contenans les omelies et certaines canteries que les enfans de cuer cantent . . .	
1461/2	Item audit Jehan [Rongnet] pour avoir reloyet le livre du magnificat des enfans d'autel . . .	LAN, 4G 4669, fol. 29^r
1463/4	Item au devantdit sire Simon Meslet . . . escript et notte pour les enfans de coer teneurs et contres xii feulles de petit papier . . .	LAN, 4G 4671, fol. 24^v
1467/8	Item eidem [Jehan de la Fontaine]^c pro similiter^d unus antiqui graduale [sic] in quo cantant pueri feriales [sic] . . .	LAN, 4G 4675, fol. 20^v
1472/3	Item eidem Simoni Mellet pro scriptura viii codices librorum cantus puerorum altaris in quo ponuntur gradualia et alleluia totius anni etc	LAN, 4G 4680, fol. 21^v
1474/5	Item domino Iohanni de Fontaines pro ligatione libri puerorum altaris deservientes misse d'Anchin . . .	LAN, 4G 4682, fol. 22^r
1476/7	Item audit sire Jehan de Fontaines pour recoller et notter en plusieurs lieux le grant antiphonier des enfans de cuer . . .	LAN, 4G 4684, fol. 25^v
1479/80	Item a Jehan Vassal pour avoir consu sur versus certains cohiers de mottes et de magnificats estans en manis de Hemart pour les enfans de cuer . . .	LAN, 4G 4687, fol. 28^r
1481/2	Item domino Roberto Carnen pro additione unius codice ad graduale puerorum chori . . .	LAN, 4G 4688, fol. 27^r
	Item domino Iohanne de Fontaine pro ligatura dicti gradualis ac . . . pro ligature et reparatione martrologii [sic] dictorum puerorum	

1500/01	A Iohannes Regnart pour avoir reloyet timpanet	LAN, 4G 4699, fol. 29ᵛ
	? et remis a point ung grand antiphonaire	
	appartenant aux enfans de coeur	

ᵃ "Simil factionem," refers to binding, glueing, and writing new texts, detailed in an earlier entry.
ᵇ The clerk of Ste. Croix in Cambrai.
ᶜ The clerk of St. Géry.
ᵈ Binding and covering.

century and later, usually contained ordinary chants (which had become part of the troper during the period when most proper chants had tropes or verses) as well as graduals, alleluias, proses, and offertory verses in those churches where the practice had not become extinct. These chants were copied in groups in roughly the order in which they appeared in the Mass: Kyries, Glorias, graduals, alleluias, proses, offertory verses, Sanctus, and Agnus. One such late troper survives from the cathedral (Cambrai, Mediathèque municipale, MS 78), and it is unusual for containing all categories mentioned above except for the offertory verses (which were no longer sung by the late twelfth century) and the graduals.[1] Cambrai 78 provides evidence that by the twelfth century, one of the two responsorial chants of the Mass was apparently not sung by the *cantores*, that is, the soloists of the choir who used Cambrai 78, but by another group of singers.[2] When this is put together with the existence in the fifteenth century of collections of alleluias unique to the choirboys, one must conclude that choirboys sang the solo parts of one of the responsorial chants of the Mass. What appears to have happened, however, during the more than two centuries between the copying of Cambrai 78 and the first mention of a book of alleluias for the choirboys in 1417, is that the chant assigned to the choirboys was shifted from the gradual in the twelfth century to the alleluia in the fifteenth. It is probable that the references of 1417, 1429, and 1454 refer to the same book, which is qualified, in 1454, as "un viel alleluyer." The entry in 1472 may indicate a possible change in some feasts to the earlier tradition suggested by the repertory of Cambrai 78. Such changes apparently took place in the late fifteenth century, although no study of them has been made.[3]

[1] The best description of this manuscript is in Lori Kruckenberg, "The Sequence from 1050–1150: Study of a Genre in Change" (Ph.D. dissertation, University of Iowa, 1997), 189–94. Kruckenberg voices reservations about calling Cambrai 78 a cantatorium because of the absence of the graduals, but at the time she was unaware, as were all other scholars, of some of the traditions of the choirboys in the cathedral.

[2] One should note that the "solo" parts of the chant were seldom sung by just one singer. What most of the surviving *ordines* indicate was that a group of two or three men instead of the entire choir sang these sections. See Alejandro Enrique Planchart, *The Repertory of Tropes at Winchester*, 2 vols. (Princeton, 1977), 1:51 and nn. 1–2.

[3] The best study of the Cambrai liturgy in the fifteenth century is Barbara Haggh, "Nonconformity in the Use of Cambrai Cathedral: Guillaume Du Fay's Foundations," in *The Divine Office in the Latin Middle Ages*, ed. Margot Fassler and Rebecca Baltzer (Oxford, 2000), 372–400, but she downplays the changes that took place in the liturgy *in choro* of

The second type of book is mentioned in entries from 1417/18 and 1479/80 that refer to collections of "motets." However, what was meant by "motet" in 1417 and in 1479 were two different (albeit loosely related) kinds of pieces. In this context, in 1417, a "motet" was most likely a cantus firmus setting of a sacred — though not necessarily liturgical — text, composed either along the lines of what modern scholars have called isorhythmic procedures, or else a freely composed *cantilena* work such as Nicolas Grenon's *Novae vobis gaudia*. By 1479, an entirely new repertory of works had emerged consisting of settings of liturgical or devotional texts, some with a cantus firmus, others freely composed, exemplified in the first instance by Du Fay's well known *Ave regina caelorum* of 1463,[1] and in the second the setting of *O proles hispaniae / O sidus hispaniae*, which the composer describes in his will as "motetum *O sydus hispanie*."[2]

In both types of piece, the choirboys probably sang the top voice, with their master taking one of the lower parts and one or more of the *petits vicaires* taking the third and, if needed, the fourth voice. This is precisely the kind of ensemble described by Du Fay in his request that his *Ave regina caelorum* of 1463 be sung to him as his final hour approached.[3] Du Fay's request suggests a performance of the *Ave regina caelorum* by six choirboys on the top part and one adult singer on each of the lower parts. It is probable that in situations other than in the private rooms of a dying canon, there would be more than one singer in the lower parts. The Burgundian ordinance concerning the duke's chapel in 1469 indicates that the performance of four-part polyphony called for six singers in the *cantus*, two in the contratenor (*moiens*), three in the tenor, and three in the bass (*basse contre*),[4] and David Fallows has argued that the nine singers that Du Fay requested in his will for the performance of his mass for St. Anthony of Padua, which is largely in three voices, would probably be distributed 5–2–2.[5] In these cases five or six choirboys — or five or six adult falsettists — were intended to balance two or three singers in the lower parts. Here it may be useful to note the passage in Du Fay's will: "if time permits, let eight of the fellows of the church by my bed sing softly (*voce submissa*) the hymn *Magno salutis gaudio*."[6] Because the composer's death came swiftly, this request could not be carried out, but the executors paid singers for singing these

---

the cathedral, ascribing some of them to the peculiar liturgies of the side chapels, which indeed differed from the main liturgy of the cathedral.

[1] Edited in *Guglielmi Dufay Opera omnia*, ed. Heinrich Besseler, 6 vols. (Rome, 1951–66), 5: no. 51.

[2] LAN 4G 1313, p. 72: "Sex autem pueri, qui post completorium in profesto ipsius sancti responsum *Si quereris miracula* cum verso et gloria, necnon motetum, *O sydus hispanie* de eodem sancto."

[3] LAN 4G 1313, p. 70: "quo hympno finito pueri altaris una cum magistro eorum et duobus ex sociis, inibi similiter presentes, decantent motetum meum de *Ave regina celorum*."

[4] David Fallows, "Ensembles for Composed Polyphony, 1400–1474," in *Studies in the Performance of Late Medieval Music*, ed. Stanley Boorman (Cambridge, 1983), 149.

[5] Ibid., 117–20.

[6] LAN 4G 1313, p. 70: "hora pati possit, sint octo ex sociis ecclesie iuxta lectum meum, qui submissa voce cantent hympno Magno salutis gaudio." This request is followed immediately by the request to have the *Ave regina* sung as well.

pieces during the obsequies and the passage in the execution reads as follows: "Item: Because the said deceased had asked in his testament that if time permitted as soon as he had received the last rites, eight of the fellows of the choir should sing near him in falsetto (*en fausset*) the hymn *Magno salutis gaudio*."[1]

What is important here is that the term *voce submissa* is rendered by the executors in French as *en fausset*. On this and other documentation, Craig Wright has noted that the use of falsettists was already known in northern French cathedrals in the late fifteenth century.[2] But there is also another conclusion that one can derive from the translation of *voce submissa* as *en fausset* by the executors. *Voce submissa* is a common term with a literal meaning of "in a soft voice" or "in a low voice" used in hundreds of medieval *ordines*, particularly with references to utterances by the priest during the celebration of the Mass. Thus it would appear that in the fifteenth century the normal sound of the falsettists was a soft one. This would be in sharp contrast with the relatively loud sound produced by modern countertenors and sopranists, whose singing tradition derives from that of the Anglican choirs of the late nineteenth century, and it begins to explain the proportions of singers one encounters in the ordinances of the Burgundian chapel and those proposed by Fallows for the performance of the St. Anthony mass of Du Fay. By extension, it is possible to postulate that choirboys were most likely taught to sing softly as the default manner of performance.[3] This would, again, explain why it was a common practice to have six or more choirboys in a treble part in polyphony when the lower parts were sung by one or two adults.

There is no consistent source of information as to the repertory of polyphonic music that the choirboys sang at the cathedral in the fifteenth century. It is possible that they took the treble part when polyphony was sung *in choro* at Cambrai, a practice that apparently began with some consistency in the 1440s — that is, almost two decades before it became common in other northern French cathedrals.[4] But what survives of the Cambrai repertory from that period, namely the collection of movements for the ordinary of the Mass in Cambrai, Mediathèque municipale, MSS 6 and 11, and the scattered propers of the Mass that can be attributed to Du Fay and survive in Trent 88,[5] could easily be sung entirely by

---

[1] LAN 4G 1313, p. 19: "Item ad cause que le dict deffunct avoit done par son dict testament que se l'eure le pooit souffrir tantost apres qu'il aroit receu son darrain sacrement viii des compagnons du coer cantassent en pres lui en fausset le himpne *Magno salutis gaudio*."

[2] Wright, "Performance Practices," 308–9.

[3] This is most likely a continental tradition; the kind of singing required from the treble voices in the late fifteenth-century English repertory, which is represented by the pieces in the Eton Choirbook and other insular manuscripts, is probably very different. In continental music of the first three quarters of the fifteenth century, the treble part very rarely goes above *e″* (Du Fay's *Ave regina* of 1463 hits *f″* only five times in a piece 267 breves long, and in the mass based upon the motet there are twelve instances of the *f″* in a work 1,124 breves long: Kyrie 0, Gloria 6, Credo 4, Sanctus 2, Agnus 0).

[4] On this see Alejandro Enrique Planchart, "Institutional Politics and Social Climbing Through Music in Early Modern France" (forthcoming in *Analecta Musicologica*).

[5] See Alejandro Enrique Planchart, "Guillaume Du Fay's Benefices and his Relationship to the Court of Burgundy," *Early Music History* 8 (1988), 142–68; and Alejandro Enrique

adult singers. Most of the polyphonic repertory of the choirboys, however, probably came from special endowments by clerical and lay patrons who paid for the
performance of specific services for the benefit of their own souls. Consequently,
one would assume that much of this information could be found in the numerous
wills from the canons and chaplains of all the Cambrai churches still preserved in
the Archives départementales du Nord — but in fact this is seldom the case, and
Du Fay's will is exceptional, perhaps because he waited until very late in his life to
endow his own obit.[1] Most canons set their own endowments well within their
lifetimes, and the descriptions of the performances were included in appendices to
the liturgical books belonging to the chapels where these services were performed
or as appendices to the obituary calendars of the community. A number of such
obituaries survive from Cambrai,[2] but in many of them the final pages (where
these endowments are described in some detail) are among the most damaged
sections (as with many medieval liturgical books subjected to constant use) or
are simply missing.[3] Still, from what does survive, we can get a sense of many of
these foundations. It is particularly interesting, however, to note that within the
calendar section of these obituaries, in which many of the obits and endowed
Masses are described in some detail (including the payments to the *grands* and
petits vicaires and to the *chorista*), we find only two instances in which the choirboys are mentioned (in both cases as *pueri altaris*), and these are two of the seven
foundations by Du Fay, namely the Mass for St. Anthony of Padua and his obit in
the chapel of St. Stephen on 5 August.[4] But in the pages that survive at the end of

---

Planchart, "Guillaume Du Fay's Second Style," in *Music in Renaissance Cities and Courts:
Studies in Honor of Lewis Lockwood*, ed. Jessie Ann Owens and Anthony M. Cummings
(Warren, Mich., 1996), 307–40.

   [1] See Alejandro Enrique Planchart, "Notes on Guillaume Du Fay's Last Works," *The
Journal of Musicology* 13 (1995), 63–66.

   [2] For the fifteenth century the most important of these are CBM, MS 39 (a fourteenth-
century obituary of the cathedral with numerous fifteenth-century additions), MS 196
(a fifteenth-century obituary of St. Géry), and MS 197 (a fifteenth-century obituary of Ste.
Croix); and LAN 4G 2009, as well as fragments of two obituaries, one from the cathedral
(a double of Cambrai 39) and another for the Chapel of St. Stephen. On Cambrai 39 and
Lille 4G 2009, see Haggh, "Nonconformity," 372–76.

   [3] This can be determined from notes in the main body of the obituaries, set often in the
form of a liturgical calendar, where an obit or foundation is noted and a remark added such
as we find in the obituary of the *grands vicaires*, LAN 4G 2009, concerning the mass for St.
Anthony of Padua endowed by Du Fay on 13 June (fol. 6r), with the remark "sicut ad longum
declaratur in fine hoc libri." The leaf where that description was entered does not survive.

   [4] LAN 4G 2009, fol. 6r (St. Anthony of Padua); this is an added entry in the obituary
of the Chapel of St. Stephen: "Anthonii de Padua. Habemus missam de beato Anthonio in
capella nostra fundatam per magistrum G. du fay ubi sunt revestiti / et omnis socii de com-
munitate ibi convenimus cum pueris altaris / sicut ad longum declaratur in fine hoc libro
[the pages where the declaration *ad longum* was have not survived]; fol. 11v, the obit of Du
Fay, in the chapel on 27 November with no mention of choirboys; fol. 38v, obit of Du Fay
on 5 August: an extended entry following the dispositions of the will, including a payment
to the choirboys, "ut dicant post viia lectionem in eadem capella psalmus *De profundis* et
collecta *Inclina*." This last entry is part of the choir obituary, and the choirboys are in this

the obituary of the choir we encounter some declarations *ad longum* that mention the choirboys (Table 7.2).

From the entries in Table 7.2 we can see that at Cambrai there was an apparently stable tradition according to which the choirboys, their master, and possibly one or more of the *petits vicaires* sang a polyphonic hymn and a "motet" at both First and Second Vespers in a number of newly endowed feasts. That the obituary does not mention specifically any of the *petits vicaires* beyond the master in this connection is probably no more than a matter of convenience; in all of these entries, the *petits vicaires* are also paid for singing throughout the entire service, and probably the duty of one or more of them would have been to sing the hymn and the motet with the choirboys and their master. This, in fact, would agree with the relatively detailed request in Du Fay's will.[1]

In this context, it is interesting to note that the only mention of choirboys in connection with the singing of the Mass is in Du Fay's foundation for St. Anthony of Padua noted above. This is also reflected in the accounts of the *grands vicaires*. The accounts for most of the fifteenth century are lost, except for an apparently atypical register for 1440/41[2] with no information on any of the payments for the celebration of the endowed feasts. Beginning with 1501/2, however, a considerable number of the accounts survive for the sixteenth century.[3] The accounts of 1501/2 indicate that all of the obits and foundations by Du Fay held in the chapel of St. Stephen are declared *ad longum* at the end of the missals of that chapel, but either said missals have not survived or their final pages are lost. However, the expenses for the community list several dozen endowed Masses sung by the community, including several endowed by Du Fay, and only in one instance is there a mention of the choirboys — as in the obituary, a reference to the mass for St. Anthony of Padua.[4]

Since Fallows identified this mass as consisting of the Ordinary that Besseler published in the second volume of the *opera omnia* as the *Missa Sancti Anthonii Viennensis*[5] plus the propers for St. Anthony of Padua found in Trent 88 and

---

case singing plainsong and a spoken prayer. See Haggh, "Nonconformity," 373; Haggh's transcription of the entry in fol. 6ʳ (p. 392 n. 8) is incorrect.

[1] See p. 134 above.

[2] LAN 4G 6748.

[3] LAN 4G 6749 (accounts from 1501 to 1557, with small lacunae), 6750 (1563/4), 6751 (1573–89, with some lacunae).

[4] LAN 4G 6749 (1501/2), fol. 9ʳ: "Item xiii iunii pro missa sancti Anthonii de Padua ex fundatione magistri Guillermi du Fay presbytero celebranti Iohannes de Quellerie 3 s 4 d sex pueris choris cum magistro eorum cuilibet 20 d et residuum sociis cantantibus cum magistro puerorum 41 s 8 d."

[5] *Guglielmi Dufay Opera omnia*, ed. Besseler, 2: no. 3. On the mass itself, see Fallows, *Dufay*, 182–86; David Fallows, "Dufay, la sua messa per Sant'Antonio da Padova e Donatello," *Rassegna veneta di studi musicali* 2–3 (1986–87), 3–19; David Fallows, "Dufay's Most Important Work: Reflections on the Career of his Mass for St Anthony of Padua," *Musical Times* 123 (1982), 467–70; Alejandro Enrique Planchart, "The Books that Du Fay Left to the Chapel of Saint Stephen," in *Sine musica nulla disciplina: Studi in onore di Giulio Cattin*, ed. Franco Bernabei and Antonio Lovato (Padua, 2006), 175–212.

Table 7.2: Mentions of the choirboys in the choir obituary

LAN, 4G 2009, fol. 58ᵛ	Greater double of First Sunday in Advent
	Founded by Gilles Du Bois, Sr. (canon 1398–1435)
	To 6 choirboys and the master for a motet, 4s.
LAN, 4G 2009, fol. 59ʳ	Greater double of St. Gregory
	Founded by Grégoire Nicolai, official (canon, 1439–1469)
	Hymn and motet before the image of St. Gregory by the choirboys and the master at both Vespers, 6s.
LAN, 4G 2009, fol. 59ᵛ	Greater double of St. Gilles
	Founded by Gilles Carlier, dean (canon, 1431–1472)
	Motet by the choirboys and the master at both vespers, master 2s., choirboys 6s.
LAN, 4G 2009, fol. 60ʳ	Greater double of Sts. Fabian & Sebastian
	Founded by Gilles Flannel, alias L'Enfant (canon, 1438–1466)ᵃ
	Hymn and motet by the master and the choirboys at both vespers, 5s.
LAN, 4G 2009, fol. 60ᵛ	Feast of the Visitation
	Founded by Michiel van Beringhen (canon, 1438–1457)
	Hymn and motet by the choirboys and the master, 5s.
LAN, 4G 2009, fol. 60ᵛ	Greater double of the Recollectio
	Founded by Michiel van Beringhen
	As in the Visitation
LAN, 4G 2009, fol. 61ᵛ	Dedication of the Cathedral
	Celebrated after the first Sunday after the Translation of St. Thomas
	Hymn and motet by the choirboys and the master, 5s.

^a First received in 1433, but his first prebend was lost in litigation.

published by Laurence Feininger with an attribution to Du Fay,[1] a considerable literature has developed around it. Concerning its performance, Fallows arrived at a group of nine singers by cleverly dividing the number of 30 *sous* that Du Fay provided for each performance by the payment specified in Du Fay's will of 3s. 4d.[2] From this Fallows concluded that the singers were all adults. Still, Du Fay's mention of the *magister puerorum* among the singers is curious,[3] and the payments

[1] Laurence Feininger, ed., *Auctorum anonymorum Missarum propria* xvɪ *quorum* xɪ *Gulielmo Dufay ascribenda sunt*, Monumenta polyphoniae liturgicae sanctae ecclesiae romanae, ser. 2/1 (Rome, 1947), no. xɪ.

[2] Fallows, "Ensembles," 118.

[3] The will reads: "in qua assint magister puerorum et alii quiscumque sufficientiores

recorded from 1501 on include choirboys as well. This is clarified by a passage that follows shortly after the one establishing the mass in Du Fay's will:

> Moreover, the six choirboys who on the eve of said saint would sing the responsory *Si quereris* [*recte: quaeris*] *miracula* with its verse and doxology, as well as the motet *O sydus hyspaniae* of the same saint, and the next day at the Mass the *Et in terra pax*, are to receive 10s., therefore each 20d.[1]

Du Fay's responsory *Si quaeris miracula* and a cantilena motet, *O decus Hispaniae / O sidus Hispaniae*, to which Du Fay refers by its second text, as was common, have survived.[2] These pieces formed part of a set of Vespers for St. Anthony and for St. Francis, complete with a plenary mass for each, which Du Fay bequeathed in a manuscript to the chapel of St. Stephen, where all his endowments were to be performed.[3] From a number of other endowments cited above in Table 7.2, it is clear that the choirboys sang the hymn and a motet at Vespers during many feasts, and this coincides with Du Fay's mention of their singing *O sidus Hispaniae*, though Du Fay's endowment does not require them to sing the hymn, but rather the responsory *Si quaeris miracula*, indicating that the Vespers had a procession. A number of the endowments in Table 7.2 specify that the hymn and the motet were to be sung by the choirboys at First and Second Vespers. Du Fay's endowment in his will specifies only the Mass and not the Vespers, but the manuscript he left to the chapel most likely included both First and Second Vespers, and from the payments in the accounts of the *grands vicaires* in the sixteenth century, it becomes clear that in addition to the Mass, both First and Second Vespers for the saint were sung as part of Du Fay's endowment.[4]

---

de choro, sive sint magni vicarii, seu parvi, vel capellani, ad provisionem tamen dictorum magnorum vicariorum. (At which are present the master of the boys and several other of the better singers of the choir, whether they be *grands vicaires*, or *petits*, or chaplains, at the provision [i.e. determination] of the *grands vicaires*)." LAN 4G 1313, p. 73. The final part of the endowment was there because all of Du Fay's endowed Masses were to be administered by the *grands vicaires*.

[1] LAN 4G 1313, p. 73: "Sex autem pueri, qui post completorium in profesto ipsius sancti responsum *Si quereris miracula* cum verso et gloria, necnon motetum, *O sydus hispanie* de eodem sancto, et in crastinum ad missam *Et in terra pax* decantabunt, percipient 10 s, inde cuilibet 20 d."

[2] *Guglielmi Dufay Opera omnia*, ed. Besseler, 5: no. 45 and 1: no. 6.

[3] Planchart, "The Books," 185–90.

[4] In this case, the accounts of the *grands vicaires* present a curious case: from 1501 on, the payments for the Mass of St. Anthony, including the six choirboys, are entered in every surviving account, but the first mention of Vespers, and in this case of both first and second Vespers (cum utriusque vesperis *ex fundatione dicti Dufay*), appears more than seventy years afterwards in the accounts for 1573/4 (LAN 4G 6751, fol. 9ᵛ), although from the contents of Du Fay's manuscript and the mention of both the responsory and the motet in the will, it is clear that the foundation included Vespers. Here it should be noted that it is clear from a comment by the executors that this foundation was a continuation of something Du Fay had been doing for a good number of years before his death, apparently paying for it each year out of his own pocket and treating the celebrants and the singers to dinner afterwards (LAN 4G 1313, p. 30: "Item pour les despens fais par les dessus dictes executeurs et aultres

The last sentence in Du Fay's establishment of the celebration of St. Anthony requires the choirboys to sing in the Mass, but only in the Gloria. Endowments of the fifteenth century, some of which do not survive in contemporary documents but were recorded by eighteenth-century historians, record a number of Masses in both plainsong and in polyphony that required the use of choirboys.[1] The assumption has been that in those Masses in which the choirboys sang polyphony, they sang the cantus part.[2] Unfortunately, none of the other endowments is as detailed as that of Du Fay. Craig Wright has surveyed the majority of the surviving Mass endowments from the fifteenth and early sixteenth centuries that mention choirboys. These are:

1. A weekly Mass in plainsong celebrated in the chapel of the Trinity, directly behind the choir, sung by the *petits vicaires* and the choirboys.[3] The Mass followed Lauds, as did most of the endowed Masses; the main Mass *in choro* followed Terce.[4]

2. A votive Mass for the Holy Ghost in polyphony, endowed in 1516 by canon Jehan le Lievre (d. 1 February 1415), sung in the chapel of St. Lawrence.[5]

3. A Mass of Our Lady to be sung every Saturday, and on the vigil of all six feasts of the Virgin, endowed by Jehan, abbot of the monastery of Anchin near Douai, first mentioned in an entry on 14 May 1457. This Mass, like Du Fay's Mass for St. Anthony, was not only polyphonic, but appar-

---

qu'ilz appelerent au digner le jour Saint Anthoine de Pade, apres le messe dicte et descantee en la capelle dessus dicte de Saint Estiene comme avoit acoustume de faire chacun an le dict deffunct, 4 lb 2s 6d.")

[1] Cambrai had the good fortune to have three excellent liturgical and local historians during the eighteenth century, all whom left extensive notes of their own research in the archives and annotated the calendars and necrologies of the cathedral (as well as the chapter acts) with erudite and, insofar they can be checked with surviving material, astonishingly accurate notes. They were Denis-Henri Mutte (1706–1774), dean of the chapter, Albert de Carondelet (1720–1784), canon, and François-Dominique Tranchant (1722–1794), chaplain and librarian.

[2] Fallows, however, in discussing the performance of the Du Fay mass for St. Anthony, was unaware of the disposition in the will; see "Ensembles," 118 and 121. The mass, of course, could be performed entirely by adult singers, and this may well be how Du Fay intended it to be performed in Padua in 1450 if Fallows's hypothesis concerning his travel to Italy in that year is correct (see Fallows, *Dufay*, 185–86).

[3] Wright, "Performance Practices," 301, citing the accounts of the *petits vicaires* for 1483/4 (LAN 4G 6791, fol. 4ᵛ), and the chapter acts of 1546 (CBM 1072, fol. 36ᵛ). The earliest appearance of these Masses is in the accounts of the *petits vicaires* for 1458/9 (LAN 4G 6789 [1458/9], fol. 6ʳ), where they are mentioned as part of the heading for the weekly distributions. Since there is a lacuna in these accounts between 1411/12 and 1458/9, we have no way of knowing when these Masses began to be celebrated.

[4] Wright, "Performance Practices," rendered in all cases "laudes matutinales" as "matins," which was normally called "matutinum."

[5] Ibid., 301, citing CBM 1062 (Carondelet's notes), p. 365. The Mass was celebrated by the grand community of chaplains, and the endowment appears in Le Lievre's will (LAN 4G 1468, fol. 6ᵛ), but the accounts of the chaplains are curiously silent on this foundation.

ently had specific works attached to it, since one of the entries in Table 7.2 above records repairs to the book of the choirboys who sang in this Mass. The entry in the chapter acts is particularly informative in that it indicates the composition of the ensemble: the Mass was to be said by one of the [*grands*] *vicaires*, and sung in polyphony by the choirboys, their master, and two contratenors. After Mass, which was said in front of "the principal image" of the Virgin, the ensemble would repair to the chapel of the Trinity, where the famous painting of Notre-Dame de Grace was, and sing the prose *Ave sponsa*.[1] The mention of the prose might in fact explain why the chapel needed its own books, as none of the Cambrai chant books contain a prose entitled *Ave sponsa*. Indeed, a search through the *Analecta hymnica* and the *Repertorium hymnologicum* turned up only one such work, the immensely long *Ave sponsa deitatis*, which was part of the repertory of the Victorines in Paris, and which the abbot of Anchin probably had come to know.[2] It is very unlikely that the prose was sung in polyphony.

4. A Mass for the Virgin celebrated "alta voce" on 20 August and endowed by Pierre d'Ailly, who was bishop of Cambrai from 1397 to 1412 and was buried in the cathedral.[3] The earliest notice we have is from 1454/5, in the accounts of the *petits vicaires*,[4] but there is a lacuna in these accounts from 1411/12 to 1453/4, and since the entry specifies that the Mass was endowed by d'Ailly, it probably goes back to around 1420, the year of d'Ailly's death.

5. In 1515 or 1516, Jehan de la Pierre established a foundation to have the Requiem Mass of Du Fay sung in his memory by the choirboys and the master (and most likely another adult singer, since the Requiem, according to one description, was for three voices).[5] But apparently the foundation did not have the necessary money, for every entry referring to it until 1521 reports that nothing was paid, and the foundation later disappeared.

6. Louis van Pullaer, former *petit vicaire* and *magister puerorum* at Cambrai and later at Notre-Dame in Paris, and finally a canon in the cathedral, directed in his will that at his obsequies the requiem was to be sung by the *magister puerorum* and the choirboys.[6]

---

[1] Wright, "Performance Practices," 301, citing the chapter acts (CBM 1057, fol. 267ᵛ).

[2] Clemens Blume, ed., *Analecta hymnica* (Leipzig, 1904; repr. New York, 1961), 44: no. 337, for the Visitation.

[3] Wright, "Performance Practices," 301, citing Tranchant's notes in CBM 1064, p. 562, and chapter acts of 1538 (CBM 1069, fol. 233ʳ).

[4] LAN 4G 6789 (1453/4), fol. 3ᵛ.

[5] Wright, "Performance Practices," 303, citing the accounts of the community of chaplains for 1516/17 (LAN 4G 7008, fol. 33ʳ⁻ᵛ; Wright gives 32ʳ, which is the folio for LAN 4G 7009, 1517/18). There is no mention of this in the accounts for 1514/15, and those for 1515/16 are lost.

[6] Wright, "Performance Practices," 303, citing Van Pullaer's will (1528), LAN 4G 1548, fol. 19ʳ.

7. Louis van Pullaer endowed the singing of the responsory *Gaude Maria* by three choirboys *in contrapuncto*.[1]

8. Jacques Charité endowed the singing of the antiphon *Ave Maria* after Christmas compline *in contrapuncto* by the choirboys.[2]

9. Gilles Carlier endowed the singing of the responsory *Homo quidam* by the choirboys in polyphony during the octave of Corpus Christi.[3]

10. In 1460 the choirboys sang in a motet by Charles the Bold.[4]

11. In 1483 the choirboys sang in a motet and the *Benedicamus Domino* at the abbey of St. Aubert.[5]

Items 7–9 in Wright's list require some qualification. The documents he cites imply that the choirboys are to sing the polyphony by themselves (or at most, together with the *magister puerorum*), but these documents, with the exception of CBM 1069 (the chapter acts for 1525), are all notes and compilations made by the eighteenth-century canons, who present the information in a very compressed form. It is more likely that in the case of items 8 and 9, the choirboys formed part of the kind of ensemble indicated by other fifteenth-century documents, namely an ensemble of the choirboys, their master, and one or two other adult singers.

In the case of item 7, there can be no doubt that Van Pullaer wanted an ensemble consisting of the choirboys and perhaps their master, but this was in fact not a normal practice at Cambrai. The endowment comes from the very end of Van Pullaer's life, when he was preparing to return to Cambrai following his tenure as *magister puerorum* at Notre-Dame in Paris (1509–27), where such an ensemble was a common tradition.[6]

None of the information we have on these foundations indicates that the choirboys were to sing in just one movement or another of the Mass or the Requiem, as Du Fay's does. In the Mass of d'Ailly, however, we find traces of the traditions of the performance of the plainsong Mass at Cambrai that date back to the twelfth century, in that the choirboys were to sing the gradual,[7] a request that coincides with the absence of the graduals in the twelfth-century cantatorium of the cathedral mentioned above and with the copying of collections of graduals and alleluias for the choirboys in the course of the fifteenth century.

Nonetheless, the picture that emerges from the remarks in the acts and from the endowments is that the choirboys had a definite but limited role in the plainsong liturgy *in choro*, singing some of the propers of the Mass, either the gradual or the alleluia (probably depending on the feast), and in the hymn at Vespers,

---

[1] Wright, "Performance Practices," 305, citing CBM 1069, fol. 202ʳ, and CBM 1060, p. 307.

[2] Wright, "Performance Practices," 305, citing CBM 1060, p. 318.

[3] Wright, "Performance Practices," 305, citing CBM 1019, pp. 72 and 97, and CBM 1260, p. 319.

[4] Wright, "Dufay at Cambrai," 209.

[5] Wright, Performance Practices," 306, citing LAN H36 431, fol. 83ʳ.

[6] See Craig Wright, *Music and Ceremony at Notre-Dame of Paris, 500–1550* (Cambridge, 1989), 180–89.

[7] Wright, "Performance Practices," 301, citing CBM 1019, p. 562.

which probably was done in polyphony fairly consistently.[1] From early in the fifteenth century, they also sang a "motet" during Vespers, since by 1417 there was already a book of motets copied specifically for them, and a number of the foundations cited in Table 7.2 mention their singing of a motet as Du Fay's will does. If the motet was in three voices, the choirboys probably sang it with the master and perhaps another adult singer; if it was in four voices, they sang it with the master and two or more adult singers, as Du Fay indicates in his will, which is also the ensemble specified for the Lady Mass endowed by the abbot of Anchin. In this context it is worth noting that Du Fay's last isorhythmic motet, *Fulgens iubar ecclesiae Dei*, and the only one definitely written for Cambrai,[2] implies such an ensemble: the triplum includes a number of chords, indicating that it was sung by several singers, and the text of the motetus has an acrostic that reads "Petrus de Castello canta" (Pierre de Castel, sing), indicating that Pierre, who was *magister puerorum* from 1437 to 1447, was the singer assigned to this part, with two others evidently assigned to the first and second tenor of the piece. Given the context provided by the endowments in Table 7.2 and the fact that the cantus firmus, *Virgo post partum quem genuit adoravit*, is taken from the responsory *Adorna thalamum* (which was normally sung at Matins of the Purification but could be used also in the procession at Vespers),[3] the motet was likely intended for Vespers of Purification and, as such, would fit well within the tradition of music sung by the choirboys at the cathedral.

The repertory that the choirboys at St. Géry and Ste. Croix sang cannot be identified as easily as that at the cathedral, since the liturgical books of Ste. Croix have, by and large, not survived, and those of St. Géry are rather less informative than those of the cathedral and have not been studied in any detail. Still, the likelihood is that these repertories were very similar to what the choirboys sang in the cathedral. In the case of Ste. Croix, this was because the church was a dependency of the cathedral, and the ten canons of the former were often the senior chaplains of the latter; indeed, some of these men eventually became canons at the cathedral when a canonry became vacant, and no clerics with connections to the papacy or to secular lords had a prior claim to it. St. Géry was an independent foundation, with its church lying outside the walls of the city on the mount where the Emperor Charles v eventually built a citadel in 1507, requiring the demolition of the church and the transfer of the canons to the church of St. Vaast inside the city. This church is, to this day, the church of St. Géry and St. Vaast. But it is probable

---

[1] This is a conclusion one can reach from the addition of polyphonic hymns to CBM 29, the cathedral psalter and antiphoner for Vespers from the fourteenth and fifteenth centuries.

[2] Fallows, *Dufay*, 62, places both this motet and *Moribus genere* in 1442 and both for Cambrai. Laurenz Lütteken, *Guillaume Dufay und die isorhythmische Motette*, Studien zur Musikwissenschaft aus Münster, 4 (Hamburg, 1993), 297–99, makes a far more convincing argument for the motet having been written in 1442 or 1443; he also argues that it was composed for the Sainte-Chapelle in Dijon. Planchart, "Guillaume Du Fay's Second Style," 314–15, makes a case that *Fulgens iubar* must date from between 1445 and 1447 and was composed for Cambrai.

[3] CBM 38, fol. 248ᵛ; CBM, Impr. xvi C 4, fol. 171ʳ.

that the training and repertory of the choirboys at St. Géry were virtually identical to those of the cathedral. In fact, two of the most important *magistri puerorum* of the cathedral in the late fifteenth century, Jehan Hemart (1468–84) and Denis de Hollain (1485–1502), were *magistri puerorum* at St. Géry immediately preceding their appointments as such in the cathedral. An entry in the registers of the fabric of St. Géry for 1361–62 records payment to a Magister Nicolas, who was sub-cantor or *succentor* at the church (and thus most likely *magister puerorum*), for composing and notating a motet for St. Géry and copying it into the books of the church.[1] This is the earliest reference we have to composed polyphony in any of the Cambrai churches and, in fact, the next reference we have from the city is the repairing of the "book of motets" for the choirboys of the cathedral in 1417 listed in Table 7.1.

We know almost nothing of the life of the choirboys after they left the *maîtrise*, because we have so few of their names for the entire century. Unlike the *petits vicaires*, who were listed twice a year by name in their accounts and virtually week by week in the bread-and-wine accounts (as noted above), the choirboys were often mentioned only as a group. Exceptions are occasionally made when they received a gift, usually at the end of their careers as choirboys, or when they were supernumeraries placed in the house of the *magister puerorum* or another of the singing-men. Often, they are referred to by a simple baptismal name or a diminutive, and only rarely can we discover the patronymic of a choirboy unless by chance the accounts of the *aumosne* or the chapter acts provides it. Still, from the evidence that does survive it is clear that in general three paths of advancement, which were not mutually exclusive, were open to them. First, they were provided with some support for a few years to undertake further instruction. This could be at the *grandes écoles* in Cambrai itself or at one of the *studia generalia* in Paris, Louvain, or elsewhere. In the first of these cases, they very often continued to live with the *magister puerorum* or another one of the clerics of the cathedral (though apparently never with one of the canons), while in the second, they essentially disappeared from the historical record at Cambrai itself, and only very rarely can we trace them in later life. In the second case, they became clerics in the cathedral (or in St. Géry or Ste. Croix if they had been in those *maîtrises*), usually serving as *petits vicaires* and eventually as chaplains or *grands vicaires*. Before 1439, since the lists of *petits vicaires* are so infrequent, their progress is hard to follow, even when we have a full name. Since the progression from minor cleric to chaplain was relatively common, however, when we have a case such as that of Jehan le Caron I[2] (documented as a choirboy in 1421/2,[3] as a former choirboy living in Grenon's house in 1423–34,[4]

---

[1] LAN 7G 2223 (1361/2), fol. 14[r].

[2] The cathedral records give us two different men by this name, both of them musicians and probably related. Jehan le Caron II is the better known "Jehan Caron," who became *sommelier* of the Burgundian chapel.

[3] LAN 4G 7760 (1421/2), fol. 7[v].

[4] LAN 4G 7760 (1423/4), fol. 7[v].

as "foreign" chaplain in 1433/4,[1] and then as a member of the grand community of chaplains in 1438/9[2] until his death in October 1438[3]), we can safely assume that he was most likely a *petit vicaire* in the late 1420s. The third instance consists of choirboys who left the service of the cathedral and sought employment as clerics (musical or otherwise) in other churches, either in Cambrai or elsewhere. As with those who left to go to a *studium generale* they disappear entirely from the historical record at Cambrai (with some exceptions).

Most of the choirboys who did not serve later as *petits vicaires* in the cathedral are far more difficult to trace. One can find random entries in the *aumosne* or the acts, mentioning boys only by their first name, and when they left Cambrai, most of them disappear from the historical record. There are, however a number of exceptions, and they are worth examining because, among other things, they point to a relationship between the cathedral and the papal chapel that was apparently cemented early in the fifteenth century. That, however, is another story.

---

[1] LAN 4G 6006, fol. 85ᵛ. A foreign chaplain was not necessarily a non-resident chaplain but rather was not yet a member of the grand community of chaplains.

[2] LAN 4G 6908, fol. 30ʳ.

[3] CBM 1057, fol. 80ᵛ.

8

CHOIRBOYS AND *VICAIRES*
IN THE *MAÎTRISE* OF CAMBRAI
A SOCIO-ANTHROPOLOGICAL STUDY (1550–1670)

Sandrine Dumont

B

Y the end of the Middle Ages and during the Renaissance, Franco-Flemish
polyphony had been established as a preeminent style throughout Europe,
a splendid and immense repertory inaugurated by Guillaume Du Fay,
who was trained in the choir school of the cathedral of Notre-Dame in Cambrai
before beginning an international career in the most prestigious princely courts
and other chapels (Milan, Florence, Rome). An ample bibliography attests to
the interest historians have taken in this period and to musicologists' interest in
the northern school. Since the development of the Franco-Flemish school is well
known, I have chosen to study the period after the Council of Trent, focusing on
sacred music, the most conservative tradition. What became of this brilliant institution? Why do most studies overlook the vast and complex subject of Franco-
Flemish polyphonic sacred music beginning in the seventeenth century? Why and
how was Cambrai forgotten?[1] All these questions must be approached through
the context of musical institutions and social structures.[2]

At court and in urban centers, children from the social backgrounds most
privileged by class or fortune received instruction in the arts as part of their intellectual formation at home — particularly in music, as instrumental performance
was considered integral to the education of a respectable man.[3] However, very
few children were well-born; those from less affluent backgrounds could not pay
for a private teacher but could still enter into the service of a church and join its

---

[1] For example, see the article "Cambrai" in *The New Grove Dictionary of Music and Musicians* (London, 1980), 3:641–42: "by the seventeenth century Cambrai had dwindled to
insignificance both as a city and as a cultural centre."

[2] Jean-Pierre Ouvrard, *Josquin Desprez et ses contemporains, de l'écrit au sonore* (Arles,
1986), 33: "We can gain insight into religious compositions only by taking the trouble to
understand them in the context of the institutions — the places, the people, and the actions
— that engendered them."

[3] F. Grenaille de la Chatounière, *L'Honneste Garçon, ou L'Art de bien élever la noblesse
à la vertu, aux sciences et à toutes les carrières convenables à sa condition* (Paris, 1642).

maîtrise (choir school), which then assumed responsibility for them, providing room and board, thorough training, a comfortable standard of living, and a suitable career path. In short, cathedral choir schools, in assisting the many parents with only meager resources, offered choirboys better living conditions and a future profession. In exchange, the choirboys thus employed were required to sing at Mass and Vespers, since the principal function of cathedral and collegiate choir schools was musical performance in the liturgy.

The number of children in the choir school of Notre-Dame at Cambrai remained fixed at eight, as seen every year beginning in 1602 in the account registers of the office of the *petits vicaires* and the choirboys of the cathedral, which mention the expenses of the "music master and his eight choirboys" ("maistre de musique et ses huict enffans de cœur"). Nevertheless, some references in the registers of the chapter acts[1] confirm the presence of additional boys by reporting that "the canons ordered that two more choirboys be accepted, making the total ten."[2] It is not so much the figure itself but rather its stability over the centuries (beginning in the sixteenth) that attests to the wealth of the cathedral chapter; in fact, in some difficult periods, the number of choirboys in other cathedrals often varied, sometimes reduced by half.[3] At Rouen in September of 1584, for example, the cathedral chapter decided not to replace the departing choirboys because of the "cherté des vivres," and thus the number fell from ten to eight, then to six in July 1592.[4] The chapter at Grenoble decided on May 5, 1654, to discontinue "the music in this church, which is in disorder because of the priests and choirboys who have abandoned the choir."[5] This was not the case of the choir school at Cambrai, where the number of boys remained fixed until the French Revolution. During hard times, in fact, the number of boys there did not diminish, and the master's income actually increased.[6]

---

[1] These registers are Latin manuscripts comprising the minutes of the weekly meetings of the chapter. They list in chronological order all sorts of events tied to the daily life of the chapter, "capturing both the essential and the most trivial aspects"; Philippe Loupès, *Chapitres et chanoines de Guyenne aux XVIIᵉ et XVIIIᵉ siècles*, Civilisations et sociétés, 70 (Paris, 1985), 499.

[2] Médiathèque municipale de Cambrai (hereafter BMC), MS 1085, fol. 134ᵛ: "Les seigneurs ont ordonné [que] soient reçus encore deux enfants de chœur jusqu'à ce qu'ils soient dix."

[3] At the beginning of the sixteenth century, the choir school had six boys; see Craig Wright, "Performance Practices at the Cathedral of Cambrai, 1475–1550," *The Musical Quarterly* 44 (1978), 295–328 at 310. In the sixteenth century, the number stabilized at eight.

[4] Armand Collette, *Histoire de la maîtrise de Rouen*, part 1: *Des origines jusqu'à la Révolution française* (Rouen, 1875), 57.

[5] Louis Royer, "Les Musiciens et la musique à l'ancienne collégiale Saint-André," *Humanisme et Renaissance* 4 (1937), 250: "la musique qui se fait dans cette église [et qui] y apporte un grand désordre par l'abandonnement du chœur que font les sieurs prestres et habitués ou enfants de chœur."

[6] For example, Archives départementales du Nord (hereafter ADN), 4G 6809, account book for the office of the *petits vicaires* and choirboys for 1634–38: "a m[aît]re Jan

The recruitment of choirboys

How were candidates informed of vacancies? Unlike other French choir schools, at Cambrai there is no trace of a public announcement of the recruitment of boys, at least for the period studied here.[1] Nevertheless, in the registers of the chapter acts, the selection of boys is almost always formulated in the same way: "from the boys presented to the chapter today, the canons have chosen N." But the repeated expression *ex pueris* (from the boys) signifies that several boys were presented to the chapter at the same time. "From the boys presented today in the chapter, the canons chose Guillaume . . . for the choir on the condition that he improve his voice, or on the condition that he be returned to the lectern."[2] The parents went to the chapter to present their child(ren), as seen in the minutes: "those [of the parents] who have children . . . to apply for these positions (as choirboys) can present them to the chapter on the day indicated above around 9:00 am."[3] In reality, some minutes from the end of the eighteenth century stipulate that "the public is alerted that the metropolitan chapter of Cambrai has chosen August 1, 1777, to make appointments for two choirboy positions, one of which is current, and the other will be vacant next September."[4] How did they sign up? What were the criteria by which the chapter received them? A systematic listing of each arrival and departure of boys in the choir school enables one to draw up a table of the choirboys' movements (Figure 8.1). Even though arrivals were spread out over the year, the month of September remained the most important period for recruitment.

"In general, choirboys left the choir school on the evening of the Nativity of the Virgin,"[5] September 8; but the changeover at Notre-Dame of Cambrai actually took place on the feast of St. Remi, October 1: "the canons consent that Cyprien des Lettres, choirboy sent out to study, may leave the college . . . and draw his scholarship until the next feast of St. Remi."[6] In short, at the end of the sixteenth century, the general population knew the period for the recruitment of choirboys (the month of September coincided with the departures for college of the oldest choirboys). This suggests that the population was informed of the days the chapter received applicants and very probably was aware of the two days a week that the chapter met to deliberate.

Richart a raison de la chertez des prouisions par ordon[nance] . . . ont esté paiez C l[ivres] t[ournois]." For 1634: "autre mises po(u)r dons et graces durant lan de ce compte 1634."

[1] At Rouen, for example; see Collette, *Histoire de la maîtrise de Rouen*.

[2] BMC 1083, fol. 107ʳ: "Ex pueris hodie in (capitulo) (presentatis) (domini) elegunt Guillelmum . . . in choralem sub spe meliorationis eius vocis, alioqui sub conditione reponendi eum ad pulpitum."

[3] ADN 4G 1087, 14 July 1777.

[4] ADN 4G 1087, announcement of the nomination of choirboys, 14 July 1777.

[5] Anne-Marie Yvon, "La Maîtrise de Notre-Dame aux xviiᵉ et xviiiᵉ siècles," in *Huitième Centenaire de Notre-Dame de Paris: Receuil de travaux sur l'histoire de la cathédrale et de l'Église de Paris* (Paris, 1967), 365; BMC 1081, fol. 163ᵛ.

[6] BMC 1081, fol. 163ᵛ.

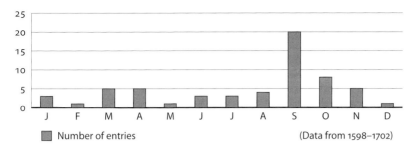

Figure 8.1: Distribution of entries of choirboys by month

Admission procedures for choirboys

The canons examined the applicants according to various criteria, the most essential obviously being the voice, since the primary function of the choir school was above all the liturgy — the purpose of the choir school, as a singing school, being to prepare the singers who would later remain in the service of the cathedral. When the chapter finally admitted a boy to its ranks, after auditions and trial performances, it informed the boy and his parents. The official announcement of the recruitment did not always coincide with the actual entry of the boy; a delay often intervened between these two operations, meaning that the boy's actual entry took effect some time later, because the applications for the next vacancy had to coincide with a departure in order to maintain a fixed number of boys in the choir school: "Stéphane Vasseur, resident of Cambrai, is engaged in the small choir in the place of Jean Francis Manié, who was removed."[1] In this way, the choir school replenished itself gradually, with senior boys and new arrivals side by side. The older ones, who were about to leave for college, were responsible for educating their juniors; they recited the daily prayers with them,[2] regulated their own behavior, helped the younger boys with their introductory courses, and assisted the master in rehearsals of liturgical chant.

A choirboy's admission was often conditional, meaning that the chapter accepted him for a trial period during which he had to meet the requirements stated at the time of his selection, most often the obligation to improve his voice; otherwise, he could be dismissed. For example, on 29 May 1609, the canons accepted the son of the custodian[3] on a trial basis, but he did not fulfill the requirements they had set for him; after a week in the choir school he was dismissed.[4] During the trial period, which could last several months, if a boy's first performances garnered

---

[1] BMC 1088, fol. 22ᵛ.

[2] ADN 4G 94, pièce 1372, rules for the choir school of choir boys, 28 Aug. 1739: "Après leurdicte messe, le plus grand rendu en la maison recitera tout haut à genoux ainsi que les autres la prière du matin modestement et distinctement."

[3] BMC 1081, fol. 276ᵛ.

[4] BMC 1081, fol. 280ᵛ.

the chapter's approval, he was very quickly employed; if, on the other hand, he did not satisfy the requirements he had been given, he was immediately let go.[1]

Nevertheless, when the boy was dismissed, whether he had immediately failed to fulfill the prescribed conditions, or had failed to meet them at the end of his musical education, the chapter regularly gave him a donation of a garment or a little money before his departure, to help cover his travel expenses (*pro viatico*).[2] Similarly, before a boy's departure, he might undergo a new examination to determine whether he had intellectual promise.[3] If so, the chapter kept him as an acolyte (or another function linked to the liturgy), which enabled him to remain at the institution and possibly to receive a scholarship. In the case of *defectus vocis*, the chapter could release the boy from his daily service while preserving his position in the choir school.[4]

The boys' social origins

Archival sources almost never state the professions of the parents, but the almonry records regularly contain either the parents' or childrens' names or a request linked to a particular circumstance (such as death or illness). Whatever the reason, this recourse to the almonry strongly suggests the parents' poverty when it is not explicitly stated.[5] With the exception of three children from Douai recruited between June 27, 1650, and January 22, 1652,[6] all others were from the city of Cambrai itself. In the context of urban poverty, the cost of maintaining a child was higher in the city than in the country, where children traditionally helped their parents with fieldwork. Thus the chapter enabled urban parents to free themselves of a financial burden while attempting to secure professional placement for their children.

---

[1] BMC 1081, fol. 276ᵛ. One such boy's name is not specified here, but it appears on fol. 278ʳ: "Joanni Tiran patri Antonii minimi choralis licentiati domini ordinant pro viatico quinquaginta patardos ab officio paruorum vicariorum."

[2] For example, BMC 1084, fol. 53ʳ: "to Guillaume Benoit, choirboy dismissed because of a defective voice, the canons grant a garment and 50 florins."

[3] For instance, BMC 1089, fol. 172ʳ: "Nicolaus Prevost choralis defectu vocis licentiatur et examinetur an sit capax studiorum." This Nicolas was judged capable of undertaking higher education and left four months later, fol. 187ᵛ: "Die veneris 13a septembris 1658."

[4] This was the case of Adrien Pasque, whom the chapter authorized to commence his studies because he "could no [longer] carry out his duties due to a vocal defect" (BMC 1080, fol. 13ʳ).

[5] BMC 1089, fol. 103ʳ: "Jacobo Lasne novissime recepto in choralem supplicanti in subsidium togae et vestis domini concedunt duodecim florenos ab officio eleemosinae: idque de gratia et intuitu paupertatis parentum."

[6] Laurent Caulier (27 June 1650), Jean Arnould (7 Nov. 1650), and Jean-Baptiste Dumont (22 Jan. 1652).

Employment contracts

There is no trace of any employment contract that would link the institution to the family, for such mutual agreements were apparently tacit. On the one hand, the chapter agreed to give the child room and board, clothing, education, medical care, and salary; on the other, the family agreed to cut off all familial bonds with the child: "never may the choirboys walk around in the church, even to speak with their parents, no matter who they are ... none of the children may leave the house to dine in the city, whether at the home of their parents or elsewhere, for any reason at all, without permission."[1] The child was thus totally separated from the family, but entrusting a child to the chapter ensured a professional future that the family could never have offered him otherwise in this period. The high rate of infant mortality in cities shows that families did not always have the means to ensure even the survival of their children, whereas the institution to which they relinquished all responsibility offered much more: a real education and the possibility of a good life.

Upon arrival in the choir school, a young chorister was probably seven or eight years old; he was almost immediately ready to sing in the liturgy, the main purpose for which he had been hired. His was the age of basic apprenticeship, and also an age of mental flexibility and rapid adaptability to his new situation. As soon as he was installed in the choir school, the boy received new and used clothing that the chapter changed yearly, and he received his own room on the second floor of the *domus choralium*, situated just behind the cathedral.

The boys' day

The boys woke up at 6:00 am in the winter and at 5:30 in the summer.[2] They dressed in their rooms before going down to the classroom to put on their vestments. After the master checked the state of their clothing, he also made sure they had satisfied the call of nature "inasmuch as possible, because they will not be allowed to leave the choir for this kind of need except after asking and obtaining the permission of the master." Then he accompanied them to the cathedral for Matins; they took their places in the choir "with great attention and modesty, without turning the head or looking boldly ahead or to the side, but instead they must always have their eyes lowered." The office of Matins was followed immediately by Lady Mass sung by all the boys in the choir school.[3] In reality, although the sources do actually indicate the participation of the choir school in this morning service on several occasions,[4] they were not all required to perform at this Mass:

[1] No permission for such a visit has been found.

[2] ADN, 4G 2004. See also the outline presentation in Alejandro Planchart's contribution to this volume, pp. 127–28 above.

[3] ADN, 4G 2004: "messe capitulaire ... qu'ils [les enfants] chantent avant de retourner à la maison."

[4] BMC 1080, fol. 55[r]: "Moneantur itis simphoniaci qui sacerdoti quotidie post matutinas missam de Nostra dama celebranti."

only the four eldest[1] (and thus the most experienced) were at the disposal of the chapter for this service. The same situation obtained for the weekly Mass dedicated to St. Anne, founded by the canon Vandermeersche on 19 November 1604;[2] only four of the boys from the choir school are paid, one *patard* each, to perform the chant for this foundation.[3] This individual payment raises the question of how the boys' income was managed.

The administration of the choir school's income fell to the master and formed an integral part of his duties. This obligation to keep the accounts of the choir school was sometimes a source of conflict between the chapter and its master of music, the latter arguing (as at the cathedral of Saint-Quentin, for example) that he was a musician, not a banker, and that the chapter should entrust this task to the master of grammar, who had nothing else to do![4] Later, several injunctions of the chapter established the master as a manager of individual property belonging to the children in the choir school. The most explicit of these injunctions refers to the "purse" (the savings account), which the master was required to return when he left, so that the chapter could give it to a future student.

Returning to the *domus choralium*, the oldest student recited the morning prayer, after which the choirboys could finally eat breakfast. Afterwards came the day's rehearsal, where they worked primarily on the music for the subsequent offices and reviewed the previous day's music lesson. The office of Prime was at 9:00 am, and as soon as the bells sounded for Prime, the schoolmaster began to give the Latin lesson that would be finished at noon in time for the midday meal. After the meal, the children could "walk or play modestly in the court behind the house." At 1:00 pm the second rehearsal was held in preparation for Vespers at 2:30 pm, followed immediately by Compline. After these two offices, in which the children participated actively, they returned to the house, where they had a music lesson until the evening meal. Supper, at 6:00 pm in the winter and 6:30 in the summer, was the last meal of the day and was followed by thirty minutes of recreation. During the third rehearsal, which was directed by the master at 7:00 pm, the boys prepared for the next morning's Matins, office of the Virgin, or obits. After the evening prayer, which was recited at 8:00 pm by the oldest of the boys, "they retired, each to his own room, and there they observed strict silence until the next day."

Leaving the choir school

After the separation from his family, the departure from the choir school was another important rupture in a boy's life: the child, having become an adolescent, left a completely confined universe and entered the reality from which he had been totally protected for three to eleven years. The references in the chapter acts to the

---

[1] BMC 1080, fol. 258ʳ: "Item deinceps quotidie decantentur per quatuor chorales seniores cum Petro Lefebvre habituato missa De Beata finitis matutinis."

[2] BMC 1080, fol. 201ʳ (celebrated on Tuesday).

[3] BMC 1081, fol. 124ʳ.

[4] Denise Launay, "L'Enseignement de la composition dans les maîtrises en France aux XVIᵉ et XVIIᵉ siècles," *Revue de musicologie* 68 (1982), 79–90.

petits vicaires or *exchorales* show that in many cases, rejoining public life was not without its difficulties, at least at the beginning.

Nearly all the references to the dismissal of the boys in the cathedral school give *defectus vocis* as the reason, which does not necessarily mean that the voice was no longer melodious; voice change at puberty justified a leave (often provisional) during which the boy was assigned non-vocal tasks. In certain cases, the adolescent's dismissal was definitive, though this kind of expulsion was exceptional. Most often, vocal service was interrupted only for a period determined by the chapter. After the voice changed, the adolescent rejoined the chapter as a member of the professional ensemble of the *petits vicaires* in his new vocal register. Thus a young adolescent could be dismissed as *superius* or *contratenor*, then rejoin as a bass. In the case of other dismissals, the secretary usually did not report the reasons for expelling the child.[1]

Before boys left the choir school, they were systematically tested by former choirboys (now students) to determine whether they were capable of undertaking further studies.[2] If the choirboys about to leave school were not yet ready for higher education, they were kept in the choir school until the next assessment, and they continued to be evaluated periodically until they were judged competent. Those capable of study were "given a suit, four shirts, a dozen collars, one pair of shoes, one pair of slippers, and some money at the discretion of the chapter for paper, ink, and some initial books . . . with the sum of 120 florins that the canons give them each year."[3] In exchange for these donations from the chapter, the young students were obliged to report to the canons each year on the results they obtained in their studies; the boys were monitored very closely by the chapter.[4] Moreover, the chapter had three scholarships at the Collège d'Artois in Leuven, which were allocated to boys upon leaving the choir school so that they could begin their studies completely free of professional responsibilities.[5] These scholarships were granted to the choirboys in turn; as soon as one finished his studies,

---

[1] The exception is something close to the *defectus vocis* in BMC 1085, fol. 37ʳ: "Domini . . . dimissionem tertii choralis voce carentis ad pascha proximum"; and BMC 1083, fol. 124ᵛ: "Antonii . . . choralis licentiatur," where the boy is expelled because of an unspecified lack of ability.

[2] BMC 1088, fol. 210ᵛ: "Les enffans de chœur sortans hors de service seront examinez devant les envoyer aux estudes."

[3] BMC 1088, fol. 210ᵛ.

[4] BMC 1088, fol. 210ᵛ: "Lesdicts enffans seront tenus d'apporter tesmoingnage de leur comportement et leurs (résultats), et de surplus seront (ré)examiné pour scavoir quel prouffict ilz auront faict et s'ilz doibvent continuer."

[5] BMC 1089, fol. 150ᵛ: "Antonius Portesteulle exchoralis mittatur lovanium ad studiendum et gaudendum una ex tribus bursis in collegio attrebatensi ibidem fundatis pro choralibus dictae huius ecclesiae vacante per dimissionem magistri Joannis Leroy." Besides the usual scholarship, the chapter gave boys "who are sent to Louvain . . . the robe they have to wear in the college; and for whatever needs they might have . . . every year 40 florins each" (BMC 1088, fol. 210ᵛ).

he left the college, and his scholarship was immediately given to another boy who would use it to begin studying.[1]

When the choirboys left the choir school, they had only two choices: either they obtained a scholarship, usually at the Collège d'Artois in Leuven (or Douai, in two cases), or they entered the Jesuit order. In addition to scholarships, some boys received a daily income from the chapter.[2] Finally, most boys who left the choir school were admitted immediately into the chapter's choir, where with their new status of *petit vicaires* they obtained the status and the salary of professional singers.[3] This position enabled them to remain in the chapter and to receive supplementary income.

The *Vicaires* of the Cathedral

THE Latin word *vicarius* signifies a "substitute," "deputy," or "proxy," referring to anyone employed to perform a particular function belonging to someone else (and by extension a junior officer); it implicitly connotes subordination. This definition includes the metropolitan *vicaires*, who sang in place of the canons. How did this notion of substitution take shape at the cathedral of Notre-Dame at Cambrai?

The *vicaire* was above all a professional musician with specific technical ability, either vocal or instrumental, which he used to earn a living in the service of a cathedral. Furthermore, one sometimes finds the telling expression *parvus vicarius et cantor*,[4] referring to the freelancers, whether clergy or lay,[5] who generated instability because at the end of their musical training they had to take study trips to refine their skills and practical knowledge before auditioning and establishing themselves permanently.

The *vicaires* were recruited either by the chapter or by the music master; the recruiters placed the musician in the choir for several days among the other performers, so as to hear and evaluate his capacity during the services. Recruited as specialized musicians, the *vicaires* were thus required to participate in all the

---

[1] BMC 1084, fol. 25ᵛ: "Ad bursam collegii atrebatensis lovanii vacantem per dimissionem Toussani Robert domini nominarunt Jacobum Delattre."

[2] BMC 1081, fol. 173ᵛ: "Carolo Laurens chorali deportato (studia) supplicanti domini concedunt ab officio eleemosinae unum patardum dietim ad prosequendum studia vallencenis."

[3] BMC 1081, fol. 144ᵛ: "Cyprien Des Lettres choralis deportatus (ad studia) et ad presens parvus vicarius." BMC 1088, fol. 367ʳ: "Franciscus Mention choralis novissime licentiatus studens."

[4] BMC 1080, fol. 126ᵛ: "Hodie domini post summum sacrum capitulariter congregati receperunt Paschasium Benit diaconum diecesis cameracensis in paruum vicarium et cantorem sub stipendio quinque patardos dietim et mica cum turno ad beneficia vicarialia."

[5] Even though some of the musicians were not tonsured, they were nevertheless required to wear the cassock and surplice inside the church during the liturgy. However, some lay *vicaires* accepted the tonsure, not because of a true vocation but in hopes of receiving a chaplaincy.

sung day and night offices where they complemented and reinforced the participants both quantitatively and qualitatively, especially the beneficed clergy and the canons, one of whose principal duties was the singing of the canonical hours. However, these "canon-singers"[1] intoned and sang only plainchant, paradoxically leaving the polyphony to the *vicaires*, the substitutes. Finally, the *vicaires'* responsibility for professional musical support is linked to the etymology: the *vicarius* supplements the officiating clergy; he is responsible for the sung office. However, this supplementary function of representing the rights and responsibilities of another is the reason for the connection between the literal definition of the term and its function — as real as it was symbolic.

The chapter records frequently mention the *vicaires'* studies, suggesting that the vicariate did not automatically represent an end in itself, at least for young singers, but rather a professional stepping stone, a concrete means of access to an education or to a deeper knowledge of singing when the family could not pay for private teachers. Like the choirboys of the choir school from which most of them came, the *vicaires* were often poor, coming mainly from underprivileged social backgrounds.[2] The young *vicaires* sang the daily offices in rotation, so that they could study outside of working hours while remaining in the chapter under the protection of the canons.[3]

The grands vicaires or vicaires perpétuels

There were *petits vicaires* who were also *grands vicaires*, and *petits vicaires* who were not *grands vicaires*, and vice versa, even if this situation was reversible over the course of a career because a *grand vicaire* could become a *petit vicaire*![4] Consequently, despite their homonymous names and the uniformity of their status, these two professions did not *a priori* fulfill the same functions,[5] and the entirety of the criteria that distinguished them was contained in the modifier. The *petits vicaires*, professional musicians, were concerned only with the sung part of the liturgy, even if in addition to their position they received one or more chaplaincies. The *grands vicaires*, for their part, sometimes took on responsibilities fairly remote from singing itself; for example, while the canons dedicated themselves only to the choral chant of the divine office, they left the exercise of their ministry to certain *grands vicaires* (or *vicaires perpétuels*). Moreover, according to canon law, when a bishop died, resigned, or was stripped of his title, his jurisdiction was transferred

---

[1] Chapter sources sometimes refer to certain canons by the dual designation "canonicus et cantor."

[2] BMC 1080, fol. 204ʳ; BMC 1081, fol. 144ᵛ:"Cyprien Des Lettres choralis deportatus (ad studia) et ad presens paruus vicarius."

[3] The *petits vicaires* who were students arranged their schedules with the chapter: "Domini permittunt ut Joannes Marteau vocis superioris possit frequentare scholas diebus quibus non cantatur musica in choro" (BMC 1087, fol. 164ᵛ).

[4] BMC 1080, fol. 221ʳ: Abraham Wagon maintained the salary and portion of bread from his *grande vicairie*, which is why he was recruited without bread at a salary of only three *patards* a day.

[5] The master of music was recruited most often among the *grands vicaires*.

to the cathedral chapter, which then had "to prepare an inventory of the properties of the vacant church and appoint administrators to receive the revenues, and account for these revenues to the proprietor."[1] The Council of Trent gave the chapter eight days to designate an official or *grand vicaire* capable of carrying out this task; in this case, being a *vicaire* became a dignity (an office of the chapter), and the general *vicaire* acted as the right hand of the archbishop in the administration of the diocese and the archbishopric. We do not know the precise number of *grands vicaires*;[2] they were much less numerous than the *petits vicaires*, but their number likewise remained fixed because of gradual recruitment. The *grands vicaires* took on two completely different types of duties: liturgical and musical.

Thus, some of them beat time on each side of the altar,[3] an essential musical function that required a regular rhythm, familiarity with the music, and attentive listening. However, lack of information prevents us from discerning more than the most general outline of this job: the choir school was divided into a minimum of two choirs, probably conducted by two different people who were separated by the altar situated between them. There was theoretically a third conductor in the person of the choirmaster, since this responsibility was one of his duties. Moreover, choirmasters were often recruited from among the *vicaires*,[4] meaning that at least some of them had a musical education before taking up their positions. In this case, however, why did some of them (if they were in fact educated to be musicians) not join as singers before becoming *grands vicaires*?[5] Were their musical skills judged inadequate?

The recruitment of vicaires

Chapters generally selected young men under forty,[6] "men of good morals, instructed in plainchant and music, priests, clergy or laymen; however, when their merits are equal, priests are preferred to clergy and clergy to laymen."[7] The references in the chapter registers of Cambrai show that the *petits vicaires*, like the boys in the choir school, were recruited gradually; thus an incoming *vicaire* inevitably

---

[1] Pierre Toussaint Durand de Maillane, *Dictionnaire de droit canonique et de pratique bénéficiale*, rev. ed. (Lyon, 1787), 6:340.

[2] In the fifteenth century there were nine (three deacons, three subdeacons, and three priests), according to Wright, "Performance Practices," 296.

[3] BMC 1080, fol. 4ʳ: "Magistro Antonio de Penne magno vicario (huius) ecclesiae . . . a parte sinistri lateris chori mensuram tenenti domini accordant tres patardos in singulos dies cum mica." This is the sole reference to beating time, although someone must have been beating time on the other side of the choir.

[4] This was the case, for example, of Antoine de Penne, whom the chapel asked to abandon his position as *grand vicaire* (BMC 1082, fol. 8ʳ).

[5] For example, A. Wagon.

[6] References in the chapter records to the recruitment of *vicaires* never specify the exact age of the recruit but sometimes indicate that he was young. See Loupès, *Chapitres et chanoines*, 167.

[7] Archives départmentales de la Gironde, G 1010, Statutes of the chapter of Saint-Seurin; see Loupès, *Chapitres et chanoines*, 168.

replaced a departing one.[1] However, the procedure of periodically bringing in new singers without regulating turnover rates suggests that the adult choir, like that of the choirboys, was composed of an invariable vocal force. The number of musicians was determined by the chapter with great precision. If the chapter was concerned to preserve a specific number of singers in the choir, then it must also have carefully monitored the balance of vocal registers. In fact, a departing *vicaire* could not be replaced by just any other singer; the changeover had to maintain the vocal register of the departing *vicaire*.[2]

There is no evidence of an official audition or of a series of examinations of any kind that would enable the chapter to select the best singer for the choir from among several singers. Applications were thus considered on an individual basis and probably resulted from geographic and strategic circumstances.[3] The absence of an official audition call is notable in the chapter minutes themselves: just as the references to the acceptance of boys are explicit ("ex pueris hodie in capitulo presentatis domini elegerunt . . ."), references to the entry of *vicaires* confirm that there were no auditions. One finds thus the verbs "to receive," "to admit," and "to welcome," but not the expressions "to select," "to elect," or even "to choose," which would imply a selection from among a group of the candidates examined. Without an official audition, those applying to become *vicaires* must have undergone a series of examinations, the most important concerning the quality of his voice. Although no reference to these examinations is extant, there must have been at least one or more steps. Moreover, in a process similar to the selection of the choirmaster, the *vicaires* sang in the services for a trial period of a few days before their recruitment.[4]

When a young *vicaire* was admitted to the roster, his name was cited in the chapter registers, the selection examination having preceded the written report. Furthermore, the numerous statements from the chapter associating the *vicaires* with the roster[5] (without a specific contract) recall the reasons for recruiting the *vicaires* even if there were some cases of "failed" musicians reported in the chapter acts.[6] The absence of an employment contract binding the musicians to the chapter means that we do not know for how long they were engaged, nor do we know whether the contracts were reviewed regularly or if the singer was

---

[1] BMC 1082, fol. 301ᵛ: "Magister Gérard Du Gardin presbiter secliniensis bassus recipitur in paruum vicarium stipendio septem patardos et unus micae dietim cum turno ad beneficia vicarialia loco domini Jacobi Roussel . . . qui licentiatur."

[2] BMC 1082, fol. 172ᵛ: "Domini admittunt Michaelem Cordier ad officium petit dessus honorario trium patardorum . . . et licentiatur Andreas Fontaine (ancien petit dessus)."

[3] The new *vicaires* were generally from the surrounding towns. Ambitious *vicaires* (freelancers) wishing to obtain certificates of quality had to go through the most prestigious chapters, whose reputation was enough to guarantee the quality of their musicians.

[4] This poses a new problem: if the chapter as a unit officially represented the employer, who was appointed to hire the applicant? Who actually made the selection? Was it the cantor, a canon mainly charged with the organization of the liturgy? Or was it the *phonascus*/music master, who could evaluate the applicant technically, but who had no vote in the chapter, because he was not himself a canon?

[5] BMC 1080, fol. 46ʳ: "Clementi Gillet cantori basse vocis."

[6] BMC 1082, fol. 69ᵛ: "Magistro Joanni Baulduin filio clerici donomensis."

confirmed in his position or fired. The lack of explicit texts leaves these questions open, although some data shed light on a few questions. There would at least have existed a "moral" contract stipulating the vocal conditions for which the *petits vicaires* were recruited, to the extent that, in case of *defectus vocis*, the singer could be provisionally or definitively fired. Otherwise, certain references to the *vicaires'* salaries specify that they are only valid "until the next Jean-Baptiste," which would confirm that at least part of the musical personnel was under a system of annually renewable contracts.[1] Certainly, once recruited, most musicians were hardly attached to their functions or to their "employer."[2] The fact that the salaries were considered low must have led the performers to play truant and leave the canons in the lurch fairly often.

Salaries and remuneration

It is difficult to determine with precision the fixed salary of the *petits vicaires* when they entered the service of the cathedral chapter because each recruitment resulted in a specific sum that varied from one individual to another. For instance, Nicolas du Perrois was recruited at 15 *patards* a day,[3] like Michael Le Kien[4] and Julien Le Cocq,[5] whereas Pierre Le Cocq joined the chapter to perform a similar function for six *patards*.[6] The chapter maintained the salary of Nicolas Verneuil at only one *patard* per day.[7] What criteria enabled them to differentiate the starting salaries to this extent? A systematic analysis of all the salaries of the *vicaires* and their diverse variations enable us to formulate certain hypotheses. First of all, the chapter paid its singers in proportion to their professional abilities, correlated with the quality of their voices, the number and quality of their performances. Thus, several *vicaires* of the same vocal register recruited at the same time could have different starting salaries.[8] Furthermore, in the event of *defectus vocis*, the chapter reserved the right to reduce the salary gradually in proportion to the degradation of the voice, until they terminated it completely.[9]

[1] BMC 1081, fol. 108ᵛ: "Nicolao Verneuil parvo musico vulgo petit dessus continuantur stipendia unus patardi et micae dietim usque ad festum nativitatis sancti Joannis Baptistae proximum."

[2] Loupès, *Chapitres et chanoines*, 168.

[3] BMC 1080, fol. 7ʳ: "Hodie receperunt domini in parvum vicarium Nicolaii Du Perrois binchiensis sub emolumentis consuetis cum mica et quinque patardis cum turno ad beneficia vicarialia."

[4] BMC 1080, fol. 69ᵛ.

[5] BMC 1080, fol. 70ᵛ.

[6] BMC 1080, fol. 61ᵛ: "Petrus Le Cocq cameracensis cantorem basse vocis domini receperunt in paruum vicarium sub stipendio sex patardorun et mica dietim ac solitis emolumentis cum turno ad beneficia vicarialia."

[7] See n. 1 on this page.

[8] BMC 1083, fol. 150ᵛ: "Nicolaum Hucquet juvenem atrebatensis in paruum vicarium gallice petit dessus . . . necnon Laurentum Segart et Joannem Legrand."

[9] BMC 1082, fol. 29ʳ: "Magistro Roberto de Paris basso attento defectu eius vocis." The amount of salary reduction is not indicated but we know that it was four *patards* because Robert of Paris had been recruited at twelve *patards* a day (BMC 1081, fol. 195ᵛ).

At the same time, salary may also have been related to vocal register, inasmuch as basses were often recruited at more than 10 *patards* a day, while the higher voices were generally paid less than 10 *patards*. Nevertheless, even though some new recruits earned only half as much as others, there was a minimum salary. Thus, despite the disparities in wages, there was in fact a "standard" salary,[1] and references to the recruitment of musicians show that in general this amount corresponded to a portion of bread and five *patards* a day as well as a place in the rota for receiving the benefits due the *vicaires*.[2]

Even though most initial salaries were usually modified (by a raise, for example),[3] the *petits vicaires* still had relatively limited incomes and in certain cases no salary at all,[4] which raises the question of how they survived. It was probably because of their mediocre salaries that they combined their *vicairie* with related duties within the chapter, or with occasional services; in both situations, their regular income was expanded by gifts resulting from extracontractual services. Other benefits of association with the chapter likewise compensated for the *vicaires'* meager salaries. For example, the chapter covered all or part of the poorest singers' living expenses (aside from lodging) through the office of *petit vicaire* and also through the distribution of alms, which demonstrates the charitable and occasional character of the donation, since the amount would have varied from one person to another.

Lodging

Some privileges of the chapter could temporarily compensate for the inadequacy of a *vicaire's* salary. For instance, the large number of canonial houses owned by the chapter were reserved primarily for the use of the canons but could be rented to the *vicaires* at favorable rates by means of a system of renewable contracts for a limited period (leases).[5] This rental system was all the more attractive because the canons assumed responsibility for the maintenance of the canonial buildings and thus financed all repairs. However, the leases stipulated that if one of the canons wished to use a house temporarily inhabited by a *vicaire*, the latter had to make way for the canon and thus find another canonial house that would be free at the end of his lease, or if necessary, some outside lodging.[6] Nevertheless, the sources do not refer to any such cases of abrupt departure. The contracts governing the

---

[1] BMC 1083, fol. 7ᵛ: "Joannes Clos orchicensis recipitur in paruum vicarium stipendio ordinario." BMC 1083, fol. 109ʳ: "Philippo Carpentier domini concedunt ordinarum."

[2] See the document quoted in p. 158 n. 3 above.

[3] All the manuscripts contain numerous references to "auctio stipendii."

[4] BMC 1080, fol. 138ᵛ: "Fiant due cappae pro duobus vicariis non beneficiatis ab officio eleemosinae."

[5] BMC 1080, fol. 13ᵛ: "The canons appointed to examine a house for which the *grands vicaires* requested a lease must note and report to the chapter any repairs that need to be made and the terms of the lease to be signed."

[6] BMC 1080, fol. 179ʳ: "Magistro Petro de Bonnières basso huius ecclesiae domini accordant domum canonicalem . . . solvendo quatuor florenos ad acquittandum canonem conditione quod debebit ex ea migrare si per aliquem canonicum optetur."

rentals are in fact extremely specific and unambiguous: the departing tenant preserves his lodging until the end of the lease. Moreover, in case of a dispute between the resident and the postulant, it was up to the chapter to deliberate or to deputize canons to intervene at the site in order to resolve the conflict. In any case, it may have been because of residential instability that some *vicaires* opted to live outside the chapter's houses: musicians could live together in small groups and thus share the costs of the lodging.

Clothing

The sources show that, like the choirboys at entry into the choir school, certain *vicaires* (probably the poorest) received a set of clothes furnished according to need;[1] here again, the size of the ensemble depended on the generosity of the canons. Furthermore, considerable sums were regularly spent to maintain these clothes, as seen in the almonry accounts. Even though the chapter generally provided most of the choir vestments for the musicians, in theory the *vicaires* had to cover the costs of their clothing, whether lay or liturgical.

Discipline

The numerous abuses denounced by the Council of Trent related to the performance of the liturgy, ignorance, irreverence, non-abstinence, the other faults of some clerics (musicians or not), and finally the quality of musical performance. Notre-Dame of Cambrai was no exception; already in the fifteenth and sixteenth centuries, and probably earlier, the large number of chapter documents entitled *monitiones vicariorum* proves that the singers were not always orderly in their ranks; some *vicaires* on the left were reproached for throwing bones over the altar onto their counterparts on the right![2] The *monitiones* asked the two choirs to sing the divine office together, in the same rhythm, to "beat time, and the two sides to sing together"![3] These innumerable reproaches, followed by sanctions that were determined according to the gravity of the violation but also according to the amplitude of the scandal the offense had provoked, persisted throughout the seventeenth century and beyond — *monitiones* still appear in the eighteenth century concerning the *petits vicaires* as well as the *grands vicaires*. Consequently the singers' names often appear in the chapter acts in the *monitio* register.[4] The

---

[1] The chapter recruited Pierre Sohier, soprano, Friday, Feb. 6, 1609, "stipendio quinque grossorum cum mica dietim" and the same day, the chapter gave "dicto Petro Sohier . . . ab officio eleemosinae usum unius togae culcitrae, duorum parvum lintea-[ ] . . . duorum superpelliceorum et cappae et dant ab eodem officio unum par calceorum" (BMC 1081, fol. 245ᵛ).

[2] Wright, "Performance Practices," 297.

[3] BMC 18, injunction on the first folio of a manuscript of polyphony.

[4] Each chapter assembly began with a series of general injunctions addressed to the entire membership, using the meetings to remind those serving in the liturgy of their duty and of the importance of their service. Perhaps because these admonitions appear in a ritual manner and are addressed to no one in particular, they usually were without consequence.

sermons, reprimands, threats, and sanctions ranging from the minor punishment of *panis doloris et aqua* to imprisonment with suspension of benefits show that at least some of the *vicaires* constituted serious problems for the chapter.

First of all, the proximity of the numerous inns and taverns on the square right across from the *parvis* of the cathedral posed the problem of alcohol.[1] Thus many *vicaires* and chaplains were frequently reprimanded for alcohol abuse and the consequences of drunkenness, even during the liturgy. In fact, the problem of alcohol led directly to that of absenteeism from services,[2] especially in the morning.[3] It was perhaps as a result of these repeated absences that the chapter appointed a timekeeper responsible for daily roll-call and a regular list of all unexcused absences;[4] his work was so efficient that he managed to flush out those absent from services and also from processions,[5] despite the number of participants in both. When the *vicaires* were present, the second problem inherent to alcohol abuse surfaced, that of violence: some offices ended in free-for-alls laced with violent insults and sometimes even oaths among the combatants! The other recurrent problem presented by taverns was that of *feminae male famatae*, women who led the young men away from their vow of chastity. These women are often mentioned in the chapter acts with the name of the guilty party (the chapter secretary almost seems to have enjoyed reporting the details of the chapter's lawsuit against these incriminated couples). Nevertheless, it remains impossible to determine with any precision the real state of relations between these men and women, or to ascertain the nature or extent of their punishments; the chapter seems never to have had formal proof of wrongdoing, because its assessment was often based only on eyewitness testimony. Besides prostitutes, there was also the simple problem of the concubinage of some lay *vicaires* who had not taken vows of chastity; they were still asked to cease all relations or be expelled.[6] In general, departures from the chapter were extremely rare despite a few exceptions, such as resignation.

Certainly, an association with Cambrai conferred unmatched social prestige; several years after the departure of a boy, he was still called *exchoralis*. The

However, for truly serious faults that deserved condemnation, admonitions generally led to more or less severe sanctions, most often the chapter prison or dry bread and water for three weeks, with complete or partial suspension of salary but required attendance at all daily services.

[1] For references to the drunkenness of the *exchorales*, see BMC 1088, fol. 36ʳ.

[2] BMC 1081, fol. 208ʳ: "Messieurs ordonnent que tous vicaires indifferemment estans aux gaiges faisans maranches ou faultes s'abstenans de l'eglise sans congé seront mulctez comme il est declaré."

[3] BMC 1081, fol. 208ʳ: "Ceulx [les vicaires] qui ne seront a la premiere psalme de prime et a Christe filie dei unii perdent comme s'ilz avoient estez toute l'heure absens."

[4] The *vicaires*, like the other members of the choir (except the boys) were allowed to be absent for various periods and reasons, on condition that they had made a request to the chapter in advance and that the chapter had accorded the leave.

[5] BMC 1080, fol. 209ᵛ: Guillelmus des Ourmeaulx, *vicaire*, appears very frequently in the *monitiones*.

[6] According to BMC 1080, fol. 7ᵛ, Charles de Lannoy had to separate from his concubine.

famous choir school of Cambrai had not really changed its mode of operation since the time of Du Fay. Perhaps it was precisely for this reason that the choir school passed into obscurity; the persistence of tradition could have favored the "decadence" of musical practices by limiting creative impulses in order to preserve ancient customs, thereby ignoring contemporary musical developments.

[translated with revisions by Susan Boynton from "Enfants de chœur et vicaires de la maîtrise de Cambrai: Étude socio-anthropologique (1550–1670)," *Mélanges de sciences religieuses*, 61 (2004), 51–70, with permission of the author and the publisher.]

9

CHOIRBOYS, MEMORIAL ENDOWMENTS, AND EDUCATION AT AACHEN'S *MARIENKIRCHE*

Eric Rice

WHEN Charlemagne built what was to become the Collegiate Church of St. Mary in Aachen in about 800, he endowed the institution substantially. Since no document recording the initial endowment of the church or the establishment of its college of canons survives, however, the exact nature of the institution at the time of its founding has been the subject of debate. On one side, scholars such as Josef Fleckenstein believe that the church was a private chapel — essentially an itinerant court chapel that was installed in Aachen's *Marienkirche*.[1] Other scholars have been more cautious, expressing doubt that Charlemagne's chaplains would have lived according to a religious rule like that of Aachen's collegiate church and citing the difficulty of distinguishing between monks and canons in the religious culture of the eighth and ninth centuries.[2] On the other side, scholars such as Ludwig Falkenstein believe that Aachen's *Marienkirche* was founded as a collegiate church, noting that the charter of Compiègne's collegiate church cites its Carolingian forerunner as a model.[3] Though it may not be possible to determine the true nature of the *Marienkirche* at its founding, the distinction is important for my present subject: collegiate churches were more likely to have schools associated with them than were itinerant chapels, and though choirboys were usually present in both cases, provisions for their care and education were generally more substantial in collegiate churches. Given the nature of Charlemagne's educational and liturgical reforms, however, it is very likely that

---

[1] Josef Fleckenstein, *Die Hofkapelle der deutschen Könige*, Teil 1: *Grundlegung: Die karolingische Hofkapelle*, MGH Schriften, 16 (Stuttgart, 1959), 40–41.

[2] Michael McGrade, "Affirmations of Royalty: Liturgical Music in the Collegiate Church of Saint Mary in Aachen, 1050–1350" (Ph.D. diss., University of Chicago, 1998), 19; Rudolf Schieffer, "Hofkapelle und Aachener Marienstift bis in die staufische Zeit," *Rheinische Vierteljahrsblätter* 51 (1987), 16–20.

[3] Ludwig Falkenstein, *Karl der Große und die Entstehung des Aachener Marienstiftes* (Paderborn, 1981).

choirboys were present and provided for in exemplary fashion in Aachen during his lifetime, regardless of the nature of the *Marienkirche* at its founding.[1]

Once the *Marienkirche* became a collegiate church, much of the Aquensian liturgy evolved, as such liturgies often did, through memorial endowments. The church's canons, fully ordained priests who were part of the governing structure of the church and who were not required to hold property in common, could establish funds in their wills for the founding of new feasts or for the increase of an existing feast's rank; the funds would be used to pay the additional canons or chaplains who appeared for the additional singing they were required to perform as part of the change in liturgy, and the donor's soul would benefit from the donation after his death. Few Aquensian wills from the High Middle Ages survive — indeed, I am only aware of canons' wills from the fourteenth century and later — but these endowments were generally recorded in the church's necrologies along with the death dates of their donors. Additionally, a canon might endow a Mass for the Dead to be sung over his grave on the anniversary of his death, and such ceremonies also required payments to canons or lay singers for services rendered. It is through endowments of this kind, which are recorded in necrologies and in wills, that we can begin to discern a trend in the funding of the choirboys' education. Though the picture is far from complete, it appears that the canons slowly came upon the idea of funding the education of individual choirboys through memorial endowments in part because of the role of choirboys in the singing of polyphony in memorial services and on high feast days. These endowments evolved into complex scholarships involving service to the collegiate chapter as a choirboy, attendance at the church's school, and subsequent study at universities in Liège (the seat of Aachen's diocese) and Cologne (the seat of its archdiocese).

The later of the *Marienkirche*'s two surviving necrologies, now in the Stadtarchiv Aachen, dates from the first half of the fourteenth century. Subsequent additions record endowments created as late as 1700. Beginning in the early fourteenth century, such endowments contain specific instructions and payments for various aspects of the endowed service. In one such endowment, created by William de Pomerio (of Alsace), we read that the donor, who died in 1307,[2] funded additional singing for the major hours of the Office and for the high Mass on the feast of St. Catherine, with specific payments to the cantor and his assistants as

---

[1] A lively discussion of the ruler's interest in education is Donald A. Bullough, "A Court of Scholars and the Revival of Learning," in *The Age of Charlemagne* (New York, 1966), 101–29. Charlemagne's *Admonitio generalis* of 789, a decree addressing church procedures within his realm, included several rules on liturgical practice. One called for higher educational standards in conjunction with greater liturgical conformity. Another sought the suppression of the Gallican liturgy in favor of the Roman, so that the rituals within the Frankish realm would correspond with those of Rome. The entire edict is edited in *Monumenta germaniae historica Capitularia*, 1:52–62 (no. 22), 60–61, and in McGrade, "Affirmations of Royalty," 42–43. On the general significance of the edict, see Rosamond McKitterick, *The Frankish Church and the Carolingian Reforms, 789–895* (London, 1977), 1–79.

[2] All supplemental information on the Aquensian canons in this article was gathered from Peter Offergeld, "Die persönliche Zusammensetzung des alter Aachener Stiftskapitels bis 1614" (Ph.D. diss., Rheinisch-Westfälische technische Hochschule Aachen, 1972).

well as to the celebrant, deacon, and subdeacon at Mass.[1] Many such endowments refer to candles, and indeed William specified a payment of six *solidi* "to the *custos*, that he may light the *corona*," a reference to the twelfth-century crown-shaped chandelier donated by Frederick Barbarossa.[2] The incense bearer and the organist also receive payment, but payment to the choirboys is indicated almost as an afterthought: "that which remains of the four marks is given to the choirboys *pro focis*," that is, for their own hearth and home.[3]

In a somewhat later endowment by the canon Alardus de Monte (of Mons), whose activity between 1331 and 1385 has been detected in the documents, we read one of the first indications in this context of a payment "for singing in polyphony (*in organis*)."[4] While it is indeed possible that boys were employed for monophonic singing or for other tasks in conjunction with such services, later sources tend to refer to choirboys and polyphony in close proximity to one another, suggesting that boys were employed in special services specifically for polyphonic singing (which was probably improvised in most cases). During the fourteenth century, however, choirboys and polyphony are seldom mentioned in the same entry, and

---

[1] Aachen, Stadtarchiv, K St. Marien 204, fol. 71ᵛ (1307): "William of Alsace, canon, gave two marks for the feast of blessed Catherine. To those singing First Vespers, one *obolus*; for Matins, one *obolus*; and for Second Vespers, one *obolus*. To the cantor with those assisting him, eight *denarii*; to the celebrant of the Mass, six *denarii*; to the deacon, four; to the subdeacon, four; to the *custos*, that he may light the *corona*, six *solidi*; to the incense-bearer, three *denarii*; to the organist, six *denarii*. That which remains of the four marks is given to the choirboys for their own hearth and home." ("Willelmus de pomerio canonicus dedit nobis in festo beate katerine virginis ii marcas. Socijs in i vesperis obolum. In matutinis obolum. Et in ii vesperis obolum. Cantori cum sibi astantibus cuilibus viii denarios. Missam celebranti vi denarios. Dyaconi iiii et subdyaconi iiii denarios Custodi ut coronam accendat vi solidos. Incensori iii denarios. Organiste vi denarios. Quod super est de iiii marcis dabitur scolaribus pro focis.")

[2] On this chandelier, see Georg Minkenberg, "Der Barbarossaleuchter im Dom zu Aachen," *Zeitschrift des Aachener Geschichtsvereins* 96 (1989), 69–102; on its use in the liturgy, see Eric Rice, *Music and Ritual at Charlemagne's* Marienkirche *in Aachen*, Beiträge zur Rheinischen Musikgeschichte (Kassel, 2008), 55–57.

[3] While William's endowment provides two marks, the final sentence refers to four, perhaps indicating an existing endowment of two marks for the feast of St. Catherine. The relationship between the various currencies in use in Aachen in the late Middle Ages and early modern period is extremely complex; since the economics of the endowments are not central to my discussion, I have translated currency names literally and have not calculated currency equivalents.

[4] Aachen, Stadtarchiv, K St. Marien 204, fol. 72ᵛ (ca. 1385): "Alardus de Monte, canon of the Church of Blessed Mary in Aachen, gave us for the feast of blessed Agatha, virgin, to the canons present for First Vespers, Matins, and the Mass, one mark; to their associates, six shillings; to the director of the choir at Mass, six *denarii*; to the celebrant at Mass, one mark; to the subdeacon replacing a canon, six *denarii*; to the deacon, six *denarii*; for singing in polyphony, twelve *denarii*." ("Alardus de Monte canonicus ecclesie beate Marie Aquensis dedit nobis in festo beate Agathe virginis canonicis presantibus in primis vesperis in matutinis et in missa unam marcam. Sociis sex schillinge. Custodienti chorum in missa vi denarios. Celebranti missam vi denarii. Subdiacono existenti canonico vi denarii. Dyacono vi denarii. Cantanti in organis xii denarii.")

it is probably the case that the indication of payments "for singing in polyphony" implied payments to choirboys as well as to adult singers.

By the fifteenth century, the sheer number of specific stipulations in some wills required that endowments be recorded in necrologies by means of an extract from the will itself. In one such extract from the will of Theodoric Snydwuit, who died in 1472, the specifics concerning the testator's memorial services are immediately followed by a paragraph that deserves quotation in full:

> A passage from the will of the honorable former lord of this church Theodoric Snydwuit, while he lived a canon, who died in the year 1472 .... I leave twelve Rhenish florins by inheritance for and to my cloistered house for the two first choirboys appointed by the chapter, who are under obligation to stand near the pulpit reading and singing continuously without disturbing the service in the choir, and either one of them will sing the *cursus* and Office of the Blessed Virgin Mary every day for the well-being of my soul and for those who have been overlooked.[1]

The specificity of these instructions is significant. The money was to be used for the "first two choirboys," presumably meaning the best two; it stipulates their duties and behavior, but also ultimately makes clear that the endowment was meant for the benefit of the deceased. As we shall see, the emphasis on the boys' duties and education increases during the sixteenth century, though the canons' desire to secure the well-being of their own souls is never wholly absent from the picture.

The fact that Snydwuit's endowment was for two choirboys rather than one is perhaps related to the tradition — a relatively old one in Aachen by this time — of establishing similar funds for pairs of chaplains of new altars.[2] By 1474, the year the second-oldest ordinal was probably copied, the church had thirty-three active altars, each with at least two chaplains or canons associated with it. Many of these altars and the prebends associated with them were established in the wills of local nobles or, as time passed, in the wills of the canons themselves. Indeed, Snydwuit's will goes on to establish a weekly Mass sung by the chaplains at the Altar of the Holy Cross, probably one increase among many in the chaplains' activity at that altar. With one exception, every subsequent endowment I have read for the education and well-being of choirboys funds two positions in the church.

---

[1] Aachen, Stadtarchiv, K St Marien 204, fols. 80ᵛ–81ʳ (1472): "Clausula ex testamento honorabilis quondam domini Theodericj Snydwuit huius ecclesie dum viveret Canonici qui decessit Anno domini millesimo quadranigentesimo septimagesimo secundo. . . . ℂ Item lego duodecim florenos renensis hereditare ad et super domum meam claustralem pro duobus primis vicarijs scholaribus per capitulum instituendis/ qui continuo stando juxta pulpeta legendo et cantando remanens debent absque officijs exercendis in choro/ et quilibet eorum dicat cursum et officium beate marie virginis singulis diebus pro salute anime mee et pro neglectis."

[2] Several altars are known to have been founded with two rectors. The oldest example of which I am aware is the altar of St. Simon and St. Jude, which was founded by Henry, duke of Lorraine and Brabant, in 1223; the foundation document is printed in Christian Quix, *Geschichte der Stadt Aachen, nach Quellen . . . mit einem Codex diplomaticus aquensis*, 2 vols. (Aachen, 1840), 2:98, no. 136.

The nature and specificity of endowments for choirboys, as for other endowments, is wholly dependent on the wealth of the testator. The exceptional endowment for the support of one choirboy rather than two was established by Thomas Tzamen, also known as Thomas Aquanus, who was active as choirmaster and subsequently also as a priest from 1485 until his death in 1517. Tzamen is perhaps the only person mentioned in this article whose name might be familiar to a musicologist: in addition to his presumed activity at Aachen, a motet attributed to him is preserved in Heinrich Glarean's treatise *Dodecachordon* of 1547, but until recently nothing else about him had come to light.[1] The name "Thomas" is listed for the choirmaster in the church's payment records from 1485 to 1487 and then again from 1493 to 1501, when a twenty-nine-year lacuna begins. The choirmaster listed after the lacuna, beginning in July of 1530, is one "Adam," who probably can be identified as Adam Luyr, a student of Tzamen's who transmitted the latter's work to Glarean at the University of Cologne between 1510 and 1514.[2] Tzamen's heretofore unknown will is located in the *Marienkirche*'s archives, and the document transmits not only Tzamen's death date (5 April 1517), but also the fact that he was raised in Maastricht and served as a parish priest in the village of Mortier east of Liège.[3] His inventory is substantial enough that he must have died a relatively wealthy man, and yet the fact that he established an endowment for only one choirboy suggests that he was perhaps not quite as wealthy as some of the canons. As one might expect, his will offers a bit more specificity as to the activities of the choir. He refers to eight choirboys, a somewhat unusual number for the churches within the diocese of Liège, and offers to endow a position for a ninth:

> I also leave 100 horn guilders to support a young ninth vicar, and it will be his task to prepare the censer or incense vessel, and to carry the cross and to serve in the Mass in the choir, and he will be somewhat senior to the other boys, just as in Maastricht and Liège in all secondary churches there are two, and if my honorable dear lords [of the chapter] do not need or approve [of a ninth vicar], then the 100 horn guilders shall be provided for *elmissen* or for distributing bread at Mortier every year when the annual service in my commemoration shall be held, according to the determination of my executors, or my dear lords of the chapter, or the churchwardens of Mortier.[4]

[1] Tzamen's motet *Domine Jesu Christe* is transcribed in Heinrich Glarean, *Dodecachordon*, 2 vols., trans. Clement A. Miller, Musicological Studies and Documents 6 (n.p., 1965); Glarean's brief discussion of Tzamen and the latter's student Adam Luyr is 2:256–57.

[2] Luyr matriculated at the University of Cologne on 23 Nov. 1510; see Clement A. Miller, "Aquanus, Adam," *New Grove Dictionary of Music and Musicians*, 2nd ed., 29 vols. (London, 2000), 1:792.

[3] In his will, Tzamen leaves sums to the Collegiate Church of St. Servais, where he notes that he had been a choirboy, and the parish church of St. Mark, where he notes that his parents are interred; Aachen, Domarchiv, Stiftsarchiv, vi.4.2, fol. 3ᵛ. Tzamen and Luyr receive fuller treatment in Rice, *Music and Ritual*, chap. 5.

[4] Aachen, Domarchiv, Stiftsarchiv, vi.4.2, fol. 3ʳ (1516): "Noch besett ick hondert hornsgulden om eenen jongen negende vicarius te sien, ende die sall belast syn, den cencer of wyerichs vaet te maicken, ende dat cruytz te dragen ende die choer messe te dienen, ende he sal wat meerder syn dan die ander jongen, gelyck te Triecht ende tot Luyck in alle

This paragraph suggests that Tzamen wanted Aachen's collegiate church to emulate the practices of others in the area. Curiously, it also suggests that some members of the chapter might not approve of such an endowment, since Tzamen offered to fund alms for the poor of Mortier instead.

If such endowments were not well regarded in the early years of the sixteenth century, the reverse was true by the second quarter of the century. The Pollart family, landholders in Exaten and Roggenbosch, became important donors and canons within the church, and a relatively complex network of uncles, brothers, and nephews developed, each emulating the others in his will. The level of detail is perhaps at its height in the will of Hugo Pollart, dated 1527, wherein we read that the choirboys receiving scholarships from his endowment will be released from their singing responsibilities (presumably after their voices have broken) by the cantor or succentor, so that they will subsequently be able to study for a total of six continuous years.[1] Hugo then names his top choices for the first recipients of his scholarship before turning back to its conditions: every day the boys must read

secundarj kirchen esser twee, ende oft myn erwerdige lieve herrn niet alsoe en belieft of guet en dunckt, soe salmen die hondert hornsgulden ordineren tot elmissen of broit te deylen tot Mortiers alle jaer als men myn jairbeganck halden sal, nae disposicien mynre testamentoire, of mynre lieven herren vanden capittel off kerckmeesters van Mortiers." My thanks to Rob C. Wegman for his translation of Tzamen's will.

[1] Aachen, Domarchiv, Stiftsarchiv, IV.6.A.1 — Hugo Pollart Will, fol. 4^{r-v}: "These ten florins I wish to be applied in perpetuity and in future times for the use of two superior choirboys; [the sum] should reach those most worthy to be presented to my lords of the chapter by our venerable lord cantor and succentor of the same church with a time of release from singing. These two will enjoy the presented aforementioned ten florins for [the purpose of] six continuous years of specific and general study, five florins [for each to study] simultaneously at any place. Once these six years have been completed, they will enjoy the rest of the remaining [florins] as prescribed. Upon the establishment [of this fund], I want one of the sons of Master Nicholas to enjoy it first, with the approval of the church, so that the latter should nominate one of his offspring, either John or Nicholas, for my lords. And I want these two choirboys to be compelled to read the seven Penitential Psalms daily, and the Requiem and collect for the founder at the end of the day, and other collects normally recited for the faithful. What remains of the ten florins, if at any time it should happen to be returned, I wish the same sum of this redeemed amount to be applied in and beyond the city of Aachen, so that the sons of the city of Aachen can enjoy the same memorial in perpetuity." ("Quos decem florenos desidero perpetuis et futuris temporibus applicari ad usum duorum vicariolum proborum, quos tempore absolutionis a cantu per venerabilem dominum nostrum cantorem et succentorem ejusdem ecclesiae dominis meis de capitulo idoneiores praesentari contigerit. Qui duo praesentati praedictis decem florenis ad sex annos continuos in studio particulari et universali gaudebunt; pro quolibet quinque similes floreni. Quibus sex annis finitis gaudebunt de eisdem alii ad hoc praestandi, prout praescriptum est. Ad quam fundationem volo quod in primis gaudeat unus de filiis Magistri Nicolai, eccelesiae testificis, prout idem eisdem dominis meis nominaverit, de Joanne vel Nicolao prolibus. Et volo quod dicti vicarioli quotidie sint obligati ad legendum septem psalmos poenitentiales, in fine cum Requiem et collecta pro fundatore, et aliis collectis pro fidelibus dici consuetis. Quos dictos redditus decem florenorum, si aliquando redimi contingat, desidero quod eadem summa ex redemptione proveniens applicetur in et supra urbem Aquensem, qui subditi filiorum civium Aquensium eadem memoria in perpetuum gaudebunt.")

the seven Penitential Psalms as well as the Requiem and a collect customarily said for the dead on his behalf, and any residual funds must be reapplied to the endowment so that it grows and can be enjoyed by the boys of Aachen in perpetuity.

Hugo's endowment seems to have begun a significant trend, one that three more examples will serve to illustrate. By 1573, Protestantism was a serious threat to Aachen and its collegiate church, and Dutch rebels had already besieged the city once.[1] In Jacob Hochtmann's will from that year, the canon specifies that two poor boys should receive scholarships to attend schools in which "sound and Catholic doctrine flourishes."[2] Like Hugo's endowment, Hochtmann's fund was designed to educate the boys in a school not associated directly with the *Marienkirche*, though clearly it had to be Catholic. Hochtmann also tries to ensure that there will be sufficient funds so that if one boy is deemed deficient, another may receive the scholarship. Perhaps in response to Hugo's suggestion that boys funded through his endowment be released from singing, Hochtmann insists that the scholarship be given to boys who were good singers or who served the church in some other way, though he also insists on their low station. The two senior canons rather than the cantor or succentor would have ultimate authority over the boys.

---

[1] Rice, *Music and Ritual*, chap. 9; see also Eric Rice, "Two Liturgical Responses to the Protestant Reformation at the Collegiate Church of Saint Mary in Aachen, 1570–1580," *Viator* 38/2 (2007), 291–318.

[2] Aachen, Domarchiv, Stiftsarchiv, iv.7.3 — Jacob Hochtmann Will (1573): "A clause from the will of lord Jacob Hochtmann of blessed memory, formerly a canon of the Church of the Blessed Virgin Mary, established 17 November 1573. . . . If any of my goods should remain, I leave and bequeath [them] to the poor in the study of letters and especially scripture for sustenance and nourishment; and this [is to be done] in towns and schools for specific and general study in which sound and Catholic doctrine flourishes. If it be that this subsidy is able to endure in perpetuity and future times, I seek and desire that the sum and assessment be obtained every year from the money that remains and is left after the completion of the bequests of this my will and the payment of my debts, so that even if one boy falls short in his studies, another youth of good nature might succeed him. But I want the boys who benefit from this subsidy to be those from this our Church of the Blessed Virgin Mary and to be the best at singing and in any other way that they serve or minister. Nevertheless, I wish that those who are joined to me by blood in any degree be preferred over others. However, I release any power or authority that these two recipient boys of good character might owe for the enjoyment of this my subsidy for study to the two senior priest canons of this church." ("Clausula testamenti Domini Iacobi Hochtmanni piae memorie quondam canonici Ecclesiae Beatae Mariae Virginis Anno 1573 die 17 Novembris conditi. . . . Si quid in bonis meis residui fuerit, lego et relinquo pauperibus in studio literarum et maxime sacrarum alendis et nutriendis: et hoc in locis et gymnasiis particularibus vel generalibus in quibus vigeat sana et Catholica doctrina. Sit ut hoc subsidium durare valeat perpetuis futuris temporibus peto et cupio ut emantur annui singuli redditus et census ex pecunia quae superfuerit et restabit post complementum legatorum cuius mei testamenti et debitorum meorum solitionem ut sit uno a studiis deficiente succedat alius bonae indolis iuvenis. Volo autem ut hoc subsidio gaudeant illi iuvenes qui huic Ecclesiae nostrae Beatae Mariae Virginis et in primis canendo, aut aliquo alio modo inservierint aut ministraverint. Attamen illis praeferri volo, quos constabit mihi aliquo gradu esse sanguine iunctos. Horum autem bonis indolis iuvenium assumendorum qui hoc meo studii subsidio gaudere debeant, facultatem et autoritatem relinquo duobus senioribus cuius ecclesiae canonicis sacerdotalibus.")

The will of Hermanus Pollart, Hugo's nephew, is dated 1576 and is even more clear about the relationship of the boys' work at the church and their education. After explaining that the endowment is for the benefit of his soul and those of his parents as well as for the advantage of the church, he writes that two equal portions of his fund should be used to educate two choirboys *after* they had served the church studiously and earnestly, and that they must also be proficient in polyphonic singing.[1] This is especially significant for Aachen's history as a center for the cultivation of polyphony, for it was also during this decade that the Liégeois composer Johannes Mangon was employed as succentor, leaving behind three substantial manuscripts of liturgical polyphony by composers such as Orlande de Lassus, Jacobus Clemens non Papa, Thomas Crecquillon, and himself. As I have shown elsewhere, the insistence on maintaining a high quality of music despite limited funds is evident from many other documents in the church's archives, and Aachen's importance as a flourishing musical center in the period is underscored not least by the canon's consistent endowments for the education and maintenance of the church's choirboys.[2] The fact that Hermanus was unwilling to release choirboys whom he had funded into the wider world for their studies until they had become proficient in polyphonic singing suggests that he wanted to maintain the chapter's reputation as a musical center. The will also specifies that the recipients of his scholarship could only go on to university studies in Liège with the express

---

[1] Aachen, Domarchiv, Stiftsarchiv, IV.7.5 — Hermanus Pollart Will (1576): "After these, I leave and bequeath, from the goods manifestly left by me, five hundred gold florins in gold, or indeed their value; for a comparison sum I approve twenty-five of the similar golden florins for use in the foundation described below. Desiring indeed to be mindful of the well-being of my soul and those of my parents, and the setting out earnestly of this letter or testament of mine, for future times in perpetuity, [and] the improvement of the church and scholastic study, I order and constitute out of the fund described two equal portions for two choirboys, that after they have served studiously and earnestly with the choir in our church in Aachen, have progressed excellently in polyphony, are seen to be of good nature and prospects — both in their propensity for their studies and for their utility — and are favorable for the study of letters and devotion to the choir, they might be sent forth, with express permission of the chapter, and have a four-year stipend. I also want the first year to be a review in the rudiments of grammar in this our school of the Blessed Virgin Mary, but the three remaining years [to be spent] in the city of Liège in its present disposition and inclination." ("Post haec lego et relinquo ex promptioribus bonis per me reliquentis quingentos florenos aureos in auro, vel verum illorum valorum; pro comparando redditu annuo viginis quinque similium florenorum aureorum in usum fundationis subscriptae. Cupiens enim animae meae et parentum meorum saluti consulere, harum literarum sive testi huius mei serie, pro perpetuis futuris temporibus in profectum Ecclesiae et seminarii studii scholastici augmentum. Ordino et constituo ex redditu praescripto: Duas equales portiones pro duobus Iuvenibus Vicariolis, ut postquam in Ecclesia nostra Aquensi choro studiosi et graviter inservierint, et in Cantu figurativo probe profecerint, bonae indolis et expectationis, ac ad studia propensi seu utiles esse videantur; et studii literari gratia a servilis chori/ de expresso consensu Capituli/ remissi fuerint quadriennale habeant alimoniae subsidium. Volo autem ut priori anno in schola hac nostra Beatae Mariae Virginis in rudimentis grammatices sese exerceanti reliquis vero tribus, in civitate Leodiensis de praesentia dispositione et voluntate.")

[2] Rice, *Music and Ritual*, chap. 9.

consent of the chapter, and then only after they had spent one year studying the rudiments of grammar, further suggesting that Hermanus did not want the boys to be seen as deficient in any way.

Such stipulations also stood as efforts to preserve the chapter's reputation and to combat provincialism among its own members, for it was logical that some of the chapter's choirboys would return to Aachen to become canons. The will of Robert Wachtendonck, who held a benefice at the church of St. Martin in Liège and was elected dean of Aachen's *Marienkirche* in 1565, is significant in this regard as well as in several others. It was likely Wachtendonck who, through his two positions, brought Mangon and other Liégeois musicians to Aachen, so we would expect his interest in liturgical polyphony to be manifest in his will. His document was written during one of the deadliest plagues in Aachen's history, one that took the life of Johannes Mangon and was to take that of Wachtendonck as well. Just as in some of the earliest wills, provisions for Wachtendonck's memorial service include specific payments to choirboys.[1] He also funded university studies for two boys, who were to spend three years studying in Liège and another three in Cologne, and he specifies that the three years at the University of Cologne should be spent in the *Bursa Laurentiana*, a venerable society that provided financial and logistical support, housing, and an approach to the liberal arts curriculum that accorded with the views of Albertus Magnus.[2] Given the turbulent times in which

---

[1] Aachen, Domarchiv, Stiftsarchiv, VI.4.28, fols. 1ᵛ–2ʳ, 4ʳ — Robert Wachtendonck Will (1578): "Moreover, for my memory and for that of my uncle, lord Gisbert Wachtendonck, an anniversary is to be made and observed in the said Church of the Blessed Virgin Mary of the town of Aachen every future year in perpetuity. I want the sum of four guilders annually assigned to my venerable lord brothers, and similarly three guilders of fair weight to the vicars, the men of the choir, the singing choirboys, for which the said memorial will be performed at first light on All Saints Day. . . . Item, I also leave, for the support of two choirboys [who have] served decently and fluently, in support of their studies in Liège for three years, then for three years in Cologne at the Bursa Laurentiana, 600 gold guilders, which they shall have and enjoy for their use and yearly pension in the same amounts as those ordered by Hermanus Pollart. The disposition of these funds will be ordered by my nephew, Reinhardt von Wachtendonck, as long as he lives, and once he has died, by the dean, or in his stead, the senior deacon or senior subdeacon." ("Insuper pro mea patruique mei memoria Domini Gisberti à Wachtendonck anniversaria in dicta beatae Mariae Virginis oppidi Aquensis Ecclesia annis futuris singulis perpetuis temporibus fienda et observanda. Volo de bonis meis mobilibus per executores infra nominandos assignari venerabilis dominis confratribus meis quatuor aureos annui redditus, similiter vicarius, chori sociis, cantoribus vicariolis tres aureos justi ponderis comparandos, quae quidem memoria servabitur die primae omnium sanctorum. . . . Item noch besetz ich zu unterhaltung zwey vicariolis so zuchtig und fleissig gedienet zu unterhaltung in studiis Leodii ad Triennum, deinde Coloniae in Bursa Laurentiana ad Triennum 600 goltgulden derer abnutzung und jahrliche pension sich zu erfreuen haben sollen, in massen wie dominus Hermanus Bollart verordnet. Zu welche disposition meinen Neven Reinhardt von Wachtendonck die Zeit er lebt verordnen, illo mortuo, Decanus senior, in altari, senior diaconus senior subdiaconus residens wider disponieren sollen.")

[2] Maarten J. F. M. Hoenen, "Late Medieval Schools of Thought in the Mirror of University Textbooks," in *Philosophy and Learning: Universities in the Middle Ages*, ed. Maarten J. F. M. Hoenen, J. H. Josef Schneider, and Georg Wieland, Education and Society in the Middle Ages and Renaissance, 6 (Leiden, 1995), 329–69, esp. 330–34; see also Rainer Christoph

Wachtendonck composed his will, he may have felt that such specific stipulations were an effective way to prevent the corruption of his endowment's recipients and thus combat the spread of Protestantism in the region. The boys' yearly allowances were to be the same size as those stipulated by Hermanus Pollart, exemplifying the kind of emulation that took place in the creation of such endowments. Wachtendonck goes on to specify that his nephew Reinhardt will administer the endowment, and that, should Reinhardt die, the dean of the chapter would succeed him, in conjunction with various deacons.

Endowments for the education of choirboys continued well into the seventeenth century, and university study persisted as a significant element in the stipulations. The nearly constant increase in the specificity of the educational provisions in such endowments may have been part of an effort to combat increasing insularity of the collegiate chapter. By the close of the sixteenth century, Aachen's choirboys were called *vicarioli*, a plural diminutive of *vicarius* that reflected the hope that they might progress to become adult vicars and perhaps even canons. Even if the majority of the choirboys did not enter the priesthood or otherwise serve the church in subsequent years, they presumably derived significant benefits from the education they received in conjunction with their ecclesiastical service. Such benefits were surely used to recruit the most talented young singers from the surrounding region, as was the case in every other collegiate church with a choir school. Indeed, the comparison between Aachen's *Marienkirche* and the collegiate churches of Liège — which we saw above in conjunction with the will of Thomas Tzamen — demonstrates a concern that the institution's musical stature had fallen below that of its neighbors. Endowments designed to improve the situation of the *Marienkirche*'s choirboys are especially well recorded, and they surely indicate a more widespread practice in other collegiate churches in the area.

Today, Aachen's *Domsingschule* cites a twelve-hundred-year history and names Alcuin among its founders.[1] While such a statement is a specious suggestion that the institution has functioned uninterruptedly from Charlemagne's era to ours, it is clear that a long tradition of education in both music and grammar persisted at Aachen's collegiate church. The evolution I have just traced of memorial endowments gradually developing into scholarships for choirboys demonstrates the canons' efforts to bolster the importance of their institution not only through the maintenance of a rich liturgico-musical culture but also through the promotion of education (whether at Aachen or nearby) for the boys who were potential future canons. While these men used their money to ensure the well-being of their souls in the hereafter, they also found means to continue, in an increasingly thoughtful and detailed fashion, the traditions of the institution that had nurtured them in this life.

Schwinges, "Sozialgeschichtliche Aspekte spätmittelalterlicher Studentenbursen in Deutschland," in *Schulen und Studium im sozialen Wandel des hohen und späten Mittelalters*, ed. Johannes Fried, Vorträge und Forschungen, 30 (Sigmaringen, 1986), 527–64.

[1] The statement can be found on the website of the Domsingschule Aachen at http://www.aachener-dommusik.de/index16-0.aspx (accessed 9 Aug. 2007).

10

THOMAS MULLINER
AN APPRENTICE OF JOHN HEYWOOD?

Jane Flynn

THIS chapter will examine the further musical education and training of English choristers (after their voices had broken) between 1500 and 1560. It was customary to place the most talented young men in an apprenticeship with a master of choristers or a musician associated with a prominent ecclesiastical or collegiate institution. Using archival sources that document the activities of masters of choristers, the autobiographical manuscript produced by Thomas Whythorne,[1] an apprentice of John Heywood from 1545 to 1548, and the famous miscellany by the singer and organist Thomas Mulliner, I will argue that Mulliner was in turn Heywood's apprentice from 1559 to 1563 and that he compiled his miscellany during that time.

Like Whythorne, who had been a chorister at Magdalen College School, Oxford, before he studied with Heywood, Mulliner had presumably trained as a chorister, although it is not known where. In general, such musical apprentices would have been expected to continue their study of pricksong, faburden, descant, organ-playing, and Latin grammar,[2] and in addition, to serve their master by teaching younger choristers or by assisting in the production of pageants and other civic or royal entertainments. In this way, Whythorne learned from Heywood how to play dances and songs on the virginals and lute; how to write verse; and how to set lyrics to music. Since Mulliner's miscellany can be shown to include examples of all the various kinds of subject matter associated with choristers' and musical apprentices' training — Latin poetry and translation exercises, organ versets arranged in order of increasing difficulty, transcriptions of motets and other vocal and instrumental pieces, moralistic songs and dances, and consort parts of

---

[1] Oxford, Bodleian Library, MS Eng. misc. c. 330; published as Thomas Whythorne, *The Autobiography of Thomas Whythorne*, ed. James M. Osborn (Oxford, 1961).

[2] See Jane Flynn, "The Education of Choristers in England during the Sixteenth Century," in *English Choral Practice, c.1400–c.1650*, ed. John Morehen, Cambridge Studies in Performance Practice, 5 (Cambridge, 1995), 180–99.

pieces for cittern and gittern, and so on — it comprises a rich and invaluable source that illustrates and supplements the archival and documentary evidence.[1]

When the average chorister's voice broke at around the age of fourteen or fifteen,[2] he would usually return to the society from which he had come.[3] For example, both John and Symond Byrd, who were listed as choristers at St. Paul's in 1554, later became wealthy London merchants and financiers.[4] The few choristers (including their brother William) who hoped to become vicars choral or organists remained at their cathedral or collegiate chapel, usually living in the choristers' house and assisting in various capacities while continuing their education. Thus, in 1517, William Saunders, "late child of the Chapel," remained with William Cornish, master of choristers at the Chapel Royal, who was paid for "finding [i.e., housing, feeding, and clothing] and teaching" him.[5] In 1511, in Exeter, where each "clerk of the second form" or "secondary" was maintained by a senior canon, the secondaries were permitted to be absent from choir in order to attend the cathedral song school or the city grammar school.[6] At Lincoln in 1542, three of the adolescents, who "contrary to custom, had their chambers in taverns and other houses of laymen in the close and outside," were ordered to take their meals in the vicars' house, the choristers' house, or one of the chantries, and to attend the grammar school, but were forbidden to "wander round hither and thither as they now did."[7] Nevertheless, in 1545, another adolescent, William Smythe, was brought before the chapter for boarding outside the close and "being very remiss in getting up for mattins and reading the holy Scriptures and attending the grammar school as he is bound."[8]

Presumably because of the mixed nature of their duties, the official title for such adolescents varied from place to place, but their duties often included reading the lessons or looking after the organ. The two "yeomen" at the Chapel Royal were also "called pistellers groweing from the children of the chappell by succession of age and after that theire voices change";[9] at Northumberland's chapel, the

---

[1] British Library, Add. MS 30513; the keyboard music is transcribed in Denis Stevens, ed., *The Mulliner Book*, Musica Britannica, 1 (London, 1973).

[2] Roger Bowers, "The Vocal Scoring, Choral Balance and Performing Pitch of Latin Church Polyphony in England, c.1500–58," *Journal of the Royal Musical Association* 112 (1987), 38–76 at 48.

[3] Nicholas Orme, "Education and Learning at a Medieval English Cathedral: Exeter, 1380–1548," *Journal of Ecclesiastical History* 32 (1981), 265–83 at 279.

[4] John Harley, "Merchants and Privateers: A Window on the World of William Byrd," *Musical Times* 147 (2006), 51–66 at 51.

[5] John Stevens, *Music and Poetry in the Early Tudor Court* (Cambridge, 1979), 305.

[6] Nicholas Orme, "The Medieval Clergy of Exeter Cathedral, II: The Secondaries and Choristers," *Reports and Transactions of the Devonshire Association* 115 (1983), 79–100 at 82–84.

[7] William Page, ed., *The Victoria History of the County of Lincoln*, vol. 2 (London, 1906), 432–33.

[8] Ibid., 433.

[9] *A Collection of Ordinances and Regulations for the Government of the Royal Household* (1780 [all catalogues give date of 1790]), 50–51, as cited in Frank Ll. Harrison, *Music in Medieval Britain*, 2nd ed. (London, 1963), 24.

"yeoman of the chapel" was "responsible for the removal of the instrument [organ] every time the peripatetic household moved on from one location to the next, and for blowing the organ when it was being played."[1] The (presumably adolescent) ancillary staff at Thomas Wolsey's household chapel comprised "a yeoman and two grooms of the vestry, and a servant of the master of choristers to assist him in looking after the boys."[2] At Wells in 1507, Richard Bramston, a probationary vicar choral continuing his studies, was deputizing for the master of choristers, Richard Hygons, in playing the organ, teaching the choristers, and serving as "keeper of the organ."[3]

If an adolescent stayed at the same cathedral where he had been a chorister, the transition to "secondary" was more or less informal and left little documentary record. However, a detailed indenture was drawn up in 1503 between John, Abbot of Rushen Abbey, Isle of Man, and authorities at Chester, wherein John Darcy (Darse) was provided with an exhibition to Chester Abbey to "abide & dwelle," to study for six years with William Park, and to be his "servant":

> Wyllm Parke . . . shal fyrste informe hym of his dayly s[er]vice anenst God also to instructe hȳ in dyscyplyne of good man[ne]rs & also to tech hȳ to synge prykkytsong, Descant of all man[ner] mesurs & to syng upon a pryksonge fawburdon to cownter of ev[er]y mesur, & to set a songe of thre p[ar]ts iiij or v sbstancyally, and also to play upon the organs any man[ner] plaȳsong or prykkytsonge two pts or thre
>
> And yf the said Willm c[om]mand ye said John his s[erva]unt . . . to tech or instruct any of þe said Willmi scolers . . . that ye said John schall wt good wyll indev[our] hȳself deligently to doo ye same wtout gruggyng or gayn-sayyng[4]

A similar arrangement is suggested by the bill of complaint in Exeter in 1547×51 of another musical apprentice, John Yeo, and the reply of his master, the organist Thomas Wyncott, who had been given 40s. by "Friends" of Yeo to

> teche & instructe . . . [him] to play apon the vyalles vyrginalles & Organs and also to wrytte & Rede and to doo all maner of other occupacions whiche thesayd Thomas Wyncote dyd then use . . . and that [Yeo] shuld contynue & remayne wyth thesayd Thomas Wyncote by the space of syxe yeres[5]

[1] Bowers, "Vocal Scoring," 72.

[2] Roger Bowers, "The Cultivation and Promotion of Music in the Household and Orbit of Thomas Wolsey," in *Cardinal Wolsey: Church, State and Art*, ed. Steven J. Gunn and Phillip G. Lindley (Cambridge, 1991), 178–218 at 180.

[3] W. H. Grattan Flood, "New Light on Early Tudor Composers, xiv: Richard Bramston," *Musical Times* 62 (1921), 17–18.

[4] British Library, Harley MS 2095, fol. 106ᵛ, cited in J. R. Oliver, trans. and ed., "Indenture 1503" in *The Manx Society 9: Monumenta [III] de insula Manniae, or A Collection of National Documents relating to the Isle of Man* (1862); see also http://www.isle-of-man.com/manxnotebook/manxsoc/msvol04/v3p025.htm. (Accessed 14 October 2007.)

[5] London, Public Record Office [now The National Archives], C 1/1284/11. Darcy and Yeo were both apprenticed for six years; see John M. Wasson, ed., *Devon*, Records of Early

the said Defendaunt sayeth that he did the best he could do therin but the said Complaynant was so vnapt to lorne ... [that he] put the said Complaynant from the house and service of the said Defendaunt[1]

The arrangement that John Heywood (ca. 1497 – ca. 1578) made with his "servant and skoller" Thomas Whythorne in 1545 must have been similar to this (though mutually satisfying).[2] Whythorne was born about 1528 into a prominent family in Ilminster, Somerset, and had learned to read, write, and "also to sing Muzik" in the local school.[3] When he was ten years old, he was sent to Oxford to live with an uncle who was a priest. The uncle's initial suggestions for Thomas's education were for him to train as a priest, physician, or lawyer. When these options did not appeal to Thomas, his uncle asked whether he would like to study "Grammer, with þe knowleȝ in þe latten toong? or els to Muzik, az to learn to sing, and to play on þe O[r]gans, þe which be good qualitiez and be much esteemed in þez daiez."[4] Since Whythorne chose music, his uncle sent him to Magdalen Col-lege School as a chorister for six years, where he learned grammar first and then music. In 1544, at the age of sixteen, he was old enough to progress to the Col-lege as a student (demy). But a year later, when his uncle died and left him some money, Whythorne decided to leave Oxford and go to London, where "a frend" placed him with Heywood. According to Whythorne, Heywood

> waz not only very well skylled in Muzik, and playeng on þe virȝinals but also such an english poet, az þe lýk, for hiz witt and invension, with þe quantitie þat hee wrot, waz not az þen in England, nor befor hiz tým sinse Chawsers tým. with mr haywood I remayned three yeer and mor. in þe which tým I learned to play on þe virginals, þe liut, and to mak english verses.[5]

Heywood was probably born in Coventry, where his father was a coroner and an associate of John Rastell (ca. 1475–1536), who was a member of the Corpus Christi guild and who continued his theatrical interests after moving to London about 1508/9.[6] Rastell's wife, Elizabeth,[7] was the sister of Sir Thomas More, who recreated the kind of humanist education in his own home that he had experi-

---

English Drama (Toronto, 1986), 140–41. In 1562 it is evident from "An Acte towching dyvers Orders for Artificers Laborers Servantes of Husbandrye and Apprentises" (which applied to musicians), that the length of indenture was to be a minimum of seven years (paragraph xix of the Statute of Artificers). See Lynne Hulse, "The Musical Patronage of Robert Cecil, First Earl of Salisbury (1563–1612)," *Journal of the Royal Musical Association* 116 (1991), 24–40.

[1] London, Public Record Office, C 1/1284/12; Wasson, *Devon*, 141–42.

[2] Whythorne, *Autobiography*, 13.

[3] Ibid., 7.

[4] Ibid., 11.

[5] Ibid., 13.

[6] E. J. Devereux, *A Bibliography of John Rastell* (Montreal, 1999), 6; see the Introduction to *The Plays of John Heywood*, ed. Richard Axton and Peter Happé, Tudor Interludes, 6 (Cambridge, 1991), 2.

[7] They were married by 1504; Heywood, *Plays*, ed. Axton and Happé, 2.

enced in Cardinal Morton's house.[1] One of More's "pupil-servants," John Clement, attended and then taught in More's "school" (after he had left John Colet's St. Paul's school under William Lily).[2] Since Heywood was "multis annis familiarissimus" with More,[3] and since the latter died in 1535, Heywood was presumably another "of the young people More loved to have about him."[4] Heywood's brother Richard (1509–1570), another of More's protégés,[5] became a protonotary of the court of King's Bench (1498–1523) and a colleague of William Roper (1496–1578), who was also a protégé;[6] Richard Heywood was one of the lawyers who supported More at his trial.[7]

More's own love of drama is well attested: according to his friend Erasmus, "in his youth [he] wrote and acted in little comedies,"[8] and it is not surprising that he is traditionally believed to have introduced Heywood at court. In 1519, after Henry VIII made some changes to his entourage, More became more active at court, and this period (Michaelmas 1519 to Christmas 1520) coincides with a series of payments to Heywood as a "synger" in the king's household accounts.[9] (There are also various payments between March 1529 and Christmas 1545 to "John Heywood, player of the virginals.")

There is therefore some doubt about whether Heywood was the "Iohn Haywoode" who received a special payment on Twelfth Night, 1515, when he would have been about eighteen years old. A. W. Reed suggests that this is the same man who appears in the accounts of the duke of Buckingham (Edward Stafford, 1478–1521) in 1520: "to oon John Haiwode oon of the yomen of the Crowne bringing tithings unto the said duk . . . from therle of Surrey out of Ireland."[10] This man is included on a list of 1528 of the *garciones nuper de hospicio* (grooms of the chamber).[11] As far as I know there is nothing to suggest that he is not Heywood

---

[1] More was a page between the ages of twelve and fourteen in Morton's household, where the chaplain, the Rev. Henry Medwall, presumably wrote his *Fulgens and Lucres* (printed by John Rastell, London, ca. 1514). See R. J. Schoeck, "Sir Thomas More and Lincoln's Inn Revels," *Philological Quarterly* 29 (1950), 426–30.

[2] Thomas More, *Utopia*, ed. E. Surtz and J. H. Hexter (New Haven, 1965), vol. 4, The Yale Edition of the Complete Works of St. Thomas More, 41. In 1525, Clement, like Heywood, became a sewer of the chamber at court; see A. W. Reed, "John Clement and his Books," *The Library* 4th ser., 6 (1926), 329–39.

[3] The Latin is quoted from Johannes Pitseus, who knew Heywood's son Jasper. See W. Bang, "Acta Anglo-Lovaniensia: John Heywood und sein Kreis," *Englische Studien* 38 (1907), 234–50 at 237.

[4] A. W. Reed, *Early Tudor Drama: Medwall, the Rastells, Heywood, and the More Circle* (London, 1926), 47 and 155.

[5] Ibid., 155.

[6] Sebastian Westcote was one of the witnesses of William Roper's will (1577).

[7] R. J. Schoeck, "William Rastell and the Protonotaries: A Link in the Story of the Rastells, Ropers and Heywoods," *Notes and Queries* 197 (1952), 398–99.

[8] Erasmus, Letter to Ulrich von Hutten (1519), cited in Elizabeth Story Donno, "Thomas More and Richard III," *Renaissance Quarterly* 35 (1982), 401–47 at 413–14.

[9] Reed, *Tudor Drama*, 40–41.

[10] Ibid., 235.

[11] According to Reed (ibid., 44), it was not until 1552 that Heywood was made *dapifer camerae* or sewer of the royal chamber, and "superintended the arrangement of the table,

the singer. Musicians were often employed to carry messages, and he may even have had personal reasons for travelling to Ireland: his future father-in-law, John Rastell, had only recently returned from an extended stay there and may even have maintained some connections in the country. In March 1517, Rastell had been given permission to go on an expedition to Ireland (and beyond), and this would have been known to the earl of Surrey, the lord admiral.[1] Rastell remained happy and prosperous in Ireland (perhaps in Cork) until late 1519. While he was there, he wrote *A New Interlude and a Mery of the Nature of the iiij Elements*, which he printed about 1520 on his return to London.[2] Moreover, in 1520 (the same year he paid John Heywood for bringing news), Buckingham and his retinue were in attendance at the revels for the Field of Cloth of Gold.[3] Rastell was also there, since Sir Edward Belknap and Sir Nicholas Vaux requested that he make and decorate the roofs of the banqueting hall,[4] and according to W. H. Grattan Flood, there is "a notice of [Thomas] Farthing [a singer in the Chapel Royal] as having taken part in the Revels at Greenwich on December 9, 1520," an entertainment at which John Heywood also assisted.[5] Another indication that Heywood was involved in court entertainments before 1519 is that Farthing's annuity was transferred after his death (1520) to Heywood "in consideracione boni et fidelis servicii quod serviens noster Johes Haywode," and, according to De la Bère, "faithful service generally implies long service."[6]

By 1523, Heywood had married Rastell's daughter, Joan (who was also the niece of Thomas More); he was also presumably involved with productions performed on Rastell's own theatrical stage at Finsbury Fields, which was built about 1524. For the visit of Francis I to Greenwich Palace in 1527, Heywood "probably worked" with Rastell,[7] who most likely devised the "pageant of the father of heaven" (Jupiter) in which four young choristers of the Chapel Royal supported "Riches" and another four supported "Love" in a debate concerning whether the former were better than the latter (the result eventually being that both were necessary for princes).

In 1530, "J. Heywood citizen and Stationer of London and one of the king's servants" was presented by Sir Rauff Warren as common measurer and adjudicator of

seating of the guests, and the tasting and serving of the dishes" in Edward's household; see Andrew Ashbee, "Groomed for Service: Musicians in the Privy Chamber at the English Court, c.1495–1558," *Early Music* 25 (1997), 185–97 at 194.

[1] Devereux, *John Rastell*, 9–10.
[2] Reed, *Tudor Drama*, 202–3.
[3] W. R. Streitberger, *Court Revels, 1485–1559*, Studies in Early English Drama, 3 (Toronto, 1994), 121.
[4] Reed, *Tudor Drama*, 13; Streitberger, *Court Revels*, 107.
[5] W. H. Grattan Flood, "New Light on Early Tudor Composers, XIII: Thomas Farthing," *Musical Times* 61 (1920), 814. Reed (*Tudor Drama*, 40) says there is no record of Heywood's attendance, however.
[6] R. de la Bère, *John Heywood, Entertainer* (London, 1937), 24.
[7] Richard Axton, "Royal Throne, Royal Bed: John Heywood and Spectacle," *Medieval English Theatre* 16 (1994), 66–76 at 67.

disputes in the Mercers' Company,[1] the foremost livery company; other mercers then included Thomas More, Thomas White, William Gyfford, and John Bramston. At court, Heywood was also a good friend of Sir Anthony Cooke of Gidea Hall, Romford, Essex, and of his daughter Mildred Cooke (1526–1589), who married William Cecil in 1545 (Lord Burghley in 1572). Heywood was also described in the will of Sir Thomas Pope (1507–1559) as "my trewe frynd."[2] Heywood would have been acquainted with the Franco-Flemish lutenist Philip van Wilder, the Italian organist Dionisio Memo, the composers and musicians of the Bassano family, and the composer Philip de Monte from Mechelen,[3] among others, and through them had access to French and Italian music such as chansons and fantasias.

During the 1530s, Heywood was involved in several artistic activities. For example, his *Play of the Wether*, which was printed by William Rastell (John Rastell's son) in 1533, "may be the only survivor of his plays written for acting by boys," as it requires ten players, one of whom is "A Boy, the lest that can play."[4] Music is "played," and probably sung, by "sirs" while Jupiter withdraws into his throne,[5] and the Vice, Mery Report (possibly Heywood himself), sings a solo accompanied by instruments, presumably viols. In January 1537, "Heywood's servant" (likely an apprentice) was paid "for bringing my lady grace's [Princess Mary's] Regalles to Greenwich"[6] (recall that secondaries were often responsible for moving and "keeping" organs); in March 1538, Heywood was paid for "playing an interlude with his children before my lady grace."[7] In February 1539, he performed a *Masque of King Arthur's Knights* for Thomas Cromwell and again at court: Cromwell paid the "Bargeman that carried Heywoods maske to the court and home again."[8]

Heywood's "children" are most likely the choristers of St. Paul's:[9] his connections with St. Paul's during this period are indicated by the contents of British Library, Additional MS 15233, which include the interlude *Wit and Science* by John Redford, master of choristers (d. 1547), with its cues for four songs, two of which are accompanied by viols, and a galliard on a ground bass, also played on viols. The manuscript also includes poems, most of which are by Redford and Heywood. The refrain in one of Heywood's poems ("I desyre no number of manye thynges for store / But I desyre the grace of God, and I desyre no more!") is marked "corus,"

---

[1] Reed, *Tudor Drama*, 46.

[2] Daniel Bennett Page, "Uniform and Catholic: Church Music in the Reign of Mary Tudor (1553–1558)" (Ph.D. diss., Brandeis University, 1996), 311.

[3] In 1554, de Monte lived in London as a member of Phillip II's private chapel; see Willem Elders, *Composers of the Low Countries*, trans. Graham Dixon (Oxford, 1991), 8.

[4] Heywood, *Plays*, ed. Axton and Happé, 11.

[5] Axton ("Royal Throne," 67), suggests that "even if it [Jupiter's throne] was not recycled [from Rastell's 1527 pageant] in Heywood's *Play of the Weather*, the device surely suggested a scenario for the play."

[6] Princess Mary's Book of Expenses (British Library, Royal MS 17 B xxviii, fol. 7b), cited in Reed, *Tudor Drama*, 58.

[7] Reed, *Tudor Drama*, 58.

[8] Andrew Ashbee, ed., *Records of English Court Music*, vol. 7: (1485–1558) (Snodland, Kent, 1993), 416.

[9] Reed, *Tudor Drama*, 61.

which suggests performance by choristers. Another of his poems, *Yf love for love of long tyme had*, "could not be better suited for use in . . . *A Play of Love*, at the following cue:'here they both go out and the Lover beloved entreth with a song.'"[1] The play, which has "strikingly heavy legalistic language," "was doubtless written for a special audience in the Inns of Court"[2] and possibly performed at Lincoln's Inn at Christmas, 1529.[3] John Milsom, who found a single inner voice part of a polyphonic setting of it written on a flyleaf in Cambridge, Trinity College, MS 0.1.30, rightly points out that "Duple metre prevails, and the cluster of rests before the phrase 'my love hath loved me' implies an imitative texture, pointing to the mid-sixteenth century as a likely date of composition."[4] In fact, the setting is very similar to the only other setting of a Heywood poem that survives (also from British Library, Add. MS 15233), *What harte can thynke or tonge expresse the harme that groweth of idleness*. British Library, Additional MS 4900 includes an adaptation for voice and lute of the presumably "original" four-voice consort song for voice and viols;[5] as John Ward points out, "the accompaniment is in no way appropriate to the lute."[6] Regals, on the other hand, could substitute well for viols with no adaptation, and we recall Heywood's "servant" transporting regals to Greenwich for Princess Mary. Indeed, it is possible they were for accompanying choristers' songs: the 1559–61 accounts of Tallowchandlers indicate payment to Maister Phillippes for "playeng of the Regalles and for the gouernement of the Children."[7] Master Phillippes may be Phillip ap Rhys, organist of St Paul's until 1561,[8] and the same "master phelpes" who worked with Heywood and Westcote in 1559 (see below). If so, it is also possible that he is the composer of three pieces that have been attributed (though doubtfully) to Philip van Wilder (d. 1553); these are a piece entitled "Philips song," an untitled "galliard-like setting à 4 of something like a metrical psalm tune . . . [that] resembles nothing else by van Wilder, in style or spirit" and a "Dump / philli" in Marsh MS no. 164, which "is remarkably archaic in style."[9] (But see another possible identification below.)

During the early 1540s, Heywood was in serious trouble: in 1542–43 he and several others, including John More (son of Thomas More) and William Roper,

---

[1] John Milsom, "Songs and Society in Early Tudor London," *Early Music History* 16 (1997), 235–93.

[2] R. J. Schoeck, "A Common Tudor Expletive and Legal Parody in Heywood's 'Play of Love," *Notes and Queries* n.s. 3/9 (1956), 375–76 at 376.

[3] Heywood, *Plays*, ed. Axton and Happé, p. xiv.

[4] Milsom, "Songs and Society," 293.

[5] Mary Joiner, "British Museum Add. MS 15117: A Commentary, Index and Bibliography," *Royal Musical Association Research Chronicle* 7 (1969), 51–109 at 60.

[6] John M. Ward, *Music for Elizabethan Lutes* (Oxford, 1992), 33.

[7] R. Mark Benbow, "Sixteenth-century Dramatic Performances for the London Livery Companies," *Notes and Queries* n.s. 29/2 (1982), 129–31. Another reference is a record for the Lord Mayor's pageant in 1556, in which the Merchant Taylors paid "ij boyes which played & sung to the Regalles"; see Robert T. D. Sayle, *Lord Mayors' Pageants of the Merchant Taylors' Company in the 15th, 16th & 17th Centuries* (London, 1931), 30.

[8] Page, "Uniform and Catholic," 296.

[9] Ward, *Elizabethan Lutes*, 4–5.

were involved in the so-called Prebendary Plot, an unsuccessful effort to over-throw Archbishop Thomas Cranmer by attempting to charge him with failing to enforce the Six Articles, an act of Parliament reaffirming six essentially Catholic beliefs within the newly established Church of England. In *A New Discourse of a Stale Subject* (London 1596), Sir John Harington reports that Heywood "scaped hanging with his mirth," for Henry was "truly perswaded, that a man that wrate so pleasant and harmlesse verses, could not have any harmfull conceit against his proceedings."[1] After recanting publicly, Heywood was back in favor: the royal accounts of 1544/5 (BL Add. MS 59900) include payments to him as "virginals player."[2]

One of Whythorne's first duties (in 1545) was to make a fair copy for Heywood of his *Dialogue of Proverbs* (described as a dialogue that is both debate and mock trial;[3] published by Berthelet, the King's Printer, in 1546) and of his interlude *Parts of Man*, a play written for Cardinal Wolsey, apparently as a peace offering. Why-thorne describes this and quotes a few lines from the otherwise lost interlude in his *Book of Songs and Sonetts, with Longe Discoorses Sett with Them, of the Chylds Lyfe, togyther with A Yoong Mans Lyfe, and Entring into the Old Mans Lyfe.*[4] In this interlude, Reason disputes with Will about which has "þe siuprem government in man. Whervpon, in þe end, þei both ar dryven to graunt þat man kan do nothing withowt will, and withowt reazon man kan do no good thing."[5]

Whythorne's "autobiography" takes the form of "songs and sonnets" (written in italic script)[6] interspersed with "discourses" (in secretary hand) that he claims to have written at the time the events occurred and later "augmented" as memories returned to him. He describes how he kept a book of his own, which unfortu-nately has not survived:

> Whyll I waz with him, he [Heywood] mad diverz dittiez to bee sung vnto muzikall instruments . . . and I hav þe copiez of most of þem in A book at þis present of mýn own wrýting. Also, whýll I waz with him, I did wrýt owt for him diverz songs and sonets þat wer mad by þe erll of Surrey, sir Thomas Wiatt þe elder, and mr [William] Moor þe exsellent Harper besýd sertain salms þat wer mad by þe said mr wyatt, and also mr Sternold. þe which be also in my said book. by þe which okkazions of wryting & reading,

---

[1] Cited in James Holstun, "The Spider, the Fly, and the Commonwealth: Merrie John Heywood and Agrarian Class Struggle," *English Literary History* 71 (2004), 53–88 at 83 n. 32.

[2] Reed, *Tudor Drama*, 65.

[3] John Heywood, *John Heywood's 'A Dialogue of Proverbs'*, ed. Rudolph E. Habenicht (Berkeley, 1963), 50.

[4] Whythorne, *Autobiography*, [1].

[5] Ibid., 74.

[6] In this period, secretary hand was the everyday script; italic was learned at a later age. For example, in 1507 it was decreed that when the choristers at St. George's Chapel, Windsor, were given their annual allowance for ink and paper, they were to be exhorted "to learn in writing to copy the Roman characters after the Italian style"; see F. G. E[dwards], "A Famous Choir School: St. George's Chapel, Windsor," *Musical Times* 44 (1903), 166–69 at 168.

I afterward gav my self to imitat and follow þeir trads and devẏses in wry-
ting az okkazions moved me.[1]

As Osborn points out, Whythorne had access to these verses before they were
published.[2] Apparently, at that time he also had access to works by Heywood's
friends, works from which he quoted later. For example, he wrote "az I did ons
read (in effekt) in þe book [by Elyot] kalled þe banket of Sapiens,"[3] and he refers
to a song "which I devẏzed vpon A sentens þat I took owt of A book [by Baldwin]
named (az I do remember) *De treatis of philosophie* þe which sentens þus begin-
neth. *If þow dezier þat þi frendz loov may kontinew*."[4]

Whythorne later published settings of some of these songs in *Songes, for Three,
Fower, and Five Voices* (London: John Day, 1571).[5] For example, he had written
the song "Prefer not gret bewty befor vertew: / Þe much gazing þeron many may
rew" after he had left Heywood and was setting up his own chamber in London
to begin teaching; he was recalling what he had learned about women's wiles from
authorities such as Seneca and Ovid.[6] The setting is in four voices, "For Children,"
with an overall range of *c* to *c*".[7] Another example, this one from between 1560 and
1562 while he was tutor to William Bromfield at Cambridge, was written when
Bromfield's other tutor was being friendly face to face, yet speaking "most spẏtefull
wurdz, and reprochfull tawnts" behind his back. Whythorne wrote a verse based
on Socrates on the subject of malicious words: "Lẏk az þe smok owtwardly seen,
doth gyv knowle3 whẹr þat fier iz / So all evl wurdz diskouer plain, þe hatfull hart
whẹr þat ier iz."[8] These settings of these poems are very similar in style to Heywood's: they are mostly homophonic, they begin with the pavan rhythm (long,
short, short), and brief imitation occurs at the beginning of some of the phrases.
Whythorne describes how he "yuzed to sing [his] songs and sonets sumtẏm to þe
liut and sumtẏms to þe virginals,"[9] but during the late 1550s and early 1560s, he
taught himself how "to play on þe Gyttern, and Sittern. which ij instruments wẹr
þen stran3 in England, and þerfor þe mor dezyred and esteemed,"[10] and which, like
the lute and virginals were "instruments which do go with songs."[11]

Although Whythorne does not report on playing the virginals except as ac-

---

[1] Whythorne, *Autobiography*, 3.

[2] Ibid., 14.

[3] Ibid., 65; Thomas Elyot's *Bankette of Sapience* (London, 1539).

[4] Whythorne, *Autobiography*, 165–66; William Baldwin, *Treatise of Morall Phylosophie,
Conteyning the Sayinges of the Wyse* (London, 1547). Baldwin was also a lawyer.

[5] Thomas East later published Whythorne's 52 *Duos, or songs for two voices* (London,
1590), which were "for beginners."

[6] See Heywood, *Dialogue*, ed. Habenicht, 5, for a discussion of this tradition, which
was followed also by Heywood in his *Dialogue of Proverbs*.

[7] Whythorne, *Autobiography*, 27; Thomas Whythorne, *Songes for fower voyces*, ed.
Robert McQuillan (Newton Abbot, 2004), no. 28, pp. 28–29. (This song is for triplex and
medius voices.)

[8] Whythorne, *Songes*, no. 22, pp. 16–17.

[9] Whythorne, *Autobiography*, 51.

[10] Ibid., 19.

[11] Ibid., 19–20. Another example: "Apon the said clarycorde Sir Edward Stannely playd

companiments to songs, the discovery of a short piece entitled "a morys . . . finis quod Thomas whythorne" is evidence that he also played keyboard dances.[1] The eight-bar dance survives on a folio bound with manuscript copies of two legal treatises by Filips Wielant (1441–1520), a jurist in Mechelen.[2] The folio has the same watermark as the treatises, and the handwriting of the "morys" looks similar enough to the handwriting in his autobiography to suggest that it is Whythorne's autograph.[3] In his autobiography, Whythorne describes his travels of 1554 and refers in a poem to Mechelen as being known for its lawyers.[4] The manuscript could have been taken there by Whythorne himself, but as there is an annotation at the bottom of folio 300 recto that reads "finem huic praxi criminali imposui 24 aprilis anno 1565, pridie supplicationis Mecliniensis," I think that Bouckaert's other possibility, "that Whythorne's music found its way to the Low Countries through his teacher John Heywood, who stayed in Mechelen from 1564" is more plausible.[5]

Between about 1548, when Whythorne left Heywood, and about 1558, when I suggest Mulliner joined him, Heywood associated closely with Westcote (ca. 1520–1582), who had become yeoman of the King's chamber in 1545 and vicar choral and acting almoner at St. Paul's in 1547, by which time he "had already become acquainted with the circle of writer-musicians associated with Redford and Heywood."[6] For example, in 1551 both Heywood and Westcote were dinner guests at the London house of Sir William Paget (1505–1563), who had attended St. Paul's school;[7] in February 1552, expenses were "Paid in rewarde to . . . Mr Heywoodde . . . and to Sebastian, tawards the charge of the children with the carriage of the plaiers garments";[8] in 1553, for Mary's entry procession, "in Pauls Churchyard against the Schoole, one Mr. Heywod sate in a pageant under a vine

---

a ballade and sange therewith" to entertain Princess Margaret on her visit to Scotland in 1503 (John Leland, cited in Stevens, *Music and Poetry*, 268–69).

[1] Morris dances were performed in entertainments. For example, on Twelfth Night in 1511 "a Morice" was danced by the king's young gentlemen; see Streitberger, *Court Revels*, 69.

[2] Bruno Bouckaert and Eugeen Schreurs, "A New Fragment with 16th-century Keyboard Music: An Unknown Composition by Thomas Whythorne (1528–1596) in a Manuscript from the Low Countries (Gent-Rijksuniversiteit, MS G11655)," in *Music Fragments and Manuscripts in the Low Countries*, ed. Eugeen Schreurs and Henri Vanhulst, Yearbook of the Alamire Foundation, 2 (1997), 121–28.

[3] See facsimile ibid., 125. The end of another keyboard piece at the top of the folio is in a different hand.

[4] Whythorne, *Autobiography*, 66.

[5] Bouckaert and Schreurs, "New Fragment," 127. Heywood's letter of request to Lord Burleigh in 1575 is from Mechelen; Reed, *Tudor Drama*, 35–37.

[6] Streitberger, *Court Revels*, 355 n. 39.

[7] John Leland, a classmate of Paget at St. Paul's, wrote a long poem about him in 1540s, detailing his life and education; see Page, "Uniform and Catholic," 401.

[8] Percy Clinton Sydney Smythe Strangford, ed., *Household Expenses of the Princess Elizabeth during her Residence at Hatfield, October 1, 1551, to September 30, 1552*, Camden Society, 2 (London, 1853), 37. In May 1553, Heywood's play with twelve unidentified choristers and William Baldwin's play *The State of Ireland* were performed for Edward VI; see Streitberger, *Court Revels*, 293–94.

and made to her an oration in Latin and English";[1] on 26 May 1554, both Heywood and Westcote witnessed the will of Richard Bramston;[2] on 2 June 1557, "Johenn Heywood de London generosus et Thomas Predioxe de medio Templo London generosus" (whose poem Dido's Lament appears in British Library, Add. MS 15233) signed a £40 bond to support Westcote's acquisition of the lease of Wickham St. Paul, Essex;[3] and in July 1559, the earl of Arundel, Sir Thomas Pope, entertained Elizabeth with a play by the Children of Paul's "and ther master Se[bastian], master Phelypes, and master haywod."[4]

Like Whythorne, Mulliner would most likely have been educated as a chorister until his voice began to break. If he were the "Mulliner" who was one of the eight clerks at Magdalen College, Oxford, from April 1557 to July 1558[5] (who were to be "of sufficient and competent literature, well-conditioned, and of honest conversation and . . . are to have competent voices, and be well or at least competently instructed in singing and reading"[6]), this would indicate that his date of birth was around 1541 or 1542. In addition to his stipend, "Mulliner" was paid for copying fourteen pages of music (antiphons) in March 1558. The cantor at Magdalen at that time was Edmund Molyneux (mr mullinax), who had arrived at Magdalen two terms before Mulliner did, and left two terms before him.[7] Edmund went to London, where he was employed as secretary by Sir William Cecil (mentioned above as the husband of Mildred Cook, a good friend of Heywood's). Mullinax the cantor and Mulliner the clerk may have known Heywood's son Jasper, who was a probationer at Merton from 1554 until 1558, when he resigned his fellowship. It is probably not coincidental that all three left Oxford in 1558 and that after the Visitation of Magdalen College in September that year, the chaplains, clerks, and most of the choristers chose to leave or were expelled for religious reasons.[8]

Six years later, in March 1564, a Thomas Mulliner went to Corpus Christi College, an institution with close connections to Magdalen and also known to have had Roman Catholic leanings at the time. This Mulliner would have been about twenty-one years old, and he matriculated as a student as well as serving as the "modulator organorum." He was still young, and this particular post was not a prestigious one: the chapel had only two priests, two acolytes, and two choristers. Of the two "Acolytes . . . one of them is to be the organist, and the other the

---

[1] John Stow, *The Annales of England* (London [1592]), 1044.

[2] David Mateer, "The 'Gyffard' Partbooks: Composers, Owners, Date and Provenance," *Royal Musical Association Research Chronicle* 28 (1995), 21–50 at 44–45.

[3] Ibid.

[4] Henry Machyn, *The Diary of Henry Machyn, Citizen and Merchant-Taylor of London from AD 1550 – AD 1563*, ed. John Gough Nichols, Camden Society, 42 (London, 1848), 206.

[5] Francis Knights, "Thomas Mulliner's Oxford Career," *The Organ* 297 (1996), 132–35.

[6] John Rouse Bloxam, *A Register of the Presidents, Fellows, Demis . . . of Saint Mary Magdalen College in the University of Oxford*, 8 vols. (Oxford, 1857), 2:xiv.

[7] He was clerk and cantor for four terms in 1557 and one term in 1558 (Oxford, Magdalen College, LCD/1, fols. 138r, 156v; LCE/5, fol. 202r, draft *Liber computi*).

[8] Bloxam, *Register*, 2:lxv.

sub-sacristan ... to ring the bells."[1] (At around this age Whythorne was preparing to teach music privately and learning to play the cittern and gittern.) In July 1564, just four months after Mulliner went to Corpus Christi, Heywood was forced to leave England with his wife and Catholic friends. He was in no position to help advance Mulliner's career, though perhaps he or Westcote assisted in placing Mulliner at Corpus Christi, which shared the same humanist ideals as St. Paul's.[2]

I believe that it was sometime during the intervening five years, between mid 1558 and early 1564, that Thomas Mulliner was a servant and scholar of John Heywood and compiled his commonplace book (as Whythorne did his). There are several indications in Mulliner's book to suggest this. Folio 2 bears the inscription "Sum liber thomae mullineri'/ iohanne heywoode teste," which uses similar vocabulary to inscriptions written on other student books. For example, on what had been an "end-paper of a book that was once in the library of Westminster Abbey, or perhaps of Westminster School," is written: "John [one word illegible] monachus Westmonasteriensis / Est custos huius libri teste Thoma."[3] On folio 129, Mulliner wrote a Latin poem (in italic script), translated as follows: "Woe to you who shall steal [my] book with a swift hand, for your thefts can not hide from God. If anyone sees it straying and lacking its lord, return the book to me. You have my name in the margin."[4] A less erudite but similar verse is written in another sixteenth-century schoolbook: "He that steals this book, / Shall be hanged on a hook."[5]

Warnings like these suggest that there was a possibility that other students might gain access to prized books, and through Heywood, Mulliner was likely to come into contact with the choristers of St. Paul's. He may even have assisted their master Westcote, perhaps as one of the "deputies" Wescote was given at his reappointment on 1 December 1559.[6] If Mulliner were Westcote's deputy in 1559, it would go some way to explaining the annotation on folio 2 that "T Mulliner was master of St Paul's school," written by John Stafford Smith, the antiquarian and owner of the Mulliner Book about 1774. There are several examples of deputies being erroneously named as "master": for example, "Edward Kirkham [was paid

---

[1] G. R. M. Ward, trans. and ed., *The Foundation Statutes of Bishop Fox for Corpus Christi College, in the University of Oxford*, A.D. 1517 (London, 1843), 77–78.

[2] Jonathan Woolfson, "Bishop Fox's Bees and the Early English Renaissance," *Reformation and Renaissance Review* 5 (2003), 7–26.

[3] A. Hyatt King, "The Significance of John Rastell in Early Music Printing," *The Library* 5th ser., 26 (1971), 197–214 at 209: "John monk of Westminster is the guardian of this book by the witness of Thomas Phyllyp."

[4] BL Add. MS 30513, fol. 129ʳ, 'Ve tibi qui rapida librum furabere palma / nam tua non possunt furba latere deum. / Si quis eum errantem videret dominoque carentem / redde mei librum. margine nomen habes'.

[5] Cited in J. Howard Brown, *Elizabethan Schooldays: An Account of the English Grammar Schools in the Second Half of the Sixteenth Century* (Oxford, 1933), 52.

[6] Reavley Gair, "The Conditions of Appointment for Masters of Choristers at Paul's (1553–1613)," *Notes and Queries* n.s. 27/2 (1980), 116–24 at 117–18.

as] one of Mrs of the children of Pawles . . . for presenting by them two playes or Enterludes" during Edward Pearce's tenure as master of choristers (1599–1600).[1]

Mulliner's book includes Latin verses that are also indicative of adolescent authorship. His "intercessory prayer to God" requests "fine sailing to my beginning, that I may explore what are the most gracious muses." The references to classical images ("muses" and "fine sailing," with its pun on *vela, vellum*, i.e., his book) suggest that he was using phrases he had learned at school. On the penultimate folio, Mulliner wrote *De beata Maria versus*, which is evidence that he could fulfill the requirement at Corpus Christi College, where students (including clerks) were to have been "instructed to such an extent in Latin grammar, and the approved authors of the Latin tongue, that they can dictate Latin letters off hand, and make verses, at least in a middling way."[2] On the last folio of his book, folio 129, Mulliner wrote out two short translation exercises (in secretary hand) that concern "conscience."[3] They are similar to the *sententiae* arranged under headings in Elyot's *Bankette of Sapience*, which Whythorne studied. Heywood professed to be unlearned, but he gave Latin orations and would no doubt have been capable of teaching his apprentices at this level.

Most of the music in Mulliner's book comprises liturgical versets for organ: there are seventy-eight of them. This may indicate that Mulliner was preparing for a musical career in church rather than at court, although his master Heywood does not appear to have been involved with the performance of liturgical music. Whythorne also seems to have had little interest in liturgical music, at least early in his life:[4] he chose to leave Magdalen College at the first opportunity, and the only reference to organ playing in his autobiography is the description (cited above) concerning music studies at Magdalen. And although one of Heywood's "servants" was paid for transporting regals, which suggests that Heywood played them, it is likely that he played non-liturgical music on them. But since Mulliner's book is a major source of Redford's organ music, perhaps Mulliner studied organ playing with Westcote, who played at St. Paul's.[5] Mulliner may even have been assigned the task of making copies of music by the famous and much-loved master Redford, and took the opportunity to copy examples into his own book (much as Whythorne did when he copied texts for Heywood). It is surely no coincidence that, apart from Redford's, most if not all of the versets were written by organists who were working in London at that time; for example, it includes all but one of

---

[1] Harold Newcomb Hillebrand, *The Child Actors: A Chapter in Elizabethan Stage History*, University of Illinois Studies in Language and Literature, 11/1–2 (Urbana, 1926), 196; see also Jane Flynn, "A Reconsideration of the Mulliner Book (British Library Add. MS 30513): Music Education in Sixteenth-Century England" (Ph.D. diss., Duke University, 1993), 90–92.

[2] Ward, *Foundation Statutes*, 64.

[3] Another student, Richard Mynshall, aged about fifteen years old, "tried out his Latin tags on the end-papers" of the lute book he compiled during the 1590s; see Robert Spencer, "Three English Lute Manuscripts," *Early Music* 3 (1975), 119–24 at 119.

[4] He later became Archbishop Parker's master of music.

[5] Nicholas Sander's report in 1561 to Cardinal Morone includes "Sebastianus qui organa pulsat apud D. Paulum Londini," cited in Page, "Uniform and Catholic," 274.

the surviving organ works by John Blitheman, who was a member of the Chapel Royal by December 1558 and who is listed as head of the lay clerks at Christ Church, Oxford, from 1563 to 1578.[1] Mulliner's book is also a major source of Thomas Tallis's keyboard pieces; it does not include any music by William Byrd (ca. 1543–1623), who was presumably a "secondary" right up until 1563, when he was appointed organist at Lincoln.

The organ versets in Mulliner's book are interspersed among other genres, and they apparently chart how he progressed from studying two- and three-voice organ versets that have the *cantus firmus* in long notes to those in three and four voices with figuration of the chant (as described by Thomas Morley),[2] then on to versets based on faburden, and so on. A few examples must suffice here: the (untitled) *Miserere* settings M7[3] (by Redford) and M8 (an unattributed *unicum*) are unusual in the repertoire in having only two voices with the chant presented in long equal notes. Mulliner may have modelled M8 on Redford's (M7), as the two versets not only share the same first six consonances, they also include repetition of a figure (or point) on three or more of these consonances; in addition, the descants begin with the same six notes and use one note value continuously, which is one of the first ways in which florid counterpoint was taught. According to Morley, after learning note-against-note counterpoint, descanters learned how to sing two notes to each one of chant, then three and so on: "Quadrupla and quintupla they [descanters of the past] denominated after the number of black minims set for a note of the plainsong."[4] This presumably explains the reference to singing "Discant of all man[ner] mesurs" in the Chester indenture cited above, as well as to teaching choristers "Descant to four minims" in Robert Heywood's contract at Christ Church, Dublin, in 1546,[5] and to "descant of two mynymes at the lest" required at the College of Middleham.[6] M9, Tallis's *Natus est nobis*, is quite unusual in that it is a written example of Morley's first kind of chant figuration, in which one note of the chant is performed long and the next is short, even though they are not presented as such in the chant book.[7] Perhaps this — and the other two kinds of chant figuration — explain the reference in the Chester indenture to playing "upon the organs any man[ner] plaȳsong." M18, *Claro pascali gaudio* by Allwood, is the first example in Mulliner's book to have some breaking of the chant (Morley's second kind of figuration), which is placed in the lowest voice. It is also an example of a descant that comprises an ostinato: a skillful descanter would try to repeat the

[1] Andrew Asbee and David Lasocki, eds., *A Biographical Dictionary of English Court Musicians, 1485–1714* (Aldershot, 1998), 160.

[2] Thomas Morley, A *Plaine and Easie Introduction to Practicall Musicke* (London, 1597), 90.

[3] "M" refers to the number given to pieces in *Mulliner Book*, ed. Stevens.

[4] Morley, *Introduction*, 91.

[5] Harrison, *Medieval Britain*, 197.

[6] James Raine, ed., "The Statutes Ordained by Richard Duke of Gloucester for the College of Middleham, dated July 4, 18 Edw. IV. [1478]," *Archaeological Journal* 14 (1857), 160–70.

[7] John Caldwell, "Keyboard Plainsong Settings in England, 1500–1660," *Musica Disciplina* 19 (1965), 129–53 at 138.

same short motive or point at various pitch levels and at various rhythmic intervals over the chant.[1] Moreover, the point in *Claro pascali*, like many other ostinato points, is designed to fit many contexts.[2] M41, a *Miserere* by Shelbye, involves the repeated-note method of chant figuration, this time placed in the top part, and is the first appearance in Mulliner's book of difficult proportions: the two counters (descants below the chant) are in the proportions 3 : 2 and 9 : 2 (i.e., they are further examples of "discant of all man[ner] mesurs"). By Morley's day this style was unappreciated: "those Superparticulars and Superpartients carry great difficulty, and have crept into music I know not how; but it should seem that it was by means of the Descanters who, striving to sing harder ways upon a plainsong than their fellows, brought in that which neither could please the ears of other men, nor could by themselves be defended by reason."[3] M49, Blitheman's *Eterne rerum* [1] is the first example in Mulliner's book that uses Morley's second kind of chant figuration in which all of the chant is "broken" so that both voices are more or less equal. This is similar to Christopher Simpson's description of "2 viols descanting on a ground," in which one breaks the ground and the other descants on a third or fifth (sixth where required). In this way, Simpson explains, "two Viols may move in *Extemporary* Division a whole Strain together, without any remarkable clashing in the Consecution of *Fifths* or *Eighths*."[4] The most contrapuntally complex versets in Mulliner's book are towards the end of the book, M97–105, all by Tallis, and they are in four equal, imitative voices (with the chant broken).

Mulliner himself may have composed M109, the anonymous *Psalmus: O Lord turn not away*, which is a unique setting for organ of a psalm tune.[5] It has two counters, one in parallel sixths below the *cantus firmus* and the other in even running notes that are very similar in figuration to those in the anonymous *Miserere* (M8). It is apparently modelled on Redford's *Salvum fac* (M62), but as the *cantus firmus* is a psalm tune, with its notes of mixed rhythmic value as printed in the *English Psalter* (1561) for Sternhold and Hopkins's *Lamentation of a Sinner*, the piece demonstrates an advanced technique of improvised counterpoint — that of making counterpoint on "figured song." Several treatises refer to the practice of applying descanting techniques to *cantus firmi* that were notated mensurally: according to Tomás de Santa Maria, "he who wishes to become a consummate performer must devote himself to playing counterpoint of rhythmic elegance and

---

[1] See Morley's derogatory remarks in his *Introduction*, 121–22.

[2] Denis Stevens, *The Mulliner Book: A Commentary* (London, 1952), 34 and 38, points out that *Eterne rerum* and M75 *Jam lucis* use a similar point, and that [*Clarifica me pater*] (M101) "has a point very similar to that of the following piece, *Veni Redemptor*. Obviously the complete organist should be perfectly capable of fitting any point to any plainsong."

[3] Morley, *Introduction*, 90.

[4] Christopher Simpson, *Division-Viol, or, The Art of Playing Ex Tempore upon a Ground*; [1667] *Lithographic Facsimile of the Second Edition* (London, 1955). See also the example of "plane sang figurateuff" in British Library, Add. MS 4911, "The Airt of Musicke," fols. 92ᵛ–93ʳ.

[5] Nicholas Temperley, "Organ settings of English Psalm Tunes," *Musical Times* 122 (1981), 123–28 at 125.

melodic grace over plainsong and, above all, over mensural music" ("sobre canto llano y sobre todo de organo").[1]

The next largest category of pieces in Mulliner's book comprises keyboard versions (accompaniments) of part-songs or consort songs by masters of choristers and others (such as Heywood and Whythorne) who wrote moralistic or pedagogical texts. Perhaps when Whythorne accompanied himself on the virginals he played from similar "arrangements"; the fact that the texts are not placed in Mulliner's book does not argue against this, as lyrics were often written out separately and punctuated to indicate how they were to be fitted to music (and not for sense). MII, *Whose faithful service* (text not identified), and M12 (untitled) are both lacking their top parts, which indicates that Mulliner was copying from partbooks such as the four described by Sainliens that contain songs by Richard Edwards, "maister of the children of the Queenes chapel" from 1561 until his death in 1566.[2] Denis Stevens points out that the repeated notes at the end of MII show "the influence of the keyboard, or of viols" (rather than of voices).[3] Several texts of songs in Mulliner's book are found in the collection of Edwards, which was published posthumously in 1576 as *The Paradise of Dainty Devices*.[4] For example, *O the silly man* is a unique setting by Edwards of a poem by Francis Kinwelmarch; in *Paradise* its heading is a proverbial distich used in teaching grammar and morals (for example, in Elyot's *Bankette of Sapience*): "Most happy is that state alone / Where woordes and deedes agree in one." Like Whythorne's songs "for children" (and some songs by Thomas Ravenscroft written for choristers' plays[5]), this song has a high tessitura (*d–f''*). The refrain of *In going to my naked bed* by Edwards (and included in *Paradise*)[6] is "The fallyng out of faithfull frends, is the renuyng of loue," which is one of the *sententiae* used in the *Grammar* of 1542 by William Lily (master at St. Paul's school): "Amantium irae, amoris redintegratio est / The variance of lovers (saith Terence) is the renuying of love."[7] Indeed, Whythorne quotes both of these proverbs in his autobiography.

Like John Darcy, who learned from William Parke how "to set a songe of thre p[ar]ts iiij or v," and as did Whythorne from Heywood, Mulliner apparently

---

[1] Tomás de Santa María, *Libro llamado Arte de tañer fantasia*, 2 vols. (Valladolid, 1565), part 2, chap. 52.

[2] Claudius Hollyband [Claude de Sainliens], *The French Schoolmaister* (London, 1573), fol. 28ᵛ, cited in David Wulstan, *Tudor Music* (London, 1985), 81–82.

[3] Stevens, *Commentary*, 52–53.

[4] Richard Edwards, *The Paradise of Dainty Devices (1576–1606)*, ed. Hyder Edward Rollins (Cambridge, Mass., 1927).

[5] Linda Phyllis Austern, *Music in English Children's Drama of the Later Renaissance* (Philadelphia, 1992), 212–18. See also "Sith all our grief is turned to bliss", the (incomplete) last song from John Jeffere's *The Bugbears*, a play performed at court by boys between 1563 and ca. 1570; Andrew J. Sabol, "Two Songs with Accompaniment for an Elizabethan Choirboy Play," *Studies in the Renaissance* 5 (1958) 145–59; and Flynn, "Mulliner Book," 57–58, for a reconstruction. M27 also has a high tessitura.

[6] Sir John Hawkins located the text and included the setting in the appendix to vol. 5 of *A General History of the Science and Practice of Music* (London, 1776).

[7] Quoted in Beatrice White, ed., *The Vulgaria of John Stanbridge and the Vulgaria of Robert Whittinton*, Early English Text Society, o.s. 187 (London, 1932), 39.

practiced how to set texts to music. The four-voice setting written in score on folio 1 verso, signed TM, is of Vaux's poem, "The higher that the Ceder tree, vnto the heauens doe growe, / The more in danger is the top, when sturdie winds gan blowe." It was published in *Paradise* with the title "Of the meane estate," and is based on a proverb: "The hyer a man ascendeth the more nede he hath to loke about him: / for yf he fayle of hold or slyppe þe greter is his fall. Quo altius quisquam ascendit: eo oculatiori vigilantia opus est sibi. / Quippe si manus aut per deficiat: in preceps ruit."[1] Like Heywood's songs discussed above, this setting begins with the chanson rhythm and is basically homophonic.

Another example of a song in Mulliner's book that has distinct pedagogical interest is *O ye tender babes*, a unique setting by Tallis of part of the address "To the reader" in the English part of Lily's *Grammar*, beginning "You tender babes of Englande, shake of slouthfulnes, set wantonnes a parte, apply your wyttes holy to lernyng and vertue." Stevens, who located the text, suggests that Tallis may have written the setting while he was assisting Richard Bowers, master of choristers at the Chapel Royal.[2] *My Friends* is a setting of a translation of one of Martial's epigrams (10:47, "Ad Seipsum") by Henry Howard, earl of Surrey; Whythorne copied some of his poems for Heywood. Surrey's poem (in the version beginning "My friends") is included in Baldwin's *Treatise of Morall Philosophie*, and a musical setting, with the same heading, is in a part-book (London, Public Record Office, State Papers, 1/246), both of which Mulliner may have had access to through Heywood.[3]

Another genre associated with choristers' education and also popular in their plays was the lament (for example, the lawyer Prideaux's *Dido's Lament*, mentioned above). Mulliner's book includes the laments *When shall my sorrowful sighing slake*; *The bitter sweate that straines my yelded harte*, which is by Heywood's son Jasper (printed in *Paradise*) and is musically very similar to the elder Heywood's; *Like as the doleful dove*, by William Hunnis of the Chapel Royal (also printed in *Paradise*); *Defiled is my name*;[4] Thomas Howell's *Like as the chained wight*;[5] and Edwards's *When griping griefs* (also printed in *Paradise*, and cited in Shakespeare's *Romeo and Juliet*). In choristers' plays, such songs were often accompanied on viols or regals: in Redford's *Wit and Science*, the lament *Exceeding mesure with paynes continewall* is sung by four singers and accompanied by viols, and in Edwards's

---

[1] Quoted in White, ed., *Vulgaria*, 77.

[2] Denis Stevens, "A Musical Admonition for Tudor Schoolboys," *Music and Letters* 38 (1957), 49–52.

[3] Other versions of Surrey's poem, beginning "Warner . . ." or "Martial . . ." are described by A. S. G. Edwards, "Surrey's Martial Epigram: Scribes and Transmission," in *Scribes and Transmission in English Manuscripts, 1400–1700*, ed. Peter Beal and A. S. G. Edwards, British Library English Manuscript Studies, 1100–1700, 12 (London, 2005), 74–82. See Denis Stevens, "A Part-Book in the Public Record Office," *Music Survey* 2 (1950), 161–70.

[4] G. E. P. Arkwright, "Elizabethan Choirboy Plays and their Music," *Proceedings of the Musical Association* 40 (1913/14), 117–38 at 131.

[5] This appears to be an earlier version of "Like as the wofull wight" by Howell; see Flynn, "Mulliner Book," 333–35.

only surviving play, *Damon and Pithias*, performed by Chapel Royal choristers in 1564,[1] Pithias sings *Awake ye wofull wights* accompanied by regals.

English metrical psalms (such as those by Sternhold that Whythorne copied for Heywood) were for non-liturgical use and thus belong in the genre of moralistic part-song.[2] Sternhold wrote his translations of the psalms for the edification of Edward VI and sang them to him while accompanying himself on the organ. Nicholas Temperley points out that "Sternhold's didactic purpose is further emphasised by the extra couplet [i.e., distich] which he added at the beginning of each psalm, driving home its moral significance."[3] Mulliner's book includes *The man is blest*, Sternhold's Psalm 1, which has a musical concordance (British Library Add. MS 15166, fols. 1r–2v) by Sheppard. This and other psalm settings by Shepherd in Additional 15116 are similar to M55–57,[4] which are also by Sheppard and labelled *Versus*. These could have been used for singing the psalms or similar texts in the same meter. M112, *When that the fifty day*, is from Christopher Tye's *Actes of the Apostles*, the verses of which "were patterned on those of Sternhold"[5] and were "to synge and also to play upon the Lute, very necessarye for studentes after theyr studye." Choristers most likely used a psalm setting like Sheppard's for the last song in the play *Pacient Grissell*, by John Phillips, which was "offered for acting" between 1558 and 1561, though it is not known by whom:[6] *How greatly am I bound to prayse / My God that syts in Throne* is in the most common psalm metre used by Sternhold (the same as *The man is blest*). Perhaps the unknown play performed before Elizabeth in July 1559 by the Children of St. Paul's "and ther master Se[bastian], master Phelypes, and master haywod" (to which I referred above) was this play, and "master Phelypes" was John Phillips.

Six short pieces comprising only one point of imitation are in a musical style similar to these psalm settings: the *Points* M68 and M69 are from Tye's *Praise ye the Lord, ye children*,[7] a setting of Psalm 113, vv. 1–6, 8 in British Library, Additional MS 30480. As M64–65 and M33 (by Sheppard) are very similar to these two, perhaps their sources will eventually be located.

M24, Sheppard's *Quia fecit*, M43, Tallis's *Remember not*, and M44, Sheppard's *I give you a new commandment*, are transcriptions of basically homophonic vocal polyphony, but towards the end of the book, Mulliner copied several transcriptions

[1] Yoshiko Kawachi, *Calendar of English Renaissance Drama, 1558–1642*, Garland Reference Library of the Humanities, 661 (New York, 1986), 16.

[2] Philip Brett, ed. *Consort Songs*, Musica Britannica, 22 (London, 1974), p. xiv, writes that one kind of early consort song "comprises settings of metrical psalms . . . and poems from the courtly anthologies of the time."

[3] Nicholas Temperley, *The Music of the English Parish Church*, 2 vols. (Cambridge, 1979), 1:23.

[4] Stevens, *Commentary*, 69, refers in particular to M57.

[5] Leonard Ellinwood, "Tallis' Tunes and Tudor Psalmody," *Musica Disciplina* 2 (1948), 189–203 at 189.

[6] Kawachi, *Calendar*, 2.

[7] Jason Smart, private communication. See John Morehen, ed., *Christopher Tye, 1: English Sacred Music*, Early English Church Music, 19 (London, 1977), 200–15, bars 49–51(1) and bars 15(3)–19(3) with adaptations towards the end to make a cadence.

of more intricate, imitative vocal "pricksong," perhaps for the purpose of study: M76, *Rejoice in the Lord always*, M117, Tye's *I lift my heart* (the only five-voice piece in Mulliner's book); M119, *Per haec nos* (part of Tallis's *Salve intemerata virgo*); and in particular M120, *Tres parts in una* (from William Munday's *Exsurge Christe*). Mulliner may also have "scored" them in preparation for learning how to play them from a choirbook[1] (recall the remark in the Chester indenture, cited above, "to play upon the organs . . . prykkytsonge two p[ar]ts or thre"; this skill was often required of candidates applying for organist positions).

Like Whythorne, Mulliner most likely studied the virginals with Heywood. His book includes an arrangement for virginals (with written-out virginalist-type ornamentation) of the lament *O ye happy dames*; two variations of *The Maiden's Song* (untitled in the manuscript); and an untitled galliard with varied repeats (M2). M116, a *Pavan* by Newman, though apparently for keyboard (as it has a varying number of voices), is simple and without ornamentation, similar in style to the French dances M13–15 (of which only two voices are notated), *La bounette*, *La doune cella* (a pavan), and *La shy myze*. Mulliner's source could have been part-books for viols: he would easily have been able to add inner parts, especially when playing for dancers. Mulliner transcribed several other pieces from sources notated for viols; as noted above, such music was often transferable to the organ.

The *In nomines* by Johnson (M45) and Robert White (M87) include a few large stretches for the hands, and Stevens suggests convincingly that Mulliner's source was for viol consort, such as Oxford MS Mus. Sch. d. 212–16, which includes both pieces, as well as John Taverner's famous *In nomine* (M35). M32, *An excellent meane* by Blitheman, also includes large stretches, and if Mulliner's source was for viols, perhaps this explains the title of what is a *Felix namque*. M10, a "fansye of master newmans" à 3, survives in two versions as a lute piece (Ireland, Archbishop Marsh's Library MS Z3.2.13, ca. 1595, nos. 22 and 93), but since it appears to be a parody (in part) of M. A. Cavazzoni's *Salve Virgo*,[2] a viol consort version would likely have been Mulliner's source. As Peter Holman suggests, it is possible that Mulliner copied these versions for accompanying purposes.[3]

Towards the end of Mulliner's book are eight pieces for four-course cittern, one for five-course that "require the tuning of Le Roy, but with a chromatic fretting," and two pieces for gittern:[4] *A songue*; *A pavion*; [*Chi passa*]; [*pavan*]; [*galliard*]; *Che passa*; *Was not goode Kinge Solomon* [an alman]; [*pavan*]; *The Queen of Scottes gallyard per TM*; *The Frenche gallyard*; *Venetian gallyard*. It appears that Mulliner had originally intended to learn to play the lute, as he had ruled the last two gath-

---

[1] Gerald Gifford, "The Mulliner Book Revisited: Some Musical Perspectives and Performance Considerations," *The Consort* 58 (2002), 13–27 at 23.

[2] Christopher D. S. Field, "Fantasia, §1 (viii): To 1700: Great Britain," *The New Grove Dictionary of Music and Musicians*, 2nd ed., ed. Stanley Sadie (London, 2001).

[3] Peter Holman, "'Evenly, Softly, and Sweetly Acchording to All': The Organ Accompaniment of English Consort Music," in *John Jenkins and his Time: Studies in English Consort Music*, ed. Andrew Ashbee and Peter Holman (Oxford, 1996), 353–82 at 361.

[4] James Tyler, "Cittern, §3: History and repertory from 1500," *New Grove Dictionary*, ed. Sadie.

erings with three staves of six lines each, appropriate for six-course lute tablature, and thus crossed the extra lines out. Like Thomas Cecil (the son of Heywood's friend Mildred), he may have developed an interest in the newly popular instruments: in July 1561, Thomas's tutor Thomas Windebank wrote to William Cecil that his son did not have "any mind to learn the lute, but to the cithera he has."[1] Like Whythorne, who apparently learned the cittern and gittern primarily to accompany himself singing and not for solo playing, Mulliner intabulated pieces that are appropriate for accompanying a voice or voices or in consorts, in that they are incomplete harmonically (lacking the bass): *A songe* lacks its melody, and all but *Venetian galliard* by Churchyard are in a strumming style characteristic of consort music.[2]

Lyrics could be fitted to well-known tunes or grounds such as these: F. J. in Gascoigne's *The Adventures of Master F. J.* (1573), who, "taking into his hand a Lute that lay on his Mistres bed, did unto the note of ye *Venetian* galliard applie the Italian dittie . . . *Rugier qual sempre fui.*"[3] The "tune of *King Salomon*," a ballad registered for publication in 1558/9,[4] was used for Egistus and Clytemnestra's song beginning "And was it not a worthy sight" in *A New Enterlude of Vice conteyning the Historye of Horestes* by John Pickering, which was printed in 1567 and may have been the play performed by St. Paul's boys in 1567/8.

The gittern or cittern were sometimes used in choristers' plays: for example, in *Cambyses* by Thomas Preston (possibly performed in 1560 by St. Paul's boys), a Lord suggests to his Lady that they proceed "in field to walk abroad / On lute and cittern there to play a heavenly harmony." She agrees, and the stage direction reads: "heer [they] trace up & down playing." I assume that the part played by the cittern in this duet would be similar to those in the Mulliner Book, and that the lute could play the bass (perhaps with other chord notes and the melody). *An Enterlude Intituled Like wil to like Quod the Devel to the Colier, Very Godly and Ful of Plesant Mirth*, made by Ulpian Fulwell, was offered for acting between 1562 and 1568, and although the players are not known, Peter Happé suggests that "the phrase 'in the shroudes' (l. 248) may be a hint that . . . [it] was in fact designed (and perhaps produced) as a boys' play at St Paul's."[5] A cue reads: "Nichol Newfangle must have a Gittorn or some other instrument (if it may be) but if hee have not they must daunce about the place all three, and sing this song that followeth which must bee doon also although they have an instrument." As Ward points out, the first eight bars of the *Venetian galliarde* by Churchyard provide the first strain of a textless piece for three voices added in manuscript to the last leaf of the Folger

[1] Flynn, "Mulliner Book," 87.

[2] Ivan F. Waldbauer, "The Cittern in the Sixteenth Century and its Music in France and the Low Countries" (Ph.D. diss., Harvard University, 1964), 333.

[3] John M. Ward, "Music for *A Handefull of pleasant delites*," *Journal of the American Musicological Society* 10 (1957), 151–80 at 170–71.

[4] Edward Arber, ed., *A Transcript of the Registers of the Company of Stationers of London 1554–1640*, 5 vols. (London, 1875), 1:96.

[5] Peter Happé, ed., *Two Moral Interludes*, Malone Society Reprints (Oxford, 1991), 55–56.

Library's copy of the play (printed in London, ca. 1570),[1] and Sabol suggests convincingly that it is "a setting for the concluding lyric."[2] This vocal arrangement has open fifths and ungraceful voice-leading, which could, however, be filled out by the gittern that had been played earlier in the play.[3]

In conclusion, Mulliner's book includes examples of almost all of the kinds of pedagogical material that one might expect an apprentice musician to study, based on the documentary evidence (such as the Chester indenture) and Whythorne's autobiography: Mulliner learned Latin grammar and translation exercises and how to write Latin verse. One assumes that he also wrote moralistic English verse similar to that of Redford, Heywood, Edwards, and Whythorne (and presumably Sebastian Westcote, whose lost "book of ditties, written," that he presented to Queen Mary as a New Year's gift were probably secular songs, since she kept them among her personal possessions).[4] Mulliner also learned how to set lyrics to music (recall that Darcy learned "to set a songe of thre p[ar]ts, iiij or v"). He collected examples of "discant of all manner of measures," as well as of progressively intricate vocal polyphony and music for viols, which he most likely learned to play (recall that Darcy was to learn "to play upon the organs any man[ner] plaÿsong or prykkytsonge two p[ar]ts or thre"). Mulliner learned to play the virginals and plucked stringed instruments, perhaps for accompanying himself in solo songs or for use in assisting with entertainments put on by masters Heywood, Westcote, Philips, and their choristers. His book thus illustrates vividly and comprehensively the use of material from the few other sources we have concerning the further education of older choristers in England in the period up to Elizabeth's religious settlement.

---

[1] Ward, *Elizabethan Lutes*, 48.

[2] Andrew J. Sabol, "A Three-Man Song in Fulwell's *Like Will to Like* at the Folger," *Renaissance News* 10 (1957), 139–42.

[3] Flynn, "Mulliner Book," 535–36.

[4] Page, "Uniform and Catholic," 272.

11

CANTANDO TUTTE INSIEME
TRAINING GIRL SINGERS IN EARLY MODERN
SIENESE CONVENTS

Colleen Reardon

I N one of his gossipy letters from 1697, the Sienese aristocrat Fabio Spannocchi described for Cardinal Francesco Maria de' Medici, the absent governor of
Siena, the ceremony to welcome a new novice into one of the city's convents:

> Yesterday evening at the door of that same convent [of Monnagnese], which
> faces the palace of Your Highness, those little nuns performed the most
> beautiful polyphony as the bride made her entrance into the cloister.[1]

Spannocchi's description of the singers as "little nuns" (*monachine*) seems not at
all remarkable when one remembers that he, along many other writers of the time,
employed the word *cantarine* to refer to fully grown female opera singers.[2] The
diminutive can also be found in earlier records from female sacred institutions.
The historical chronicles from the institution of Santi Abbondio e Abbondanzio,
for example, label the performers at the 1564 consecration ceremony as *citole* or
"little girls."[3] Although it could be argued that such diminutives were a stylistic
tic of the age, it is also possible that, in this case, they acknowledge the youth of

---

[1] Florence, Archivio di Stato, Mediceo del Principato 5835, #675: "Siena 28 dicembre
1697 . . . ier sera dalla porta del medesimo convento [di MonAgnese] che riesce in faccia
al palazzo di Vostra Altezza fecero quelle monachine una bella musicha nel tempo che la
sposa vi fece l'entrata." Thanks go to Nello Barbieri for his help with the translations in this
essay.

[2] Fabio Spannocchi's observations on opera in Siena are the subject of a forthcoming
article.

[3] Siena, Biblioteca Comunale (hereafter BCS), MS E.v.19, "Storia del monasterio di
S. Abundio e Abundanzio," fol. 92ʳ. Although the consecration ceremony was supposed to
include only those nuns who had reached the age of twenty-five, the women often asked
authorities for permission to include all professed nuns who had not yet been consecrated,
even those still in their teens; see, for instance, Siena, Archivio di Stato (hereafter ASS),
Conventi soppressi 918 (Sant'Abbondio), fol. 194ᵛ. For more on the music at consecration
ceremonies in Siena, see Colleen Reardon, *Holy Concord within Sacred Walls: Nuns and
Music in Siena, 1575–1700* (Oxford, 2002), 58–74.

the performers in question. Indeed, the nunnery provided one of the few places in early modern Italy where one might regularly hear the characteristic timbre of girls' voices, either as soloists or in a choir. The tender age at which female children were placed in convents suggests that the majority received a thorough musical training there, one that enabled them to enchant even a cynical and experienced dilettante such as Fabio Spannocchi, among others.

Just how did these littlest members of the cloistered community learn to sing? By piecing together the sparse documentation on music education and the girls' general activities, and by linking those activities to a few extant musical sources from Siena, I will sketch the outlines of a training program for youngsters in a convent. My arguments are necessarily conjectural, and I do not wish to imply that they apply to all Sienese nunneries or to all girl singers. We know of girls whose training must have been as unusual as either their musical talent or their family situation. The trio of ten-year-olds who performed a three-act sacred opera at San Girolamo in Campansi in 1686 must have received intensive, extraordinary instruction at the hands of teachers employed by their powerful, aristocratic parents.[1] Here, however, I want to concentrate on what might have been the normal procedures and the usual repertory used in the cloister to transform musically talented girls into proficient singers.

BOARDERS AND NOVICES

A DOCUMENT preserved in the records of the Sacra Congregazione dei Vescovi e Regolari helps establish the number of female religious in Siena around the beginning of the seventeenth century and offers some insight into the number of girls who lived as boarders in the city's convents.[2] The unnamed apostolic visitor was attempting to establish the maximum number of *bocche* ("mouths") that each institution could support and wanted to mandate a reduction in the population of nearly every nunnery in the city. As part of this process, he wished to impose a limit on the number of girl boarders (called *educande* or *secolari*) the nuns could admit. If we look at the convents with strong musical traditions, we see that both the numbers of prescribed boarders and the ratio of nuns to boarders varied widely (see Table 11.1). For example, the writer mandated only five *educande* at Sant'Abbondio, despite the fact that he thought the institution could maintain eighty nuns, but allowed as many as twelve at Ognissanti, notwithstanding his directive to reduce the number of nuns paying normal dowries from sixty to fifty. The apostolic visitor did not explain his logic. Perhaps it was traditional to admit more boarders at Ognissanti than at Sant'Abbondio, or perhaps Sant'Abbondio had a higher number of servant nuns who neither sang nor taught. Of one thing,

---

[1] For more on this work, see Reardon, *Holy Concord*, 129–53.

[2] The figures in Table 11.1 are taken from Vatican City, Archivio Segreto, Sacra Congregazione dei Vescovi e Regolari, Pos. 1600, Lett. P–T, letter of Oct. 16, 1600. The document is published in full in Gian Ludovico Masetti Zannini, *Motivi storici della educazione femminile*, vol. 2: *Scienza, lavoro, giuochi* (Naples, 1982), 358–61.

Table 11.1: Recommended *bocche* for selected Sienese convents, 1600

	Nuns (normal dowries)	Supernumeraries (double dowries)	Educande
Augustinian			
S. Maria degli Angeli (Santuccio)	44	10	10
S. Maria Maddalena	50	10	10
S. Marta	50	5	5
S. Paolo	30	10	10
Benedictine			
SS. Abbondio e Abbondanzio	70	10	5
Cistercian			
Monastero delle Trafisse	45	5	6
Clarissan			
S. Petronilla	45	5	6
Gesuate			
S. Sebastiano in Vallepiatta	33	7	10
Olivetan			
Ognissanti	50	10	12

however, we can be sure: the fact that the visitor was trying to lay down the law probably indicates that the nuns were admitting more girls than he thought optimal. I have not come across a similar document from later in the century, but other records make it clear that some institutions were able to grow dramatically (e.g., Santuccio, which housed seventy-three nuns by ca. 1650). We can posit that the number of *educande* increased as well, despite official recommendations. Santa Petronilla, whose population appears to have increased only to about fifty-five nuns by the mid *Seicento*, housed fourteen girls in 1644 and was home to eight boarders even as the population declined in 1693.[1]

The *educande* came in all sizes. Families were allowed to board their daughters in convents once the girls reached the age of seven. If the girls were destined for marriage, they might remain in the cloister, safe from the world's temptations until the age of seventeen or eighteen. Most of the boarders were, however, girls whose families had deemed them unmarriageable. In Siena, they often took the veil when they reached the age of twelve. At that point, they became novices and were supposed to be separated from the other boarders so that they could concentrate

---

[1] See ASS, Conventi soppressi 3514, unn. fol., payment from Dec. 25, 1644; and 3400, unn. fol., payment from April 1693. For more on the Sienese convent population, see Reardon, *Holy Concord*, 15–19.

on their preparation for the religious life. Each group of girls was assigned to a nun. A "mistress of the novices" (*maestra delle novizie*) supervised the teenagers who were studying for profession. A "mistress of the girls" (*maestra delle fanciulle*) looked after the youngsters who either had not yet taken vows or would never take vows.[1] Although there must have been some older brides-to-be in this group, it was undoubtedly composed mostly of girls between the ages of seven and eleven.

If convents with vigorous performing traditions were to maintain their reputation for musical excellence, it is clear that training had to begin with the youngest members of the community and continue throughout the novitiate and beyond.[2] We can surmise that the *maestra delle fanciulle* and the *maestra delle novizie* both served as tutors, but they were not the only music teachers to which the girls had access. As the girls became more musically competent, it is also possible that they came into contact with the nun who supervised the performance of Gregorian chant and the nun who directed the polyphonic choir in those convents that appointed women to such positions.[3] Licenses permitting men to teach music at female monastic institutions sometimes mention the anticipated participation of girls.[4] Nuns could also offer individualized training to a boarder, usually a relative.[5] Depending on the particular institution, *educande* might have had access to musical training in many different forms, from many different teachers.[6] What repertory, then, best suited the very youngest and most inexperienced of the girl boarders as they first entered the cloister?

[1] The information on *educande* and novices is taken from *Decreti e costitutioni generali dell'illustriss. e reverendiss. Monsignore Alessandro Petrucci Arcivescovo di Siena per il buon governo delle monache della sua città e diocesi* (Siena, 1625). Although these decrees do not mention a "mistress of the girls," nuns with this title appear in records of individual houses; see, for example, ASS, Conventi soppressi 3403 (Santa Petronilla), unn. fol., payment of July 1693.

[2] The sheer amount of noise that such activity entailed could try the patience of less musically inclined nuns; see Reardon, *Holy Concord*, 34. For the story of one exceptionally talented girl organist, see Colleen Reardon, "The Good Mother, the Reluctant Daughter, and the Convent: A Case of Musical Persuasion," in *Musical Voices of Early Modern Women: Many-Headed Melodies*, ed. Thomasin LaMay (Aldershot, 2005), 271–86.

[3] At S. Sebastiano, a "maestra di coro" and a "maestra di cappella" (or a "maestra del canto figurato") are listed among the officers regularly elected in two-year cycles from 1629 through 1699; see Siena, Archivio dei Conservatorî Riuniti Femminili (hereafter ACRFS), S. Sebastiano in Vallepiatta 1 (old 1248); and Reardon, *Holy Concord*, 30–35.

[4] Reardon, *Holy Concord*, Doc. 7c, 194–95.

[5] Craig A. Monson, *Disembodied Voices: Music and Culture in an Early Modern Italian Convent* (Berkeley, 1995), 49.

[6] In some cases, parents gave their daughters music lessons before they entered the convent in order to qualify them for dowry reductions. This "darker side of musical education" is discussed in Robert L. Kendrick, *Celestial Sirens: Nuns and their Music in Early Modern Milan* (Oxford, 1996), 181–82, and in Colleen Baade, "'Hired' Nun Musicians in Early Modern Castile," in *Musical Voices of Early Modern Women*, 287–310. In Siena, however, dowry reductions appear to have been rare; see Reardon, *Holy Concord*, 41.

Devotional Songs

A LATE-SEVENTEENTH-CENTURY document offers some indirect evidence for the repertory the nuns might have taught their youngest singers. It describes the festivities surrounding an annual Sienese procession by lay religious companies. In 1684, the holy women of Sant'Abbondio, located several miles outside the walls of Siena in the area of Munistero, lent their most important relic, the body of the Blessed Giovanni Colombini, for the procession. Two days after Easter, the members of the congregation of San Michele Arcangelo came to take Colombini's body to Siena Cathedral, where it lay in state for the rest of the week. On the day of the procession, the Sienese were "moved to devotion" by a charming spectacle:

> On Low Sunday, the authorities in Munistero had someone teach some of the girls words appropriate for that saint [Colombini], words to the effect that "we have lost him" and similar things. The girls, dressed as angels, went into the city [of Siena] searching for the blessed one and singing all together.[1]

The "little angels" (who might have included *educande* at Sant'Abbondio) were probably singing a *lauda*: a strophic, devotional song in Italian. It seems clear that they had memorized the words and the tune, which they sang unharmonized. Some devotional songs probably circulated widely in an oral tradition; from the description above, for example, it seems that the girls learned new words to a well-known (perhaps secular) melody.[2] Other songs were newly composed for specific occasions. The *lauda* repertory so permeated cloisters throughout Italy that it not only played a role in liturgical services, it was also often the soundtrack for holy women's mystic visions.[3] Devotional songs were highly suitable repertory for even

---

[1] For a discussion of nuns' musical contributions to this annual procession, see Reardon, *Holy Concord*, 44–47. For more on the symbolism inherent in processions of young people dressed as angels, see Marica S. Tacconi, *Cathedral and Civic Ritual in Late Medieval and Renaissance Florence: The Service Books of Santa Maria del Fiore*, Cambridge studies in palaeography and codicology, 12 (Cambridge, 2005), 214–17.

[2] Robert Kendrick provides an overview of spiritual music and its cultural function in "Devotion, Piety and Commemoration: Sacred Songs and Oratorios," in *The Cambridge History of Seventeenth-Century Music*, ed. Tim Carter and John Butt (Cambridge, 2005), 324–77.

[3] Patrick Macey, "*Infiamma il mio cor*: Savonarolan *Laude* by and for Dominican Nuns in Tuscany," in *The Crannied Wall: Women, Religion, and the Arts in Early Modern Europe*, ed. Craig A. Monson (Ann Arbor, Mich., 1992), 161–89. Macey examines the role *laude* played in keeping the Savonarolan spirit of religious reform alive. Kimberlyn Montford discusses devotional music in Roman nunneries in "Music in the Convents of Counter-Reformation Rome," (Ph.D. diss., Rutgers University, 1999), 161–220. See also Masetti Zannini, "'Suavità di canto' e 'purità di cuore': Aspetti della musica nei monasteri femminili romani," in *La cappella musicale nell'Italia della Controriforma. Atti del Convegno internazionale di studi nel IV Centenario di fondazione della Cappella Musicale di S. Biagio di Cento, 13–15 ottobre 1989*, ed. Oscar Mischiati and Paolo Russo (Florence, 1993), 123–41. Zannini transcribes texts of

the youngest *educande*: the texts promoted religious ideals and the settings were often simple and tuneful.[1]

Laude seem to have figured prominently in the plays staged in many of Siena's female monastic institutions. Certainly, a good number of *sacre rappresentazioni* that were published in Siena and might have provided scripts for convent plays include directions to sing a devotional text in Italian at high points in the drama. Perhaps these musical moments were assigned to the *educande* as a way to include them in the theatrical proceedings.[2]

The singing of a devotional song also seems to be at the core of a dramatic practice reserved exclusively for the girl boarders, one that was separate from the complex theatrical productions mounted by novices and professed nuns. Nuns in at least four Sienese houses cultivated the old Tuscan tradition of having their girls sing the "May song" (*cantare maggio*). At Santa Petronilla the custom is documented from about 1623, and at Santa Maria degli Angeli (Santuccio) records begin in 1634. Traces of the practice also surface at Santissima Concezione and at Sant'Abbondio, the latter an institution that, like Santa Petronilla and Santuccio, had a reputation for excellence in musical performance.[3]

The term "cantare maggio" originates, of course, in a tradition celebrating the return of spring; in the convent it might have involved just singing, or singing and dancing, or singing, dancing, and acting out a brief story with devotional content.[4] Records from all four institutions named above consist only of the briefest of entries in the debit registers, which show money disbursed to buy snacks and to give a small gratuity to the young performers.[5] Records from Santa Petronilla suggest that the term "cantare maggio" might have had the specific meaning of honoring the Virgin Mary during the month dedicated to her. In 1681, for example, registers record a small payment to the girls "which we usually give them in May for the

---

Italian devotional songs performed as part of liturgical rites; he also includes the story of a novice who saw the Virgin and Child springing out of a church wall accompanied by the music of a *lauda*. The Sienese mystic Caterina Vannini, too, heard *laude* during her visions; see Reardon, *Holy Concord*, 106.

[1] Kendrick, "Devotion, Piety and Commemoration," 343, quotes from a Catholic hymnal whose purpose was "to draw small children, with their innate desire to sing (like a small bird with a little pipe), to Christian children's doctrine."

[2] See, for example, *La rappresentatione di Santa Agata vergine e martire* (Siena, 1606), *La rappresentatione di Santa Orsola vergine e martire* (Siena, 1608), and *La rappresentatione e festa di Rosana* (Siena, 1626), all preserved in BCS. Alessandro D'Ancona, ed., *Sacre rappresentazioni dei secoli XIV, XV, e XVI*, 3 vols. (Florence, 1872), 2: 323–24, suggests that the *Rappresentazione di Santa Teodora* (Siena, 1614) might have been performed entirely by *educande*; this play, too, ends with a devotional song.

[3] Reardon, *Holy Concord*, 79.

[4] D'Ancona, *Origine del teatro in Italia*, 2 vols. (Florence, 1877), 2: 364–91, discusses the tradition of "maggi spirituali."

[5] ASS, Conventi soppressi 2326 (Santuccio), fol. 92v: "A dì primo maggio (1660). A dì detto £. quattro date alle nostre secolare quando ànno cantato maggio, due lire li si devevano e £. 2 pagatoli il prosciutto, £. 4."

Most Sacred Virgin."[1] Between 1687 and 1690, the girls likewise received the same amount of money for "the most Holy Virgin."[2]

Unfortunately, no seventeenth-century "May songs" from Siena appear to survive. One late Sienese source preserves the text of a May song performed "in honor of the Annunciation of the Virgin Mary."[3] The poem consists of twenty-two stanzas of four lines each, clearly inviting a strophic musical setting so characteristic of the *lauda*. Although the work begins as a paean to the joys of spring, it eventually turns into a hymn in praise of the Madonna:

Stanza 1:

Ecco riede il piacevole	Here once again is pleasant
Maggio ad ognun gradito	May, to all most welcome,
E ci fa dolce invito	Who extends to us a sweet invitation
Al canto e al carolar.	To sing and to dance.

Stanza 14:

Ave donna purissima	Hail woman most pure;
Ave di grazia piena	Hail full of grace;
Fonte tu sei, Tu vena	You are a fountain and a spring
D'infiniti tesor.	Of boundless treasure.

It might be that spring was not the only time of year that the *educande* staged a miniature performance based on devotional songs. A Sienese manuscript containing a number of *laude* for the Christmas season includes a short late-seventeenth-century playlet of thirteen folios in which all the dramatic action plays out in strophic devotional songs.[4] It begins with shepherds named Favilla and Narciso, who are "singing as they go to the manger." These two characters perform alternate stanzas of a *lauda* in which they describe the appearance of the angel announcing the birth of Christ, then decide what gifts they will take to the child, and finally express the duty to praise God at all times. This is followed by a "*lauda* the shepherds sing when they have reached the manger," a "*lauda* to Baby Jesus," a "*lauda* for Mary, mother of Baby Jesus," and finally a "*lauda* on the birth of Baby Jesus." In all but one case, each multi-stanza text appears first, followed by

[1] ASS, Conventi soppressi 3394, fol. 158ʳ: "1681. Giugno. Il 2 dato alle fanciulle lire due soldi 13 e denari 4 per la Santissima Vergine quale siamo solite il darli il maggio, £. 2.13.4."

[2] ASS, Conventi soppressi 3397, fols. 105ʳ, 109ʳ, 111ʳ, 114ʳ.

[3] *Maggio cantato l'anno 1796 in onore dell'annunziazione di Maria Vergine* (Siena, n.d.), preserved in BCS. The connection between the Virgin Mary and Spring was venerable; see David J. Rothenberg, "The Marian Symbolism of Spring, ca. 1200 – ca. 1500: Two Case Studies," *Journal of the American Musicological Society* 59 (2006), 319–98.

[4] BCS, MS G.x.43, "Laudi per il natale di nostro Signore." Lorenzo Ilari dates this manuscript to the eighteenth century, but I believe he looked only at the first five folios. The playlet with Favilla and Narciso begins on fol. 6ʳ and continues through fol. 18ʳ. The scribe here is not the same person who copied the first five folios; the hand looks similar to that found in MS G.xi.58, a seventeenth-century manuscript containing a convent play with music. See Ilari, *La Biblioteca pubblica di Siena disposta secondo le materie: Catalogo*, 7 vols. (Siena, 1844–48), 1:182; and Reardon, *Holy Concord*, 79–87. My heartfelt thanks to Frank A. D'Accone, who brought the little Christmas play to my attention.

the musical score. All settings feature a single melody line; most are accompanied by basso continuo and framed by an instrumental ritornello, although the first song for Favilla and Narciso is endowed with a ritornello but no basso continuo and the second song for the shepherds has a basso continuo but no ritornello.[1]

Although many of the texts preserve the masculine endings appropriate for an apparently heterogeneous group of males and females, the final verse of the last *lauda* in the manuscript implies that the "maleness" of the performers might have gone only costume-deep. In that verse, the singers ask to be made "worthy" of eternal glory; the word "worthy" is rendered in the feminine plural (*degne*). If the mini-drama was intended for an all-female cast, the most probable context for its staging is a female monastic institution. Furthermore, given the brevity of the work and the simplicity of the melodic style, it seems tailor-made for young singers. It is true that the first song for Favilla and Narciso does calls for more ex-perienced performers who can sing unaccompanied and solo; perhaps this was as-signed to two of the older and more musically secure *educande*. The rubrics in the manuscript also do not clarify whether the other *laude* in the manuscript were to have been performed by these two singers alone. It is possible, however, to imagine a staging where Favilla and Narciso convince other shepherds to accompany them on their journey. This larger group of "shepherds" (that is, all the girl boarders) would have then sung the remaining *laude* together with Favilla and Narciso.

Example 11.1 provides a transcription of the song the shepherds sing upon their arrival at the manger. The text is set in a straightforward manner, with each sylla-ble receiving one note of the tune.[2] The melody moves for the most part in semim-inims, and it only once exceeds the range of a sixth (at the leading tone in measure four). The second melodic phrase is constructed as a varied sequence of the first, with a short refrain-like tag at the end. The harmonies are likewise basic, and the singers proceed directly from stanza to stanza with no intervening ritornello. The *lauda* performed in honor of the Virgin Mary (Example 11.2) is slightly more dif-ficult, as if challenging the girls to show off more of their skills as they settle into the performance.[3] Here, a mostly stepwise melody is enlivened with an upward leap of a sixth to the last phrase. The tune has a more varied rhythmic profile and is set to a wider harmonic palette. An instrumental ritornello separates each of the eleven stanzas; the singers' reward for getting through all of them is a lively refrain, *Viva, viva Maria del ciel Regina*.

We can imagine that girl boarders easily learned attractive strophic songs such

---

[1] MS G.x.43, fol. 6ʳ: "Favilla e Narciso pastori vanno cantando al presepio" (text on fols. 6ʳ–7ʳ, music on fol. 7ᵛ); fol. 8ʳ: "Laude che si canta dai pastori giunti al presepio" (text on fols. 8ʳ–9ʳ, music on fol. 9ᵛ); fol. 10ʳ: "Laude al bambino Gesù" (text on fols. 10ʳ–12ʳ, music on fols. 12ᵛ–13ʳ); fol. 16ʳ: "Laude a Maria Madre di Gesù bambino" (text on fols. 16ʳ–17ʳ; music on fol. 15ʳ); fol. 18ʳ: "Laude al Natale di Gesù bambino" (text on fols. 18ʳ–19ᵛ; no music provided).

[2] Translation of the text in Example 1: "Who makes us worthy of such favor? / O what happiness! / Who fills us with such sweetness? / O what joyousness!" My thanks to Tim Rolls who computer-processed all the musical examples for this article.

[3] Translation of the text in Example 2: "Rejoice, O Great Maiden, / While the heavens rejoice / At the birth of your noble and divine child. / Long live Maria, Queen of heaven."

Example 11.1: *Laude che si canta dai pastori giunti al presepio* (BCS, MS G.x.43, fol. 9ᵛ)

Example 11.2: *Laude a Maria Madre di Giesù bambino* (BCS, MS G.x. 43, fol. 15ʳ)

as these, especially when they were associated with a familiar story. The music could be taught by rote, and the texts could provide fodder for reading lessons and memory exercises.[1] Singing in unison was an excellent means to cultivate the most basic singing skills: accurate pitch and rhythm, a sense of meter, clear diction, and good ensemble. Finally, the use of the vernacular allowed even the youngest boarders to understand and to begin to find ways to communicate the meaning of what they were singing, an essential step in cultivating singers able to deliver musically compelling performances.

PART-SONGS

AFTER the girls had developed a sure sense of pitch and rhythm as well as good memorization skills by singing theatrical *laude* such as those examined here, the next step in their musical education might also have taken place within the context of convent drama. Four of the six extant plays that can be definitively associated with Sienese monastic institutions include directions for the performance of secular part-songs; these are sometimes labeled generically (e.g., madrigal, canzonetta) and sometimes not. In a number of cases, the sections of the play featuring such music focus on minor characters who have little to do with the unfolding drama; they appear to sing and then leave the stage to the principal actresses.[2] Such scenes would seem appropriate both dramatically and musically for those slightly older *educande* who were ready to progress beyond unison singing and venture into simple multi-part works.

No scores are extant for any of these monastic plays, so we must guess at the style of the music performed. One work does, however, suggest that the nuns might have drawn on published secular repertory to supply some of their musical needs. The early-seventeenth-century convent drama *Eufrosina* ends with a choir of "young men"; the rubrics indicate that the music they sang was for more than one part (*Qui Giovanetti cantino in musica*). More interestingly, the text of this composition begins by quoting the text of a three-voice *canzone alla napolitana* that Girolamo Scotto published in 1571:

Scotto, 1571

> Dolc'amorose e leggiadrette ninphe
> Che col vostro cantar e dolci accenti
> Fat'Ecco risonar placar i venti
> Venit'a cantar meco

---

[1] Both Sharon T. Strocchia, "Learning the Virtues: Convent Schools and Female Culture in Renaissance Florence," in *Women's Education in Early Modern Europe: A History, 1500–1800*, ed. Barbara J. Whitehead, Studies in the History of Education, 7 (New York, 1999), 3–46 at 26–27, and Susan Boynton, "Training for the Liturgy as a Form of Monastic Education," in *Medieval Monastic Education*, ed. George Ferzoco and Carolyn Muessig, (London, 2000), 7–20 at 11, discuss the use of rote learning and "sight-sound drills" for teaching children in monastic settings to read.

[2] For more on Sienese convent drama, see Reardon, *Holy Concord*, 75–97.

Notte felice e bella
Che mi guidast'in bracci'alla mia stella.[1]

Eufrosina, 1608

Dolci amorose, e leggiadrette Ninfe,
Che col dolce cantar, e dolci accenti
Fate ecco risonar, placar i venti,
Venite a cantar nosco.
Nozze per noi bramate
Felici più d'ogn'altro hoggi ci fate.[2]

The "young men" in this scene make no previous appearances in the play; they are brought on just to sing the final chorus, an appropriately circumscribed role for the girls who might have been assigned this scene. Scotto's three-part musical setting, which adapts easily to the new text (Example 11.3), displays two upper lines that lie well within the range of youthful sopranos and altos (despite the designation of the second part as "tenore"). The bass line is also quite high, and, although it could have been played by an instrumentalist, it might also have been performed by a few (perhaps older) low altos.[3] The texture is homophonic, and piquancy is added to the basically diatonic harmonic scheme in D minor by frequent vacillation between F-natural and F-sharp. Phrases are generally short and clearly defined by cadences. The uppermost melodic lines often move by step, and the rhythmic motion unfolds in semiminims, slowing to even minims as a cadence approaches. Here is attractive music that girls with pleasant voices, good ears, and some experience as performers of the "May song" might have learned easily by rote. Learning and performing such repertory would have developed their ability to hear, recognize, and correctly tune intervals and would have further refined their sense of pitch and rhythm. It would also have introduced them to a formal structure that was not strophic.

Gregorian Chant

I HAVE surmised that early musical training for girls in the convent might have begun with unison devotional songs and then progressed to simple part-music, all of it setting Italian texts and all of it connected in some way with theatrical

---

[1] I wish to thank Vera Möllering for helping me obtain a microfilm of *Corona: Il secondo libro delle canzoni alla napolitana a tre voci* (Venice, 1571). Both the text given here and the music for Example 11.3 are taken from the microfilm reproduction of the print held in Munich, Bayerische Staatsbibliothek, Musikabteilung, Mus.pr. 10 — Beibd. 5.

[2] BCS, MS G.XI.59, "Eufrosina comedia spirituale nuova 1608," fol. 54ʳ. Translation of text (see also Example 11.3): "Sweet, loving and graceful nymphs / Who with your sweet songs and sweet words / Make echoes resound and calm the winds, / Come to sing with us. / O wedding that we longed for, / You make us happier than anyone else today."

[3] Kendrick notes the importance of the three-voice setting for seventeenth-century spiritual madrigals; see "Devotion, Piety and Commemoration," 332, 346.

Example 11.3: *Dolci, amorose e leggiadrette ninfe* (music: Scotto, 1571, from Munich, Bayerische Staatsbibliothek, Musikabteilung, Mus. pr. 10 — Beibd. 5; text: BCS, MS G.xi.59, fol. 54ʳ)

contexts. Clearly, however, any girl destined to become a nun needed to learn to sing Gregorian chant. The scandal that arose in 1644 when one woman at Santa Caterina del Paradiso refused to learn to read or sing, and her cloistered sisters in turn declined to grant her the full privileges of a choir nun, demonstrates how essential musical expression was to the cultivated women within most monastic communities and how connected it was to literacy in general.[1] Instruction in singing chant also began very early on. Craig Monson has brought to light several cases of precocious musical behavior, one of which involved a girl in a Bolognese convent who at eight years old could sing the office with the nuns in the choir.[2] Documents from Sienese convents are not so specific, but they do suggest that, when male musicians came to the convent parlors to teach plainchant, their pupils (who were separated from them by a wall with grated openings) often included not just nuns and novices but also the girl boarders.[3] And certainly, by the time an *educanda* became a novice, Gregorian chant was supposed to be her only daily musical bread.[4] As Archbishop Alessandro Petrucci decreed in 1625, "because [polyphonic] music is of little use during the probationary period, novices should learn only plainchant, which they should practice in the choir."[5]

As Anne Yardley notes in her contribution to this volume, girls could and did memorize chant repertory through repeated listening.[6] But it seems logical to assume that for musically talented novices, learning plainchant was inextricably tied up with the development of musicianship skills. A sixteenth-century manu-script from the convent of Santa Maria Maddalena is a reminder of this fact, for it appends a treatise on the "Rules for Singing" to a book containing Gregorian chant. The treatise addresses philosophical questions concerning the definition

---

[1] See Reardon, *Holy Concord*, 30–31.

[2] Monson, *Disembodied Voices*, 49.

[3] ASS, Conventi soppressi, 3290 (San Paolo), unn. fol.: "Facci gratia conceder licenza di venire al nostro monasterio il reverendo signor Lazzaro ad effetto di insegnare il canto fermo alle novisie de' Buonsignori . . . Si concede . . . 19 maggio 1687"; unn. fol.: "Si prega Vostra Signoria Illustrissima a volere concedere licenza di venire al nostro monasterio il reverendo signor Francesco Neri maestro di canto fermo del Duomo per insegnare a cinque o sei monache giovane la medesima virtù del canto fermo . . . Si concede . . . 17 maggio 1692"; Conventi soppressi 3289 (San Paolo), unn. fol.: "Si prega Vostra Signoria Illustrissima e Reverendissima a conceder licenza di poter venire al nostro monasterio per canto e suoni il reverendo signor Giuseppe Fabbrini, il reverendo signor Andrea Pontolmi, il reverendo signor Giuseppe Cavallini et ancho il reverendo signor Neri maestro di canto fermo per in-segniare ha le monache e fanciulle fino al santo Avento . . . Si concedono . . . 1 maggio 1697."

[4] Gregorian chant was so much a part of a novice's life that it, too, seems to have had a featured role in mystic auditory experiences. In 1542, for example, as a novice at Sant'Abbondio lay sick in bed, the sound of sweet disembodied voices singing the Requiem announced her impending death. See BCS, MS E.v.19, fol. 77ᵛ: "Ne morì una di queste non professa che si domandava S. Agnesa Finetti, la quale il giorno che s'ammalò si udirno nell'aria suavissime voci cantare *Requiem eternam* con tutto quello che segue."

[5] *Decreti e costitutioni generali*, 62–63: "Et essendogli nel tempo della probatione poco utile la musica, doveranno nel novitiato solamente imparare il canto fermo, dove però s'eserciti nel coro."

[6] See "The Pedagogy of Music in Medieval English Nunneries" in this volume. See also Boynton, "Training for the liturgy," 11.

of music and tackles practical issues of mode, consonance and dissonance, and the principles of solmization.[1] Over a century later, not much had changed. The first chapter of Lorenzo Penna's 1684 treatise, *Li primi albori musicali*, provides a sequence of lessons for training young musicians of the early modern era. Penna explains the Guidonian hand and goes on to show neophytes how to read the lines and spaces of the staff according to the clef used. He furnishes exercises for reading scales and for mutating hexachords and elucidates the meaning of accidentals.[2] Thus, we can assume that at least some of the *educande* and many of the novices who went to the grated parlors or to the convent *maestra* or to their cloistered aunt to learn to sing chant were also taking basic theory lessons — learning to identify clefs, accidentals, and modes, and from there how to sing at sight — proficiencies that were not necessarily required to sing *laude* or to commit to memory a part-song for a theatrical performance. These musicianship skills were necessary to prepare girls not only for the chant choir but also for eventual participation in the ensemble responsible for performing small-scale and large-scale polyphonic Latin works that were a staple of Sienese monastic houses during this time.

Singing chant also meant developing or refining a number of other skills. The youngsters would have had to adjust to an ensemble composed of girls and women of all ages. They were now reading text and music from a liturgical book (even if they possessed only what Yardley describes as "level two" literacy).[3] Different chants called for different performance styles. The Constitution of Santa Marta addresses the special problems of singing antiphonal psalms: the two groups needed to listen and respond without interrupting one another or allowing their voices to hold notes so long that they interfered with devotion.[4] Plainchant such as Example 11.4, a Magnificat antiphon for First Vespers on the feast of All Saints of the Augustinian Order, copied in 1675 for the nuns at Santa Maria Maddalena, was considerably more complex than a devotional tune.[5] Its notation demanded that the singers be able to negotiate both an F clef and a C clef (Example 11.4 reproduces the change of clef in the original version with a modern treble substituting for the C clef). The range is wide, spanning an octave and a fifth. The tune itself is not strophic in form but rather is held together by the irregular repetition

---

[1] BCS, MS I.vιιι.29, fols. 152ʳ–156ʳ.

[2] P. F. Lorenzo Penna, *Li primi albori musicali per li principianti della musica figurata* (1684; repr. Bologna, 1969), 4–29.

[3] Yardley, "The Pedagogy of Music," this volume.

[4] BCS, MS E.11.8, "Costitutioni delle molto reverende monache di Santa Marta," p. 2: "Et havertino le monache et altre che si trovano al coro di recitare l'offitio divino con honestà et attentione e di fare le pause talmente che per in fin che non è finito il rosso del salmo da una banda non cominci l'altra e nel fine del verso non tirino tanto oltre la voce che possa infastidire alcuna acciò non li facci perdere il vigore della devotione."

[5] ACRFS, Santa Maria Maddalena 131 (old 1331). Translation of text in Example 11.4: "O victorious army of triumphant martyrs, / O sacred gathering of holy confessors, / O noble group of blessed monks, / O virgins of the Lord and holy women, / And all inhabitants of our monastery/ Intercede for us, alleluia." For more on this manuscript, see Reardon, *Holy Concord*, 32.

In festo omnium Sanctorum ordinis nostri ad primas Vesperas, antiphona ad Magnificat

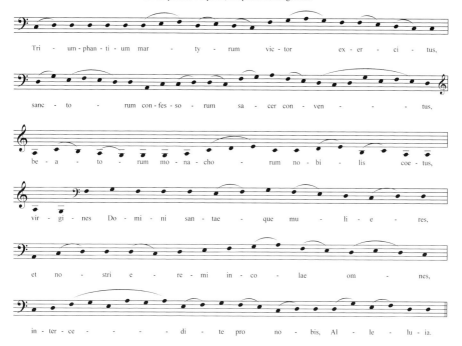

Example 11.4: Magnificat antiphon, First Vespers, Feast of All Saints of the Augustinian Order (ACRFS, Santa Maria Maddalena 131)

of short motives. The language, too, would have been a challenge, for instead of the vernacular, girls had to begin to learn and understand church Latin.[1]

Plainchant also included sections designed to spotlight soloists, sometimes even the younger soloists.[2] A sixteenth-century plainchant manuscript for an unnamed female monastic house in Siena includes the customary hymn for the procession on Palm Sunday.[3] Following a tradition that can be found in cathedral schools for boys, rubrics assign an important role in the performance of the *Gloria, laus* to two novices.[4] They are directed to enter the church, to wait for the doors to be closed, and then to begin the hymn (Example 11.5). During the course of the procession, the novices sing one complete stanza of the hymn and introduce the final iteration of the refrain:[5]

[1] Literacy rates in Sienese convents seem to have been high, but see Kendrick's cautionary note in *Celestial Sirens*, 182, and also Yardley, "The Pedagogy of Music," in this volume.

[2] See Yardley, "The Pedagogy of Music," this volume.

[3] BCS, MS F.vi.20, fols. 12ᵛ–14ʳ. See Reardon, *Holy Concord*, 31.

[4] Osvaldo Gambassi, *"Pueri cantores" nelle cattedrali d'Italia tra medioevo e età moderna: Le scuole Eugeniane; Scuole di canto annesse alle cappelle musicali* (Florence, 1997), 34.

[5] For the complete text, see the *Liber Usualis* (Paris, 1964), 586–87. Translation of the text in Example 11.5: "Glory, praise and honor be yours, Christ the King, Redeemer. / The

Circa finem evangeli duae novitiae intrent ecclesiam et ianuis clausis dicant versum usque "Cui puerile":

Deinde duae novitiae dicant versum "Plebs hebrea":

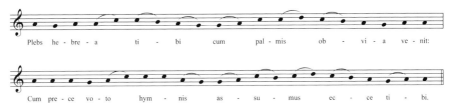

Example 11.5: *Gloria, laus* (BCS, MS F.vi.20, fols. 12ᵛ, 13ᵛ–14ʳ)

Two novices:	Gloria, laus . . . tibi sit,
Choir:	Cui puerile . . . osanna pium.
Two nuns:	Israel es tu rex . . . rex benedicte, venis.
Choir:	Cui puerile . . . osanna pium.
Two nuns:	Cetus in excelsis . . . creata simil.
Choir:	Gloria laus . . . osanna pium.
Two novices:	Plebs hebrea . . . ecce tibi.
Choir:	Cui puerile . . . osanna pium.
Two novices:	Gloria laus . . . tibi sit,
Everyone:	et honor . . . osanna pium.

If the girls already had experience in convent drama, it doubtless served them well in this liturgical setting, allowing them to take on their featured musical role with the ease of seasoned theatrical professionals.

Singing Exercises

Plainchant certainly widened a girl's repertory, developed her theoretical knowledge and sight-singing skills, and honed her sense of ensemble. It was still quite a leap to singing polyphonic music or a virtuoso solo, however. At the very least, the girls had to have already practiced reading note values, rests, and time signatures before they could tackle, for example, an imitative Latin motet.[1] Documents from Sienese convents suggest that acquiring such skills required

---

Hebrew people came to meet you with palms: we are before you with prayers, offerings, and hymns."

[1] Penna, *Li primi albori musicali*, 30–50, supplies exercises and examples for teaching these skills, too.

dedicated lessons unconnected with chant repertory.[1] In some cases, this instruction might have taken place in the time-honored fashion: the director charged with preparing a choir for performance might have simply hacked out parts one at a time and then put them together. In Siena, however, at least two musicians, Cristofano Piochi and Giuseppe Cini, developed pedagogical tools for helping youngsters become accustomed to the demands of performing polyphonic compositions and acquire confidence and expertise as soloists in extended works.

Piochi was one of the longest-serving directors of the Siena Cathedral choir during the seventeenth century. He took over leadership of the ensemble in 1646 and died on the job in 1677 at the age of eighty-three. In 1671, 1672, and 1674 he appears in an account book from the convent of Santa Marta, where he received payments for teaching the nuns and composing music for them.[2] Piochi published three books of *Ricercari* (1671, 1673, 1675), the first two of which were dedicated to his students at the cathedral school, and all three of which were intended for their use. The books contain canons as well as two- and three-part compositions clearly meant to increase dexterity at singing polyphony.[3]

Piochi's pupil Cini was a violinist and singer at the cathedral in the 1670s and 1680s and *maestro di cappella* at Santa Maria in Provenzano in the mid-1690s. In 1708, shortly after his appointment as music director at Siena Cathedral, Cini abruptly died. From 1683 to 1695, Cini was associated with the Augustinian convent of San Paolo, where he taught viola, violin, and singing.[4] Following his teacher's example, Cini composed a volume of *Solfeggiamenti* for his cathedral pupils, published in the year of his death by his nephew Tommaso Redi.[5] The twenty-four solfège exercises are scored for nearly all possible combinations of

---

[1] Licenses from Santa Petronilla and San Paolo, for example, always differentiate between the men who taught plainchant and those who instead instructed the cloistered women in "musica" or "suono e canto." See p. 207 n. 3 above and Thomas Culley, *Jesuits and Music: A Study of Musicians Connected with the German College in Rome during the 17th Century and of Their Activities in Northern Europe*, Sources and Studies for the History of the Jesuits, 2 (Rome, 1970), 70–72.

[2] See Reardon, *Agostino Agazzari and Music at Siena Cathedral, 1597–1641* (Oxford, 1993), 51; Reardon, *Holy Concord*, 41.

[3] The titles and dedications of all three of Piochi's volumes of *Ricercari* are reproduced in Gaetano Gaspari, *Catalogo della Biblioteca musicale G. B. Martini di Bologna*, 5 vols. (1905; repr. Bologna, 1961), 4:220–21. I would like to thank the staff of the Biblioteca del Conservatorio in Bologna for providing impeccable service on a miserably hot June day while the library was undergoing reconstruction. I was able to see microfilm copies of the incomplete 1671 volume and of the 1675 volume. The transcription provided as Example 11.6 is taken from the Conservatorio's microfilm copy of Piochi's work.

[4] See Rinaldo Morrocchi, *La musica in Siena* (Siena, 1886), 102–03; Siena, Archivio dell'Opera della Metropolitana, 1089–1090 (payment registers); and ASS, Conventi soppressi, 3289, 3290 (license books, San Paolo). The latter registers show Cini's intense teaching activity at San Paolo and confirm his acquisition of the music directorship at Provenzano.

[5] For the complete title and dedication to the volume, see Gaspari, *Catalogo della Biblioteca musicale G. B. Martini di Bologna*, 1:316–17. I again offer thanks to the staff at the Biblioteca del Conservatorio. Examples 11.7 and 11.8 were transcribed from the original print preserved in the library.

two voices and the pieces include up to three sharps in the signature as well as various permutations of duple, triple, and quadruple meter.

Neither composer mentions nuns in his dedication or in the body of the works. Clearly, however, works scored for sopranos and altos are as equally suited to girls' voices as they are to boys'. Since both Piochi and Cini worked as teachers in convents, it might well be that the exercises they published were not only appropriate for girl singers but that they indeed grew out of their pedagogical experiences involving *educande* and novices at Santa Marta and San Paolo.[1]

Piochi's *Ricercare ottavo a tre* (1675) offers an exercise whereby two sopranos, accompanied by either a male teacher singing the bass line or by an instructor or colleague playing the part on an instrument, could begin to learn how to sing simple, imitative polyphony (Example 11.6). The upper parts present few difficulties: the opening upward leaps of fourths evolve into straightforward melodic lines that frequently move by step when not presenting variations on the opening motive. The two soprano parts cross only occasionally. The rhythmic motion is even and steady to allow the girls time to hear the interplay of voices and to read ahead. Dissonance is, as to be expected, very carefully prepared, and chromatic alterations are few. The textless music allows students to focus fully on singing correct intervals and rhythms.

Once the two sopranos had mastered Piochi, they could move up to Cini's *Solfeggiamento decimo*, which challenged them to stretch their abilities even further (Example 11.7). This exercise requires great vocal range and flexibility, for in the first two and a half measures, each singer has to descend an octave and then quickly ascend a tenth. The melodic line is much more disjunct than Piochi's: leaps of thirds, fifths, and octaves are common. The voices frequently cross and each singer must listen carefully to the other, for they are often engaged in imitation. The sixteenth-note figures require clean articulation at high speed. Unison and octave intervals, suspension chains, and the lack of a supporting bass test the performers' ability to maintain accurate pitch over the course of the work.

Cini's *Solfeggiamento quarto*, on the other hand, seems designed to help a budding alto attain confidence as a soloist by interacting with a bass line that is easily played instrumentally (Example 11.8). The young singer must explore fully her richest register. Leaps of fifths, sixths, and octaves demand smoothness and consistency in vocal production as well as accuracy of pitch. The performer must sing a passage of parallel tenths in tune with the continuo line. The use of triple time allows for a syncopated melody against an unsyncopated bass (and vice versa). And once again, the singer must understand how to bring out imitative lines.[2]

---

[1] For an example of a pedagogical motet volume that does mention girl pupils, see Kendrick, *Celestial Sirens*, 181.

[2] It would be interesting to know if nuns transformed any of Piochi's or Cini's exercises into motets by supplying the wordless music with Latin texts. The practice is suggested in a letter that Suor Lutugarda Chigi, a nun at S. Margherita in Castelvecchio, wrote in 1670 asking either Flavio or Sigismondo Chigi to send her a book of motets. She blithely noted, "It does not matter to me if the words are missing . . . just as long as they are for soprano and alto." See Reardon, *Holy Concord*, 35.

Example 11.6: Cristofano Piochi, *Ricercare ottavo a 3* (1675), mm. 1–21

From Student to Teacher

THE talented performers who populated Siena's convents in the *Seicento* did not all enter with their musical talents fully formed. Many began their studies within the cloister.[1] The efficacy of the system of music education in Sienese convents was of no small importance to the denizens of those institutions. This is apparent in a record from May 1644, when Suor Maria Niccola and Suor Maria Candida Tolomei, two novices at Santa Petronilla, participated in the rite that made them fully fledged members of the Clarissan house. Institutional records show payments both before and after the profession ceremony to buy and bind

---

[1] See Reardon, *Holy Concord*, 33–42.

Example 11.7: Giuseppe Ottavio Cini, *Solfeggiamento decimo a 2 canti* (1708), mm. 1–17

volumes of polyphonic music and to purchase psalters and music staff paper; these items were apparently intended for use by the newly minted sisters.[1] If Suor Maria Niccola and Suor Maria Candida followed the normal schedule for entering and joining the monastic house — *educande* at age seven and novices at age twelve — then they were both around sixteen years old when they professed

[1] ASS, Conventi soppressi, 3389 (Santa Petronilla), p. 566: "1643/44. Addì detto (30 gennaro), £.8.6.8 per due corpi di libri di musica e per supplimento di due salterii che si comprorno per S. Maria Niccola e S. Maria Candida, £.8.6.8; 1644. Addì stante (10 maggio) £. tre soldi 10 per legatura di 2 corpi di libri musicali e fogli rigati, £.3.10." A record of these same payments is found in Conventi soppressi 3514, and there they seem to be linked to the other expenses surrounding the profession ceremony for Suor Maria Niccola and Suor Maria Candida. Conventi soppressi 3565, fol. 101ᵛ, provides the surname for the two women.

Example 11.8: Cini, *Solfeggiamento quarto: alto e basso* (1708), mm. 1–23

in 1644. I should like to think that they came up through the ranks of the convent and received the kind of training I have suggested here. The gift of polyphonic music books and music paper suggests that by this time they had grown into accomplished singers and formidable musicians who were expected to transmit their skills to others in the cloister so that the Sienese public who flocked to hear the nuns sing could not help but compare them to choirs of angels.

12

CHOIRBOYS IN EARLY MODERN ROME

Noel O'Regan

A s in other cities, choirboys played an essential role in the soundscape of early modern Rome. With the exception of the Cappella Pontificia,[1] all institutions with regular choirs made use of a small number of boys. Their musical training, which was entrusted to the *maestro di cappella*, played an important role in the transmission of repertory and in the development of Roman styles of composition; many of these boys in turn became singers and *maestri* in the city's institutions. The instruction of the Nanino brothers, Giovanni Maria and Giovanni Bernardino, who both served as *maestri* at San Luigi dei Francesi as well as at other churches, was particularly well known, and some of their teaching materials survive. This chapter reviews the evidence for the use of boys in performances of sacred music during the sixteenth and early seventeenth centuries, based on the archival records of various institutions and on notarial agreements between parents and institutions or *maestri*. It also surveys the repertory they would have sung and the methods used in their musical training. The use of boys' voices was not confined to singing polyphony and chant in major churches; they also sang the popular *laude spirituali* at devotional gatherings, performed in *sacre rappresentazioni*, and were regularly heard in Christian doctrine classes.

---

[1] The archives of the Cappella Pontificia contain no payments to boys nor any indication that boys were employed to sing in the papal chapel. The engraving by Étienne Dupérac of a papal ceremony in the Cappella Sistina during the reign of Gregory XIII (r. 1572–85) does, however, seem to show a few boys in the cantoria. See Christopher A. Reynolds, "Rome: A City of Rich Contrast," in *The Renaissance: From the 1470s to the End of the Sixteenth Century*, ed. Iain Fenlon, Music and Society (London, 1989), 63–101. Dupérac may have depicted boys because he thought he was hearing boys' voices or perhaps because boys were occasionally present as listeners — possibly in the care of members of the choir who were teaching them, such as Giovanni Maria Nanino.

ROME'S CHORAL INSTITUTIONS

At the beginning of the sixteenth century, Rome had relatively few permanent choirs other than the Cappella Pontificia, and comparatively little is known about them. Christopher Reynolds, who has studied the choir of St. Peter's Basilica prior to its refoundation as the Cappella Giulia by Pope Julius II in 1513, sees the reign of Pope Nicholas V (reigned 1447–55) as a turning point in the development of polyphonic music and notes the earliest surviving reference to boys at the basilica in 1447, when the singer Rubino twice collected extra wages to cover the expenses of two boys.[1] Reynolds cites the Florentine practice of singing *laude* with organ accompaniment in connection with the first Roman reference to Italian boys (during the reign of Alexander VI in the late 1490s), who are mentioned as singing "in organo," "cum organis," or "in sul'organo."[2] In 1506, Nicholas de Furnis received extra wages for the care of two boys, while one Bernardino di Modena was designated "magister" for the same period, a significant pairing, in Reynolds' view, of a northern European music master with an Italian master for grammar. Such combinations are also to be seen in other Roman institutions, with northern *maestri di cappella* occupying positions at most Roman churches until at least the 1550s and in some cases into the 1560s and beyond.[3] Reynolds also cites evidence that two other churches in the city, Santa Maria Maggiore and Sant'Agostino, employed northern European choirboys ("garzoni tedeschi") in the 1470s and 1480s as a result of the patronage of the influential French Cardinal d'Estouteville.[4] He suggests that since northern churches had a much fuller liturgical life with more polyphony, the boys who were training there acquired more singing experience and hence were in more demand in Italy than the locally trained boys.

The first decades of the sixteenth century saw the reorganization or establishment of choirs on a firmer footing in major Roman basilicas and a few other institutions. Most significant was the refounding of the choir at St. Peter's in 1513. Julius' plan was to maintain a group of twelve Italian boys in training so as to reduce papal dependence on foreign singers.[5] The actual number was initially only two or three, rising to four or five in the mid 1550s and eventually to six, when the

---

[1] Christopher A. Reynolds, *Papal Patronage and the Music of St. Peter's, 1380–1513* (Berkeley, 1995), 132.

[2] Ibid., 133.

[3] For example, François Roussel served successively at St. Peter's (1548–50), San Lorenzo in Damaso (1564–66), San Luigi dei Francesi (1566–71), and San Giovanni in Laterano (1572–75). See Greer Garden, "François Roussel: A Northern Musician in Sixteenth-Century Rome," *Musica Disciplina* 31 (1977), 107–33. Probably the last significant northern musician to serve in Rome was the Fleming Francesco Martini, *maestro di cappella* at the Chiesa Nuova from 1604 until at least 1623. See Arnaldo Morelli, *Il tempio armonico: Musica nell'Oratorio dei Filippini in Roma (1575–1705)*, Analecta Musicologica, 27 (Laaber, 1991).

[4] Reynolds, *Papal Patronage*, 132–33.

[5] Ariane Ducrot, "Histoire de la Cappella Giulia au XVIᵉ siècle," *Mélanges d'archéologie et d'histoire* 75 (1963), 179–240, 467–559.

choir became the largest user and trainer of choirboys in the city. From 1551 the presence of Giovanni Pierluigi da Palestrina and Giovanni Animuccia as *maestri di cappella*, with responsibility for training the boys, ensured its stature as both choir and training ground, though surprisingly few of its choirboys ended up in the Cappella Pontificia, as had originally been intended by Julius II.[1] In the bull *De communi omnium ecclesiarum* of 1578, Pope Gregory XIII reorganized the Cappella Giulia, confirming the number of singers at twelve adults (four each on alto, tenor, and bass) and twelve boys (called "cappellani scolari").[2] Some months later this was revised to six boy sopranos and six adult *cappellani*. The boys were often joined on the top line by one or two adult falsettists such as Giovanni Battista Bovicelli (served 1578–81).[3]

The choirs in San Giovanni in Laterano and Santa Maria Maggiore were also reformed early in the sixteenth century, in both cases with fewer singers than at St. Peter's: two adults per part and three to four boys.[4] The parsimony of the chapter of San Giovanni in supporting music, and in particular in supporting its choirboys, was a major reason for Palestrina's move to Santa Maria Maggiore in 1561.[5] Both choirs often sang under strength and hired additional singers for important feast days or processions.[6] The basilica of San Lorenzo in Damaso was one of the most important parish churches in the heart of the city and the only such church to have a permanent choir. This distinction was the result of its having been rebuilt into the new Palazzo della Cancelleria by Cardinal Riario in the late fifteenth century, becoming the palace chapel of the powerful Cardinal

---

[1] Among the few who did move on to the Cappella Pontificia were Alessandro Merlo and Carlo Vanni. See Giancarlo Rostirolla, "La Cappella Giulia in San Pietro negli anni palestriniani," in *Atti del Convegno di studi Palestriniani, 28 settembre – 2 ottobre 1975*, ed. Francesco Luisi (Palestrina, 1977), 99–283. Some papal singers had previously served in the Cappella Giulia as adults, such as Tomasso Benigni (who may also have been there as a boy) and Ercole Ferruzzi.

[2] Giancarlo Rostirolla, "La bolla 'De communi omnium' di Gregorio XIII per la restaurazione della Cappella Giulia," in *La cappella musicale nell'Italia della controriforma: Atti del Convegno internazionale di studi nel IV Centenario di fondazione della Cappella Musicale di S. Biagio di Cento, Cento, 13–15 ottobre 1989*, ed. Oscar Mischiati and Paolo Russo, Quaderni della Rivista italiana di musicologia, 27 (Florence, 1993), 39–65.

[3] Rostirolla, "La Cappella Giulia," 228.

[4] The fourth major basilica, San Paolo fuori le mura, was in the care of Benedictine monks and so far nothing is known about any regular choir there. For San Giovanni in Laterano see Raffaele Casimiri and Laura Callegari, eds., *Cantori, maestri, organisti della Cappella lateranense negli atti capitolari (sec. XV–XVII)*, Biblioteca di Quadrivium, 6 (Bologna, 1984), 26, 30–33, 49–50. For Santa Maria Maggiore, see Vito Raeli, *Nel secolo di G. P. da Palestrina nella Cappella Liberiana* (Rome, 1920).

[5] Raffaele Casimiri, *Giovanni Pierluigi da Palestrina: Nuovi documenti biografici* (Rome, 1922), 24–25.

[6] For instance, at Santa Maria Maggiore in 1561 Palestrina (as *maestro di cappella*) was given four *scudi* to pay for outside singers (the number is not specified but was most likely four) for the basilica's two main feasts, which fell close together — that of St. Mary of the Snow on 5 August and the Assumption of the Virgin on 15 August (Rome, Archivio di S. Maria Maggiore, A IV 1, unfoliated, 15 Aug. 1561).

Vice-Chancellors, who took a strong personal interest in its choir.[1] The earliest information on the choir there comes from 1510, when a surviving list of payments to singers includes fifteen *baiocchi* "pro expensis nicolao soprano" (for the costs of the soprano Nicholas),[2] and there are records of two or three other sopranos who seem to have been boys. Archival information from the early decades of the century remains scarce, but a payment in 1539 refers to "il banco de li putti cantori" (the bench of the boy singers). In 1564 the *maestro* François Roussel was paid 1.20 *scudi* "per il salario di un putto cantore" (for the salary of a boy singer). Like San Giovanni in Laterano and Santa Maria Maggiore, the desired size of the choir was two singers per part on alto, tenor, and bass, as well as two or three boy sopranos. Each boy was normally paid half the salary of an adult singer, which helps to identify the boys here, as in other institutions.

One of the most significant churches for music in Rome was, paradoxically, not Italian but the French national church, San Luigi dei Francesi.[3] In the battle between French, Spanish, and German groups for political influence in the city, music became an increasingly important weapon, and so the French émigrés were prepared to pay for a regular choir, despite having to finance the building of the church and also having to support French pilgrims and the sick. While there may well have been some singers of polyphony earlier, the first named singer was Desiderius/Johanino Babel from Toul, called *cantor* from 1 May 1514. By 1515 he was being referred to as *maestro di cappella*, and, by the time he left in 1519, he had been joined by a tenorista, another singer, and a boy soprano, as well as the organist. Like other choirs, that at San Luigi had to be rebuilt after the Sack of Rome in 1527. Herman-Walther Frey has singled out the achievement of Firmin Lebel, *maestro di cappella* from 1545 to 1561, who saw the choir expand and start to undertake regular outside work for other confraternities and institutions. By 1552 there were seven adult singers and two boys, with three boys in 1555–57 and four by 1583. Nevertheless, as in other choirs, the number of boys actually in service at any one time could vary. The choir continued to operate until 1622, when it was reduced in size, and from 1623 it farmed out its choirboys to *maestri* at other institutions.

At least two of the city's confraternities had regular choirs in the early years of the sixteenth century: the Arciconfraternità del Gonfalone and the Arciconfraternità dello Spirito Santo. The 1495 statutes of the former indicate that a *maestro di cappella* had to provide singers and "to teach singing to all the men in the confraternity who wished to learn, or to their sons" ("insegniare de canto ad tutti li uomini della compagnia o loro figlioli che volessero imparare"). The type of singing is not specified, but since these were ordinary confraternity members and

---

[1] These included Cardinals Alessandro Farnese and Alessandro Montalto.

[2] Luca Della Libera, "L'attività musicale nella Basilica di S. Lorenzo in Damaso nel Cinquecento," in *Rivista italiana di musicologia* 32 (1997), 25–59.

[3] Herman-Walther Frey, "Die Kapellmeister an der französischen Nationalkirche San Luigi dei Francesi in Rom im 16 Jahrhundert," *Archiv für Musikwissenschaft* 22 (1965), 272–23; 23 (1966), 32–60; Jean Lionnet, *La Musique à Saint-Louis des Français de Rome au XVIIe siècle* (Venice, 1985–86).

their sons, the teaching would have concentrated on what they needed to know to chant the offices in the oratory and to sing in processions rather than polyphony. Confraternity oratories like that of the Gonfalone needed a certain number of *coristati*, laymen experienced enough to lead the singing of some of the offices, e.g., the Office of the Blessed Virgin. One of the Gonfalone's main activities was the mounting of a *sacra rappresentazione* of the Passion in the Colosseum on Good Friday of certain years.[1] Various surviving versions of the text make it clear that considerable portions were sung; while there is no direct evidence of female parts being taken by boys, this is very likely to have been the case.

From 1517 until the Sack of Rome a decade later the confraternity maintained a regular choir of three to four adults and two to three sopranos. Although the records do not specify whether or not the sopranos were boys, there is a clear distinction between sopranos paid a single ducat per month or thereabouts and those called "cappellano" and paid more. The latter were presumably falsettists or perhaps castrati, while the former were boys.[2] On one occasion in 1519 the payment specifically names a boy ("Baldo cantore et Nicolo soprano suo put[t]o"), and a similar payment in 1518 ("Fulminotto maestro di cappella con il suo soprano") also implies an apprentice-like role for the boy.[3] The choir regrouped after the Sack and continued until it was disbanded in the early 1530s, the confraternity subsequently relying on *cappellani cantores* and on hiring musicians for its major feast-day celebrations and processional commitments. During the 1580s, a new attempt was made to set up a regular choir, increasing to two adult singers per part and two to three boys by the early 1590s under Asprilio Pacelli as *maestro di cappella*. Once again, financial constraints led to the disbanding of the choir in 1593 and a return to the situation that had existed prior to 1580.[4]

Santo Spirito in Sassia combined a number of institutions under one umbrella: confraternity, hospital, order of the Hospitallers, and male and female orphanages. Its large church was the center of a considerable liturgical cult, maintaining a small regular choir throughout the period. Unlike the situation of the Gonfalone, archival materials for Santo Spirito are scarce in the sixteenth century, but the *Libro de mandati* for 1569 records a payment to one "Stazio, a Roman singer in our church, one *scudo di moneta* . . . for helping teach the boys polyphony."[5] An undated document from this period states that the most able boys were provided with "an appropriate teacher to instruct them in grammar, music, and in some mechanical art

---

[1] Nerida Newbiggin is currently engaged in a study of the Gonfalone's *sacre rappresentationi*. My forthcoming book on music at Roman confraternities, 1486–1650, treats music at the Gonfalone in detail.

[2] Newbiggin has suggested (in private communication) that one of the singers employed at the Gonfalone during this period, called Ferminotto but sometimes referred to as "Ruinotto" or "Rovinato," may have been a castrato.

[3] Archivio Segreto Vaticano, Fondo Arciconfraternità del Gonfalone, 134, 135.

[4] Ibid., 52.

[5] Archivio di Stato di Roma, Fondo Ospedale S. Spirito in Sassia, 1900, unfoliated, 29 June 1569: "Stazio romano, cantore in nostra chiesa, scudi uno di moneta . . . per aiutare a insegnare a li putti la musica." (The confusingly named *scudo di moneta*, literally "in coin," was a money of account and not a coin.)

according to their capacity and inclination."[1] The specific mention of music confirms that this was one of the careers for which the orphans were being prepared. In 1579 Giovanni Battista Locatelli, organist in the church, was paid three *scudi* a month, two for playing the organ and one for teaching the harpsichord to "li nostri putti."[2] It is not clear whether these were the *putti* who served in the regular choir or those in the orphanage being trained in music but it is likely that both groups were the same. In 1635 the *maestro di cappella* Orazio Benevoli was paid for "a *cartella* and a book to learn to play the organ, for the soprano Alessandro, son of the house"[3] while in 1638 the clothier Bastiano Manenti was paid two *scudi* and thirty *baiocchi* for the expense of two short cloaks, two pairs of shoes, and two coats for the *cantorini* who are learning to sing in the house of the *maestro di cappella* (Benevoli).[4] An undated document from the period when Francesco Beretta was *maestro di cappella* (1669–91) speaks of his duties, including "teaching some of the boys in school, that is, those who have the most ability."[5] These surviving documents, while sketchy, indicate that at Santo Spirito in Sassia a small number of talented boys from the orphanage were trained in music and some or all sang in the choir of the associated church. The choral foundation at Santo Spirito was never rich and often struggled to survive; the availability of these orphaned boys must have played a part in maintaining its viability.

The situation in other Roman confraternity churches in the sixteenth century was mixed. A number of churches set up choirs during the late sixteenth and early seventeenth centuries but most did not last very long. San Rocco was a typical case, which, like many such bodies, relied mainly on *cappellani cantores* to supply a minimum of polyphonic music.[6] In 1581 two boy sopranos were hired there, and one of the chaplains was given the role of *maestro di cappella*. Sometime in or before 1593, three adult singers (alto, tenor, bass) were hired to go with the two boys, as well as a trombone player, but this small group was disbanded once more in 1594. Two boy sopranos were again hired for the Holy Year of 1600, presumably to sing with some of the chaplains, but in April the choir was again disbanded

---

[1] "un maestro adatto li istruisse nelle lettere, nella musica ed in qualche arte meccanica in corrispondenza alla loro capacità ed inclinazione"; Giancarlo Rostirolla, "L'Archivio musicale della Chiesa annessa all'Ospedale di Santo Spirito," in *Atti del Convegno: L'antico ospedale di Santo Spirito dall'istituzione papale alla sanità del terzo millennio, Roma 15–17 Maggio 2001* in *Il veltro: Rivista della civiltà italiana* 46 (2002), 279–343 at 283.

[2] Antonio Allegra, "La cappella musicale di Santo Spirito in Saxia di Roma: Appunti storici (1551–1737)," *Note d'archivio per la storia musicale* [hereafter *Note d'archivio*] 17 (1940), 26–38 at 29.

[3] Ibid., 32: "una cartella et uno libro per imperar a suonare nel organo ad Alessandro soprano figlio di casa."

[4] Ibid., 33.

[5] Ibid., 36: "imparare a qualche putto di scuola, cioè a quelli, che sono più abili al mestiero."

[6] For references here and further information, see Noel O'Regan, "Music at the Roman Archconfraternity of San Rocco in the Late Sixteenth Century," in *La musica a Roma attraverso le fonti d'archivio: Atti del convegno internazionale, Roma, 4–7 giugno 1992*, ed. Bianca Maria Antolini, Arnaldo Morelli, and Vera Vita Spagnuolo, Strumenti della ricerca musicale, 2 (Lucca, 1994), 521–52.

because of financial problems, as had been the case in 1594. One of the members of the confraternity offered to pay for one of the *putti*, and this led to a reprieve for the small choir until after July 1601. Other institutions that had small choirs, all with two or three boys, for some of the period under discussion (the dates of their known existence appear in parentheses) included Santa Maria di Monserrato (1583–88), San Giovanni dei Fiorentini (from 1586), Santissima Trinità dei Pellegrini (1591–93), Santa Maria di Loreto dei Fornai (from 1592), San Gerolamo della Carità (from 1593), Santa Maria della Consolazione (1597–1617), Santa Maria in Trastevere (from 1607), and San Giacomo degli Spagnoli (1614–23).[1] This list is not exhaustive. One rare example of a confraternity paying for a boy's singing lessons is Santissimo Crocifisso in 1573–74; the boy, Oratio "di musica" or Oratuccio, must have been singing in its oratory.[2]

Two of the city's seminaries were important musical institutions for training boys and students.[3] Most significant for music was the German College, largely because of the enthusiasm of its rector from 1573 to 1587, Michele Lauretano, who had himself been a choirboy at the Santa Casa in Loreto.[4] In the early years, the students provided the polyphony with some support from one or two papal or other singers residing in the College, but from the early 1580s three or four boys were taken on and put in training with the *maestro*, Annibale Stabile.[5] The Seminario Romano, which was set up to train priests for the Roman archdiocese in the

[1] For further details, see Noel O'Regan, "Tomás Luis de Victoria's Roman Churches Revisited," *Early Music* 28 (2000), 403–18; Helene Wessely-Kropik, "Mitteilungen aus dem Archiv der Arciconfraternità di San Giovanni dei Fiorentini," *Studien zur Musikwissenschaft* 24 (1960), 43–60; Noel O'Regan, *Institutional Patronage in Post-Tridentine Rome: Music at Santissima Trinità dei Pellegrini, 1550–1650*, RMA Monographs, 7 (London, 1995); Arnaldo Morelli, "Filippo Nicoletti (ca. 1555–1634) compositore ferrarese: Profilo biografico alla luce di nuovi documenti," in *Musica Franca: Essays in Honor of Frank A. D'Accone*, ed. Irene Alm, Alyson McLamore, and Colleen Reardon, Festschrift Series, 18 (New York, 1996), 139–50; Eleonora Simi Bonini, *Il fondo musicale dell'Arciconfraternità di S. Girolamo della Carità* (Rome, 1992); Jean Lionnet, "La Musique à Sancta Maria della Consolazione de Rome au 17ème siècle," *Note d'archivio* n.s. 4 (1986), 153–202; Graham Dixon, "The Cappella of S. Maria in Trastevere (1605–45): An Archival Study," *Music and Letters* 62 (1981), 30–40; Jean Lionnet, "La Musique à San Giacomo degli Spagnoli au XVIIème siècle et les archives de la Congrégation des Espagnols de Rome," in *La musica a Roma attraverso le fonti d'archivio*, 479–505.

[2] Archivio Segreto Vaticano, Arciconfraternità del SS. Crocifisso in S. Marcello, A XII 1573 and A XII 1574, unfoliated. This could have been Oratio Caccini, brother of Giulio, who was paid for singing at Santissimo Crocifisso soon after this.

[3] A third institution, the Venerable English College, had a regular choir for only short periods: 1579–88 and again in the first decade of the seventeenth century. See Thomas Culley, "Musical Activity in Some Sixteenth-Century Jesuit Colleges, with Special Reference to the Venerable English College in Rome from 1579 to 1589," *Analecta musicologica* 19 (1979), 1–29.

[4] Raffaele Casimiri, "'Disciplina musicae' e 'mastri di capella' dopo il Concilio di Trento nei maggiori istituti ecclesiastici di Roma: Seminario Romano — Collegio Germanico — Collegio Inglese (sec. XVI–XVII), VI. II: Il Collegio Germanico," *Note d'archivio* 16 (1939), 1–9.

[5] For full details of music at the German College, see Thomas Culley, *Jesuits and Music: A Study of the Musicians Connected with the German College in Rome during the 17th Cen-*

wake of the Council of Trent, maintained a small choir of six to eight adults and a few boys from the mid 1560s; the first *maestro* was Palestrina, who also taught plainsong and the rudiments of singing to the students (including two of his sons), some of whom would probably have had unbroken voices when commencing their studies.[1]

The majority of Roman religious institutions did not have a regular choir and were content to make do with plainchant, *falsobordone*, or simple polyphony sung by chaplains on all but one or two major patronal feast-day celebrations. For these and their associated processions, singers were hired — including boy sopranos — from one or more of the city's regular choirs. From the early 1580s, when polychoral music became the norm, the numbers of hired singers increased markedly and usually included adult falsettists or castrati as well as a small number of boys. The boys normally came in the care of the *maestro di cappella*, or another singer hired for the occasion, who accepted their payments.

Santa Maria della Visitazione degli Orfani

One institution involved in the training of Roman choirboys has so far mostly escaped the notice of historians of Roman music. The Confraternità di Santa Maria della Visitazione degli Orfani was founded in 1540 as a confraternity for cardinals, prelates, and curial officials to house, train, and look after the spiritual needs of orphans. Particularly significant was the role given to the musical training of the boys and the use made of these boys by other institutions. Archival materials are patchy (many books and especially payment records are missing), but the surviving *libri di decreti* and other books provide useful insight, especially into the early years when such information is missing for Santo Spirito in Sassia. By 1547 there were 160 male and 50 female orphans,[2] while by 1552 the number of boys had risen to 264.

As at Santo Spirito, the orphans were given board and lodging and were taught catechism and the rudiments of a trade in order to prepare them for work. Training in music appeared remarkably early: already on 14 July 1541 the ruling congregation approved the hiring of a *maestro di canto* for the orphans.[3] On 4 August a salary of 2 *scudi* was decided upon, and the same was set for a *maestro di grammatica*.[4] The success of the (unnamed) *maestro di canto* in training the boys

---

tury and of *Their Activities in Northern Europe*, Sources and Studies for the History of the Jesuits, 2 (Rome, 1970).

[1] Casimiri, "'Disciplina musicae' e 'mastri di capella' . . . , VI. 1: Il Seminario Romano," *Note d'archivio* 12 (1935), 1–26.

[2] While there is no evidence that the orphaned girls were taught music at Santa Maria della Visitazione, the girls at Santa Caterina dei Funari were taught to sing polyphony. A payment of two *scudi* survives from Dec. 1582 to the singer and scribe Alessandro Pettorini for having "insegniato cantare di musicha alle zitelle."

[3] Archivio di S. Maria in Aquiro (Biblioteca Corsiniana, housed at the Accademia dei Lincei, Rome), 263, fol. 2ᵛ.

[4] S. Maria in Aquiro, 263, fol. 5ʳ.

bore rapid fruit; in November 1545 the ruling congregation agreed to send two of the orphans to sing with the choir of San Lorenzo in Damaso at a monthly salary of two *scudi* per *putto*.[1] In February of 1546, the first payment was recorded for January, but at an initial level of only one *scudo* per boy, which was raised to 1.50 *scudi* in April.[2] The February payment speaks of "dui nostri orfani quali servono a cantar et impararano in San Lorenzo" (two of our orphans who sing and studied at San Lorenzo), implying that the boys were also being taught by the then *maestro* at San Lorenzo, Antonio Medina.[3] In January 1548, a payment of 3.40 *scudi*, including a Christmas bonus of 0.40 *scudi*, speaks of "two of our boys who sing soprano at San Lorenzo."[4] We know little about the choir in San Lorenzo in these years but the arrangement continued until 1550 after which the regular monthly payments no longer appear.

Singing in San Lorenzo was, however, only one of the activities undertaken by the *putti* of the orphanage. From 1546 there is a steady stream of payments for singing at processions, Masses, and Vespers at a variety of Roman institutions, mostly confraternities. Most common were the processions held during the octave of Corpus Christi, but the orphans also sang in the Good Friday procession for Santissimo Crocifisso and at the patronal feasts of other confraternities. The largest number of such payments was for the Holy Year of 1550, when the orphans were hired to sing in processions around the four major basilicas held by various Roman confraternities and also by visiting groups from other Italian cities, in order to gain the Holy Year indulgence. Table 12.1 lists the payments for that year, divided into various categories.[5]

The orphans also took part in the monthly Blessed Sacrament procession organized by the Confraternity of that name at Santa Maria sopra Minerva and were paid 0.50 *scudi* per occasion. In February the orphans accompanied the choir of San Lorenzo in Damaso to the house of Cardinal del Reno, receiving 1.10 *scudi* and in June they made a similar visit to the house of Signor Cesarini, this time getting the larger sum of 3.30 *scudi*. Finally on 8 September a payment of 0.50 *scudi* was made to "Guglielmo Orbo nostro orfano per haver sonato l'organo alla chiesa di S. Maria dell'Orto el di della Madonna" (blind Guglielmo, our orphan, for playing the organ in the church of Santa Maria dell'Orto on the feast day of the Virgin Mary), showing that organ lessons were also proving useful.

It is not at all clear how many *putti* were involved or whether they all sang polyphony. It is difficult to match payments and numbers very precisely. Santissimo Crocifisso had four *orfani cantori* for their dowry procession, earning 0.50 *scudi* each. On the other hand, in 1553 Santa Maria Maggiore only paid 0.10 *scudi* to each of four orphans — perhaps payment depended on the amount of singing

---

[1] S. Maria in Aquiro, 263, fol. 44[r].

[2] S. Maria in Aquiro, 405, fol. 113[v] (modern foliation).

[3] From May 1545 to May 1546, the *maestro di cappella* at San Lorenzo in Damaso was Antonio Medina. See Della Libera, "L'attività musicale," 55.

[4] S. Maria in Aquiro, 406, fol. 28[v] (modern foliation): "doi nostri putti che cantano soprano in S. Lorenzo."

[5] These payments come from S. Maria in Aquiro, 406, passim.

Table 12.1: Payments for boys from Santa Maria della Visitazione in 1550

Jubilee processions by Roman confraternities:	
S. Anna dei Palafrenieri	5 *scudi*
Compagnia dei Bussolari	4
Compagnia dei Macellari	1.20
S. Lucia del Gonfalone	2
S. Maria dell'Orto	3
S. Maria del Pianto	1.50
S. Maria in Campo Santo	1.50
S. Maria sopra Minerva	2
Jubilee processions by visiting confraternities from:	
Asprascoli	2.20
Bergamo	4.80
Milano	3
Palomba	4
Velletri	0.60
Vicavaro	4
Corpus Christi processions:	
Compagnia dei Cochi	1.20
S. Giovanni dei Fiorentini	1.50
S. Lorenzo in Damaso	1.10
S. Marcello	0.99
S. Maria del Pianto	1.50
S. Valentino	1
Good Friday procession:	
SS. Crocifisso	0.85
Patronal Feast days:	
S. Lorenzo Martire degli Spetiali (10 August)	1.20
SS. Crocifisso (14 September)	2
(four *orfani cantori* for the procession of the *zitelle*, girls to whom dowries were being given)	
S. Omobono dei Sarti (13 November)	1

involved.[1] We may also conclude that in addition to those children able to sing polyphony, other orphans also took part in the processions, perhaps singing well-known pieces of plainchant or *laude*. A payment of September 1556 was made to "two singers who went with our boys to the procession of [Santa Maria sopra] Minerva, because [those of] our boys who sing went to Sant'Apollinare."[2] This would imply that the orphanage had only a limited number of singing *putti* but could also provide non-singing *putti*. Indeed a payment of one *scudo* is recorded from Sant'Apollinare on 25 August for a sung Mass and Vespers. That the boys sang polyphony is confirmed, for example, by a 1554 payment recorded in the archives of Santissimo Crocifisso "ad li orfani ch'accompagnorno la compagnia con musica" in the Good Friday procession, a payment which also appears in the archives of the Confraternità degli Orfani.[3]

All of this activity brought the confraternity the considerable sum of over 60 *scudi* in 1550 as well as raising the profile of the orphanage. Gaps in the archival records mean that it is not possible to say how long this practice of hiring out singing orphans continued. Payments can no longer be found after the mid 1550s, but payments to orphans from Santa Maria continue to appear sporadically in the records of other confraternities. Payments to a *maestro de canto* appear inter-mittently throughout the surviving books at Santa Maria, as well as payments to a *maestro di grammatica* or a *maestro da scrivere*. The *maestro di canto* is rarely named, but in 1579 one Amico Jacobetto (a name not otherwise known) was paid two *scudi* per month from 16 May to 8 November "for having taught our boys to sing."[4]

The archives provide little direct information about musical activity at services within the orphanage and its associated church of Santa Maria in Aquiro before 1628. While there is no evidence for a full musical *cappella* as at Santo Spirito in Sassia, there are some payments to adult singers. From June to August of 1556, a "Don Giovanni Paolo cantor" was paid one *scudo* per month, which implies that some polyphony was sung, but this appears to have been just a short-term arrangement.[5] In 1628–30, Francesco Foggia was paid as *maestro di cappella* along with a *maestro di cembali* and a bass singer.[6] This state of affairs continued thereafter and may well have existed for some time before, but the lack of archival information makes it difficult to be certain. The scarcity of payments to outside

[1] S. Maria in Aquiro, 408, fol. 20r (modern foliation)

[2] S. Maria in Aquiro 409, fol. 37r (1556 facsicle — no modern foliation): "due cantori che andorno coli nostri putti alla processione della Minerva per esser andati li nostri putti che cantano a S. Apollinare."

[3] Archivio Segreto Vaticano, Arciconfraternità del SS. Crocifisso in S. Marcello, A xi 15, fol. 99r; S. Maria in Aquiro, 408, fol. 113v (modern foliation).

[4] S. Maria in Aquiro, 438 (unfoliated), 27 July 1579: "per havere insegnato li putti nostri a cantar."

[5] S. Maria in Aquiro, 409, fol. 33r (1556)

[6] Giancarlo Rostirolla, "Vita di Francesco Foggia musicista romano basata sui documenti superstiti," in *Francesco Foggia, "fenice de'musicali compositori" nel florido Seicento romano e nella storia: Atti del primo convegno internazionale di studi nel terzo centenario della morte (Palestrina e Roma, 7–8 ottobre 1988)*, ed. Ala Botti Caselli (Palestrina, 1988), 25–90.

musicians would imply that the orphanage produced its own singers for major feast days.[1] This hypothesis is supported by the purchase in December 1581 of Tomás Luis de Victoria's book of Magnificat settings published in that year, acquired directly from the composer.[2]

In 1582, one Leonardo Cerusi set up a hostel for homeless boys, and this institution quickly developed into the Ospedale or Compagnia del Lettorato, near the Piazza del Popolo.[3] Its boys regularly sang in processions in pairs, by themselves at their home institutions or at other institutions, accompanied by a wooden cross inscribed "Caritas." At the *possesso* of Pope Paul v in 1605 (when the pope went in solemn procession from the Vatican to San Giovanni in Laterano to take official possession of the See of Rome), it is recorded that along the way a platform representing "Carità" (Charity) was positioned holding twenty-five poor boys from the Compagnia del Lettorato, who from time to time sang songs in praise of His Holiness ("cantavano canzonette in lode di Sua Santità").[4]

Training of Boys and Relations with *Maestri*

THE working and learning relationship between choirboys and their *maestro di cappella* was crucial to the smooth functioning of musical life in the city. Boys were not free agents; they were subject to legal contracts drawn up between their parents or guardians and an institution or individual *maestro*. Many of these documents survive, providing detailed information on the contractual obligations on both sides and the mechanisms of the training process itself. One example is the contract drawn up on 16 November 1589 between Rodolfo Bonese, *berrettario* (cap-maker), and Girolamo de Nobili, *gallo, musico*, in which Bonese entrusted his son Cesare for three years to de Nobili so that he would learn to sing "musica e contrapunto" (polyphony and improvised counterpoint). Any money that the boy earned for the first year and a half by being hired out to sing for patronal and other feast days would go to the teacher and would thereafter be divided equally

---

[1] The archives only preserve two payments over the whole period for outside musicians. In 1554 1.10 *scudi* were paid to "Flaminio et altri cantori per esser stati alla processione del Sacramento della nostra chiesa" (S. Maria in Aquiro 408, fol. 126ʳ [modern foliation]). This was probably Firmin le Bel, *maestro di cappella* at San Luigi dei Francesi. The second payment comes from 1612, when, for the patronal feast of the Visitation, Sisto Ionio was paid six *scudi*, four for providing singers and two for bringing in an organ and an organist for three services — First Vespers, Mass, and the ending of the Forty Hours' devotion — as well as singing motets "nell'organo" at a Mass for the Conservatori of the city of Rome (S. Maria in Aquiro, 446 [unfoliated], 11 July 1612). This second payment would imply that there was no regular *maestro di cappella* at the orphanage at this time.

[2] S. Maria in Aquiro 438 (unfoliated), 18 December 1581.

[3] Pio Pecchiai, *Roma nel Cinquecento*, Storia di Roma, 13 (Bologna, 1948), 384–85.

[4] Francesco Cancellieri, *Storia de' solenni possessi de' somme pontefici: Detti anticamente processi o processioni . . .* (Rome, 1802), 181.

between the singer and the boy's father. If the boy's improvement was not satisfac-
tory, Bonese would be obliged to pay de Nobili one *scudo* a month.[1]

The same Girolamo de Nobili turns up in a 1594 contract between the German
College and Domenico Orgas, father of Annibale Orgas, who went on to achieve
success as a composer. The father promised that Annibale

> would not leave the service of the college as long as he shall be able to serve
> with his voice in the choir of the said college as soprano and also as con-
> tralto (when he shall no longer have a soprano voice), for four or five years,
> if it shall be the pleasure of those Fathers to keep him, and if it shall please
> the said Annibale to stay; and that the said college shall not be molested by
> Maestro Girolamo de Nobili, nor by others to whom the said *putto* might
> be obligated; and that instead, he [the father] will take every litigation upon
> himself and finish it at his own expense.[2]

Boys could be bound to an institution with a regular choir, like the German College, or to an individual teacher like de Nobili who clearly had a continuing financial interest in Orgas's progress.

Some of the most detailed information concerning contracts comes from the
systematic examination of notarial documents for the years 1589–90 undertaken
by Vera Vita Spagnuolo and her co-workers at the Archivio di Stato in Rome.
Many of the documents concern the Nanino brothers, Giovanni Maria and Giovanni Bernardino, who made a family business out of the musical training of boys,
taking in individuals and subsequently looking after the boys in the institutions
in which they themselves served as *maestro*. This practice continued even after
the cleric Giovanni Maria became a member of the Cappella Pontificia in 1577,
thereafter having no direct responsibility for boys in a *cappella*. As *maestro* at a succession of churches, his younger married brother Giovanni Bernardino continued
to share such responsibilities with his extended family: the two brothers and Giovanni Bernardino's wife lived in the same house adjacent to San Luigi dei Francesi
where they boarded choirboys.

A contract of 4 May 1589 between the Naninos and one Costantino Alii is of
particular importance for illuminating the master–apprentice relationship, which
effectively gave the *maestro* complete control over the boy's professional life. For
example, the latter's son Gregorio was assigned to the brothers for six years to be
taught singing. If the boy were to run away or no longer wished to attend, the father was obliged to return him by force, or else to pay one *scudo* per month for the
remainder of the six years. He was further bound to pay the Naninos the money
he might have earned for them in the remaining period, the sum to be assessed
by two experts. During training, the father had to provide the boy's shoes, clothes,

[1] Vera Vita Spagnuolo, "Gli atti notarili dell'Archivio di Stato di Roma: Saggio di spoglio sistematico — L'anno 1590," in *La musica a Roma attraverso le fonti d'archivio*, 19–65,
esp. 33: "Se invece Cesare non imparasse, il Bonese si obbliga a pagare al maestro Girolamo
uno scudo al mese."

[2] Culley, *Jesuits and Music*, 57. This translation is by Culley, who gives details of many
such contracts.

and other expenses. At the end of six years the boy had to be able to "cantare e fare il contrappunto al improviso" (sing and improvise counterpoint). The father was not allowed to profit from the boy during the six-year period, nor could he send him to sing anywhere, by day or by night, unless he paid one *scudo* to the Naninos. It would be unusual for a boy to be paid more than this per hired occasion, but if the father could obtain more, he could make a small profit on the boy in the short term. The boy was forbidden to take up a regular position until the six years had passed, unless the *maestro* was paid for all that he had taught the boy and for all that he might have earned from hiring out the boy, the amount again to be estimated by the two experts. For an entire year after the training was finished, the *maestro* was required to continue to house the boy, dividing his earnings equally between the *maestro* and the father. An identical contract was drawn up between the Naninos and the bookseller and printer Bernardino Donangeli, with an additional clause stating that, in the event that his son did not learn to sing after six years, the Naninos would be obliged to pay Donangeli twenty-five *scudi*.[1]

Spagnuolo points out that such provisions were customary in contracts signed between the masters and the fathers of apprentices in other trades and professions of the period. It was a two-way arrangement in which the apprentice learned the trade and the *maestro* benefitted from the apprentice's work. The *maestro* acted *in loco parentis*, housed and fed the boy, and provided his training — all in return for any profits earned from singing. As we have seen, this financial interest continued for some time after the official training period had ended. In the case of singers, these contracts normally became void once the boy's voice had broken, though some institutions might continue the employment if the boy was useful, perhaps as an alto or with an adult voice.[2] Occasionally a boy was let go because of an unsatisfactory voice: at Santa Maria Maggiore in 1606 one Giovanni Battista was sent back to his father because his voice "was not melodious or sweet, as is necessary, [and] was becoming evermore offensive to the ears of the listeners and time spent in imparting the science of music was being spent in vain"; he was given six *scudi* out of charity.[3] In the case of young castrati at Santa Maria Maggiore, a longer period of ten to twelve years of service was contracted, though there was a probationary period of between a month and a year during which the *maestro* had to be satisfied with the quality of the boys' voices.[4]

Apart from a few references to *putto castrato* or *eunuco* there is very little information in Roman archives about castration, which must have been an increasingly common practice by the early seventeenth century.[5] The archives of Santo Spirito

---

[1] Spagnuolo, "Gli atti notarili," 32.

[2] John Rosselli has reviewed various Roman and Italian contracts concerning choirboys up to the nineteenth century and found common ground in all of them. See Rosselli, "L'apprendistato del cantante italiano: Rapporti contrattuali fra allievi e insegnanti dal Cinquecento al Novecento," *Rivista italiana di musicologia* 23 (1988), 157–81 at 157–58.

[3] John Burke, *Musicians of S. Maria Maggiore, Rome, 1600–1700: A Social and Economic Study*, supplement to *Note d'archivio* n.s. 2 (1984), 95.

[4] Ibid., 98.

[5] On the introduction of *castrati* in Rome, see most recently Giuseppe Gerbino, "The

record a payment for one such operation in 1569 (which is quite early).[1] Thomas Culley has reproduced a 1630 contract between the rector of the German College and one Domenico Antonio Mocchi, father of Giovanni Battista. The latter had had some lessons from Odoardo Ceccharelli, a papal singer who also sang at the German College and who judged him to have an aptitude for singing. As a "work of charity and in order to bring this aptitude to perfection," Ceccharelli had arranged for the boy to be castrated at the father's request and had seen to his medical treatment at his own expense; he was confident in the boy's ability and backed the father's request that the College accept him as a soprano for eight years. The college accepted the boy on the condition that, if he left during that time, his father would see that he returned or, failing that, would pay the College seven *scudi* a month for the remainder of the eight years.[2] Culley records that Mocchi went on to serve at the court of the Count Palatine, Philipp Wilhelm of Neuburg-Düsseldorf.

One documented case where a boy did abscond prematurely is that of Felice Sances, removed suddenly from the German College by his father Horatio on 1 April 1614 after just under four and a half years of what was probably an eight-year contract. Horatio was jailed for refusing to pay the College the more than 400 *scudi* it claimed for the remaining term, "having kept him and educated him in Latin, in singing and in composition, so that he could already compose in two parts."[3] The College was determined that the father should pay, in case other parents might be tempted to withdraw their boys, endangering its extensive musical activity. The outcome of the affair is not known, but a cordial letter from Sances to the rector four years later would suggest that it was settled amicably. Sances went on to achieve considerable fame as a composer in Vienna. He had taken a solo part in Giacomo Cicognini's sung entertainment *L'Amor pudico* in February 1614 to mark the wedding of Prince Michele Peretti, younger brother of Cardinal Montalto, and Culley speculates that this may have persuaded the father that young Felice could make a more successful career away from the College. Culley also records cases of boys being poached from the German College by members of the nobility and even, in one case, by the Cappella Giulia, so that they could sing elsewhere in the city.[4]

Alberto Cametti has examined in detail the contracts between the governors of San Luigi dei Francesi and the parents of boys who became successful composing musicians, including three members of the Allegri family — Gregorio, Domenico, and Bartholomeo — all of whom were signed over to the church by their father. The first two, who went on to be important composers, were offered employment

Quest for the Soprano Voice: Castrati in Sixteenth-Century Italy," *Studi musicali* 32 (2004): 303–57.

[1] Archivio di Stato di Roma, Ospedale S. Spirito in Sassia, 1900, unfoliated, 22 Oct. 1569. The earliest known castrato in the Cappella Pontificia was Francesco Soto, who joined the choir in 1562.

[2] Culley, *Jesuits and Music*, 209.

[3] Ibid., 141.

[4] Ibid., 134–35, 147–48.

at San Luigi for a while after their voices broke; both lodged with the Nanino brothers at the same time as other future composers such as Paolo Agostini, Antonio Cifra, Vincenzo Ugolini, and Domenico Massenzio. Payments are recorded for the purchase of "una cartella da componere" (a *cartella* for composing) and "quattro libri da scrivere passaggi" (four books for writing out ornamentation) for the eleven-year-old Domenico Allegri in 1596, the year after he joined San Luigi. Cametti also lists purchases in connection with Latin lessons for the boys in 1599, including six grammar books, a dictionary, six and a half quires of paper, pens and ink, and erasers, as well as the epistles of Cicero.[1]

As well as benefiting from the earnings of a boy in his care, a *maestro* could gain from a *putto* in other ways, as in the case of Curtio Mancini, *maestro* at Santa Maria Maggiore in 1590. An orphaned boy soprano named Nicola Complebici died, leaving his property (which included a vineyard and his father's shoe shop) to Mancini in return for supervising his burial. The will was contested by the boy's relatives, who maintained that he was not yet fourteen (he was just one month short of that age at his death). Mancini had taken possession of the vineyard, claiming that Complebici was in fact over fourteen. Eventually Mancini ceded the vineyard in return for a payment of forty *scudi*, ten of which went to pay the expense of the boy's care and funeral.[2]

The care of boys was clearly a significant responsibility, one more easily undertaken in a family situation such as that provided by the Nanino brothers or by Palestrina. The latter's successor as *maestro di cappella* at St. Peter's, Ruggiero Giovanelli, was an unmarried cleric. He was soon accused of neglecting the boys, despite having been given a house in which to keep them, something the chapter pointed out had not been done for Palestrina.[3] It was one of the few areas where being married carried an advantage, since for other aspects of the job, institutions often preferred the greater commitment they could expect from someone without family ties, in addition to the religious reasons for preferring an unmarried cleric.[4] In the wake of the Council of Trent, the moral and spiritual welfare of the boys was an increasing preoccupation as well. John Burke quotes a number of excerpts from the *decreti* of the chapter of Santa Maria Maggiore detailing some of the problems encountered at that basilica in 1606 while Vincenzo Ugolini was maestro. He was admonished by the chapter in March of that year for taking less than good care of the boys. He was given a leave of absence for the month of May, but in June the chapter wrote to him once more suggesting that he find someone

---

[1] Alberto Cametti, "La scuola dei *pueri cantores* a S. Luigi dei Francesi in Roma e i suoi principali allievi (1591–1623)," *Rivista musicale italiana* 22 (1915), 593–641.

[2] Spagnuolo, "Gli atti notarili," 37–45.

[3] Biblioteca Apostolica Vaticana, Fondo Cappella Giulia, 427, Miscellanea, 17 (Maestri), quoted in Ducrot, "Histoire de la Cappella Giulia," 494.

[4] The chapter of San Giovanni in Laterano passed a decree on 12 Oct. 1566 stating that the choirmaster should be a bachelor. A certain Joannes A. Joanellus was dismissed from his position as choirmaster in the same year "because, burdened by wife and family, he was less able to serve the church" ("quod uxore et familia oneratus, minus inservire Ecclesiae potest"). However, this ruling was disregarded in 1570 and again in 1572. See Garden, "François Roussel," 118–19, quoting the *Liber decretorum Capitoli*, 1566, fol. 24ʳ.

who could help him take care of the boys. Ugolini was eventually dismissed in 1609, and it must have been a relief to the chapter when in June 1610 Domenico Allegri was given the post, accompanied by his married sister, who moved in with him in order to look after the boys.[1] Thomas Culley has described in detail the accusations of neglect in teaching the choirboys that led to the dismissal of Ottavio Catalani as *maestro* at the German College in 1613. Catalani seems to have been more interested in having the boys perform secular music outside the College for important patrons such as members of the Borghese family than in teaching them to perform liturgical music.[2]

Musical Training of Choirboys

THE most comprehensive description of the training of Roman choirboys comes from a 1695 document referring to training received under Virgilio Mazzocchi at St. Peter's (*maestro* 1629–46).[3] This account describes how every morning the boys spent one hour "nel cantar cose difficili e malagevoli per l'acquisto della esperienza" (singing difficult and awkward things to acquire experience), a second hour "nel essercizio del trillo," and another on *passaggi* (the ornamental figuration patterns that were memorized and practiced by singers); an hour was spent studying *lettere* and an hour exercising in front of a mirror with the *maestro* listening. Every afternoon there was a half-hour of theory, a half-hour of "contrappunto sopra il canto fermo," an hour learning "contrappunto sopra la cartella [a slate lined with staves]," and another hour on *lettere*. Any remaining time was spent practicing the *clavicembalo* or composing a psalm, motet, or canzonetta. From time to time the boys practiced in a particular spot with an echo near Monte Mario, north of the Vatican, in order to hear the sound of their own voices. The boys were also taken to hear the choirs in various Roman churches in order to observe "the manners of singing of so many famous singers who flourished during the reign of Urban VIII [r. 1623–44], to reflect on them and to give an account of them to the *maestro* when they returned home." The *maestro* also gave lectures in order to impress certain elements more firmly on the minds of the pupils. This was very intensive training indeed, involving all aspects of music at the time: virtuoso singing, improvised counterpoint, written counterpoint ("sopra la cartella"), text setting, and keyboard proficiency. The boys had the opportunity to hear their own voices as well as watching their mouths and faces as they sang.

Another useful source of information is the archive of the German-Hungarian College, which in the sixteenth century was unusual in training its more talented

---

[1] Burke, *Musicians of S. Maria Maggiore*, 93–96.

[2] Culley, *Jesuits and Music*, 121–27.

[3] Giovanni Andrea Angelini Bontempi, *Historia musica, nelle quale si ha piena cognizione della teorica, e della practica antica . . .* (Perugia, 1695; repr. Geneva, 1976), 170, quoted in Bernhard Schrammek, *Zwischen Kirche und Karneval: Biographie, soziales Umfeld und Werk des römischen Kapellmeisters Virgilio Mazzocchi (1597–1646)*, Musiksoziologie, 9 (Kassel, 2001), 338–39.

seminarians not just in plainsong but also in polyphonic music, which they performed regularly at services in the associated churches of Sant'Apollinare and
Santo Stefano Rotondo. The soprano parts were sung by four boys. A document
from the late 1580s lays out a clear program of training for both boys and students,
which, because of the pressures of academic study, had to take place during recreation periods:

> After the mass in the morning, during the time of the first table, the so-
> pranos [*putti*] go into the room of the *maestro di cappella*, where [they are
> trained] according to the capacity of each one, who sings and gives an ac-
> count of the *cartella*. After the second table, one sings in the *sala* for about
> a half hour; on Tuesdays and Fridays, two, three or more motets in the small
> [part]books, at the benches, and on the other days, some mass or Magnificat
> in the large books. And the things to be sung in church are rehearsed, with
> cautions given according to the need. Then one sings at the organ — some-
> times the sopranos, sometimes the students or others, at times each one
> separately, at times together. And if there is someone who may know how
> to play, he is trained on this occasion. In the summer, after having finished
> the said exercise, the sopranos return to the room of the *maestro di cappella*,
> where for some time, some take a lesson in playing, the others are trained,
> some in singing, some in the *cartella* — each one according to his capacity.
> In the winter, since there is not time for the said exercises after dinner, the
> sopranos go to the room of the *maestro di cappella* about an hour before the
> first table, where they stay until [the bell] rings for the second table, each one
> being trained according to his need in playing, singing, showing the *cartella*,
> and similar things. After Vespers on the feasts, and on the days of vacation
> (when convenient), they have an hour of exercise in the said things, or in
> *passaggi*, at the judgement of the *maestro di cappella*. In addition to this, it
> has been customary at times to sing some madrigals, for practice or for rec-
> reation, either in the room of the *maestro di cappella*, or elsewhere (or indeed
> at the vineyard), at the judgement of the Father Rector. At the vineyard an
> hour is also assigned to the sopranos for the practice of *passaggi* or *versetti*.[1]

This instruction follows the same basic pattern as that used by Mazzocchi, though
curtailed because of the need to fit into recreation periods. While the seminarians
were trained to sing, including polyphony from both part- and choirbooks, the
boy sopranos were given extra training in singing, playing, and composing with
the *cartella*. All were involved in practicing motets and other genres for liturgical
services.

Another document from 1611 provides more details about the seminarians'
training. Their basic instruction was in plainchant and was given initially by

---

[1] Rome, Collegio Germano-Hungarico, *Liber in quo scribuntur bullae, regulae, consuetudines et reliqua omnia que ad huius collegii disciplinam pertinent*, 176; published in Thomas
Culley, "The Influence of the German College in Rome on Music in German-Speaking
Countries during the Sixteenth and Seventeenth Centuries (1)," *Analecta musicologica* 7
(1969), 1–35 at 12–13. Culley's translation is given here.

a senior student in each dormitory for fifteen minutes after dinner. The *maestro* went from room to room checking on progress, teaching the *differentiae* of the psalm tones, how to intone a psalm, and how to project the voice ("portar la voce") well. The more advanced students were introduced to what was called the "canto secondo," which lasted for a half-hour, during which the *maestro* trained them in various types of singing, "now divided in two or three choirs, now having sung a terzetto of a hymn or of another thing (i.e., solo trio or quartet)." He also taught them to sing with organ accompaniment, to take the note from the organ, and to project the voice. The writer goes on: "now this exercise, so ancient and so necessary, which is the school and the seminary for forming singers who may afterwards help with the choir in church, how can it be managed without a *maestro di cappella* and how can the *maestro* train the students in so many varieties of songs without sopranos?"[1] The four *putti* were included in the *canto secondo* and were then given extra lessons in singing, playing, and composing.

The training of boys played an important part in the transmission of Roman sacred music. Roman musicians, particularly those in the Cappella Pontificia, perceived themselves as guardians of the sacred flame of a stylistic tradition in which Palestrina, Giovanni Maria Nanino, and Gregorio Allegri were the high priests. Handing on this tradition was the responsibility of the *maestri*. Later, a certain mythology developed around Rome as a city of choir schools around and after 1600, taking over something of the reputation that Franco-Flemish choir schools had held in the fifteenth century. In reality, while some *maestri* like the Nanino brothers did run small schools, almost all *maestri*, including the Naninos, were associated with a particular church or institution.[2] The small number of boys in each group certainly meant that each boy received considerable individual attention. The regulation of music schools was brought under the control of the revitalized Compagnia dei Musici di Roma by Pope Urban VIII in the mid 1620s.[3] The Compagnia's bull of foundation, *Rationi congruit* of 1585, included among the good works (to be rewarded with an indulgence of sixty days) "the teaching of music or grammar to boys, either by writing or reading, free of charge for the love of God."[4]

Surviving training materials are of two types: those related to the teaching of *contrappunto*, both improvised and written down, and those related to the learning of *passaggi*. Those in the former category are mainly associated with the Nanino brothers, whose *Regole di contrappunto* survives in manuscripts in libraries in

---

[1] Ibid., 17–18.

[2] Cametti, "La scuola," debunked Baini's idea of a public music school (which would have been the first opened by an Italian) run by Giovanni M. Nanino with the help of Palestrina and Francesco Soriano, pointing out that there was no evidence for such an institution but that instead each of these composers was responsible for a small number of choirboys in the *cappelle* they directed.

[3] Remo Giazotto, *Quattro secoli di storia dell'Accademia Nazionale di Santa Cecilia* (Rome, 1970), 94–96.

[4] "Pueros musicam vel grammaticam, seu ad scribendum vel legendum, gratis et amore Dei docerent"; see ibid., 11.

Bologna and elsewhere.[1] Also in Bologna is a manuscript with a set of 157 *contrappunti* on the *cantus firmus* "La Spagna" and 110 *contrappunti* on *Ave maris stella*.[2] The latter are by Francesco Soriano, *maestro di cappella* at St. Peter's (1603–20) and another distinguished trainer of choirboys. Richard Agee has convincingly shown that the first 125 *contrapuncta* on "La Spagna" are the work of Costanzo Festa, while the remainder are by Giovanni Maria Nanino, almost all of them published in 1586.[3] It is quite likely that Nanino made use of Festa's *contrapuncta* for teaching purposes — Agee has pointed out that they fulfil Festa's stated aim of "learning to sing in counterpoint, to compose, and to play all instruments" by covering different clefs and clef substitutions, contrapuntal devices, mensural and proportional problems, and by being written for two to eleven voices. Nanino added his own set on the same bass for three and five voices, adding two and four parts to the *cantus firmus* in the same manner in which he would have taught his pupils to improvise *contrappunto alla mente* or to write on the *cartella*. The training in *contrappunto alla mente* was an important part of their preparation, both as singers and as composers; this was a particularly Roman speciality, prized especially in the papal singers.[4]

A group of manuscripts preserved in the Fondo Chigi of the Vatican Library contains exercises for *contrappunti* and for *passaggi*, clearly used for teaching purposes. Typical is Chigi Q.iv.7, a small notebook from the late 1620s kept by Antonio Melendez, a singer at Santa Maria Maggiore. It contains long-note *cantus firmi* with one (and occasionally two or three) added parts, exploiting the standard formulae used in forming *passaggi* in developing *contrappunto*.[5] John Burke has speculated that this type of book was used for practicing with the organ, the *maestro* playing the *cantus firmus* and the student singing the added lines.[6] The Roman use of *passaggi* or ornamental figures is best seen in the papal singer Giovanni Luca Conforti's *Breve e facile maniera d'essercitarsi* (Rome, 1593), a manual for the instruction of singers.

---

[1] See Gaetano Gaspari, *Catalogo della Biblioteca Musicale G. B. Martini di Bologna*, Studi e testi di musicologia, 1–4 (Bologna, 1961), 1:302.

[2] Bologna, Civico Museo Bibliografico Musicale, C36.

[3] See the introduction to Costanzo Festa, *Counterpoints on a Cantus Firmus*, ed. Richard J. Agee, Recent Researches in the Music of the Renaissance, 107 (Madison, 1997).

[4] The papal singer Antimo Liberati saw Giovanni Maria Nanini as a better teacher than Palestrina: "[Palestrina] non hebbe genio di far schola o non potendo per l'assiduo impegno della compositione harmonica, ma s'unì e si conformò con la schola di giovanni Maria Nanino suo condiscepolo e amico confidentissimo." Antimo Liberati, *Lettera scritta dal [. . .] in risposta ad una del sig. Ovidio Persapegi* . . . (Rome, 1685), 24, quoted in Arnaldo Morelli, "Antimo Liberato, Matteo Simonelli e la tradizione palestriniana a Roma nella seconda metà del seicento," in *Palestrina e la sua presenza nella musica e nella cultura europa dal suo tempo ad oggi: Atti del II Convegno Internazionale di Studi Palestriniani, 3–5 Maggio 1986*, ed. Lino Bianchi and Giancarlo Rostirolla (Palestrina, 1991), 295–307 at 301.

[5] Other similar books in the same series are Chigi Q.iv.9, 20, 21, 22. All are very much working notebooks containing various types of exercise.

[6] Burke, *Musicians of S. Maria Maggiore*, 29.

REPERTORIES SUNG BY BOYS

PRECISE evidence of boys' involvement in the various musical repertories of Roman churches is difficult to come by. We know that their training prepared them for the full range of idioms: plainchant, improvised counterpoint, and polyphony, so that by the end of that period they were able to sing all of these types of music. Some useful information comes from the liturgical diaries kept by members of the German College. On the feast of the Epiphany in 1585, for instance, it was decreed that none of the boys could be absent from the choir so that a motet could be sung in place of the *Deo gratias* (presumably at the end of Lauds). The motet was Palestrina's double-choir *Surge Illuminare* sung with the organ ("in organo"), and all four boys were needed because of the two soprano parts involved.[1] This is significant evidence for the participation of boys in polychoral music. Another eight-voice motet, *Stephanus autem* (probably by Annibale Stabile), was sung in the associated church of Santo Stefano Rotondo after Compline on the Second Sunday of Lent in 1585. The diaries record that the *maestro* mistakenly told the boys to sing the incorrect versicle "Lapidaverunt Stephanum viri timorati."[2] This must have been in plainchant: the chapter from Second Vespers of St. Stephen uses the text *Stephanus autem*, which is followed by the versicle "Stephanus vidit coelos apertos." If the motet and versicle were meant as a commemoration of St. Stephen, then that may explain why the versicle chosen by Stabile was judged to be wrong. On 9 June 1592, since it was a school day, a reduced choir of two each on alto, tenor, and bass was sent to Santo Stefano, together with the *putti*; the naming of the voice parts is again direct evidence that the boys sang polyphony.[3] Further evidence for the boys singing plainchant comes from 3 August 1585 at Santo Stefano when "the boys sang the brief responsories" ("pueri cantarunt Responsoria brevia").[4] At the office of Tenebrae on the Wednesday of Holy Week in 1591 the first Lamentation was sung by a boy "who had practiced well in advance" ("bene prima essercitato"), the second by a contralto or tenor, and the third in polyphony ("musica"); the same happened in 1592, though the third Lamentation on that occasion was also in plainchant.[5] Similarly, at Santa Maria Maggiore in 1606 the chapter decreed that, during the offices of Tenebrae, the Lamentations would not be sung by the whole choir but rather "unica pueri voce recitandas," i.e., chanted by a single boy.[6] Further evidence for boys singing both polyphony ("di musica") and in *falsobordone* comes from the archives of the Arciconfraternità del Santissimo

---

[1] Archive of the German College, Rome, *Diarium ecclesiae Patris Friderick Overbeck . . . et Patris Gabriel Tibaldi . . . 1582–87*, reproduced in Culley, *Jesuits and Music*, 301.

[2] Entry in the same diary, reproduced in Casimiri, "'Disciplina musicae' e 'mastri di capella' . . . , x: Liturgia e musica in S. Apollinare," *Note d'archivio* 19 (1942), 159–68 at 163.

[3] Archive of the German College, Rome, *Diario 1591*, reproduced ibid., 164–65.

[4] Ibid., 163.

[5] Ibid., 164.

[6] Burke, *Musicians of Santa Maria Maggiore*, 93.

Crocifisso from 1599, the former at the start of a Forty Hours' devotion, the latter during a procession to the Gesù.[1]

The practice of singing with the organ, which had been first recorded at the start of the sixteenth century, continued in subsequent decades. The English Jesuit Gregory Martin's *Roma Sancta*, which describes practices he saw and heard in Rome in the late 1570s, speaks of hearing "with the organ a childes voice shriller and louder than the instrument, tuneable with every pipe."[2] Among the frequent references in the German College liturgical diaries to the singing of motets with the organ is one from April 1583, when, at a Forty Hours' devotion in the German national church of Santa Maria dell'Anima, the sopranos and the *maestro di cappella* (Annibale Stabile) sang motets "sopra l'organo."[3] Either the boys sang a small-scale motet with organ accompaniment or they improvised in *contrappunto* over a *cantus firmus* played by the *maestro* on the organ.

Not everyone was convinced that boys' voices singing polyphony or solo music was a good thing. Lodovico da Viadana, who had spent some time in Rome in the 1590s, wrote in the forward to his *Cento concerti ecclesiastici* of 1602: "per lo più i putti cantano trascuratamente, e con poca gratia" (boys mostly sing carelessly and with little grace).[4] Pietro della Valle, in his *Della musica dell'età nostra* of 1640, is particularly scathing in comparing the boys' voices of former times to the abundance of castrati in his own day:

> The best they could do in those times was to have a good *fanciullo*; but these, when they began to know something, lost their voices; and while they had [their voices], as persons of an age when they had no judgement, they sang without taste or grace, as if they had learned everything by heart, which hearing them at times gave me insupportable heartache.[5]

The small number of boys singing in choirs would have meant they had to sing with full voices without much allowance for subtlety. Certainly, boys had their shortcomings when it came to the new music of the early Baroque, which demanded both refined technique and rhetorical insight, and they were increasingly supplemented or supplanted by castrati and falsettists in the major choirs. At the same time, the church needed to continue its support for boys, who were a source of future adult singers.

---

[1] Archivio Segreto Vaticano, SS. Crocifisso, A XII 1599, unfoliated.

[2] Gregory Martin, *Roma Sancta (1581)*, ed. Gregory B. Parks (Rome, 1969).

[3] Casimiri, "'Disciplina musicae' e 'mastri di capella' . . . , x: Liturgia e musica in S. Apollinare," 160.

[4] Quoted in Gino Stefani, *Musica e religione nell'Italia barocca*, Uomo e cultura, 14 (Palermo, 1975), 101.

[5] "Il piu che si poteva fare allora era avere un buon fanciullo; ma quelli quando cominciavano a sapere qualche cosa, perdevano la voce; e mentre pur l'avevano, come persone che per l'età non avevano giudizio, anche cantavano senza gusto e senza grazia, come cose appunto imparate a mente, che alle volte a sentirli mi davano certe strappate di corda insopportabili." Taken from the transcription of Della Valle in Angelo Solerti, ed., *Le origini del melodramma: Testimonianze de contemporanei*, Piccola biblioteca di scienze moderne, 70 (Turin, 1903), 163.

As Gino Stefani has pointed out, boys' voices could represent simplicity and purity and the voices of angels to the early-modern churchgoer.[1] As such, they had a role to play in evangelization and in inspiring people to devotion. No one was more conscious of this than Filippo Neri, brought up within the *lauda*-singing tradition in Florence, which he was keen to transfer to Rome, where he arrived in the 1530s. Mindful of the value of music for both spiritual refreshment and for educational purposes, he was also aware of the attraction of boys' voices, initially for delivering memorized sermons but later for singing. One of his followers said of him: "Experience shows that when one introduces the pleasure of spiritual music and the simplicity and purity of boys into serious exercises performed by serious persons, one attracts far more people from all around."[2] In his manuscript life of Agostino Manni, one of Neri's close followers, Paolo Aringhi described how Manni introduced the practice of having boys represent some devout action or play in the oratory, which soon led to sung spiritual dialogues in *stile recitativo*, performed especially during Carnival. The most famous of these *sacre rappresentationi* was Emilio de' Cavalieri's *La rappresentatione di Anima et di Corpo* of 1600. The part of Anima was taken by a boy, who won high praise from the contemporary writer Giovanni Vittorio Rossi:

> I have praised especially the part of Anima, which, as well as having been played most divinely by that boy, I found in the music an indescribable artifice in which the affects of sadness and of sweetness were conveyed by certain false sixths which pulled onto sevenths, stealing the soul away.[3]

Silvia Casolari has pointed out that having a boy sing the part of Anima would have conveyed the state of purity and innocence necessary to confront Morte in the drama.[4] Two boys also spoke the prelude before the action began. Manni later wrote a *Rappresentatione del Figliol prodigo fatta in musica*, which was performed in January 1619. The payment for the *putti* who performed it was made through Doritio [Isorelli], a musician at the Chiesa Nuova, on the orders of Francesco [Martini], the *maestro di cappella*: this has led Arnaldo Morelli to suggest that this *rappresentatione* too was set to music.[5] Of course, boys' voices were not the only high voices to have been heard at the oratory devotions of the Chiesa Nuova: the castrati (and papal singers) Francesco Soto and Girolamo Rosini were both members of the Congregation of the Oratory and sang regularly there.[6]

---

[1] Stefani, *Musica e religione*, 101–3.

[2] "La pratica ha insegnato che, inserendosi tra gli esercitii gravi fatti da persone gravi la piacevolezza della musica spirituale e la semplicità e purità de' putti, si tira molto più popolo di ogni altra parte"; Quoted in Morelli, *Il tempio armonico*, 6.

[3] "Lodava ancora in estremo la parte del'Anima, che oltre esser stata rappresentata divinamente da quel putto, diceva nella musica esser un artifitio inestimabile, e che esprimeva gli affetti di dolore e di dolcezza con certe seste false che tiravano alla settima, che rapivano l'anima." Quoted ibid., 179. The identity of the boy seems not to have been recorded.

[4] Silvia Casolari, "Allegorie nella *Rappresentatione di Anima et di Corpo* (1600): Testo e imagine," *Rivista italiana di musicologia* 33 (1998), 7–31.

[5] Morelli, *Il tempio armonico*, 84.

[6] It is interesting in this context that there is no evidence for the use of *putti* for liturgi-

Finally, boys' voices were heard at the Christian doctrine classes held in parish churches and other churches on Sundays and feast days. The singing of *laude spirituali* was an integral part of the proceedings, alternating with rote learning of the catechism. Simple four-voice formulae for singing common prayers such as the *Pater noster*, *Ave Maria*, and the *Credo* were published by the Spanish Jesuit Jacques Ledesma in his *Modo per insegnar la Dottrina christiana* published in Rome in 1573, and additional simple *laude* were given in a companion volume *Lodi e canzoni spirituali per cantar insieme con la Dottrina christiana* published in 1576 in Milan. The preface to the latter volume spelled out the reasons for introducing singing during the catechism sessions:

> These *laude*, printed here separately from the *Dottrina*, are to be sung by the pupils at the beginning, in the middle, and at the end in the quantity and the way judged necessary by the teacher of the doctrine. Singing the doctrine and the *lodi spirituali* by two choirs is useful for a number of reasons. First, to make it easier to commit to memory, as experience has already made clear. Second, to make it more attractive for pupils to come to the *Dottrina* at times when they are otherwise invited to play games, as on feast days. Third, those who can only just speak can learn [better] through the medium of song; they do not learn as quickly without singing. Fourth, to teach with minimum effort: because when everyone sings the Credo they all take part, and readily, whereas simply listening to one after the other takes a lot of time and is boring. Fifth, to avoid the scurrilous songs that are generally sung wherever youngsters — and older people — gather when they do not know any other songs. Sixth, so that those who hear and do not come to the *Dottrina* will also learn. Seventh, so that the pupils will learn to sing with as much ease as possible so that they will know and want to sing either the *Dottrina* or the *laude* of God our Lord. Eighth, to imitate the usage of the Roman Catholic Church, which sings the canonical hours night and day. And finally to sing like the angels in heaven who continually sing: Holy, Holy, Holy to the Lord God . . .[1]

cal singing at the Chiesa Nuova, where only castrati such as Francesco Soto and Gerolamo Rosini seem to have sung.

[1] *Lodi e canzoni spirituali per cantar insieme con la Dottrina christiana* (Milan, 1576), fol. 3ʳ: "Queste lodi poste qui, come fuori della Dottrina, servono per cantare alli putti: così nel principio, o nel mezzo, come in fine: quanto e come giudicherà necessario quello ch'insegna la Dottrina. Imperoché il cantare la Dottrina, et le lodi spirituali a duoi cori è utile per più ragioni. Prima, per imparare con più facilità a mente, come l'isperienza già l'ha fatto chiaro. Seconda, per far che i putti stiano più allegramente alla Dottrina, nel tempo, che sono invitati alli giuochi, come le feste. Terza, acciò quelli ch'apena possono parlare l'imparino per mezzo del canto. Il che non imparerieno si presto senza canto. Quarta, per insegnarla con manco fatica. Percioché cantando verbigrazia il Credo tutti lo dicono, et volentieri, ma ascoltandolo a uno, a uno come sono molti, si spenderà molto tempo e fatica. Quinta, per evitar li cattivi canti, che sogliono cantare dovunque si trovano li putti, et grandi, per non sapere altri canti. Sesta per far che quelli, che sentono, e non vengono alla Dottrina l'imparino. Settima, acciò li putti sappino cantare con quell'aere più facile che si potrà, dovunque saranno, et vorranno, overo la Dottrina, overo lode a Dio nostro signore.

This is strong advocacy indeed, and Ledesma goes further, suggesting that after the catechism session the children, girls and boys, should go in procession through the streets, singing *laude* or the *Salve regina*; he even provides some simple verses that will encourage parents to send their children to the Christian doctrine session, using children as a moralizing force in instructing their parents.

CONCLUSION

WHETHER after participating in sessions of the *Dottrina christiana* or taking part in processions of confraternities, singing boys were a regular sight and sound on the streets of Rome. The number of active choirboys at any one time was not large: perhaps fifteen institutions had an average of three boys each around 1600, the number of institutions growing somewhat over the course of the seventeenth century. They were supplemented by some boys in private training with *maestri* and by boys from the orphanages who were being trained in music.

In general, the world of Roman sacred music was quite inbred. Bernhard Schrammek has examined the lives of fifty of the most significant musicians active in the city between 1600 and 1650.[1] Of these, seventeen were born in Rome and a further twenty-five in the Papal States. Twenty-seven did their training in the city, with another eight moving to Rome during their boyhood service. Most telling is that thirty-five musicians found their first employment in the city. Contacts made while singing and learning in the small number of regular choirs remained important, both for employment prospects and for the transmission of repertoire. Singing at patronal feasts in the large number of the city's institutions brought singers from various choirs together, singing under various *maestri* and performing a wide range of music. As we have seen, Virgilio Mazzocchi encouraged his choirboys to visit as many churches as possible to hear festal music. This, together with their extensive training, made them very aware of Roman styles of composition and changing trends before and after 1600. At the same time, some Rome-trained singers and composers did leave the city and take Roman repertories elsewhere, particularly to southern Germany and Austria.[2]

Ottava, per imitare l'uso della Chiesa Romana Cattolica, che canta la notte et il giorno le hore canoniche. Et ultima, per cantare gli Angioli nel cielo, che continuamente cantano, Santo, Santo, Santo, a il Signor Iddio . . ." See Giancarlo Rostirolla, "Laudi e canti religiosi per l'esercizio spirituale della Dottrina cristiana al tempo di Robert Bellarmino," in *La lauda spirituale tra cinque e seicento: Poesie e canti devozionali nell'italia della controriforma*, ed. Giuseppe Filippi et al. (Rome, 2001), 275–472 at 318–19, and Eyolf Østrem and Nils Holger Petersen, *Medieval Ritual and Early Modern Music: The Devotional Practice of Lauda Singing in Late-Renaissance Italy* (Turnhout, 2008), 57 ff.

[1] Schrammek, *Zwischen Kirche und Karneval*, 364–69.

[2] See Culley, *Jesuits and Music*; Culley, "The Influence of the German College in Rome (i)," 1–35; Thomas Culley, "The Influence of the German College in Rome on Music in German-Speaking Countries during the Sixteenth and Seventeenth Centuries (ii)," *Analecta musicologica* 9 (1970), 20–63.

GENERAL BIBLIOGRAPHY

Manuscript sources are cited in the footnotes of individual articles.

Published Primary Sources

ALPHARANUS, Tiberius. *De basilica Vaticanae antiquissima et nova structura.* Ed. Michele Cerruti. Studi e testi, 26. Rome, 1914.

ANDRIEU, Michel, ed. *Les Ordines Romani du haut Moyen-Âge.* 5 vols. Spicilegium sacrum lovaniense, 11, 23, 24, 28, 29. Louvain, 1931–61.

Anglo-Saxon Conversations: The Colloquies of Ælfric Bata. Ed. Scott Gwara, trans. with an introduction by David W. Porter. Rochester, N.Y., 1997.

Antiphonale missarum sextuplex. Ed. René-Jean Hesbert. Brussels, 1935.

ARBER, Edward, ed. *A Transcript of the Registers of the Company of Stationers of London, 1554–1640,* 5 vols. London, 1875.

ASHBEE, Andrew, ed. *Records of English Court Music,* vol. 7 (1485–1558). Snodland, Kent, 1993.

BALDWIN, William. *Treatise of Morall Phylosophie, Conteyning the Sayinges of the Wyse.* London, 1547.

BEADLE, Richard, and Peter MEREDITH, eds. *The York Play.* Medieval Drama Facsimiles, 7. Leeds, 1983.

BEADLE, Richard, ed. *The York Plays.* London, 1982.

BENSON, Larry D., ed. *The Riverside Chaucer.* 3rd ed. Boston, 1987.

BERMUDO, Juan. *Declaración de instrumentos musicales.* Osuna, 1555.

BONTEMPI, Giovanni Andrea Angelini. *Historia musica, nelle quale si ha piena cognitione della teorica, e della practica antica . . .* Perugia, 1695; repr. Geneva, 1976.

The Book of Pontiffs (Liber Pontificalis): The Ancient Biographies of the First Ninety Roman Pontiffs to AD 715. Trans. Raymond Davis. Translated Texts for Historians, 5. Rev. ed. Liverpool, 2000.

BRETT, Philip, ed. *Consort Songs.* Musica Britannica, 22. London, 1974.

CLOPPER, Lawrence M., ed. *Records of Early English Drama: Chester.* Toronto, 1979.

Codice topographico della città di Roma. Ed. Roberto Valentini and Giuseppe Zucchetti. 4 vols. Fonti per la storia d'Italia, 81, 88, 90, 91. Rome, 1940–53.

A Collection of Ordinances and Regulations for the Government of the Royal Household. London, 1780.

Constantin VII Porphyrogénète: Livre des cérémonies. Ed. Albert Vogt. 2 vols. Paris, 1935.

Consuetudines Floriacenses antiquiores. In *Consuetudinum saeculi X/XI/XII monumenta non-cluniacesnia,* 3–60. Ed. Anselme Davril and Lin Donnat. Corpus consuetudinum monasticarum, 7. Siegburg, 1984.

Consuetudines Fructuarienses. Ed. L. G. Spätling and Peter Dinter. Corpus consuetudinum monasticarum, 12. Siegburg, 1987.

Consuetudines saeculi octavi et noni. Ed. Josef Semmler. Corpus consuetudinum monasticarum, 1. Siegburg, 1963.

Corona: Il secondo libro delle canzoni alla napolitana a tre voci. Venice, 1571.

DAVIS, Norman, ed., *Non-Cycle Plays and Fragments.* London, 1970.

Decreti e costitutioni generali dell'illustriss. e reverendiss. Monsignore Alessandro Petrucci arcivescovo di Siena per il buon governo delle monache della sua città e diocese. Siena, 1625.

DUGDALE, William. *Monasticon Anglicanum: A History of the Abbies and other Monasteries . . .* New ed. 6 vols. London, 1849.

DURAND DE MAILLANE, Pierre Toussaint. *Dictionnaire de droit canonique et de pratique bénéficiale.* Rev. ed. Lyons, 1787.

EDWARDS, Richard. *The Paradise of Dainty Devices (1576–1606).* Ed. Hyder Edward Rollins. Cambridge, Mass., 1927.

ELYOT, Thomas. *Bankette of Sapience.* London, 1539.

A Fifteenth-Century Courtesy Book. Ed. R. W. Chambers. With *Two Fifteenth-Century Franciscan Rules.* Ed. Walter W. Seton. English Text Society, o.s. 148. 1914; repr. Oxford, 1962.

GLAREAN, Heinrich. *Dodecachordon.* Trans. Clement A. Miller. 2 vols. Musicological Studies and Documents, 6. n.p., 1965.

Gregorii I papae Registrum epistolarum. Ed. Paul Ewald and Ludwig Hartmann. Monumenta germaniae historica: Epistolae, 1–2. Berlin, 1887–99; 2nd ed., Berlin, 1957.

GRENAILLE DE LA CHATOUNIÈRE, F. *L'Honneste Garçon, ou L'Art de bien élever la noblesse à la vertu, aux sciences et à toutes les carrières convenables à sa condition.* Paris, 1642.

Guido d'Arezzo's Regule Rithmice, Prologus in Antiphonarium, and Epistola ad Michahelem: A Critical Text and Translation with an Introduction, Annotations, Indices, and New Manuscript Inventories. Ed. Dolores Pesce. Wissenschaftliche Abhandlungen. 73. Ottawa, 1999.

John Heywood's 'A Dialogue of Proverbs'. Ed. Rudolph E. Habenicht. Berkeley, 1963.

The Plays of John Heywood. Ed. Richard Axton and Peter Happé. Tudor Interludes, 6. Cambridge, 1991.

HOLLYBAND, Claudius [Claude de Sainliens]. *The French Schoolmaister.* London, 1573.

Iohannis Beleth Summa de ecclesiasticis officiis. Ed. Herbert Douteil. Corpus christianorum continuatio mediaevalis, 41. Turnhout, 1976.

LANDWEHR-MELNICKI, Margareta, and Bruno STÄBLEIN, ed. *Die Gesänge des altrömischen Graduale Vat. lat. 5319.* Monumenta monodica medii aevi, 2. Kassel, 1970.

Latin Colloquies from Pre-Conquest Britain. Ed. Scott Gwara. Toronto Medieval Latin Texts, 22. Toronto, 1996.

The Lenten Triodion. Trans. Mother Mary and Kallistos Ware. London, 1977.

Der Liber Benedictionum Ekkeharts IV nebst den kleinern Dichtungen aus dem Codex Sangallensis 393. Ed. Johannes Egli. Sankt Gallen, 1909.

Le Liber censuum de l'Église romaine. Ed. Paul Fabre and Louis Duchesne. Bibliothèque des Écoles françaises d'Athènes et de Rome, 2nd ser., 6/1–2. Paris, 1910.

Liber diurnus romanorum pontificum ex unico codice Vaticano. Ed. Theodor von Sickel. Vienna, 1889.

Der Liber Ordinarius der Abtei St. Arnulf vor Metz (Metz, Stadtbibliothek, Ms. 132, um 1240). Ed. Alois Odermatt. Spicilegium friburgense, 31. Freiburg, 1987.

Le Liber pontificalis: Texte, introduction et commentaire. Ed. Louis Duchesne. 2 vols. Paris, 1886–92.

The Lives of the Eighth-Century Popes (Liber Pontificalis): The Ancient Biographies of Nine Popes from AD 715 to AD 817. Trans. Raymond Davis. Translated Texts for Historians, 13. Liverpool, 1992.

The Lives of the Ninth-Century Popes (Liber Pontificalis): The Ancient Biographies of Nine Popes from AD 817 to AD 891. Trans. Raymond Davis. Translated Texts for Historians, 20. Liverpool, 1995.

MACHYN, Henry. *The Diary of Henry Machyn, Citizen and Merchant-Taylor of London from AD 1550 – AD 1563*. Ed. John Gough Nichols. Camden Society, 42. London, 1848.

Maggio cantato l'anno 1796 in onore dell'annunziazione di Maria Vergine. Siena, n.d.

MAIGNE D'ARNIS, W.-H. *Lexicon manuale ad scriptores mediae et infimae latinitatis . . .* Paris, 1866.

MARTIN, Gregory. *Roma Sancta (1581)*, ed. Gregory B. Parks. Rome, 1969.

MEDWALL, Henry. *Fulgens and Lucres*. London, ca. 1514.

The Monastic Constitutions of Lanfranc. Ed. and trans. David Knowles, rev. Christopher N. L. Brooke. Oxford, 2002.

Monumenta germaniae historica: Capitularia regum Francorum. 2 vols. Hanover, 1881–97.

Monumenta germaniae historica: Poetae latini aevi carolini. 4 vols. Berlin, 1881–1923.

MORE, Thomas. *Utopia*. Ed. E. Surtz and J. H. Hexter. New Haven, 1965.

MORLEY, Thomas. *A Plaine and Easie Introduction to Practicall Musick*. London, 1597.

OLIVER, J. R., trans. and ed. "Monumenta [III] de insula Manniae, or A Collection of National Documents relating to the Isle of Man." *The Manx Society* 9 (1862).

Ordinaire et coutumier de l'église cathédrale de Bayeux (XIIIᵉ siècle). Ed. Ulysse Chevalier. Bibliothèque liturgique, 8. Paris, 1902.

L'Ordinaire de la cathédrale d'Aoste (Bibliothèque capitulaire, Cod. 54, fol. 93–240). Ed. Robert Amiet and Lin Colliard. Monumenta liturgica ecclesiae augustanae, 4. Aosta, 1978.

Ordinaires de l'église cathédrale de Laon (XIIᵉ et XIIIᵉ siècles). Ed. Ulysse Chevalier. Bibliothèque liturgique, 6. Paris, 1897.

L'Ordinaire liturgique du diocèse de Besançon (Besançon, Bibl. Mun, MS 101): Texte et sources. Ed. Romain Jurot. Spicilegium friburgense, 38. Fribourg, 1999.

Patrologiae cursus completus: Series latina. Ed. Jacques-Paul Migne. 225 vols. Paris, 1844–55.

PENNA, Lorenzo, P. F. *Li primi albori musicali per li principianti della musica figurata*. 1684; repr. Bologna, 1969.

Le pontifical romano-germanique du dixième siècle. Ed. Cyrille Vogel and Reinhard Elze. 3 vols. Studi e testi, 226–27, 269. Vatican City, 1963–72.

La rappresentatione di Santa Agata vergine e martire. Siena, 1606.

La rappresentatione di Santa Orsola vergine e martire. Siena, 1608.

La rappresentatione di Santa Teodora. Siena, 1614.

La rappresentatione e festa di Rosana. Siena, 1626.

RASTALL, Richard, ed. *Six Songs from the York Mystery Play "The Assumption of the Virgin"*. Newton Abbot, 1985.

Il regesto sublacense del secolo XI. Ed. Leone Allodi and Guido Levi. Rome, 1885.

Registrum Henrici Woodlock diocesis Wintoniensis (A.D. 1305–1316). Ed. A. W. Goodman. 2 vols. Canterbury and York Society, 43–44. Oxford, 1940–41.

Registrum Roberti Winchelsey Cantuariensis Archiepiscopi, A.D. 1294–1313. Ed. Rose Graham. Canterbury and York Society, 52. Oxford, 1956.

RB 1980: The Rule of St. Benedict in English and Latin. Ed. Timothy Fry. Collegeville, Minn., 1980.

SANTA MARIA, Tomás de. *Libro llamado Arte de tañer fantasia . . .* 2 vols. Valladolid, 1565.

SIMPSON, Christopher, ed. *Division-Viol, or The Art of Playing Ex Tempore upon a Ground [1667]: Lithographic Facsimile of the Second Edition*. London, 1955.

SPECTOR, Stephen, ed. *The N-Town Play*. Early English Text Society, 2nd ser. II, 12. London, 1991.

STEVENS, Martin, and A. C. CAWLEY, eds. *The Towneley Plays*. Early English Text Society, 2nd ser. 13, 14. Oxford, 1994.

STEVENS, Denis, ed. *The Mulliner Book*. Musica Britannica, 1. London, 1973.

STOW, John. *The Annales of England*. London, [1592].

STRANGFORD, Percy Clinton Sydney Smythe, ed., *Household Expenses of the Princess Elizabeth during her Residence at Hatfield, October 1, 1551, to September 30, 1552*. Camden Society, 2. London, 1853.

THOMPSON, A. Hamilton, ed. *Visitations of Religious Houses in the Diocese of Lincoln*. 3 vols. The Publications of the Lincoln Record Society, 7, 14, and 21. Lincoln, 1914–29.

——. *Visitations in the Diocese of Lincoln, 1517–1531*. The Publications of the Lincoln Record Society, 35. Hereford, 1944.

TOLHURST, J. B. L., ed. *The Ordinale and Customary of the Benedictine Nuns of Barking Abbey (University College, Oxford, MS 169)*. Henry Bradshaw Society, 65–66. London, 1927.

Two Moral Interludes. Ed. Peter Happé. Malone Society Reprints. Oxford, 1991.

Christopher Tye, 1: English Sacred Music. Ed. John Morehen. Early English Church Music, 19. London, 1977.

Vetus Disciplina Monastica. Ed. Marquard Herrgott. Paris, 1726; repr. Siegburg, 1999.

VON DEN STEINEN, Wolfram. *Notker der Dichter und seine geistige Welt*. 2 vols. Bern, 1948.

The Vulgaria of John Stanbridge and the Vulgaria of Robert Whittinton. Ed. Beatrice White. Early English Text Society, o.s. 187. London, 1932.

WARD, G. R. M., trans. and ed. *The Foundation Statutes of Bishop Fox for Corpus Christi College, in the University of Oxford, A.D. 1517*. London, 1843.

WHYTHORNE, Thomas. *The Autobiography of Thomas Whythorne*. Ed. James M. Osborn. Oxford, 1961.

——. *Songes for fower voyces*. Ed. Robert McQuillan. Newton Abbot, 2004.

SECONDARY SOURCES

ADINOLFI, Pasquale. *Laterano e Via maggiore: Saggio della topografia di Roma nell'età di mezzo*. Rome, 1857.

AGEE, Richard J., ed. *Costanzo Festa: Counterpoints on a Cantus Firmus*. Recent Researches in the Music of the Renaissance, 107. Madison, 1997.

ALLEGRA, Antonio. "La cappella musicale di Santo Spirito in Saxia di Roma: Appunti storici (1551–1737)." *Note d'archivio per la storia musicale* 17 (1940), 26–38.

ANDRIEU, Michel. "La Carrière ecclésiastique des papes et les documents liturgiques du Moyen Âge," *Revue des sciences religieuses* 21 (1947), 90–120.

ARIÈS, Philippe. *Centuries of Childhood*. Trans. R. Baldick. New York, 1962.

ARKWRIGHT, G. E. P. "Elizabethan Choirboy Plays and their Music." *Proceedings of the Musical Association* 40 (1913/14), 117–38.

ARLT, Wulf. *Ein Festoffizium des Mittelalters aus Beauvais in seiner liturgischen und musikalischen Bedeutung*. 2 vols. Cologne, 1970.

——. "Das Eine und die vielen Lieder: Zur historischen Stellung der neuen Liedkunst des frühen 12. Jahrhunderts." In *Festschrift Rudolf Bockholdt zum 60. Geburtstag*, 113–27. Ed. Norbert Dubowy and Sören Meyer-Eller. Pfaffenhofen, 1990.

———. "Neues zum neuen Lied: Die Fragmente aus der Handschrift Douai 246." In *Sine musica nulla disciplina: Studi in onore di Giulio Cattin*, 89–110. Ed. F. Bernabei and A. Lovato. Padua, 2006.

ARMELLINI, Mariano. *Le chiese di Roma dal secolo IV al XIX*. Rev. ed. by Carlo Cecchelli. 2 vols. Rome, 1942.

ARNALDI, Girolamo. "Giovanni Immonide e la cultura a Roma al tempo di Giovanni VIII." *Bollettino dell'Istituto storico italiano per il Medioevo* 68 (1956), 33–89.

ASHBEE, Andrew. "Groomed for Service: Musicians in the Privy Chamber at the English Court, c. 1495–1558." *Early Music* 25 (1997), 185–97.

AUDA, Antoine. *La Musique et les musiciens de l'ancien pays de Liége*. Brussels, Paris, and Liége, 1930.

AUNGIER, George J. *The History and Antiquities of Syon Monastery, the Parish of Isleworth, and the Chapelry of Hounslow: Compiled from Public Records, Ancient Manuscripts, Ecclesiastical and Other Authentic Documents*. London, 1840.

AUSTERN, Linda Phyllis. *Music in English Children's Drama of the Later Renaissance*. Philadelphia, 1992.

AXTON, Richard. "Royal Throne, Royal Bed: John Heywood and Spectacle." *Medieval English Theatre* 16 (1994), 66–76.

BAADE, Colleen. "'Hired' Nun Musicians in Early Modern Castile." in *Musical Voices of Early Modern Women, Many-Headed Melodies*, 287–310. Ed. Thomasin LaMay. Aldershot, 2005.

BANG, W. "Acta Anglo-Lovaniensia: John Heywood und sein Kreis." *Englische Studien* 38 (1907), 234–50.

BECKER, Otto F. "The *Maître* in Northern France and Burgundy during the Fifteenth Century." Ph.D. diss., George Peabody College for Teachers, 1967.

BELL, David N. *What Nuns Read: Books and Libraries in Medieval English Nunneries*. Cistercian Studies Series, 158. Kalamazoo, Mich., 1995.

BENBOW, R. Mark. "Sixteenth-century Dramatic Performances for the London Livery Companies." *Notes and Queries* n.s. 29/2 (1982), 129–31.

BEREND, Nora. "La Subversion invisible: La Disparition de l'oblation irrévocable des enfants dans le droit canon." *Médiévales* 26 (1994), 123–36.

BERGER, Anna Maria Busse. *Medieval Music and the Art of Memory*. Berkeley, 2005.

BERGER, Karol. "The Guidonian Hand." In *The Medieval Craft of Memory: An Anthology of Texts and Pictures*, 71–82. Ed. Mary Carruthers and Jan M. Ziolkowski. Philadelphia, 2002.

BERTOLINI, Ottorino. "Per la storia delle diaconie romane nell'alto medioevo sino alla fine del secolo VIII." *Archivio della Società romana di storia patria* 70 (1947), 1–145. Repr. in *Scritti scelti di storia medievali*, 1:311–460. Ed. Ottavio Banti. 2 vols. Livorno, 1968.

BLOXAM, John Rouse. *A Register of the Presidents, Fellows, Demis . . . of Saint Mary Magdalen College in the University of Oxford*. 8 vols. Oxford, 1857.

BOITEUX, Martine. "Le feste: cultura del riso et della derisione." In *Roma medievale*, 293–96. Ed. André Vauchez. Storia di Roma dall'antichità a oggi, 2. Rome and Bari, 2001.

BORGERDING, Todd M. "Imagining the Sacred Body: Choirboys, Their Voices, and Corpus Christi in Early Modern Seville." In *Musical Childhoods and the Cultures of Youth*, 25–48. Ed. Susan Boynton and Roe-Min Kok. Middletown, Ct., 2006.

BOUCKAERT, Bruno, and Eugeen SCHREURS. "A New Fragment with 16th-Century Keyboard Music: An Unknown Composition by Thomas Whythorne (1528–1596) in a Manuscript from the Low Countries (Gent — Rijksuniversiteit MS G11655)." In *Music Fragments and Manuscripts in the Low Countries*, 121–28. Ed. Eugeen Schreurs and Henri Vanhulst. Yearbook of the Alamire Foundation, 2. Peer, 1997.

BOURDON, A., Chanoine, and l'Abbé A. COLLETTE, *Histoire de la maîtrise de Rouen*. Rouen, 1892; repr. Geneva, 1972.

BOWERS, Roger. "The Vocal Scoring, Choral Balance and Performing Pitch of Latin Church Polyphony in England, c.1500–58." *Journal of the Royal Musical Association* 112 (1987), 38–76.

——. "The Cultivation and Promotion of Music in the Household and Orbit of Thomas Wolsey." In *Cardinal Wolsey: Church, State and Art*, 178–218. Ed. Steven J. Gunn and Phillip G. Lindley. Cambridge, 1991.

——. "To Chorus from Quartet: The Performing Resource for English Church Polyphony, c. 1390–1559." In *English Choral Practice 1400–1650*, 1–47. Ed. John Morehen. Cambridge, 1996.

——. "The Almonry Schools of the English Monasteries, c. 1265–1540." In *Monasteries and Society in Medieval Britain: Proceedings of the 1994 Harlaxton Symposium*, 177–222. Ed. Benjamin Thompson. Harlaxton Medieval Studies, 6. Stamford, 1999.

BOYNTON, Susan. "The Liturgical Role of Children in Monastic Customaries from the Central Middle Ages." *Studia Liturgica* 28 (1998), 194–209.

——. "Performative Exegesis in the Fleury *Interfectio puerorum*." *Viator* 29 (1998), 39–64.

——. "The Sources and Significance of the Orpheus Myth in 'Musica Enchiriadis' and Regino of Prüm's 'Epistola de harmonica institutione.'" *Early Music History* 18 (1999), 47–74.

——. "Training for the Liturgy as a Form of Monastic Education." In *Medieval Monastic Education*, 7–20. Ed. George Ferzoco and Carolyn Muessig. London, 2000.

——. "Les Coutumes clunisiennes au temps d'Odilon." In *Odilon de Mercœur, l'Auvergne et Cluny: La "Paix de Dieu" et l'Europe de l'an mil; Actes du colloque de Lavoûte-Chilhac des 10, 11, et 12 Mai 2000*, 193–203. Nonette, 2002.

——. "Orality, Literacy, and the Early Notation of the Office Hymns." *Journal of the American Musicological Society* 56 (2003), 99–167.

BOYNTON, Susan, and Isabelle COCHELIN. "The Sociomusical Role of Child Oblates at the Abbey of Cluny in the Eleventh Century." In *Musical Childhoods and the Cultures of Youth*, 3–24. Ed. Susan Boynton and Roe-Min Kok. Middletown, Ct., 2006.

BROOKS, Lynn Matluck. "'Los Seises' in the Golden Age of Seville." *Dance Chronicle* 5 (1982), 121–55.

BROWN, J. Howard. *Elizabethan Schooldays: An Account of the English Grammar Schools in the Second Half of the Sixteenth Century*. Oxford, 1933.

BULLOUGH, Donald A. "A Court of Scholars and the Revival of Learning." In *The Age of Charlemagne*, 101–29. New York, 1966.

BURKE, John. *Musicians of S. Maria Maggiore, Rome, 1600–1700: A Social and Economic Study*. Supplement to *Note d'archivio* n.s. 2. Venice, 1984.

CALDWELL, John. "Keyboard Plainsong Settings in England, 1500–1660." *Musica Disciplina* 19 (1965), 129–53.

CAMETTI, Alberto. "La scuola dei *pueri cantores* a S. Luigi dei francesi in Roma e i suoi principali allievi (1591–1623)." *Rivista musicale italiana* 22 (1915), 593–641.

CANCELLIERI, Francesco. *Storia de' solenni possessi de' somme pontefici: Detti anticamente processi o processioni . . .* Rome, 1802.

CARRUTHERS, Mary. *The Book of Memory: A Study of Memory in Medieval Culture*. Cambridge Studies in Medieval Literature, 10. Cambridge, 1990.

CARRUTHERS, Mary, and Jan M. ZIOLKOWSKI, eds. *The Medieval Craft of Memory: An Anthology of Texts and Pictures*. Philadelphia, 2002.

CASIMIRI, Raffaele. *Giovanni Pierluigi da Palestrina: Nuovi documenti biografici*. Rome, 1922.

——. "'Disciplina musicae' e 'mastri di capella' dopo il Concilio di Trento nei maggiori istituti ecclesiastici di Roma: Seminario Romano — Collegio Germanico — Collegio Inglese (sec. XVI–XVII), VI. I: Il Seminario Romano." *Note d'archivio per la storia musicale* 12 (1935), 1–26.

——. "'Disciplina musicae' e 'mastri di capella' dopo il Concilio di Trento nei maggiori istituti ecclesiastici di Roma: Seminario Romano — Collegio Germanico — Collegio Inglese (sec. XVI–XVII), VI. II: Il Collegio Germanico." *Note d'archivio per la storia musicale* 16 (1939), 1–9.

——. "'Disciplina musicae' e 'mastri di capella' dopo il Concilio di Trento nei maggiori istituti ecclesiastici di Roma: Seminario Romano — Collegio Germanico — Collegio Inglese (sec. XVI–XVII), X: Liturgia e musica in S. Apollinare." *Note d'archivio per la storia musicale* 19 (1942), 159–68.

CASIMIRI, Raffaele, and Laura CALLEGARI, eds. *Cantori, maestri, organisti della Cappella lateranense negli atti capitolari (sec. XV–XVII)*. Biblioteca di Quadrivium, 6. Bologna, 1984.

CASOLARI, Silvia. "Allegorie nella Rappresentatione di Anima et di Corpo (1600): Testo e imagine." *Rivista italiana di musicologia* 33 (1998), 7–31.

CATTIN, Giulio. "Church Patronage of Music in Fifteenth-Century Italy." In *Music in Medieval and Early Modern Europe: Patronage, Sources and Texts*, 21–36. Ed. Iain Fenlon. Cambridge, 1981.

CHAMBERS, E. K. *The Medieval Stage*. 2 vols. Oxford, 1903.

CHARTIER, F. L. *L'Ancien Chapitre de Notre-Dame de Paris et sa maîtrise*. Paris, 1897; repr. Geneva, 1971.

CLANCHY, Michael. *From Memory to Written Record: England, 1066–1307*. 2nd ed. Cambridge, Mass., 1993.

CLAPTON, Nicholas. *Moreschi: The Last Castrato*. London, 2004.

CLERVAL, J.-A. *L'Ancienne Maîtrise de Nôtre-Dame de Chartres*. Paris, 1899; repr. Geneva, 1972.

COCHELIN, Isabelle. "Besides the Book: Using the Body to Mould the Mind — Cluny in the Tenth and Eleventh Centuries." In *Medieval Monastic Education*, 21–34. Ed. George Ferzoco and Carolyn Muessig. London and New York, 2000.

——. "Étude sur les hiérarchies monastiques: Le Prestige de l'ancienneté et son éclipse à Cluny au XIᵉ siècle." *Revue Mabillon* n.s. 11 (2000), 5–37.

——. "Evolution des coutumiers monastiques dessinée à partir de l'étude de Bernard." In *From Dead of Night to End of Day: The Medieval Customs of Cluny*, 29–66. Ed. Susan Boynton and Isabelle Cochelin. Turnhout, 2005.

COLLETTE, Armand. *Histoire de la maîtrise di Rouen*, part I: *Des origines jusqu'à la Révolution française*. Rouen, 1875.

COSTA Y BELDA, Enrique. "Las constituciones de Don Raimundo de Losaña para el cabildo de Sevilla (1261)." *Historia, instituciones, documentos* 5 (1978), 169–235.

CULLEY, Thomas. "The Influence of the German College in Rome on Music in German-Speaking Countries during the Sixteenth and Seventeenth Centuries (I)." *Analecta musicologica* 7 (1969), 1–35.

——. "The Influence of the German College in Rome on Music in German-Speaking Countries during the Sixteenth and Seventeenth Centuries (II)." *Analecta musicologica* 9 (1970), 20–63.

CULLEY, Thomas. *Jesuits and Music: A Study of Musicians Connected with the German College in Rome during the 17th Century and of Their Activities in Northern Europe.* Sources and Studies for the History of the Jesuits, 2. Rome, 1970.

——. "Musical Activity in Some Sixteenth-Century Jesuit Colleges, with Special Reference to the Venerable English College in Rome from 1579 to 1589." *Analecta musicologica* 19 (1979), 1–29.

CUNNINGHAM, Hugh. "Histories of Childhood." *American Historical Review* 103 (1998), 1195–1208.

D'ANCONA, Alessandro. *Origine del teatro in Italia.* 2 vols. Florence, 1877.

D'ANCONA, Alessandro, ed. *Sacre rappresentazioni dei secoli XIV, XV, e XVI.* 3 vols. Florence, 1872.

DE JONG, Mayke. "Growing up in a Carolingian Monastery: Magister Hildemar and His Oblates." *Journal of Medieval History* 9 (1983): 99–128.

——. "Carolingian Monasticism: The Power of Prayer." In *The New Cambridge Medieval History*, vol. 2: *c.700–c.900*, 622–53. Ed. Rosamond McKitterick. Cambridge, 1995.

——. *In Samuel's Image: Child Oblation in the Early Medieval West.* Leiden, 1996.

DELLA LIBERA, Luca. "L'attività musicale nella Basilica di S. Lorenzo in Damaso nel Cinquecento." *Rivista italiana di musicologia* 32 (1997), 25–59.

DEVEREUX, E. J. *A Bibliography of John Rastell.* Montreal, 1999.

DIXON, Graham. "The Cappella of S. Maria in Trastevere (1605–45): An Archival Study." *Music and Letters* 62 (1981), 30–40.

DOBSON, E. J. "The Etymology and Meaning of 'Boy.'" *Medium Aevum* 9 (1940), 121–54.

DOBSZAY, László. "*Pueri vociferati*: Children in Eger Cathedral." In *International Musicological Society Study Group Cantus Planus: Papers Read at the 6th Meeting, Eger, Hungary, 1993*, 1:93–100. Budapest, 1995.

DONNO, Elizabeth Story. "Thomas More and Richard III." *Renaissance Quarterly* 35 (1982), 401–47.

DOMPNIER, Bernard, ed. *Maîtrises et chapelles aux XVIIᵉ et XVIIIᵉ siècles: Des institutions musicales au service de Dieu.* Clermont-Ferrand, 2003.

DORAN, John. "Oblation or Obligation? A Canonical Ambiguity." In *The Church and Childhood: Papers Read at the 1993 Summer Meeting and the 1994 Winter Meeting of the Ecclesiastical History Society*, 127–41. Ed. Diana Wood. Oxford, 1994.

DORRELL, Margaret. "Two Studies in the York Corpus Christi Play." *Leeds Studies in English* n.s. 6 (1972), 63–111.

DUCROT, Ariane. "Histoire de la Cappella Giulia au XVIᵉ siècle." *Mélanges d'archéologie et d'histoire* 75 (1963), 179–240, 467–559.

DYER, Joseph. "The Schola Cantorum and Its Roman Milieu in the Early Middle Ages." In *De Musica et Cantu: Studien zur Geschichte der Kirchenmusik und der Oper; Helmut Hucke zum 60. Geburtstag*, 19–40. Ed. Peter Cahn and Ann-Katrin Heimer. Musikwissenschaftliche Publikationen, Hochschule für Musik und Darstellende Kunst, 2. Hildesheim, 1993.

——. "Schola cantorum." In *Die Musik in Geschichte und Gegenwart*, Sachteil 8:1119–23. 2nd ed.

EDWARDS, A. S. G. "Surrey's Martial Epigram: Scribes and Transmission." In *Scribes and Transmission in English Manuscripts 1400–1700*, 74–82. Ed. Peter Beal and A. S. G. Edwards. British Library English Manuscript Studies, 1100–1700, 12. London, 2005.

E[DWARDS], F. G. "A Famous Choir School: St. George's Chapel, Windsor." *Musical Times* 44 (1903), 166–69.

EDWARDS, Kathleen. *The English Secular Cathedrals in the Middle Ages.* 2nd ed. Manchester, 1967.

EKONOMOU, Andrew J. *Byzantine Rome and the Greek Popes: Eastern Influences on Rome and the Papacy from Gregory the Great to Zacharias, A.D. 590–752.* Lanham, Md., 2007.

ELDERS, Willem. *Composers of the Low Countries.* Trans. Graham Dixon. Oxford, 1991.

ELLINWOOD, Leonard. "Tallis' Tunes and Tudor Psalmody." *Musica Disciplina* 2 (1948), 189–203.

ESCUDIER, Denis. "Des enfants 'bien appris': L'Enseignement de la grammaire et du chant aux enfants de chœur de la Sainte-Chapelle de Paris d'apres un règlement du XIVᵉ siècle." In *La Tradition vive: Mélanges d'histoires des textes en l'honneur de Louis Holtz,* 223–33. Ed. Pierre Lardet. Paris and Turnhout, 2003.

FAIVRE, Alexandre. *Naissance d'une hiérarchie: Les Premières Étapes du cursus clérical.* Théologie historique, 40. Paris, 1977.

FALKENSTEIN, Ludwig. *Karl der Große und die Entstehung des Aachener Marienstiftes.* Paderborn, 1981.

FASSLER, Margot. "The Office of the Cantor in Early Western Monastic Rules and Customaries: A Preliminary Investigation." *Early Music History* 5 (1985), 29–51.

———. "The Feast of Fools and *Danielis ludus*: Popular Tradition in a Medieval Cathedral Play." In *Plainsong in the Age of Polyphony,* 65–95. Ed. Thomas Forrest Kelly. Cambridge, 1992.

———. "Composer and Dramatist." In *Voice of the Living Light: Hildegard of Bingen and Her World,* 149–75. Ed. Barbara Newman. Berkeley, 1998.

FLECKENSTEIN, Josef. *Die Hofkapelle der deutschen Könige,* Teil 1: *Grundlegung: Die karolingische Hofkapelle.* MGH Schriften, 16. Stuttgart, 1959.

FLOOD, W. H. Grattan. "New Light on Early Tudor Composers, XIII: Thomas Farthing." *Musical Times* 61 (1920), 814.

———. "New Light on Early Tudor Composers, XIV: Richard Bramston." *Musical Times* 62 (1921), 17–18.

FLYNN, Jane. "A Reconsideration of the Mulliner Book (British Library Add. MS 30513): Music Education in Sixteenth-Century England." Ph.D. diss., Duke University, 1993.

———. "The Education of Choristers in England during the Sixteenth Century." In *English Choral Practice, c.1400–c.1650,* 180–99. Ed. John Morehen. Cambridge Studies in Performance Practice, 5. Cambridge, 1995.

FOREST, Jean Marie H. *L'École cathédrale de Lyon.* Paris, 1885.

FREY, Herman-Walther. "Die Kapellmeister an der französischen Nationalkirche San Luigi dei Francesi in Rom im 16 Jahrhundert (1)." *Archiv für Musikwissenschaft* 22 (1965), 272–93; 23 (1966), 32–60.

GAIR, Reavley. "The Conditions of Appointment for Masters of Choristers at Paul's (1553–1613)." *Notes and Queries* n.s. 27/2 (1980), 116–24.

GAMBASSI, Osvaldo. *"Pueri cantores" nelle cattedrali d'Italia tra medioevo e età moderna: Le scuole Eugeniane; Scuole di canto annesse alle cappelle musicali.* Florence, 1997.

GARDEN, Greer. "François Roussel: A Northern Musician in Sixteenth-Century Rome." *Musica Disciplina* 31 (1977), 107–33.

GASPARI, Gaetano. *Catalogo della Biblioteca musicale G. B. Martini di Bologna.* 5 vols. 1905; repr. Bologna, 1961.

GERBINO, Giuseppe. "The Quest for the Soprano Voice: Castrati in Sixteenth-Century Italy." *Studi musicali* 32 (2004), 303–57.

GESTOSO Y PÉREZ, José. *Curiosidades Antiguas Sevillanas: serie II.* Seville, 1910; repr. 1993.

GIAZOTTO, Remo. *Quattro secoli di storia dell'Accademia Nazionale di Santa Cecilia.* Rome, 1970.

GIL, Carlos Martínez. *La capilla de música de la Catedral de Toledo (1700–1764): Evolución de un concepto sonoro.* Toledo, 2003.

GIL, Marc, and Ludovic NYS. *Saint-Omer gothique.* Valenciennes, 2004.

GILLET, Lev. "Deacons in the Orthodox East." *Theology* 58 (1955), 415–21.

GONZÁLEZ BARRIONUEVO, Herminio. *Los seises de Sevilla.* Seville, 1992.

———. *Francisco Guerrero (1528–1599): Vida y obra; La música en la catedral de Sevilla a finales del siglo XVI.* Seville, 2000.

GREATREX, Joan. "The Almonry School of Norwich Cathedral Priory in the Thirteenth and Fourteenth Centuries." In *The Church and Childhood: Papers Read at the 1993 Summer Meeting and the 1994 Winter Meeting of the Ecclesiastical History Society,* 169–81. Ed. Diana Wood. Oxford, 1994.

GRIER, James. "A New Voice in the Monastery: Tropes and Versus from Eleventh- and Twelfth-Century Aquitaine." *Speculum* 69 (1994), 1023–69.

GUIDOBALDI, Federico. "Struttura e chronologia delle recinzioni liturgiche nelle chiese di Roma dal VI al IX secolo." In *Mededelingen van het Nederlands Instituut te Rome* 59 (2000), 81–99.

HAGGH, Barbara. "Music, Liturgy, and Ceremony in Brussels, 1350–1500." Ph.D. diss., University of Illinois at Urbana-Champaign, 1988.

HANAWALT, Barbara. "Medievalists and the Study of Childhood." *Speculum* 77 (2002), 440–60.

HARLEY, John. "Merchants and Privateers: A Window on the World of William Byrd." *Musical Times* 147 (2006), 51–66.

HAWKINS, John. *A General History of the Science and Practice of Music.* New ed. 3 vols. London, 1876.

HAY, Denys. *The Church in Italy in the Fifteenth Century.* Cambridge, 1977.

HERKLOTZ, Ingo. "Der Campus Lateranus im Mittelalter." *Römisches Jahrbuch für Kunstgeschichte* 22 (1985), 1–43.

HERMES, Raimund. "Die stadtrömischen Diakonien." *Römische Quartalschrift für Antike und Christentum* 91 (1996), 1–120.

HIGGINS, Paula. "Musical Politics in Late Medieval Poitiers: A Tale of Two Choirmasters." In *Antoine Busnoys: Method, Meaning, and Context in Late Medieval Music,* 155–74. Ed. Paula Higgins. Oxford, 1999.

HILEY, David. *Western Plainchant: A Handbook.* Oxford, 1993.

HILLEBRAND, Harold Newcomb. *The Child Actors: A Chapter in Elizabethan Stage History.* University of Illinois Studies in Language and Literature, 11/1–2. Urbana, 1926.

HOENEN, Maarten J. F. M. "Late Medieval Schools of Thought in the Mirror of University Textbooks." In *Philosophy and Learning: Universities in the Middle Ages,* 329–69. Ed. Maarten J. F. M. Hoenen, J. H. Josef Schneider, and Georg Wieland. Education and Society in the Middle Ages and Renaissance, 6. Leiden, 1995.

HOLMAN, Peter. "'Evenly, softly, and sweetly acchording to all': The Organ Accompaniment of English Consort Music." In *John Jenkins and his Time: Studies in English Consort Music,* 353–82. Ed. Andrew Ashbee and Peter Holman. Oxford, 1996.

HOLSTUN, James. "The Spider, the Fly, and the Commonwealth: Merrie John Heywood and Agrarian Class Struggle." *English Literary History* 71 (2004), 53–88.

HÖRLE, Georg H. *Frühmittelalterliche Mönchs- und Klerikerbildung in Italien.* Freiburger theologische Studien, 13. Freiburg im Breisgau, 1914.

HUGLO, Michel. "Les Débuts de la polyphonie à Paris: Les Premiers Organa parisiens."

Aktuelle Fragen der musikbezogenen Mittelalterforschung = Forum musicologicum 3 (1982), 93–164.

HULSE, Lynne. "The Musical Patronage of Robert Cecil, First Earl of Salisbury (1563–1612)." *Journal of the Royal Musical Association* 116 (1991), 24–40.

ILARI, Lorenzo. *La Biblioteca pubblica di Siena diposta secondo le materie: Catalogo.* 7 vols. Siena, 1844–48.

JOHNSON, Martin H., and Barry J. EVERITT. *Essential Reproduction.* Oxford, 1980.

JOHNSON, R. W. "Noah at Hull." *The Dalesman* (1963), 105–7.

JOHNSTON, Alexandra F., and Margaret DORRELL. "The York Mercers and their Pageant of Doomsday, 1433–1526." *Leeds Studies in English* n.s. 6 (1972), 11–35.

JOINER, Mary. "British Museum Add. MS 15117: A Commentary, Index and Bibliography." *Royal Musical Association Research Chronicle* 7 (1969), 51–109.

JOSI, Enrico. "Lectores — schola cantorum — clerici." *Ephemerides liturgicae* 44 (1930), 282–90.

KAWACHI, Yoshiko. *Calendar of English Renaissance Drama, 1558–1642.* Garland Reference Library of the Humanities, 661. New York, 1986.

KELLY, Thomas Forrest. "Melisma and Prosula: The Performance of Responsory Tropes." In *Liturgische Tropen: Referate zweier Colloquien des Corpus Troporum in München (1983) und Canterbury (1984),* 163–80. Ed. Gabriel Silagi. Münchener Beiträge zur Mediävistik und Renaissance-Forschung, 36. Munich, 1985.

KENDRICK, Robert L. *Celestial Sirens: Nuns and their Music in Early Modern Milan.* Oxford, 1996.

——. "Devotion, Piety and Commemoration: Sacred Songs and Oratorios." In *The Cambridge History of Seventeenth-Century Music,* 324–77. Ed. Tim Carter and John Butt. Cambridge, 2005.

KIENZLE, Beverly Mayne. "Hildegard of Bingen's Teaching in her *Expositiones evangeliorum* and *Ordo virtutum.*" In *Medieval Monastic Education,* 72–86. Ed. George Ferzoco and Carolyn Muessig. London, 2000.

KING, A. Hyatt. "The Significance of John Rastell in Early Music Printing." *The Library* 5th ser. 26 (1971), 197–214.

KNIGHTS, Francis. "Thomas Mulliner's Oxford Career." *The Organ* 297 (1996), 132–35.

LAPORTE, M. A. "Le Souper de Jean Diacre." *Mélanges d'archéologie et d'histoire* 21 (1901), 305–87.

LAUNAY, Denise. "L'Enseignement de la composition dans les maîtrises, en France, aux XVIᵉ et XVIIᵉ siècles." *Revue de musicologie* 68 (1982), 79–90.

LECLERCQ, Henri. "Diacre." In *Dictionnaire d'archéologie chrétienne et de liturgie,* 8/2:2249–66.

LEONARDI, Claudio. "La 'Vita Gregorii' di Giovanni diacono." In *Roma e l'età carolingia: Atti delle giornate di studio, Roma 3–8 maggio 1976,* 381–93. Rome, 1976.

LIONNET, Jean. *La Musique à Saint-Louis des Français de Rome au XVIIᵉ siècle.* Venice, 1985–86.

——. "La Musique à Sancta Maria della Consolazione de Rome au 17ᵉᵐᵉ siècle." *Note d'archivio* n.s. 4 (1986), 153–202.

——. "La Musique à San Giacomo degli Spagnoli au XVIIᵉᵐᵉ siècle et les archives de la Congrégation des Espagnols de Rome." In *La musica a Roma attraverso le fonti d'archivio: Atti del convegno internazionale, Roma, 4–7 giugno 1992,* 479–505. Ed. Bianca Maria Antolini, Arnaldo Morelli, and Vera Vita Spagnuolo. Strumenti della ricerca musicale, 2. Lucca, 1994.

LLEÓ CAÑAL, Vicente. *Arte y espectáculo: La fiesta del Corpus Christi en la Sevilla de los siglos XVI y XVII*. Publicaciones de la Excma. Diputación Provincial de Sevilla, Sección historia, ser. 1a no. 9. Seville, 1975.

LOMBARDI, Ferruccio. *Roma — Le chiese scomparse: La memoria storica della città*. Rome, 1996.

LOUPÈS, Philippe. *Chapitres et chanoines de Guyenne aux XVIIe et XVIIIe siècles*. Civilisations et sociétés, 70. Paris, 1985.

LUMIANSKY, R. M., and David MILLS. *The Chester Mystery Cycle: Essays and Documents, with an Essay, "Music in the Cycle," by Richard Rastall*. Chapel Hill, N.C., 1983.

LUMIANSKY, R. M., and David MILLS, eds. *The Chester Mystery Cycle*. Early English Text Society, 2nd ser. 3, 9. Oxford, 1974, 1986.

LUO, Michael. "Memorizing the Way to Heaven, Verse by Verse." *The New York Times*, national edition (Wed., Aug. 16, 2006), A18.

McCLENDON, Charles B. *The Origins of Medieval Architecture*. London, 2005.

MACEY, Patrick. "*Infiamma il mio cor*: Savonarolan *Laude* by and for Dominican Nuns in Tuscany." In *The Crannied Wall: Women, Religion, and the Arts in Early Modern Europe*, 161–89. Ed. Craig A. Monson. Ann Arbor, Mich., 1992.

McGRADE, Michael. "Affirmations of Royalty: Liturgical Music in the Collegiate Church of Saint Mary in Aachen, 1050–1350." Ph.D. diss., University of Chicago, 1998.

McKITTERICK, Rosamond. *The Frankish Church and the Carolingian Reforms, 789–895*. London, 1977.

MAIER, Michael. "Paraphonos, paraphonia." In *Handbuch der musikalischen Terminologie*, Auslieferung 34 (2003), 6–7.

MARIX, Jeanne. *Histoire de la musique et des musiciens de la cour de Bourgogne sous le règne de Philippe le Bon*. Strasbourg, 1939; repr. Baden-Baden, 1974.

MARSHALL, John. "The Chester Whitsun Plays: Dating of Post-Reformation Performances from the Smiths' Accounts." *Leeds Studies in English* n.s. 9 (1977), 51–61.

MARTÍN ABAD, Julián. *Post-incunables ibéricos*. Madrid, 2001.

MARTYN, John R. C. "Gregory the Great: On Organ Lessons [and on Equipping Monasteries]," *Medievalia et Humanistica* n.s. 30 (2004), 107–13.

MASETTI ZANNINI, Gian Ludovico. *Motivi storici della educazione femminile*, vol. 2: *Scienza, lavoro, giuochi*. Naples, 1982.

———. "'Suavità di canto' e 'purità di cuore': Aspetti della musica nei monasteri femminili romani." In *La cappella musicale nell'Italia della Controriforma: Atti del Convegno internazionale di studi nel IV Centenario di fondazione della Cappella Musicale di S. Biagio di Cento, 13–15 ottobre 1989*, 123–41. Ed. Oscar Mischiati and Paolo Russo. Florence, 1993.

MASSIP I BONET, Francesc. "Cerimònia litúrgica i artifici teatral en el jorn de Pentecosta (segles XIII–XVI)." In *Actes del Congrés de la Seu Vella de Lleida*, 257–63. Lleida, 1991.

MATEER, David. "The 'Gyffard' Partbooks: Composers, Owners, Date and Provenance." *Royal Musical Association Research Chronicle* 28 (1995), 21–50.

MEREDITH, Peter. "John Clerke's Hand in the York Register." *Leeds Studies in English* n.s. 12 (1981), 245–71.

MILANESE, Guido. "*Paraphonia–paraphonista*: Dalla lessicografia greca alla tarda antichità romana." In *Curiositas: Studi di cultura classica e medievale in onore di Ubaldo Pizzani*, 407–21. Ed. Antonino Isoala et al. Naples, 2002.

MILL, Anna J. "The Hull Noah Play." *Modern Language Review* 33 (Oct. 1938), 489–505.

MILLER, Timothy. "The Orphanotropheion of Constantinople." In *Through the Eye of a Needle: Judeo-Christian Roots of Social Welfare*, 83–104. Ed. Emily Albu Hanawalt and Carter Lindberg. Kirksville, Mo., 1994.

——. *The Orphans of Byzantium: Child Welfare in the Christian Empire*. Washington, D.C., 2003.

MILSOM, John. "Songs and Society in Early Tudor London." *Early Music History* 16 (1997), 235–93.

MINKENBERG, Georg. "Der Barbarossaleuchter im Dom zu Aachen." *Zeitschrift des Aachener Geschichtsvereins* 96 (1989), 69–102.

MONACI, Ernesto. "Per la storia della Schola cantorum Lateranense." *Archivio della Reale Società Romana di Storia Patria* 20 (1897), 451–63.

MONSON, Craig A. *Disembodied Voices: Music and Culture in an Early Modern Italian Convent*. Berkeley, 1995.

MONTFORD, Kimberlyn. "Music in the Convents of Counter-Reformation Rome." Ph.D. diss., Rutgers University, 1999.

MORELLI, Arnaldo. "Antimo Liberato, Matteo Simonelli e la tradizione palestriniana a Roma nella seconda metà del seicento." In *Palestrina e la sua presenza nella musica e nella cultura europa dal suo tempo ad oggi: Atti del II Convegno Internazionale di Studi Palestriniani, 3–5 Maggio 1986*, 295–307. Ed. Lino Bianchi and Giancarlo Rostirolla. Palestrina, 1991.

——. *Il tempio armonico: Musica nell'Oratorio dei Filippini in Roma (1575–1705)* = *Analecta musicologica* 27 (1991).

——. "Filippo Nicoletti (ca. 1555–1634) compositore ferrarese: Profilo biografico alla luce di nuovi documenti." In *Musica Franca: Essays in honor of Frank A. D'Accone*, 139–50. Ed. Irene Alm, Alyson McLamore, and Colleen Reardon, Festschrift Series, 18. New York, 1996.

MORROCCHI, Rinaldo. *La musica in Siena*. Siena, 1886.

MUESSIG, Carolyn. "Learning and Mentoring in the Twelfth Century: Hildegard of Bingen and Herrad of Landsberg." In *Medieval Monastic Education*, 87–104. Ed. George Ferzoco and Carolyn Muessig. London, 2000.

NOBLE, Jeremy. "New Light on Josquin's Benefices." In *Josquin des Prez: Proceedings of the International Josquin Festival-Conference*, 76–102. Ed. Edward E. Lowinsky and Bonnie J. Blackburn. Oxford, 1976.

OFFERGELD, Peter. "Die persönliche Zusammensetzung des alter Aachener Stiftskapitels bis 1614." Ph.D. diss., Rheinisch-Westfälische technische Hochschule Aachen, 1972.

OGDEN, Dunbar H. *The Staging of Drama in the Medieval Church*. Newark, N.J., and London, 2002.

O'REGAN, Noel. "Music at the Roman Archconfraternity of San Rocco in the Late Sixteenth Century." In *La musica a Roma attraverso le fonti d'archivio: Atti del convegno internazionale, Roma, 4–7 giugno 1992*, 521–52. Ed. Bianca Maria Antolini, Arnaldo Morelli, and Vera Vita Spagnuolo. Strumenti della ricerca musicale, 2. Lucca, 1994.

——. *Institutional Patronage in Post-Tridentine Rome: Music at Santissima Trinità dei Pellegrini, 1550–1650*. RMA Monographs, 7. London, 1995.

——. "Tomás Luis de Victoria's Roman Churches Revisited." *Early Music* 28 (2000), 403–18.

ORME, Nicholas. *English Schools in the Middle Ages*. London, 1973.

——. "Education and Learning at a Medieval English Cathedral: Exeter, 1380–1548." *Journal of Ecclesiastical History* 32 (1981), 265–83.

——. "The Medieval Clergy of Exeter Cathedral, II: The Secondaries and Choristers." *Reports and Transactions of the Devonshire Association* 115 (1983), 79–100.

ORME, Nicholas. *Medieval Children*. New Haven and London, 2002.

———. *Medieval Schools: From Roman Britain to Renaissance England*. New Haven and London, 2006.

ØSTREM, Eyolf, and Nils Holger PETERSEN. *Medieval Ritual and Early Modern Music: The Devotional Practice of Lauda singing in Late-Renaissance Italy*. Turnhout, 2008.

OUVRARD, Jean-Pierre. *Josquin Desprez et ses contemporains, de l'écrit au sonore*. Arles, 1986.

PAGE, Daniel Bennett. "Uniform and Catholic: Church Music in the Reign of Mary Tudor (1553–1558)." Ph.D. diss., Brandeis University, 1996.

PAGE, William, ed. *The Victoria History of the County of Lincoln*, vol. 2. London, 1906.

PATALA, Zoï. "Les Chants grecs du Liber politicus du chanoine Benoît." *Byzantion* 66 (1996), 512–30.

PECCHIAI, Pio. *Roma nel Cinquecento*. Storia di Roma, 13. Bologna, 1948.

PIETZSCH, Gerhard. *Die Musik im Erziehungs- und Bildungsideal des ausgehenden Altertums und frühen Mittelalters*. Studien zur Geschichte der Musiktheorie im Mittelalter, 2. Halle an der Saale, 1932; repr. 1969.

POWER, Eileen. *Medieval English Nunneries, c.1275 to 1535*. Cambridge, 1922.

QUIX, Christian. *Geschichte der Stadt Aachen, nach Quellen . . . mit einem Codex diplomaticus aquensis*. 2 vols. Aachen, 1840.

RAELI, Vito. *Nel secolo di G. P. da Palestrina nella Cappella Liberiana*. Rome, 1920.

RAINE, James, ed. "The Statutes Ordained by Richard Duke of Gloucester for the College of Middleham, dated July 4, 18 Edw. IV. [1478]." *Archaeological Journal* 14 (1857), 160–70.

RASTALL, Richard. "Vocal Range and Tessitura in Music from York Play 45." *Music Analysis* 3/2 (1984), 181–99.

———. "Female Roles in All-Male Casts." *Medieval English Theatre* 7/1 (1985), 25–51.

———. "The Musical Repertory." In *The Iconography of Heaven*, 162–96. Ed. Clifford Davidson. Early Drama, Art, and Music Monograph Series, 21. Kalamazoo, Mich., 1994.

———. *Music in Early English Religious Drama*, vol. 1: *The Heaven Singing*. Cambridge, 1997.

———. *Music in Early English Religious Drama*, vol. 2: *Minstrels Playing*. Cambridge, 2001.

———. "Young Wives Played by Males: The Case of Percula in York Play 30." In *Mainte belle œuvre faicte; Études sur le théâtre médiéval offertes à Graham A. Runnalls*, 433–37. Ed. Denis Hue, Mario Longtin, and Lynette Muir. Orléans, 2005.

REARDON, Colleen. *Agostino Agazzari and Music at Siena Cathedral, 1597–1641*. Oxford, 1993.

———. *Holy Concord within Sacred Walls: Nuns and Music in Siena, 1575–1700*. Oxford, 2002.

———. "The Good Mother, the Reluctant Daughter, and the Convent: A Case of Musical Persuasion." In *Musical Voices of Early Modern Women, Many-Headed Melodies*, 271–86. Ed. Thomasin LaMay. Aldershot, 2005.

REED, A. W. *Early Tudor Drama: Medwall, the Rastells, Heywood, and the More Circle*. London, 1926.

———. "John Clement and his Books." *The Library* 4th ser. 6 (1926), 329–39.

REYNAUD, François. *Les Enfants de chœur de Tolède à la Renaissance*. Turnhout, 2002.

REYNOLDS, Christopher A. "Rome: A City of Rich Contrast." In *The Renaissance: From the 1470s to the End of the Sixteenth Century*, 63–101. Ed. Iain Fenlon. Music and Society. London, 1989.

———. *Papal Patronage and the Music of St. Peter's, 1380–1513*. Berkeley, 1995.

RICE, Eric. "Two Liturgical Responses to the Protestant Reformation at the Collegiate Church of Saint Mary in Aachen, 1570–1580." *Viator* 38/2 (2007), 291–318.

——. *Music and Ritual at Charlemagne's Marienkirche in Aachen*. Beiträge zur Rheinischen Musikgeschichte. Kassel, 2008.

ROBERTSON, Anne Walters. "Benedicamus Domino: The Unwritten Tradition." *Journal of the American Musicological Society* 41 (1988), 1–60.

——. "Remembering the Annunciation in Medieval Polyphony." *Speculum* 70 (1995), 275–304.

ROSA Y LÓPEZ, Simón de la. *Los seises de la catedral de Sevilla: Ensayo de investigación histórica*. Seville, 1904; repr. 1982.

ROSSELLI, John. "L'apprendistato del cantante italiano: Rapporti contrattuali fra allievi e insegnanti dal Cinquecento al Novecento." *Rivista italiana di musicologia* 23 (1988), 157–81.

ROSTIROLLA, Giancarlo. "La Cappella Giulia in San Pietro negli anni palestriniani." In *Atti del Convegno di studi Palestriniani, 28 settembre – 2 ottobre 1975*, 99–283. Ed. Francesco Luisi. Palestrina, 1977.

——. "Vita di Francesco Foggia musicista romano basata sui documenti superstiti." In *Francesco Foggia, "fenice de'musicali compositori" nel florido Seicento romano e nella storia: Atti del primo convegno internazionale di studi nel terzo centenario della morte (Palestrina e Roma, 7–8 ottobre 1988)*, 25–90. Ed. Ala Botti Caselli. Palestrina, 1988.

——. "La bolla 'De communi omnium' di Gregorio XIII per la restaurazione della Cappella Giulia." In *La cappella musicale nell'Italia della controriforma: Atti del Convegno internazionale di studi nel IV Centenario di fondazione della Cappella Musicale di S. Biagio di Cento, Cento, 13–15 ottobre 1989*, 39–65. Ed. Oscar Mischiati and Paolo Russo. Quaderni della Rivista italiana di musicologia, 27. Florence, 1993.

——. "Laudi e canti religiosi per l'esercizio spirituale della Dottrina cristiana al tempo di Robert Bellarmino." In *La lauda spirituale tra cinque e seicento: Poesie e canti devozionali nell'italia della controriforma*, 275–472. Ed. Giuseppe Filippi et al. Rome, 2001.

——. "L'archivio musicale della chiesa annessa all'Ospedale di Santo Spirito." In *Atti del Convegno: L'antico ospedale di Santo Spirito dall'istituzione papale alla sanità del terzo millennio, Roma 15–17 Maggio 2001 = Il veltro: Rivista della civiltà italiana* 46 (2002), 279–343.

ROTHENBERG, David J. "The Marian Symbolism of Spring, ca. 1200 – ca. 1500: Two Case Studies." *Journal of the American Musicological Society* 59 (2006), 319–98.

ROYER, Louis. "Les Musiciens et la musique à l'ancienne collégiale Saint-André." *Humanisme et Renaissance* 4 (1937), 237–73.

RUIZ JIMÉNEZ, Juan. *La Librería de Canto de Órgano: Creación y pervivencia del repertorio del Renacimiento en la actividad musical de la catedral de Sevilla*. Granada, 2007.

——. "Los sonidos de la montaña hueca: Innovación y tradición en las capillas musicales eclesiásticas de la corona de Castilla durante los albores del Renacimiento; El paradigma sevillano." In *La música en tiempos de Isabel la Católica*. Ed. Soterraña Aguirre Rincón. Valladolid, forthcoming.

SABOL, Andrew J. "A Three-Man Song in Fulwell's *Like Will to Like* at the Folger." *Renaissance News* 10 (1957) 139–42.

——. "Two Songs with Accompaniment for an Elizabethan Choirboy Play." *Studies in the Renaissance* 5 (1958) 145–59.

SALMON, Pierre. "La 'Ferula': Bâton pastoral de l'évêque de Rome." *Revue des sciences religieuses* 30 (1956), 313–27.

SÁNCHEZ-ARJONA, José. *Noticias referentes a los Anales del Teatro en Sevilla desde Lope de Rueda hasta fines del siglo XVII*. Seville, 1898; repr. 1994.

SÁNCHEZ HERRERO, José. "Centros de enseñanza y estudiantes de Sevilla durante los siglos XIII al XV." *En la España medieval* 5 (1984), 875–98.

SANSTERRE, Jean-Marie. *Les Moines grecs et orientaux à Rome aux époques byzantine et carolingienne (milieu du VIe s. – fin du IXe s.)*. 2 vols. Académie Royale de Belgique: Mémoires de la Classe des Lettres, 2nd ser. 66/1. Brussels, 1983.

SANZ SERRANO, María Jesús. "El Corpus en Sevilla a mediados del siglo XVI: Castillos y danzas." *Laboratorio de arte* 10 (1997), 123–38.

SAXER, Victor. "Recinzioni liturgiche secondo le fonti letterarie." *Mededelingen van het Nederlands Instituut te Rome* 59 (2000), 71–79.

SAYLE, Robert T. D. *Lord Mayors' Pageants of the Merchant Taylors' Company in the 15th, 16th & 17th Centuries*. London, 1931.

SCHIEFFER, Rudolf. "Hofkapelle und Aachener Marienstift bis in die staufische Zeit." *Rheinische Vierteljahrsblätter* 51 (1987), 16–20.

SCHIMMELPFENNIG, Bernhard. "Die Bedeutung Roms im päpstlichen Zeremoniell." In *Rom im Hohen Mittelalter: Studien zu den Romvorstellungen und zur Rompolitik vom 10. bis zum 12. Jahrhundert*, 47–61. Ed. Bernhard Schimmelpfennig and Ludwig Schmugge. Sigmaringen, 1992.

SCHNEIDER, Fedor. *Rom und Romgedanke im Mittelalter: Die geistigen Grundlagen der Renaissance*. Munich, 1925; repr. 1952.

SCHOECK, R. J. "Sir Thomas More and Lincoln's Inn Revels." *Philological Quarterly* 29 (1950), 426–30.

———. "William Rastell and the Protonotaries: A Link in the Story of the Rastells, Ropers and Heywoods." *Notes and Queries* 197 (1952), 398–99.

———. "A Common Tudor Expletive and Legal Parody in Heywood's 'Play of Love.'" *Notes and Queries* n.s. 3/9 (1956), 375–76.

SCHRAMMEK, Bernhard. *Zwischen Kirche und Karneval: Biographie, soziales Umfeld und Werk des römischen Kapellmeisters Virgilio Mazzocchi (1597–1646)*. Musiksoziologie, 9. Kassel, 2001.

SCHWINGES, Rainer Christoph. "Sozialgeschichtliche Aspekte spätmittelalterlicher Studentenbursen in Deutschland." In *Schulen und Studium im sozialen Wandel des hohen und späten Mittelalters*, 527–64. Ed. Johannes Fried. Vorträge und Forschungen, 30. Sigmaringen, 1986.

SENTAURENS, Jean. *Seville et le théâtre: De la fin du Moyen Âge à la fin du XVIIe siècle*. Lille, 1984.

SHAHAR, Shulamith. "The Boy Bishop's Feast: A Case-Study in Church Attitudes Towards Children in the High and Late Middle Ages." In *The Church and Childhood: Papers Read at the 1993 Summer Meeting and the 1994 Winter Meeting of the Ecclesiastical History Society*, 243–60. Ed. Diana Wood. Oxford, 1994.

SHERR, Richard. *Music and Musicians in Renaissance Rome and Other Courts*. Aldershot, 1998.

SIMI BONINI, Eleonora. *Il fondo musicale dell'Arciconfraternità di S. Girolamo della Carità*. Roma, 1992.

SMITS VAN WAESBERGHE, Joseph. "'De glorioso officio ... dignitate apostolica ...' (Amalarius): Zum Aufbau der Groß-Alleluia in den päpstlichen Ostervespern." In *Essays Presented to Egon Wellesz*, 48–73. Ed. Jack Westrup. Oxford, 1966.

SOLERTI, Angelo, ed. *Le origini del melodramma: Testimonianze de contemporanei*. Piccola biblioteca di scienze moderne, 70. Turin, 1903.

Spagnuolo, Vera Vita. "Gli atti notarili dell'Archivio di Stato di Roma: Saggio di spoglio sistematico — L'anno 1590." In *La musica a Roma attraverso le fonti d'archivio: atti del convegno internazionale, Roma, 4–7 giugno 1992*, 19–65. Ed. Bianca Maria Antolini, Arnaldo Morelli, and Vera Vita Spagnuolo. Strumenti della ricerca musicale, 2. Lucca, 1994.

Spencer, Robert. "Three English Lute Manuscripts." *Early Music* 3 (1975), 119–24.

Stefani, Gino. *Musica e religione nell'Italia barocca*. Uomo e cultura, 14. Palermo, 1975.

Stevens, Denis. "A Part-Book in the Public Record Office." *Music Survey* 2 (1950), 161–70.

——. "A Musical Admonition for Tudor Schoolboys." *Music & Letters* 38 (1957), 49–52.

Stevens, John. *Music and Poetry in the Early Tudor Court*. Cambridge, 1979.

Stevenson, Robert Murrell. *La música en la catedral de Sevilla (1478–1606): Documentos para su estudio*. Publicaciones de la Sociedad Española de Musicologia, Seccion B 4. Madrid, 1985.

Streitberger, W. R. *Court Revels, 1485–1559*. Studies in Early English Drama, 3. Toronto, 1994.

Strocchia, Sharon T. "Learning and Virtues: Convent Schools and Female Culture in Renaissance Florence." In *Women's Education in Early Modern Europe: A History, 1500–1800*, 3–46. Ed. Barbara J. Whitehead. Studies in the History of Education, 7. New York, 1999.

Strohm, Reinhard. *Music in Late Medieval Bruges*. Oxford, 1985.

Tacconi, Marica S. *Cathedral and Civic Ritual in Late Medieval and Renaissance Florence: The Service Books of Santa Maria del Fiore*. Cambridge Studies in Palaeography and Codicology, 12. Cambridge, 2005.

Tanner, J. M. *Growth at Adolescence*. 2nd edn. Oxford, 1962.

Temperley, Nicholas. *The Music of the English Parish Church*. 2 vols. Cambridge, 1979.

——. "Organ settings of English Psalm Tunes." *Musical Times* 122 (1981), 123–28.

Thompson, Glenda G. "Music in the Court Records of Mary of Hungary." *Tijdschrift van de Vereniging voor Nederlandse Muziekgeschiedenis* 34/2 (1984), 132–73.

Trend, John Brande. "The Dance of the Seises at Seville." *Music & Letters* 2 (1921), 10–28.

Van Orden, Kate. "Children's Voices: Singing and Literacy in Sixteenth-Century France." *Early Music History* 25 (2007), 209–56.

Waldbauer, Ivan F. "The Cittern in the Sixteenth Century and its Music in France and the Low Countries." Ph.D. diss., Harvard University, 1964.

Ward, John M. "Music for *A Handefull of pleasant delites.*" *Journal of the American Musicological Society* 10 (1957), 151–80.

——. *Music for Elizabethan Lutes*. Oxford, 1992.

Wegman, Rob C. *Born for the Muses: the Life and Masses of Jacob Obrecht*. Oxford, 1994.

——. "From Maker to Composer: Improvisation and Musical Authorship in the Low Countries, 1450–1500." *Journal of the American Musicological Society* 49 (1996), 409–79.

Weiss, D. A. "The Pubertal Change in the Human Voice." *Folia Phoniatrica* 2 (1950), 126–59.

Wessely-Kropik, Helene. "Mitteilungen aus dem Archiv der Arciconfraternità di San Giovanni dei Fiorentini." *Studien zur Musikwissenschaft* 24 (1960), 43–60.

Woolfson, Jonathan. "Bishop Fox's Bees and the Early English Renaissance." *Reformation and Renaissance Review* 5 (2003), 7–26.

Wright, Craig. "Performance Practices at the Cathedral of Cambrai, 1475–1550." *The Musical Quarterly* 44 (1978), 295–328.

———. *Music at the Court of Burgundy, 1364–1419: A Documentary History.* Henryville, Pa., Ottawa, and Binningen, 1979.

———. *Music and Ceremony at Notre Dame of Paris, 500–1550.* Cambridge, 1989.

Wulstan, David. "Vocal Colour in English Sixteenth-Century Polyphony." *Journal of the Plainsong and Mediaeval Music Society* 2 (1979), 19–60.

———. *Tudor Music.* London, 1985.

Yardley, Anne Bagnall. "'Ful weel she soong the service dyvyne': The Cloistered Musician in the Middle Ages." In *Women Making Music: The Western Art Tradition, 1150–1950*, 15–38. Ed. Jane Bowers and Judith Tick. Urbana, Ill., 1986.

———. *Performing Piety: Musical Culture in Medieval English Nunneries.* New York, 2006.

Young, Karl. *The Drama of the Medieval Church.* 2 vols. Oxford, 1933.

Yvon, Anne-Marie. "La Maîtrise de Notre-Dame aux xviie et xviiie siècles." In *Huitième Centenaire de Notre-Dame de Paris: Receuil de travaux sur l'histoire de la cathédrale et de l'Église de Paris*, 359–99. Paris, 1967.

Zieman, Katherine. "Reading, Singing and Understanding: Constructions of the Literacy of Women Religious in Late Medieval England." In *Learning and Literacy in Medieval England and Abroad*, 97–118. Ed. Sarah Rees Jones. Utrecht Studies in Medieval Literature, 3. Turnhout, 2003.

INDEX

Page numbers in **boldface** refer to illustrations or musical examples.